Generative phonology
and French phonology

Generative phonology and French phonology

FRANÇOIS DELL
CHARGÉ DE RECHERCHE, CENTRE NATIONAL DE
LA RECHERCHE SCIENTIFIQUE, PARIS

TRANSLATED BY
CATHERINE CULLEN

CAMBRIDGE UNIVERSITY PRESS

CAMBRIDGE
LONDON NEW YORK NEW ROCHELLE
MELBOURNE SYDNEY

HERMANN, PUBLISHERS IN ARTS AND SCIENCE

PARIS

Published by the Press Syndicate of the University of Cambridge
The Pitt Building, Trumpington Street, Cambridge CB2 1RP
32 East 57th Street, New York, NY 10022, USA
296 Beaconsfield Parade, Middle Park, Melbourne 3206, Australia

Original French edition, *Les règles et les sons* © Hermann, Paris 1973
English translation © Cambridge University Press 1980

First published in English translation 1980

Printed in France by Imprimerie Nouvelle, Orléans

Library of Congress Cataloguing in Publication Data

Dell, François, 1943–
Generative phonology and French phonology.

Translation of Les règles et les sons.
Bibliography : p.
Includes index.
1. Grammar, Comparative and general − Phonology. 2. Generative grammar.
3. French language − Phonology.
I. Title.
P217.D413   414   79-14139
ISBN 0 521 22484 5 hard covers

ISBN 0 521 29519 X paperback (Part I of hard cover edition)

Contents

Foreword to the English edition

This is an English version of a book published in 1973 in Paris by Hermann, *Les règles et les sons; introduction à la phonologie générative*. Where possible, the French examples of the first two chapters have been replaced by English ones. The bibliography has been brought up to date. The discussion of French phonology in chapters 5 and 6 has been modified in many places, sometimes quite radically, so as to take into account work done since 1973.

I wish to thank Catherine Cullen for translating this book into English, Elisabeth Selkirk for devising most of the English examples given in place of the French ones, Ken Safir and Laurent Sagart for proof reading, and all those who had a hand in seeing this book through the press.

To p.q.m.

Preface

By generative phonology, what is usually meant is the phonological theory developed by Chomsky, Halle and their collaborators for almost twenty-five years. This development was crowned by the publication in 1968 of a work of fundamental importance, *The Sound Pattern of English*. My ambition in writing this book is twofold : to enable a wide public with no specific knowledge of this field to get an idea of what phonology is all about, and to help linguists who were trained in former schools of thought to sort out among the accumulation of secondary (but necessary) details the few simple ideas that lie at the core of the generative approach.

This theory is still at its preliminary stage in many places, and constantly undergoing change. It would have been foolish to wish to make a complete inventory of a system that is still evolving. My aim has been, rather, to try to communicate an attitude of mind when confronted with the theories and facts. It should, therefore, not surprise the reader to find that such important subjects as the evaluation of grammars, the status of rule schemata, the principle of cyclical application, and disjunctive ordering, have been either barely touched on or totally ignored. For the aim was not to summarize the content of a certain number of basic books and articles, but to enable the reader to approach them more easily.

The book is divided into two parts. The first is an introduction to generative phonology. Chapters 1 and 2 constitute a long preamble where the fundamental notions are progressively set out. Chapter 1 explains what a generative grammar is, and the role of the phonological component. In chapter 2 the central concepts of phonology are introduced : phonetic representations, phonological representations, phonological rules. Chapter 1 is the backdrop. Chapter 2, the props; the show itself only actually begins with the third chapter. There is only one way to grasp the full implications of a system of concepts, and that is to use it. Chapter 3 is therefore entirely devoted to processing concrete examples borrowed from Zoque and Yokuts. Starting with a set of consonant or vowel alternations that occupy a central position in the phonology of these languages, I discuss the phonological rules that account for them and the manner in which these rules interact, at the same time adding various points to the notions introduced in the preceding chapters.

The second part of the book is devoted to a reassessment of certain classical problems posed by the phonology of contemporary French. Whereas in the preceding chapters it is first and foremost a question of illustrating some theoretical points with the help of limited examples, the aim of this second part is to show what a fairly wide-ranging sample of linguistic description looks like, without omitting problems of detail or ignoring gaps or areas of uncertainty that remain at this stage in the theory. The aim of chapter 4 is mostly pedagogical : I set myself the task of reconstructing step by step the process that consists of postulating a phoneme, schwa, in the underlying representations of French. Chapters 5 and 6 are more technical in nature; various rules of French phonology are examined in detail.

The readers who wish simply to encounter phonology for the first time can stop at the end of chapter 4 and go directly on to the conclusion.

My gratitude first goes to my teacher Morris Halle, for his gift of communicating to all those around him his enthusiasm in teaching and learning, and for the time and patience he devoted to me for three years. My intellectual debt to him and to Noam Chomsky is immense. I also owe much to Kenneth Hale, Paul Kiparsky and the other linguists of the MIT group.

I wish to thank Alexis Rygaloff who guided my first steps in linguistics and has since never stopped encouraging me. I also wish to thank Dan Sperber, who suggested I write this book and for whose advice on its final form I am much indebted; Venios Angelopoulos, Hans Basbøll, Jean-Elie Boltanski, Coucoune, Catherine Gipoulon, Richard Kayne, David Perlmutter, Nicolas Ruwet, Alexis Rygaloff, Elisabeth Selkirk, Dan Sperber, Ginette Tornikian, Suzanne Tyč and p.q.m., who read the manuscript either entirely or in parts and who gave me the benefit of their suggestions. I would also like to thank Maurice Gross and Anne Nau whose help was invaluable in the preparation of the French manuscript.

Notations and conventions

(The numbers in parentheses refer to the pages where the following notations are explained)

*	(14, n. 10)
+	(15)
#	(22)
→	(7)
/X/	(58)
A → B / X——Y	(53 ff.)
§	(59)
α, β, γ, etc.	(94)
$A \left\{ \begin{matrix} B \\ C \end{matrix} \right\} D$	(101)
A(B)C	(192)
X_n	(121)
[− rule R]	(117)
$\widehat{XY}$	(176)
[− seg]	(175, n. 18)
Ø	(47)
V, C, O, N, L	(47)
OBL, OPT	(198)

Pronunciation of the phonetic symbols

ENGLISH EXAMPLES

[p]	spot	[f]	face	[y]	you
[b]	ball	[v]	voice	[w]	we
[t]	stop	[s]	sin	[l]	lamp
[d]	doll	[z]	ease	[r]	rat, car
[k]	skull	[š]	shock	[D]	butter
[g]	god	[ż]	pleasure		
[c]	hats	[m]	mean		
[ƶ]	gods	[m̦]	rhythm		
[č]	beach	[n]	nut		
[ǰ]	large	[n̦]	season		
[θ]	thin	[ŋ]	lung		
[ð]	rather	[h]	hat		

[i]	feel	[ə]	balloon
[ɪ]	fill	[æ]	fat
[u]	fool	[a]	coward
[ʊ]	full	[ɑ]	father
[ɛ]	best	[ʌ]	some
[ɔ]	boy		

FRENCH EXAMPLES

[p]	part	[f]	face	[l]	alors		
[b]	barre	[v]	verre	[ļ]	peuple		
[t]	tard	[s]	serre	[r]	parole		
[d]	dard	[z]	zéro	[ŗ]	quatre		
[k]	corps	[š]	chat	[y]	avion		
[g]	gauffre	[ž]	jamais	[y̥]	papier		
[ķ]	cintième	[m]	ami	[w]	cambouis		
[ǧ]	bon **guieu**	[m̥]	atmosphère	[w̥]	bafouer		
[c]	tsar	[n]	canard	[ẘ]	nuit		
[ź]	**dz**	[n̥]	pneu	[ẅ]	fuite		
[č]	match	[ñ]	vigne	[h]	ha! ha!		
[j]	budget	[ŋ]	camping				

[i]	vie	[a]	balle	[ã]	élan	
[e]	né	[ɛ]	selle	[ɛ̃]	**bain, fin, un**	
[u]	sourd	[ɔ]	sol	[ɔ̃]	son	
[ü]	sur	[œ]	seul			
[o]	gauche					
[ö]	creux					

Pronunciation of the phonetic symbols

TABLE I

		- back		+ back	
		- round	+ round	- round	+ round
- low	+ high	i	ü		u
- low	- high	e	ö		o
+ low		ε	œ	a	ɔ

TABLE II

- syll	+ cons	- son	obstruents: stops and fricatives: t, c, s, etc.
- syll	+ cons	+ son	liquid and nasal consonants: l, r, m, n, etc.
- syll	- cons	+ son	glides : h, ʔ and semi-vowels w, y, etc.
+ syll	- cons	+ son	vowels : a, ε, ã, ε̃, etc.

TABLE III

				- cor	+ cor	- cor			
				+ ant		- ant			
				- high		+ high			- high
				- back				+ back	
- nas	- son	- cont	- voice	p	t, c	č	ḳ	k	
- nas	- son	- cont	+ voice	b	d, z	j	ǧ	g	
- nas	- son	+ cont	- voice	f	s	š			
- nas	- son	+ cont	+ voice	v	z	ž			
- nas	+ son	+ cont	+ voice		l		y, ẅ	w	r
+ nas	+ son	+ cont	+ voice	m	n		ñ	ŋ	

(all the sounds in this table are [− syll], and they are all [+ cons] except y, ẅ and w, which are [− cons])

TABLE IV

	sonorant	syllabic	consonantal	continuant	nasal	high	low	back	rounded	anterior	coronal	voiced	del rel
ã	+	+	−	+	+	−	+	+	−	−	−	+	+
ɔ̃	+	+	−	+	+	−	+	+	+	−	−	+	+
ɛ̃	+	+	−	+	+	−	+	−	−	−	−	+	+
a	+	+	−	+	−	−	+	+	−	−	−	+	+
ɔ	+	+	−	+	−	−	+	+	+	−	−	+	+
œ	+	+	−	+	−	−	+	−	+	−	−	+	+
ɛ	+	+	−	+	−	−	+	−	−	−	−	+	+
o	+	+	−	+	−	−	−	+	+	−	−	+	+
ö	+	+	−	+	−	−	−	−	+	−	−	+	+
e	+	+	−	+	−	−	−	−	−	−	−	+	+
u	+	+	−	+	−	+	−	+	+	−	−	+	+
ü	+	+	−	+	−	+	−	−	+	−	−	+	+
i	+	+	−	+	−	+	−	−	−	−	−	+	+
h	+	−	−	+	−	−	−	−	−	−	−	−	+
ʔ	+	−	−	−	−	−	−	−	−	−	−	−	−
ẅ	+	−	−	+	−	+	−	−	+	−	−	+	+
w	+	−	−	+	−	+	−	+	+	−	−	+	+
y	+	−	−	+	−	+	−	−	−	−	−	+	+
l	+	−	+	+	−	−	−	−	−	+	+	+	+
r	+	−	+	+	−	−	−	+	−	−	−	+	+
ŋ	+	−	+	+	+	+	−	+	−	−	−	+	−
ñ	+	−	+	+	+	+	−	−	−	−	−	+	−
n	+	−	+	+	+	−	−	−	−	+	+	+	−
m	+	−	+	+	+	−	−	−	−	+	−	+	−
ž	−	−	+	+	−	+	−	−	−	−	+	+	+
š	−	−	+	+	−	+	−	−	−	−	+	−	+
z	−	−	+	+	−	−	−	−	−	+	+	+	+
s	−	−	+	+	−	−	−	−	−	+	+	−	+
v	−	−	+	+	−	−	−	−	−	+	−	+	+
f	−	−	+	+	−	−	−	−	−	+	−	−	+
g	−	−	+	−	−	+	−	+	−	−	−	+	−
k	−	−	+	−	−	+	−	+	−	−	−	−	−
g̈	−	−	+	−	−	+	−	−	−	−	−	+	−
k̈	−	−	+	−	−	+	−	−	−	−	−	−	−
ǰ	−	−	+	−	−	+	−	−	−	−	+	+	+
č	−	−	+	−	−	+	−	−	−	−	+	−	+
ǯ	−	−	+	−	−	−	−	−	−	+	+	+	+
c	−	−	+	−	−	−	−	−	−	+	+	−	+
d	−	−	+	−	−	−	−	−	−	+	+	+	−
t	−	−	+	−	−	−	−	−	−	+	+	−	−
b	−	−	+	−	−	−	−	−	−	+	−	+	−
p	−	−	+	−	−	−	−	−	−	+	−	−	−

PART I

Generative phonology :
Basic concepts

1
Languages and grammars

Linguistics is the study of languages, and phonology that of their pronunciation. Humans communicate by articulating certain sounds which have a certain meaning. Each pronounced sentence has two facets: sound and meaning. Peter says to Paul: *when is Kathy coming?* The sentence's pronunciation consists of a succession of sounds that are represented by special symbols enclosed in square brackets: [wɛnɪzkæθɪkʌmɪŋ].[1] The sentence also has a meaning: 'the speaker is asking the hearer to indicate to him when Kathy is coming'. Sound, and not meaning, is going from Peter's mouth to Paul's ear. But if sound is the only thing being transmitted from Peter to Paul, how does Paul manage to grasp its meaning?

Each language associates sound and meaning through a network of correspondences regulated by a set of strict rules. Peter and Paul know English, that is to say they have the key to the particular correspondence system between sound and meaning which characterizes the English language. It is because of this key that Paul can reconstruct what Peter wished to communicate when articulating the sentence [wɛnɪzkæθɪkʌmɪŋ]. Each different sound is a material clue given by Peter to help Paul in this reconstitution. Peter, on his side, is in a somewhat symmetrical position to Paul's. Whereas Paul must discover the meaning corresponding to the sounds [wɛnɪzkæθɪkʌmɪŋ], Peter's task is to find and correctly pronounce a sequence of sounds precisely meaning 'the speaker is asking the hearer to indicate to him when Kathy is coming'. Understanding what is said and speaking are certainly two different activities, but both presuppose that the subject masters the correspondence system between sound and meaning which we call a language.

---

[1]   The phonetic symbols, especially conceived to note speech sounds. For the values attached to the main phonetic symbols used in this book, see pp. XII–XIII.

Languages are often considered as coding systems of a special kind. For example, if we take a numbered code where each letter of the alphabet is represented by an arbitrarily chosen two-digit number: 61 stands for A, 23 stands for B, 12 stands for C, and so on, the sequence of numbers 23-12-61-12 stands for the sequence of letters B-C-A-C. In other words, in this particular code, B-C-A-C is the meaning of the message 23-12-61-12. In order completely to define this code, all one has to do is to make a list – a lexicon – in which each one of the twenty-six letters of the alphabet is set opposite the number associated to it. Imagine two people, X and Y, who correspond at a distance with the help of this code. Each one has a copy of the lexicon. If X wants to communicate to Y the meaning A-A-C-B, for example, he will consult his lexicon and successively replace each letter by the desired number. He thus obtains the message 61-61-12-23, which he sends to Y. Y, on his side, deciphers the message he has received by doing exactly the reverse: he looks in his lexicon for each letter corresponding to each number of the sequence 61-61-12-23 and thus reconstructs the meaning A-A-C-B. Of course languages have a far more complex structure than this numerical code. But the analogy clearly illustrates the relationship between the sound and meaning of sentences, as well as the respective roles of the speaker and hearer during the act of communication.

Let us now suppose that a third person, Z, wishes to discover the code X and Y are using to communicate with, but has not been able to get hold of their lexicon. Z still has another means of doing so: he can get a 'bilingual' sample of their correspondence, such as the notebook in which Y writes the messages he receives from X, with the corresponding 'decoded' meanings. Z will not be long in discovering that the number 61 always corresponds to the letter A, the number 23 to the letter B, etc.... and he will in that way be able to reconstruct the lexicon used by X and Y. It is often said that linguists, when trying to describe the mechanism of a language, are in a similar situation to Z. Linguists do not have direct access to a language code, since it lies in the brain of each speaker, who is not conscious of the code he uses or of the complex mental operations at work as he speaks or interprets the speech of others. Therefore linguists think they will be able to describe the mechanism of languages by systematically examining the sentences uttered by speakers, and the meaning given them by these speakers.

What could constitute the code of the English language? The first idea that springs to mind is that it consists of a gigantic dictionary containing all the sentences of English, with a complete description of the meaning and pronunciation of each one. Learning the English language would imply learning each of its sentences individually, and describing English would imply making an exhaustive catalogue of them. Such a hypothesis is untenable. In the first place, it implies that we are capable of producing or understanding only sentences that we have already heard at least once: i.e. when we learnt them. Miller (1970: 82) calculated that English has roughly a hundred billion billion sentences of twenty words, and that it would take one hundred billion centuries to say them all one after the other. The sentences we hear or pronounce all the time sound familiar to us, and yet most of them have never been either heard or pronounced by anyone before. In fact the number of sentences of any language is not only astronomical, it can be shown to be infinite. We are all capable of saying and understanding an infinite number of sentences which we encounter for the first time, and this is what is meant by the creativity of language.[2] Ready-made sentences such as *what time is it?* or *who's speaking?* constitute but a small minority.

Creativity, when given the particular meaning it has here, is not found only in language. It is an essential feature of the human mind and manifests itself in most of the cognitive processes. Take, for example, the addition of integers. Given any two integers, adding is a correspondence by which a third integer, their sum, is associated to these first two. For example, the sum of the integers 98317501 and 134 is the integer 98317635. Since there is an infinity of integers, the number of pairs of integers of which we can calculate the sum is also infinite. It is therefore out of the question that anyone could make an exhaustive list of all the possible additions, and *a fortiori* that anyone could learn them by heart. And yet each one of us is in principle capable of adding integers, however big. The only limits to our capacity of adding are of a material kind: we have but a finite quantity of time, paper, energy, etc. The rules of addition are totally general: they are valid for all additions without exception, and unequivocally determine the sum of any pair of integers. The arithmetical work that we carry out every day is for the most part new to us, and yet we are hardly aware of this. Results are determined beforehand, since they are implicity contained in the few simple rules that we learnt at school.

We have just seen that addition rules enable us to establish a correspondence between two infinite sets: the infinite set of pairs of integers and the infinite set of integers. This correspondence is represented by the diagram below. We have also seen that speakers have the capacity to

---

[2]   A distinction is made between particular languages (Russian, English, Chinese, etc.) and *language* in general (which is the faculty that enables man to learn languages and use them to communicate with others).

Set of pairs of integers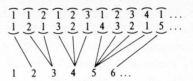

Set of integers

produce and understand an infinity of sentences, i.e. to establish a correspondence between two infinite sets: an infinite set of pronunciations and an infinite set of meanings. Let us name these two sets P and M, respectively. The correspondence is not a simple one. A sequence of sounds often has several different meanings and two different sound sequences can have the same meaning. Sentences like *my sisters left* and *my sister's left* are pronounced in exactly the same way; that is to say that the sequence of sounds [3] [maysɪstərzlɛft] has two different meanings, 'my sisters left' and 'my sister has left'.[4] Then again the phrase *the books and the car* can be pronounced in two ways, either with *and* fully pronounced, as in [ðəbʊksændðəkɑr] or with *and* reduced to a simple *n* which is syllabic, [ðəbʊksn̩ðəkɑr]. This second pronunciation is identical to one of the possible pronunciations of *the books in the car*, which can be pronounced [ðəbʊksn̩ðəkɑr] or [ðəbʊksɪnðəkɑr]. A small sample of the set of pairings that knowing English allows the speaker-hearers to establish between sound sequences and meanings is given below.

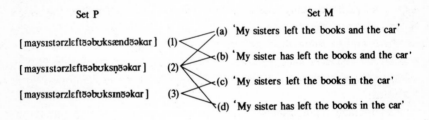

Set P
Set M

[maysɪstərzlɛftðəbʊksændðəkɑr] (1)
(a) 'My sisters left the books and the car'
(b) 'My sister has left the books and the car'

[maysɪstərzlɛftðəbʊksn̩ðəkɑr] (2)
(c) 'My sisters left the books in the car'

[maysɪstərzlɛftðəbʊksɪnðəkɑr] (3)
(d) 'My sister has left the books in the car'

The pronunciation (1) can have the meanings (a) or (b), but not (c) or (d); the pronunciation (3) can have the meanings (c) or (d), but not (a) or (b). Finally, the pronunciation (2) can have all four meanings (a), (b), (c), and (d). Of the twelve conceivable combinations, only four sound–meaning

---

[3] In this book, all the English examples are drawn from the variety of English spoken in upstate New York.

[4] *My sister's left* has yet another meaning, corresponding to the case where *left* is not a verb but the noun whose antonym is *right*. For the sake of simplification, this additional meaning will be ignored. When two forms have the same pronunciation, they are said to be homophonous. A sound sequence is said to be ambiguous when it has several different meanings.

pairs (1,c), (1,d), (3,a) and (3,b) are impossible. Remember that the pronunciations (1), (2) and (3) of the preceding example are only three elements out of the infinite set P of all the sound sequences that are possible pronunciations of English. Similarly, the meanings (a), (b), (c) and (d) are four elements out of the infinite set M of all the meanings that can be communicated in English. And our aim is to discover the exact nature of the correspondence that all those who know English can establish between P and M. But giving a precise definition of this correspondence implies having a precise definition of the sets P and M. Take P: any sound sequence is not a pronunciation of an English sentence. The sequence [aykæn] is one (*I can*), but not the sequences [ænkay], [nayæk], [yknaæ]. Ask any English speaker, and he will agree without hesitating. Anyone who knows English not only knows how to make sound and meaning correspond in a certain way, but can also, given any sequence of sounds, distinguish whether or not it is well-formed. 'Well-formed' in the sense in which we use the word here does not mean in agreement with the norms of 'correct English'. 'Correct English' is defined by normative grammars, which prescribe certain ways of speaking and forbid others: 'don't say *you can't get off so easy!*, but say *you can't avoid that so easily*'. Linguists describe the way in which people actually talk. We would differentiate between [aykæn] and [nækay] even if we had never been told that some ways of talking are more 'correct' than others. Most of the rules governing our linguistic behaviour are never explicitly taught to us. We unconsciously internalize them while learning our mother tongue. It is these rules that linguists propose to make explicit, and to them that the notion 'well-formed' refers. In this sense, sentences such as *he gets ticked off so easy* and *Gimme that*. are well-formed, and the fact that they are outlawed by purists is, from our standpoint, not relevant.[5]

To conclude, a language is characterized by a particular correspondence between two infinite sets: a set of pronunciations, say $P = \{ p_1, p_2 \cdots p_i \cdots \}$, and a set of meanings, say $M = \{ m_1, m_2 \cdots m_j \cdots \}$. Defining this correspondence amounts to defining a certain infinite set of well-formed sound–meaning pairs (p_i, m_j). *The term 'grammar of a language' is used to designate a device which gives an explicit definition of the set of well-formed sound–meaning pairs of that language. To describe a language is to construct a grammar of that language.* Usually, the term 'grammar' is understood as

---

[5]   The adjective 'grammatical' is often used in a strictly equivalent sense to 'well-formed'. Ill-formed sentences are then said to be 'agrammatical' or 'non-grammatical'. For a clear presentation of the notion of 'grammaticality', cf. Ruwet (1967: chap. 1, sec. 3.2).

designating the set of principles that governs the combination of words in sentences. Here this word is given a wider definition, so as also to embrace all aspects of pronunciation.

Describing a language requires one to define a set containing an infinity of elements (sound–meaning pairs). How, in practice, does one go about rigorously delimiting a set containing an infinity of objects, whether they are sound–meaning pairs or anything else? To accomplish this task, linguists use a method of definition that was invented by mathematicians and logicians. It will be useful to give the general idea of the method, before showing the particular use linguists make of it.

Let us call *formal language* any set of finite sequences of symbols taken out of a finite alphabet.[6] These sequences are called the *formulae* of the language in question. With mathematical or computer languages, the symbols are letters, numbers, signs of arithmetical or logical operations, parentheses, etc. The formulae of the extremely simple languages that we are going to take as examples are all constructed on an alphabet of only two letters, a and b. For example, take the language $L_1 = \{a, aa, abaa, ba\}$. L_1 is a set containing four elements, the formulae of L_1. Then take the language L_2, which is the set of sequences $\{ba, bbb, ab\}$. The sequence ba is both a formula of L_1 and of L_2. The sequence aa is a formula of L_1 but not of L_2. The sequence $ababab$ is neither a formula of L_1 nor of L_2. Let us call S the set of all the finite sequences that one can construct from the alphabet $\{a, b\}$. S contains an infinity of elements, the sequences a, b, aa, ab, ba, bb, aaa, bbb, aab, abb... $aabaaabbba$... Defining a certain language constructed from a and b is equivalent to dividing the set S into two complementary sets: on the one hand, the set of sequences of S which are formulae of the language in question and, on the other hand, the set of remaining sequences, which are not formulae of that language. The language L_1 and L_2 are sets containing a finite number of elements, and it is therefore possible to delimit them within S by making an exhaustive list of their elements. But one can conceive of languages containing an infinity of formulae.

Take, for example, the language L_3, consisting of the set of all sequences of type $a^n b^n$, i.e. sequences which are constructed by repeating a certain

---

[6]   Formal languages must not be confused with *Language*. The former are only certain types of objects, whereas the latter is a faculty (see p. 3, n. 2 above). For an elementary introduction to the study of formal languages cf. Gross and Lentin (1967).

[7] a is a sequence containing a single symbol.

number of times (n) the letter a, and the same number of times the letter b.
$L_3 = \{ab, aabb, aaabbb, aaaabbbb...\}$. Set L_3 has as many formulae as
there are distinct n integers, i.e. an infinity. It is impossible to define L_3 by
making an exhaustive list of its elements, since these are infinite in number
and a list is by definition finite. One has to go about it differently: by giving a
property, characteristic of the formulae of L_3, i.e. a property common to all
the sequences that are formulae of L_3, and which is shared by no other
sequence. For example, one could give the following definition (D):

(D) for a sequence to belong to set L_3, it is a necessary and
sufficient condition that it contain a sequence of a certain
number of as immediately followed by a sequence of the same
number of bs.

If one agrees beforehand on the meaning of the terms 'sequence',
'immediately followed by', 'same number', etc., this definition seems at
first sight sufficiently explicit to exclude any possible differences in
interpretation. This remains to be seen. Someone shown just the
definition (D) and the sequence *aaabbba* would probably say that this
sequence is a part of L_3. Indeed it contains a sequence of three as
immediately followed by a sequence of three bs, and the formulation of (D)
does not explicitly exclude the presence of anything else in addition to an
$a^n b^n$ sequence. Of course, one could alter the definition (D), but our purpose
is to give an idea of the difficulties involved in making rigorous formulations.
And it must not be forgotten that we intentionally chose a particularly
simple construction ($a^n b^n$), which can be defined without complicated
conceptual equipment. We will therefore take up another mode of definition
to characterize set L_3.

Let us take the device G, composed of an *initial symbol* J and the
rewrite-rules R1 and R2:

G
- initial symbol J
- rules
  - R1: $J \rightarrow aJb$
  - R2: $J \rightarrow ab$

The initial symbol J is the starting point of the device's operations. It is
given in the same way as the disposition of chessmen are given at the
beginning of a chess game. Rule R1 states: 'rewrite the symbol J as the
sequence of symbols aJb', or in other words, 'replace the symbol J by the

sequence of symbols *a Jb* '. Similarly, R2 states: 'rewrite *J* as *ab* '. These
rules should be operated in the following way: start by writing the initial
symbol *J*, and then apply the rules R1 and R2 as many times as is necessary
until neither is applicable. The two rules can be applied in whatever order is
chosen. Thus, to produce the sequence *aaaabbbb*, take the following steps, to
constitute the *derivation* of *aaaabbbb*:

(1)   *J*   (initial symbol)
(2)   *a Jb*   (by application of R1 to *J*)
(3)   *aa Jbb*   (by application of R1 to *a Jb*)
(4)   *aaa Jbbb* (by application of R1 to *aa Jbb*)
(5)   *aaaabbbb* (by application of R2 to *aaa Jbbb*)

Each step consists of the application of one of the rewrite-rules to the
sequence obtained by the preceding step. Step 1: the initial symbol *J* is
written; step 2: *J* is replaced by *a Jb* (rule R1), thus obtaining the sequence
a Jb; step 3: in the sequence *a Jb* obtained by the preceding step, *J* is once
again replaced by *a Jb* (rule R1), whence the sequence *aa Jbb*; step 4: in the
sequence *aa Jbb*, obtained as a result of the preceding step, *J* is once again
replaced by *a Jb* (rule R1), whence the sequence *aaa Jbbb*; step 5: *J* is
replaced by *ab* (rule R2) in the sequence *aaa Jbbb*, result of the preceding
step, whence the sequence *aaaabbbb*. The derivation comes to an end when
a sequence is obtained which does not contain any symbol that can be
rewritten. The *aaaabbbb* sequence obtained only has *a* and *b*, and rules R1
and R2 only enable the symbol *J* to be rewritten. At each step in the
derivation, one has the choice of replacing *J* by *a Jb* (rule R1) or by *ab*
(rule R2). Once one has chosen to apply rule R2, the derivation necessarily
comes to an end.

The device G – and from now on we will call it the grammar G – is a sort of
machine which builds sequences constructed on an alphabet {a, b}. What
we have described above is the succession of operations enabling the
grammar to construct the sequence *aaaabbbb*. We say that the grammar G
generates the sequence *aaaabbbb*. What is known as the 'language
generated by a grammar' is the set of sequences generated by that grammar.

Let us call L the language generated by the grammar G. It can easily be
shown that set L contains all the sequences of the a^nb^n type. For any given
integer *n*, one can produce the corresponding sequence a^nb^n by applying
the rule R1 $n - 1$ times and rule R2 once. In particular, for $n = 1$, one
directly applies rule R2 to the initial symbol *J*, thereby obtaining the
sequence *ab*. Moreover, it is easy to see that any sequence generated by the

grammar G is necessarily of the $a''b''$ type. In short, the language L generated by the grammar G and the language L_3 defined above are one and the same thing. We can now therefore define L_3 as the set of sequences generated by the grammar G, or similarly, we can say that for a sequence to be a formula of L_3, it is a necessary and sufficient condition that it be generated by the grammar G. We now possess an extremely general method of definition. *In order to define a given language, one must define a finite device (a grammar) that can mechanically construct all the sequences of that language, and those sequences only:*

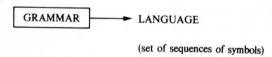

(set of sequences of symbols)

Here is another example. Take the language L_4, which is the set of all the sequences of the type $(ab)^n$, i.e. the infinite set of all the sequences formed by repeating a certain number of times the sequence *ab*, $L_4 = \{ab, abab, ababab, abababab...\}$. Here is a grammar which generates the language L_4, i.e. it generates all the sequences which are formulae of L_4, and cannot generate any others: the grammar G_4, which consists of the initial symbol J and the rules R2 (which was already represented in the grammar G above) and R3:

$$G_4 \begin{cases} \qquad\quad J \\ R2: \quad J \;\to\; ab \\ R3: \quad J \;\to\; abJ \end{cases}$$

This grammar generates, for example, the sequence *abababab* at the end of the following derivation:

J	(initial symbol)
abJ	(by application of R3 to J)
$ababJ$	(by application of R3 to abJ)
$abababJ$	(by application of R3 to $ababJ$)
$abababab$	(by application of R2 to $abababJ$)

Of course, a given grammar generates one and only one language, but the converse is not true. A given language can always be generated by several different grammars. Thus the language L_4 is not only generated by the grammar G_4, but also by the grammar G'_4, which contains the initial symbol J and the rules R2, R4, R5, and R6:

$$G'_4 \left\{ \begin{array}{l} \qquad\qquad J \\ \text{R2:} \quad J \;\rightarrow\; ab \\ \text{R4:} \quad J \;\rightarrow\; aKb \\ \text{R5:} \quad K \;\rightarrow\; ba \\ \text{R6:} \quad K \;\rightarrow\; bJa \end{array} \right.$$

This grammar contains the symbol K. K is not an initial symbol like J; it is brought into the derivation by the application of rule R4. J and K are auxiliary symbols, in the sense that they play a part in the functioning of the grammar, but unlike a and b they do not occur in the sequences generated by this grammar. Here is, for example, the derivation of the sequence *abababab* in the grammar G'_4:

initial symbol	(R4)	(R6)	(R4)	(R5)
J	aKb	$ab\,Jab$	$abaKbab$	$abababab$

The reader can verify for himself that besides G_4 and G'_4, the two following grammars also generate the language L_4:

$\{$ initial symbol J; rules: $\quad J \;\rightarrow\; ab;\quad J \;\rightarrow\; Jab\}$

and

$\{$ initial symbol J;
rules: $\quad J \;\rightarrow\; ab;\quad J \;\rightarrow\; aK;\quad K \;\rightarrow\; bJ\}$

This serves as a warning against the possible confusions that the word 'generate' often leads to. To generate a set is to define it by enumerating all its elements. Never mind the details of the practical steps leading to such an enumeration. Mathematicians can define the body of a cylinder as the volume generated by turning a rectangle around one of its axes of symmetry (fig. 1a). The same cylinder body can be generated just as well by causing a circle to undergo a translation parallel to its axis (fig. 1b). The two modes of definition in fact characterize the same object.

Lastly, just one remark on the role of initial symbols. Let us build a grammar, G_5, defined in the following way: it has the same rules R2, R4, R5, R6 as G'_4, but K is taken as its initial symbol, and not J, as in G'_4. While G'_4

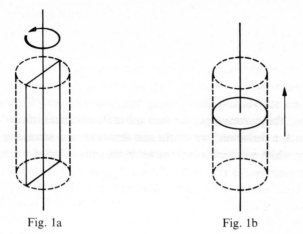

Fig. 1a   Fig. 1b

enumerates the set of sequences of the $(ab)^n$ type, G_5 enumerates the set of sequences of the $(ba)^n$ type. The language generated by a grammar depends not only on the rules of that grammar, but also on the starting point of its derivations.

If we consider an isolated symbol as a particular case of a sequence of symbols, i.e. as a sequence which contains just one symbol, we can generalize, and construct grammars where derivations no longer begin with an initial symbol, but with an *initial sequence*. Take for example the grammar which has the same rules as G_4, but an initial sequence bbJ. This grammar defines the language $bb(ab)^n$, i.e. the set of sequences composed of a bb sequence followed by a certain number of repetitions of the ab sequence. Furthermore it is possible to conceive of grammars with several initial sequences. Consider, for example, a grammar that has the same rules as G_4' and the four initial sequences J, K, bJ, aK. This grammar generates the set of sequences of at least two symbols, with a and b regularly alternating: $\{ ab, ba, aba, bab, abab, baba, ababa... \}$.

Each grammar thus defines a certain formal language in a precise way. This language is the set of sequences that it generates. The interest of grammars like G or G_4 is twofold: on the one hand they permit the enumeration of infinite sets of sequences starting from a finite list of rules and initial sequences. On the other hand, once the application of the rules has been specified, they strictly delimit the possible scope of symbolic manipulations and their final result, without leaving the least freedom of interpretation to the human operator. They therefore constitute perfectly explicit definitions of the languages they generate, i.e. definitions conceived to eliminate any obscurity.

We will see that when describing a natural language, the linguist's aim is to construct a *generative grammar*, that is to say a grammar which generates the entire set of sentences of that language. Generative grammars, constructed by linguists, are much more complex than the grammars of the formal languages presented here, but they are based on the same principle. One often sees statements of the following type in contemporary linguistic publications; 'the grammar generates such and such a sentence at the end of such and such a derivation ', where the said derivation is a succession of sequences in which each term is constructed by the application of a certain rule to the preceding term. It is a frequent mistake to believe that the derivation of a sentence is a direct representation of the psychological process taking place in the speaker's brain before he pronounces the sentence. According to this view, the step by step progression of the derivation would represent the succession in time of a certain number of elementary mental operations, and would, as it were, be like a slow motion film of a gestation at the end of which the brain would give birth to a new sentence. We do not claim anything of the sort. When we state that a grammar generates a set of sentences, all we are saying is that by systematically enumerating all its elements, it enables this set to be explicitly characterized. That is all. The grammar of a language characterizes what the subject knows of his language, and not the way in which he uses that knowledge to speak or understand. Only grammars *generate* sentences and languages; speakers, on the other hand, *produce* or *utter* sentences, and *know* languages. We all know how to multiply, i.e. we know certain rules which unequivocally determine the product of any two numbers. It is this shared knowledge which enables us to agree that the product of 99 by 9 is 891. But this does not mean that we all get to the same result in the same way. In order mentally to multiply 99 by 9, one can multiply 100 by 9 and take 9 away from the product obtained, or multiply 99 by 10 and take away 99, or again one can add the product of 90 by 9 to that of 9 by 9. What we know of multiplying determines unequivocally the final result, but not necessarily the way to obtain it.

The definition of a formal language is not concerned with the meaning attached to the symbols of the alphabet on which this language is constructed. It does not even indicate that one need give them any meaning at all. This is why one talks of 'formal' languages. They are systems of combinations in which only the ordering of the symbols is taken into consideration. The study of formal languages is a province of mathematics. The linguist, on the other hand, is directly interested only in human languages, but he borrows a certain number of his working tools from the mathematics of formal languages. The latter is to linguistics what analytical geometry is to astrophysics. It gives it a conceptual framework and a rigorous language with which to describe the empirical phenomena under study. What exactly does the linguist do with formal languages and the grammars defining them?

Suppose any sentence could be represented by a sequence of symbols precisely indicating its pronunciation and meaning. This sequence, which we will call the *description* of the sentence, could be constructed by placing one after the other the sequence of phonetic symbols indicating its pronunciation (its *phonetic representation*) and the sequence of symbols indicating its meaning (its *semantic representation*).[8] Since every sound-meaning pair now corresponds with a description that unambiguously characterizes it, defining the set of sentences of English (or of any other language) amounts to defining the set of their descriptions. Let us call E the set of sequences of symbols which are the description of an English sentence. E is a formal language, and each of its formulae is the description of a well-formed English sound-meaning pair. *Describing the English language amounts to defining the set E*. And to define E is to define a grammar that generates E (that generates all the sequences which are members of E, and no others).

Since E is an infinite set, the linguist can only ever obtain a small part of it by direct observation. He therefore has to proceed by successive extrapolations. He begins by collecting a certain number of sentences from speakers and noting their description, thus obtaining a set of descriptions: the set A of the descriptions of the (well-formed) sentences which he has collected. This set A is a finite sample of the infinite set E. Once he has the sample, he can then set himself the following problem: how exactly to define E, knowing A.[9]

The linguist then imagines a certain grammar G, and makes the hypothesis that this grammar G generates E. His task is to verify this hypothesis. G has to fulfil two conditions for it to be a possible candidate: the language it generates must be an infinite set of descriptions, since E is an infinite set of descriptions, and it must contain all the elements of A, since all the elements of A are contained in E. Suppose that the grammar G thought up by our linguist fulfils these two conditions, and thus generates all the

---

[8]   At present there is no adequate symbolic representation for meanings, for the study of meaning is still in its infancy. Consequently we simply use English sentences between inverted commas to stand for semantic representations.

[9]   See, for example, a classic problem in astronomy: having determined through observation a number of points on a planet's orbit, characterize the infinite set of points on this orbit, i.e. find an equation which defines that set.

elements of A as well as an infinity of other descriptions. It is compatible with the set A of observed data, but we still have no guarantee that it will also be compatible with any other sample of English that could be collected. When the grammar proposed by the linguist generates a given description, it makes a certain prediction: it predicts that the sound–meaning pair characterized by this description is well-formed in English. The linguist tests his grammar by checking with the speakers that each one of the descriptions it generates really does correspond to a well-formed sentence. To take a concrete example, imagine that we have constructed a grammar G, which generates, among other things, the descriptions of the following sound–meaning pairs:

(6) [ðənɛksčayld] 'the next child'
(7) [ðənɛksayl] 'the next aisle'
(8) [ðəlæskɔrnər] 'the last corner'
(9) [ðəlæsɔrdər] 'the last order'

These sentences are given one by one to the speakers. Their answers indicate that the pairs (6) and (8) are well-formed. These new data confirm the hypothesis that the language generated by G is the set E. The consulted speakers inform us, on the other hand, that the pairs (7) and (9) are ill-formed, which invalidates this hypothesis; they inform us that 'the next aisle' is not pronounced* [ðənɛksayl] [10] but [ðənɛkstayl], and that 'the last order' is not pronounced *[ðəlæsɔrdər], but [ðəlæstɔrdər].[11] So another grammar has to be found. Testing grammar G gave a negative result, but it allowed us to collect new data. We can now add to the set A the descriptions of the well-formed pairs (6), (8), (10) and (11):

(10) [ðənɛkstayl] 'the next aisle'
(11) [ðəlæstɔrdər] 'the last order'

At the same time, we can begin a new kind of list: the descriptions of ill-formed sentences. Our next grammar will therefore have to take into account both set A of descriptions of well-formed sentences, and set B of descriptions of ill-formed sentences. It will have to generate all the elements of A and none of the elements of B. For E does not contain any elements of B. In order to define the set E, it is as important to know what is *not* in it as what *is* in it. For 'negative' data, i.e. data concerning ill-formed sound–meaning pairs, is just as valuable to a linguist as 'positive' data, i.e. data concerning well-formed sound–meaning pairs. The samples A and B are finite but they can be indefinitely enriched by including new well- or ill-

---

[10] A form preceded by an asterisk is ill-formed.
[11] The grammar G predicts that more word-final consonants are dropped than actually are.

formed sound-meaning pairs collected from speakers while testing successive hypotheses. The linguist does not accumulate data by randomly questioning his informers; each new piece of data interests him only in so far as it allows him to confirm or invalidate the hypothesis that he had built to account for the data previously collected.

THE GENERAL ORGANIZATION OF GRAMMARS

In the numerical code on page 2, the messages are divided into successive groups of two digits; each one of these groups has a meaning which has been established once and for all in the lexicon. For example, group *23* always has the meaning B, group *12* always the meaning C, etc. Each one of these groups can in its turn be analysed as a sequence of two digits but these digits have no meaning of their own. When it comes to giving them a meaning, each group is taken as a whole, and the digits composing it only figure as material marks to distinguish one group from another. Natural languages have a similar property. The sounds of a natural language have no meaning in themselves. Meaningful units are not individual sounds but morphemes, represented by sound groups. To define precisely a morpheme would lead us into unnecessary complications. Let us content ourselves with saying that the notion of morpheme includes, for example, prefixes, suffixes, roots, endings, etc. For example, the sentence: *your friend recopied her notes* is composed of the following morphemes, which we separate by a + sign to indicate the morpheme boundaries: *your + friend + re + copi + ed + her + note + s.*

The morphemes of a language are finite in number. Among all conceivable morpheme sequences, only some are well-formed. The sequence *her + friend + re + copi + ed + your + note + s* is well-formed, but not the sequence **her + your + friend + note + re + s + ed + copi.* The grammar of a language must specify under what conditions a sequence of morphemes is well-formed.

The grammar of a language is not a one-piece device, directly generating the whole set of descriptions of well-formed sound-meaning pairs. It is a combination of three devices or components, each one specialized for a particular task. Each component is a system of rules. The *syntactic component* generates a set of *syntactic structures*. Each syntactic structure contains, among other things, a well-formed sequence of morphemes. A meaning is given to each syntactic structure by the *semantic component*, and a pronunciation by the *phonological component* (see diagram below).

The syntactic component is the system's backbone. It is responsible for the creativity mentioned above (p. 3), the ability to produce ever new combinations from a finite number of morphemes. The other two components merely interpret the abstract objects generated by the syntactic component by providing them with an audible aspect (pronunciation) and an intelligible aspect (meaning).

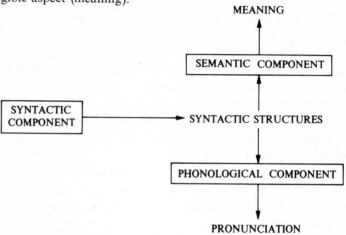

The syntactic component is a system of rules which generates an infinite set of syntactic structures. The syntactic structure of a sentence is an abstract object containing all the necessary information to enable one to deduce, with the help of rules, the meaning and pronunciation of that sentence. It has a complex structure which cannot be properly characterized without describing the syntactic component in detail. Since this book is devoted to phonology, we will only interest ourselves in those properties of the syntactic structures which play a role in the description of pronunciation. For the others, see Ruwet (1967), Lyons (1970), and the references therein. The term *surface structure* is used to describe that part of a syntactic structure which contains all the information necessary for the specification of the pronunciation of the corresponding sentence. In order to specify the pronunciation of a sentence, it is necessary (but not sufficient, see p. 22) to know the morphemes that compose it and the order in which they are arranged. Each syntactic structure generated by the syntactic component must therefore contain, among other things, a well-formed sequence of morphemes. By generating the set of syntactic structures, the syntactic component thereby generates the set of well-formed sequences of morphemes. In the case of English, this set must be defined so as to contain the sequences *you + have + copi + ed + your + note + s* and *have + you + copi + ed + your + note + s* but not *you + ed + note + have + s + copi + your*.

The *lexicon* is equivalent to a dictionary. It is the (finite) list of lexical items, or, as it were, a set of loose parts from which the syntax gets the materials it needs to construct the syntactic structures. Lexical items are isolated morphemes (*friend, copy*) or fixed combinations of morphemes (*under + take,   in + comprehens + ible,   ice + box,   soft + heart + ed, pull + his + leg*).

The meaning of each morpheme of a sentence contributes in its own right to determining the meaning of the sentence. The grammar of a language must contain general principles by which a global meaning can be attributed to any syntactic structure, given the individual meanings of the morphemes composing it, and the way in which they are combined. This task falls on the semantic rules, which constitute the semantic component of the grammar. The semantic component is a device that takes each syntactic structure generated by the syntactic component and gives it a semantic representation (see p. 13). Basing itself on the set of syntactic structures generated by the syntactic component, the semantic component constructs an infinite set M of semantic representations corresponding term for term with the set of syntactic structures.[12] The properties of the semantic component and the exact nature of its relationship to the syntactic structures is a very difficult subject, about which we still know very little.

Finally, we are left with the *phonological component*, which is the set of *phonological rules*. The phonological component gives any syntactic structure a pronunciation, based on the pronunciation of each individual morpheme and the way in which these morphemes are combined. We have said that each syntactic structure contains a surface structure consisting mainly of a well-formed sequence of morphemes. Predicting the pronunciation of a sequence of morphemes is not a trivial problem. Unfortunately, it is not enough simply to string together the pronunciations of the individual morphemes composing the sequence. Take, for example, the sequence of morphemes (12) and (14), which respectively have the pronunciations (13) and (15):

(12)   *Did + you + try + not + to + smile*
(13)   dijə-tray-nat-tə-smayl
       'Did you try not to smile?'
(14)   *Did + n't + you + try + to + smile*
(15)   dıd-nčə-tray-Də-smayl
       'Didn't you try to smile?'

[12] See p. 4.

18   *Generative phonology*

We introduced hyphens in the phonetic representations in order to facilitate the location of the sound sequences corresponding to each morpheme, except between the phonetic representations of *did* and *you* in (13) and *n't* and *you* in (15), which 'merge' together in these pronunciations. We have underlined the morphemes which are given a different pronunciation in (13) and (15).

Four of the six morphemes (*did, you, not, to*) are not pronounced in the same way in these two sentences. *Did* is pronounced [dɪd] in (15), but combines with *you* in (13) to give [dɪǰə]. *Not* is given its 'full' pronunciation [nat] in (13), but in (15) it loses its vowel and the *n* becomes syllabic. Moreover, its final *t* is modified along with *you*, giving [nč̩ə]. Finally, *to* varies between [tə] and a pronunciation where the *t* is a 'flap': [Də]. The phonological component of a grammar must be able to make explicit the general principles governing such variations.

The problem is in fact even more complicated, because the same sequence of morphemes often has several pronunciations. Apart from (13), sequence (12), for example, can have the phonetic representations (16), (17), and (18); we have underlined those pronunciations which differ from the corresponding pronunciations of (13):

(16)   [dɪǰu-tray-nat-tə-smayl]
(17)   [dɪd-yə-tray-nat-tə-smayl]
(18)   [dɪd-yu-tray-nat-tu-smayl]

Whether one pronounces (12) as (13), (16), (17), or (18), this does not affect its identity. It is the same sentence pronounced in four different ways. We will say that in such cases there is *free variation* between several pronunciations; and that the phonetic representations (13), (16), (17) and (18) are *free variants*. Some variation in pronunciation is possible in a given sequence, but not any. For example, when one pronounces (12), one can never give the morpheme *not* the pronunciation that it has in (15). The sub-sequence *try not to* of (12) cannot be pronounced *[tray-nt-tə] or *[tray-nč-tə] (*tryn't to*).

The phonological component takes the syntactic structures generated by the syntactic component and gives each one a phonetic representation (or several, in the case of free variation). The set of all the phonetic representations thus defined is the set P of all the well-formed phonetic representations of the language in question (see p. 4).

We now see how a grammar defines the infinite set of well-formed sound–meaning pairs of a language. The syntactic component generates an infinite set of syntactic structures. In a sense syntactic structures form the bridge between sound and meaning. Each syntactic structure is endowed with a semantic representation by the semantic component and with one or several phonological representations by the phonological component. Each one of the syntactic structures generated by the syntactic component thus gives rise to one or several pairs that have on the one hand a semantic representation and on the other a phonetic representation. The set of pairs thus generated is the set of descriptions of well-formed sound–meaning pairs.[13] In the case of English, an adequate grammar will, for example, have to generate the pairs (1, a) and (3, d) (see p. 4) but not the pair (3, b) since any native speaker of English knows that there is no sentence pronounced: [maysɪstərzlɛftðəbʊksɪnðəkɑr] which could mean: 'my sister has left the books and the car'.

The organization of grammars as we have described it raises several questions.

In the first place, a clear distinction is to be made between the lexicon and the syntactic, semantic and phonological components. Each one of these components is an organized set of general principles, of rules applicable to an infinity of sentences. The syntactic component of a grammar of English has, for example, a rule stating that a verb agrees in person and number with its subject. There is no need to have seen this sentence to know that one must say *he was teasing the dog* and not **he were teasing the dog*. On the other hand, the lexicon is a list of particular facts that do not arise from any general principle and which must therefore be seen and learned one by one by the subject learning the language. It is impossible for anyone who has never met the word *meniscus* [mɪnískəs] to know that it is a lens, convex on one side, concave on the other. The pronunciation [mɪnískəs] rather than **[nɪmískəs], the particular meaning attached to it, etc. are all singular features that have to be memorized by the subject. One often hears someone say: 'how odd, I don't know that word, I've never come across it before', but one never hears the same thing about a whole sentence, although one comes across many more new sentences than new words.

The distinction between language features which come from general rules and other, singular features (the term *idiosyncratic* is often used) is an absolutely fundamental distinction in linguistics. As a first approximation one can say that a lexicon is a list of all the idiosyncratic facts and that this

---

[13]   On p. 13 we did not define a description as a pair of representations, but as a sequence obtained by placing these representations one after the other. Both definitions are of course equivalent. At that point our purpose was to establish a simple analogy between natural languages and the formal languages presented in the preceding pages. Formal languages were considered as sets of sequences, and not sets of pairs of sequences.

list has to be memorized item by item by the speaker–hearer. We have already said that this list is not only composed of isolated morphemes but also of certain combinations of morphemes. In fact, there exist a great number of such combinations which possess certain global properties that cannot be deduced from those of the individual morphemes entering into their composition. Let us take a few examples. The lexical item *overtake* is composed of two morphemes: *over*, which indicates, among other things, that something is done in excess (see *overheat, overkill, overeat*, etc.), and *take* 'get a hold of'. If *over* + *take* is represented as a whole in the lexicon, it is because the grammar of English does not have a rule enabling one to deduce the meaning 'catch up with and pass' by a combination of the meanings of *over* and *take*. One must have already met the combination *over* + *take* to know that it has this meaning rather than 'take too much', for example. Or again, consider the idiom *to kick the bucket:* its meaning can certainly not be predicted by rule from those of its component parts. The sentence *he kicked the bucket* can be understood in two ways 'he died', or literally 'he kicked the bucket'. In English there are two different combinations of *to* + *kick* + *the* + *bucket* and only the first is represented in the lexicon. The second need not be learnt since it can always be reinvented by combining the lexical items *kick*, Definite Article, and *bucket*, in accordance with the rules of syntax, and it literally means 'to kick the bucket'. The reason why *he kicked the little bucket* and *that bucket which he kicked* are necessarily taken in their literal sense is that the idiom *to kick the bucket* cannot result in all the combinations which the syntactic rules normally allow in the case of a regular sequence Verb + Article + Noun.

Each lexical item is represented by a *lexical entry*, containing three categories of information: syntactic information, which specifies its ways of combining with other morphemes, semantic information, which specifies its meaning, and phonological information, which specifies its pronunciation. For example, the lexical entry of *gorilla* would include the following information:

> syntactic   :   Noun, Common, Count, Animate, etc.
> semantic   :   'an African anthropoid ape'
> phonological: /gərɪlə/

And that of *brutalize:*

> syntactic   :   Verb, Transitive, etc.
> semantic   :   'to make brutal'
> phonological: /brut + æl + ayz/

Strictly speaking, a lexical item is a set of properties: the set of properties contained in its lexical entry.[14] This lexical entry is subdivided into three sections corresponding to the three components: syntactic, semantic, and phonological. The information contained in the syntactic part defines the behaviour of the lexical item in relation to the syntactic rules, the semantic information its behaviour in relation to the semantic rules, and the phonological information its behaviour in relation to the phonological rules. A grammar is therefore a combination of three main systems: syntax, semantic, and phonology. Each of these systems has two kinds of entities: on the one hand, general principles of combination (rules) and on the other, specific information defining a certain number of elements of combination and their behaviour in relation to these rules (lexical information).

To conclude, let us say a few words on the syntactic information in lexical entries: this information indicates that the lexical item under consideration belongs to a certain number of *syntactic categories* defined by the functioning of the syntactic component, such as Noun, Verb, Adjective, Masculine, Transitive, etc. All the lexical items belonging to a given syntactic category have certain combinatory properties in common which are characteristic of this category. For instance, any lexical item belonging to the Noun class necessarily belongs either to the Animate or the Inanimate class, and it can immediately follow morphemes like *a, the, some, this*, etc.: *a boy, the silence;* all the lexical items that belong both to the Verb class and to the Transitive class take a direct object, as *the dog* and *it*, in *do + not + tease + the + dog* and *he + knows + it*. Every one of the syntactic properties of a lexical item is a constraint imposed upon the well-formed morpheme sequences in which that item can occur.

SURFACE STRUCTURES

The syntactic component generates an infinite set of syntactic structures which each contain a surface structure. The surface structure of a sentence contains all the information necessary to specify the pronunciation of that sentence. This surface structure must include a sequence of morphemes, but this is not sufficient, since it is not enough to know the morphemes which make up a sentence and the order in which they are put to predict the

---

[14] Lexical items (or morphemes) are not to be confused with their pronunciation. The sound sequence [gərɪlə] and the morpheme *gorilla* are two different things. The morpheme *gorilla* is a set of properties of which the sequence [gərɪlə] is but one element. Rather than identify each lexical item or morpheme by listing every time all the properties constituting it, it is represented by traditional spelling. The sequence of letters *g-o-r-i-l-l-a* is the name of the morpheme *gorilla* just as *Shakespeare* is the name of the author of *The Tempest*.

pronunciation of that sentence. A certain number of other syntactic properties must also be taken into account; we will examine these below.

The successive morphemes of a sentence are not simply arranged end to end like dominoes on a table. They are first of all grouped in *words*. The sentence *your friend recopied her notes* has eight morphemes grouped in five words. The sign # will be used to mark word boundaries. We will therefore write # *your* # *friend* # *re* + *copi* + *ed* # *her* # *note* + *s* #. English spelling has various symbols indicating word boundaries: spaces, hyphens, apostrophes and other punctuation marks. However, there is no sign to indicate morpheme boundaries. Phonological rules have to take into account the distribution of word boundaries when attributing a pronunciation to a sequence of morphemes. The French morpheme *galop* 'galop' is pronounced [galo] when it is used alone (# *galop* #), and [galɔp] when it is followed by other morphemes inside the same word (# *galop* + *ade* # 'galloping', # *galop* + *i* + *ez* # 'you galloped'). Similarly *cachet* 'seal' is pronounced [kaʃɛ] in # *cachet* # and [kast] in # *dé* + *cachet* + *ez* # [dekaʃte] 'unseal'.

In order to be able to predict correctly the pronunciation of a sentence, a surface structure must contain a sequence of morphemes grouped in words, and yet this is not quite sufficient. Take, for example, the sequence # *blue* # *bird* # *house* #. It is part of two different syntactic structures independently generated by the syntactic component, one characterizing the sound–meaning pair (19) and the other the sound–meaning pair (20).

(19) [blúbə̀rdhâws] 'a house for birds that is blue'

(20) [blúbə̀rdhâws] 'a house for bluebirds'

The digits 1, 2, 3, represent main stress, secondary stress and tertiary stress. Phrase (19) is pronounced with the main stress on *bird*, whereas phrase (20) has it on *blue*. The differences between the pronunciations of (19) and (20) come from the fact that although both phrases contain the same words in identical order, their syntactic relationship is not the same – *bird* is in close relationship to *house* in (19), whereas in (20) it is more closely related to *blue*. This syntactic difference can be represented by writing (*blue*(*birdhouse*)) for (19) and ((*bluebird*)*house*) for (20).[15]

Words are therefore not the only intermediary units between morphemes and sentences. The division of sentences into words is just one of the consequences of a very general fact: a sentence is a hierarchical structure

[15] On stress assignment in English, see Chomsky and Halle, *The Sound Pattern of English* (1968) (henceforth *SPE*), Liberman and Prince (1977).

composed of *constituents* embedded into one another. The biggest constituent, i.e. the sentence, is successively divided into smaller and smaller constituents until the final constituents, in other words morphemes, are reached. Words are just one type of constituent.[16]

Take for example the sentence: *my brother likes that composer*. This sentence, (S), can be divided into two constituents: *my brother* and *likes that composer*. The constituent *my brother* is a noun phrase (NP) composed of the determiner (D) *my*, and the noun (N) *brother*. The constituent *likes that composer* is a verb phrase (VP) composed of the verb (V) *likes* and a noun phrase (NP) *that composer*. The verb *likes* is composed of the verb *like* and the ending (T) *s*. The noun phrase *that composer* is composed of the determiner (D) *that* and the noun *composer*, which is in turn composed of the verb (V) *compose* and a suffix (Sx) *er* (cf. *paint/painter*, *swim/ swimmer*, etc). The hierarchy of constituents can be represented by an upside-down tree, each node representing a constituent (fig. 2a). Each node is *labelled*, i.e. it is given a symbol (a label) which is the abbreviation of that constituent's name.[17] For example, the node dominating the constituent *my brother* is given the label NP to indicate that this constituent is a noun phrase. Another kind of representation, strictly equivalent to the representation by labelled trees, consists of enclosing each constituent in a pair of labelled brackets (fig. 2b). To each of the thirteen labelled nodes of fig. 2a corresponds a pair of brackets in fig. 2b, provided with the corresponding label, giving twenty-six labelled brackets in all. Fig. 2b is set out in two lines to allow for a clearer presentation.

When figs. 2a and 2b are considered with reference to the explanation above, it can be seen that the sequences of morphemes which are constituents form organic wholes, whereas the others are just random heaps. Contrast, for example, the sequence *that composer*, which corresponds to an NP node, and *-s that compos-*, which does not correspond to any node. Although the constituents *my + brother* and *that + composer* are both adjacent to the constituent *like + s* in the morpheme sequence, the constituent *like + s* is more closely related to the constituent *that + composer*, in that they are both dominated by the VP node, and thus form a whole within the sentence, whereas to find a node that dominates both *like + s* and *my + brother*, one has to go back to the node S, which dominates the whole sentence.

---

[16] This is a gross simplification, but as the principle of cyclical application is not going to be discussed here, this simplification does not affect the coherence of our presentation. On the notion of 'word', see *SPE*:12–14 and 367–70.

[17] Groups of several letters which constitute a single abbreviation, such as NP, VP, etc. count as a single symbol.

Fig. 2a

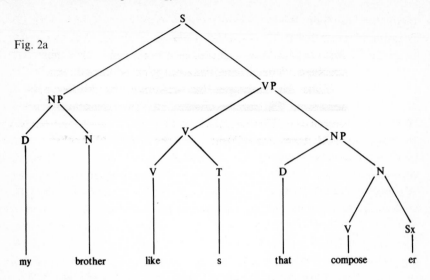

$_s[_{NP}[_D[my]_D \,_N[brother]_N]_{NP} \,_{VP}[_V[_V[like]_V \,_T[s]_T]_V \cdots$

Fig. 2b $\cdots_{NP}[\,_D[that]_D \,_N[\,_V[compose]_V \,_{Sx}[er]_{Sx}\,]_N\,]_{NP}\,]_{VP}\,]_S$

Figs. 2a and 2b (once again, these are two different but strictly equivalent ways of representing the same abstract object) contain all the necessary information for the phonological rules mechanically to deduce the pronunciation of the sentence *my brother likes that composer*. They represent the surface structure of the sentence. For purely typographical reasons, phonologists usually use the bracket representation rather than the tree. The surface structure of a sentence is a sequence of morphemes provided with a set of labelled brackets, which organize this sequence into a hierarchy of constituents. It is therefore a finite sequence composed of two kinds of symbols: morphemes (each one counting here as a single symbol) and labelled brackets. The surface structure of a sentence is one of the elements composing its syntactic structure. By generating an infinite set of syntactic structures, the syntactic component at the same time generates the infinite set of surface structures contained in the syntactic structures.[18]

[18] Any sequence of symbols with labelled brackets is called a phrase-marker. A syntactic structure is a certain set of phrase-markers generated one from the other by application of syntactic rules. A surface structure is therefore one particular phrase-marker, among all those that constitute a syntactic structure. It is said to be a 'surface' structure in contrast with another phrase-marker, the *deep structure*, which plays an essential role in the operation of the semantic component. The surface structure of a sentence is derived from its deep structure by the operation of syntactic rules called *transformations*. See Chomsky (1965, 1972).

Liaison or 'linking' phenomena in French illustrate well the way in which the pronunciation of a sentence depends on its constituent structure. There are many French words with two pronunciations, in which one is deduced from the other by dropping the final consonant. *Vous* 'you' (plur.) is pronounced [vuz] in *vous écoutez* [vuzekute] 'you are listening' and [vu] in *vous regardez* [vurgarde] 'you are watching', *petit* 'small' is pronounced [pœtit] in *petit écrou* [pœtitekru] 'small screwnut' and [pœti] in *petit bouton* [pœtibutɔ̃] 'small button', etc. The final *z* of [vuz] and the final *t* of [pœtit] are *latent consonants*. The act of pronouncing these consonants is called *liaison*. There is *liaison* between *vous* and *écoutez* but not between *vous* and *regardez*, and between *petit* and *écrou*, but not between *petit* and *bouton*. The latent consonant is never pronounced when it is at the end of a sentence (*levez-vous* [lœvevu] 'get up', *c'est trop petit* [setropti] 'it's too small'); or when it precedes a word beginning with a consonant (*vous regardez, petit bouton*). When it precedes a word beginning with a vowel, there is *liaison* only when the two words are closely enough related, syntactically speaking. One pronounces, for instance, *les* with a final *z* in *va les attendre* [valezatãdr] 'go and wait for them', since in that sentence the object pronoun *les* 'them' is syntactically closely related to the verb *attendre* [atãdr] 'to wait', whereas *les* is pronounced [le] without a final *z* in *regarde-les attendre* [rœgardleatãdr] 'look at them wait', for here *les* is more closely related to the preceding verb *regarde* [rœgard] 'to look'. To summarize, two conditions must be simultaneously fulfilled for *liaison* to take place. The first condition is of a phonological nature, by which the word containing a latent consonant must be followed by a word beginning with a vowel, and the second is a syntactic condition, by which the syntactic relation between the two words must be sufficiently close.

Liaison phenomena show that in French at least two kinds of word boundaries must be distinguished: 'weak boundaries' which allow *liaison*, and 'strong' boundaries, which prevent it. We shall represent a weak boundary by the symbol # and a strong one by the symbol ##. For instance, we write *vous#écoutez*, *petit#écrou*, *va## les#attendre*, *regarde#les##attendre*. One must remember that the presence of a single symbol # only indicates that the syntactic structure allows *liaison*, not that *liaison* actually takes place. For example, we write *vous#regardez* and *petit#bouton* because the syntactic structure is identical to that of *vous écoutez* and *petit écrou*. If *liaison* does not take place in *vous regardez* and *petit bouton*, it is because the phonological condition for *liaison* is not fulfilled: *regardez* and *bouton* do not begin with a vowel. A grammar of French must account for the fact that anyone who knows French knows how to break down a sentence into words, and where, or where not to make the *liaison*.[19] Surface structures do not explicitly separate words, since according to what we said on page 24, they do not contain # symbols. A grammar of French contains a set of rules that mechanically distribute the # and ## boundaries in any surface structure, basing itself on the disposition of the labelled brackets. This is in fact not peculiar to French. Most languages, if not all, possess facts of pronunciation which systematically depend on the closeness of the syntactic relationship between adjoining words. Selkirk (1972) studied some of the rules which distribute the # boundaries in the surface structures of English and French. We will not look into the details of their functioning here, which is rather complex. In order to make things clearer, we will assume that these rules operate in two successive steps. Some rules first insert the symbol # between each word; others then replace the symbol # by the double ## at each point where the syntactic structure prevents *liaison*, and leave a single # symbol where the syntactic structure allows *liaison*. To come back to the contrast between (19) *blue birdhouse* and (20) *bluebird house* (cf. p. 22), the surface structures of (19) and (20) are represented below in figs. 3a and 3b, respectively. We replaced the labels attached to each constituent by arbitrary numbers. The syntactic relation between *bird* and *house* is closer in fig. 3a than in fig. 3b.

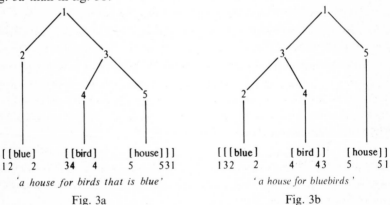

[[blue] [[bird] [house]]] 1 2 2 34 4 5 531	[[[blue] [bird]] [house]] 1 3 2 2 4 43 5 5 1
'a house for birds that is blue'	*' a house for bluebirds '*
Fig. 3a	Fig. 3b

The figures 3a and 3b illustrate an interesting property of the representation by brackets of constituent structures: the greater the number of brackets between two adjoining words, the further apart they are, from a syntactic point of view. Each bracket between two adjoining words

---

[19] Of course we are referring to norms which are inherent in the speech of native speakers, and not to those of 'correct French', imposed by schools.

indicates the existence of constituent boundaries between these words, and two words are less closely related when they do not belong to the same constituent. Two words are necessarily separated by at least two brackets, of which one is a closing bracket, indicating the end of the first word, and the other an opening bracket, indicating the beginning of the second. For instance, in fig. 3a, *bird* is separated from *house* by the closing '$]_4$' which indicates the end of the constituent *bird*, and by the opening '$[_5$' indicating the beginning of the constituent *house*. *Bird* and *house* are not separated by any other bracket, i.e. there are no constituent boundaries other than those of no. 4 and no. 5 which intervene between *bird* and *house*. On the other hand *blue* and *bird* are separated by three brackets. Apart from the closing bracket '$]_2$' which indicates the end of the constituent *blue*, and the opening bracket '$[_4$' indicating the beginning of the constituent *bird*, there is also the bracket '$[_3$' indicating the beginning of the constituent *bird house*. This bracket goes between *blue* and *bird* since *blue* is situated outside this constituent, while *bird* is inside it.

It can now be seen more clearly how the distribution of labelled brackets can be made use of by the rules which mark word boundaries as weak or strong – the rules for doubling the symbol $\#$ mentioned on page 26. If all the cases to be described were like (19) and (20), it would suffice to have one rule stating: 'replace $\#$ by $\#\#$ everywhere there is a sequence of three or more brackets'. Unfortunately, reality is much more complex. Note in particular that some *liaisons* (the so-called optional *liaisons*) depend on the type of speech. In the sentence *je vais à Paris* [žœvɛ(z)apari] 'I am going to Paris', the word *vais* is pronounced with a final *z* ([vɛz]) in careful speech, and without the *z* ([vɛ]) in everyday conversation. The syntactic structure of these sentences is the same whatever the speech style. What does change are the rules for doubling the $\#$. Each speech style is characterized by a certain system of rules for doubling the $\#$. These rules in fact are not completely at variance from one style to the other. Certain *liaison* consonants are always pronounced whatever the speech style, as the *z* at the end of *vous* in *vous écoutez* 'you listen' and others never are, as the final *n* of *Jean* in *Jean écoute* 'John listens'.

One last remark: conventional spelling has specialized symbols to indicate word boundaries: spaces, commas, etc. Each space, comma, etc. corresponds to a word boundary, and all word boundaries are indicated by a space, comma, etc. Nothing of the sort exists in speech. As far as we know, there are no sound marks specially for indicating word boundaries in any language. Instrument recordings in particular show that the voice does not pause between words, or even in general between those parts of a sentence that are separated by commas in spelling, and there is no *a priori* reason for it to be otherwise.[20] It is, therefore, perfectly illusory to want to define words in purely phonetic or phonological terms. The dividing up into words is due to certain rules operating on the constituent structure, which is defined by the syntactic component.

In our examples so far, we have been relying on the conventions of our writing system to break down sentences into words, and we will continue to do so. The breakdown into words in spelling usually matches those which it is in any case necessary to postulate in order to account adequately for the facts of pronunciation. This point deserves to be underlined: phonologists have no right to use the written language as a basis for arguing about analyses, since the object of their study is oral language, and writing is not always a faithful description of it. In many cases, English spelling does not transcribe contemporary linguistic reality but certain linguistic features of the past which have disappeared today. In order to find out whether writing is a reflection of reality or not, linguists must first study this reality for itself, without taking conventional spelling into consideration, then compare their analysis point by point with conventional spelling. The final *n* in the spelling *hymn* has a linguistic reality, for although it is not heard at the end of this word, pronounced [hɪm], it is heard in *hymnal* [hɪmnəl]. On the other hand, the final *b* at the end of *climb* [klaym] is a fiction of spelling, since it is never pronounced either in this word or in any other constructed from the same root. There is no *a priori* reason to believe that conventional spelling is any more exact in reflecting language in relation to the distribution of spaces than it is in relation to final consonants. If we accept the word analysis suggested by spelling, it is because by studying the language completely independently of its writing system, we are obliged to break up sentences into units which exactly correspond to those separated by spaces in writing. Whether we call these units words or anything else, is simply a question of terminological preference.

LINGUISTIC THEORY

When linguists attempt to construct the grammars of various languages, it is not with the intention of exhibiting them like specimens of some natural history collection, but because they hope to improve our understanding of the faculty of language.

---

[20] Spelling thus does not only note the phonetic properties of sentences, it also notes some of their syntactic properties, such as boundaries between words or between more important constituents (commas, etc.).

Of all the members of the animal kingdom, only humans are capable of learning, in their first years of life, the extraordinarily complicated system that constitutes a language. Basing himself on a small number of sentences that he has the opportunity of hearing, the child is capable of inferring the general principles governing the formation and interpretation of the infinite set of sentences of the language in question (in other words, of discovering its grammar). When one thinks of the overwhelming size of the task involved, the relative ease and rapidity with which the child accomplishes it is absolutely astounding – unless there were certain universally constant structural features, valid for all languages (*universals*), and these constants were inherent to the genetic code of the species, so that each child would be born with a built-in knowledge of the universal model on which all languages are based. When exposed to French, for example, the child would only have to discover those properties of French which are not universal. At this stage in our knowledge, the idea that language universals are determined by the genetic characteristics of the species is still a hypothesis, but the actual existence of universals is undoubtable. The languages on which we have some data are but a ridiculously small sample of all the languages that have existed since the beginning of humanity. And yet, despite their extraordinary diversity at a surface level, languages possess such deep and striking similarities, that there can be no doubt that differences between one language and another are in fact secondary variations of a single fundamental model. One way of discovering this model is by constructing the grammars of different languages and comparing them.

The linguist therefore has two different and complementary aims. On the one hand he tries to discover the grammar of particular languages and, on the other, he tries to discover the universal model on which these grammars are constructed. Constructing a grammar G of a language L amounts to proposing a definition of the notion 'well-formed sentence of L'. This definition is of the following kind: 'for a sound–meaning pair to be a well-formed sentence of L, it is necessary and sufficient that it be generated by the grammar G (and this is followed by a detailed description of the grammar G)'. A grammar of a language L is a theory of the sentences of L.

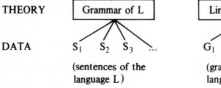
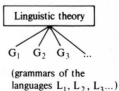

To go one degree further in abstraction, he is trying also to construct a *linguistic theory*, a theory defining the notion 'human language in general' which draws its data from the grammars of particular languages (cf. diagram).

It is easy to imagine a system of sound–meaning correspondences which would not form a possible language. Take, for example, a language in which sentences would have the same meaning as in English, but where pronunciation would be obtained by permuting the first and the last sound of normal English pronunciation (the normal pronunciation is given in parentheses)

([tɔk])	[kɔt]	'talk'
([tɔks])	[sɔkt]	'talks'
([tɔkɪŋ])	[ŋɔkɪt]	'talking'
([hitɔks])	[sitɔkh]	'he talks'
([hitɔkt])	[titɔkh]	'he talked'

One hardly needs to be an expert to see that no human language has ever been built on such a model, nor ever will be. In order to obtain the grammar of this fictitious language, one must take the grammar of English and add to the end of its phonological component a phonological rule which permutes the first and last sound of each sentence. But no known language has this type of phonological rule. The fictitious language in question is not a possible language because its grammar contains a phonological rule which is not a possible (or 'well-formed') phonological rule.

Since each particular language is characterized by a specific grammar, linguistic theory states the necessary and sufficient properties that a grammar must possess so that the set of sound–meaning pairs generated by this grammar can constitute a possible language. The remarks in the previous sections concerning the general organization of grammars in fact precisely pertain to linguistic theory.

If we transpose the terminology we have been using for sentences of a specific language to the study of languages in general, we can call 'well-formed' the grammars that generate sets of sound–meaning pairs constituting possible languages: the others are called 'ill-formed'. Just as the theory of the sentences of a particular language L (the grammar of L) must define the notion of 'well-formed sentence of L', the theory of languages in general (linguistic theory) must define the notion of 'well-formed grammar'. Needless to say, at present we are still far from our goal.

A given language, therefore, has two kinds of properties. Some of them can be found in every human language. Others, on the contrary, are particular to some languages. The description of a specific language should only mention those features that distinguish it from all other languages. The rest belongs to linguistic theory. *One cannot, therefore, claim to describe a specific language without implicitly or explicitly making hypotheses about all languages. Looking for what is common to all languages and looking for what varies from one language to another are tasks that presuppose each other.*

2

From surface structures
to phonetic representations

If X-rays are taken of a subject's mouth pronouncing a word such as *screwy*, a succession of movements can be observed which simultaneously involve different parts of the speech apparatus, the lips, the body and tip of the tongue, the vocal cords, etc. The combination of these movements produces a specific sound pattern – a signal – which then travels through the air and strikes the hearer's ear-drum. This signal is a series of sound waves, a rapid succession of fluctuations in the air pressure. To examine the movement of speech organs that produce vocal signals is to study speech from an articulatory point of view; to examine the physical properties of these signals is to study speech from an acoustic point of view. Acoustics is the branch of physics dealing with sounds.

Considered from both these points of view, the pronunciation of a sentence is a 'continuum', a set of continuous variations with no sharp boundary between one sound and the next. In order to go from [u] to [i] in [skrui] *screwy*, the lips are retracted, thus losing their roundness, and the body of the tongue is simultaneously shifted towards the front of the mouth. These movements take a certain amount of time, during which the form of the mouth cavity progressively changes and successively produces the whole range of intermediary shades between [u] and [i]. And yet we clearly hear the two vowels in succession, each one precisely delimited from the other. From continuous variations over time of the signal, our perception constructs a finite sequence s-k-r-u-i, the terms of which cannot be broken down into smaller segments, and we identify these terms as each belonging to a certain abstract category, known as a *speech sound*.[1] It is this succession of speech sounds that the phonetic representation [skrui] symbolizes.

---

[1] Our eye acts in a similar way, when it breaks down the continuous line of writing into a sequence of segments; each segment is assigned one of the letters of the alphabet.

The distinction must be carefully made between a signal – or the sequence of articulatory movements which produces it – and the phonetic representation associated with it. In the case of a signal we are dealing with a certain sequence of physical events, of sound vibrations or articulatory movements, and as such each sequence is unique. It is impossible to make exactly the same articulatory gestures or to produce exactly the same series of sound waves (the same signal) twice. From a physical point of view, two events are never absolutely identical. And yet when we repeat *they're screwy*, we have the feeling that we are pronouncing 'the same way' each time, and those who are listening have the feeling that they are hearing 'the same thing'.

Let us make a comparison. No penny is exactly identical to another, but we neglect noticeable material differences as long as they do not alter its conformity to the abstract model of 'a penny' of which each coin is a sort of material realization (a token). The only *relevant* features are the head, lettering, numbers and decorative patterns engraved on each side of the coin, and the relative size and arrangement of these. On the other hand, irregularities caused by wear or minimal differences in their production are not relevant. The same is true for the different sound patterns produced by repeating *they're screwy*. They are all tokens of a certain abstract type defined by the rules of English, and the phonetic representation [ðɛrskruɪ] refers to that type, and not to any of the concrete sound patterns we produce when we say *they're screwy*. In other words, there is the same kind of relation between a phonetic representation and the different vocal signals corresponding to it as there is between a musical score and the way in which it can be performed at different times, with different musicians or instruments. Each performance is a unique sequence of events (the performers' gestures and the sounds they produce), but they all materialize the same abstract structure. The audience can very well perceive differences in execution; these differences do not teach them anything about the tune being played, but only inform them about the musicians' performance, the quality of the instruments, etc.

Not all the physical properties of the signals are used for linguistic ends, since they cannot all be controlled by the speaker. For example, the voice quality cannot be altered, for it depends on individual anatomical characteristics, state of health, etc. The hearer, therefore, selects from what he hears, and retains what is relevant from a linguistic point of view. *It is the properties of an utterance governed by rules which are linguistically relevant.*

The linguist reduces the infinity of possible vocal productions to a finite alphabet of phonetic symbols. By this, he is making the hypothesis that the relevant linguistic properties in the pronunciation of any sentence of any language can be exhaustively described by using a finite number of parameters, each parameter describing a scale of discrete values, themselves finite in number.[2] Take for example the positions of the body of the tongue in the mouth. It can move in two directions: up and down (the vertical axis) and backwards and forwards (the horizontal axis). From its lowest to its highest point toward the roof of the mouth, there is an infinity of intermediate positions along the vertical axis. Similarly, there is an infinity of intermediate positions between the two extreme points along the horizontal axis. The complete range of positions that the body of the tongue can occupy in the mouth thus constitutes a bidimensional space made up of an infinity of points, and, for each individual speaker, an infinity of physically distinct sounds corresponds to this infinity of points. But the languages of the world actually take very little advantage of these possibilities. Only differences in sound due to fairly distant articulations are used to linguistic ends. Differences in sounds produced by very close articulations are ignored. Languages impose a discrete and finite grid of universal phonetic categories, the speech sounds, on the continuous and infinite field of articulatory and acoustic possibilities. Each speech sound is represented by a symbol from the phonetic alphabet.

Speech sounds are not unanalysable units. Each one is defined by the unique position it occupies in the universal system of *distinctive features*. For example, the sound [z] is [+ cons, + voice, − son...], i.e. a sound which is consonantal, voiced, non-sonorant, etc. (these terms will ba defined later) whereas the sound [a] is [− cons, + voice, + son...], i.e. non-consonantal, voiced, sonorant, etc. Distinctive features are established once and for all, are valid for the description of any language, and their system defines the set of articulatory and auditory possibilities that humans can use to linguistic ends. Most features represent a perceptual and articulatory dimension that can vary independently of the others. Let us simplify and assume that distinctive features are all binary, i.e. they can only have two values, which will be represented by the signs plus (+) and minus (−).[3] Each feature can be considered as a certain property P. For every speech sound which has this property P, the feature P has the *value* (or *specification*) [+ P]. For those

---

[2]   *Discrete* is contrasted with *continuous*. The integers 1, 2, 3... are discrete entities. The points of a straight line, on the other hand, form a continuous sequence.

[3]   So as to keep things fairly simple, we will say that distinctive features are binary at a phonetic level as well as at a phonological level, and we ignore the distinction usually made between their classificatory function and their function as phonetic parameters; see *SPE* (65, 169, 297) and Postal (1968; 109 ff.).

that do not have the property P, the feature [P] has the specification [− P]. Every speech sound is either [+ P] or [− P] and none can be both [+ P] and [− P]. Each speech sound is defined by the list of its specifications in relation to the various distinctive features. If φ is the total number of distinctive features proposed by linguistic theory, each speech sound is defined by a set of φ + or − specifications. The idea of a universal system of binary features was originally developed by Roman Jakobson, in a very different theoretical perspective from the one adopted here,[4] cf. Jakobson, Fant and Halle (1952), Jakobson and Halle (1956).

Table IV above is a set of the speech sounds most frequently used in this book, characterized in terms of distinctive features. The first column indicates, for example, that the speech sound represented by the letter *p* in phonetic transcriptions, is defined by the specifications [− sonorant, − syllabic, + consonantal, − continuant...]. Only distinctive features have a status in linguistic theory. The letters of the phonetic alphabet are just useful abbreviations to designate a set of specifications.[5] Thus [p] is nothing but a convenient abbreviation for the set [− sonorant, − syllabic, + consonantal, − continuant...].

The system of distinctive features must provide a universal referential framework, enabling both the different sounds of any given language to be categorized in relation to each other, and also speech sounds to be compared across languages. We are looking for a vocabulary that enables us to state precisely not only how the initial sound of *beau* 'beautiful' is different from that of *peau* 'skin' but also how it is nearer to that of the Russian word *bog* 'God' than to that of the English word *boat*. Any phonetic distinction, however slight, must have its place in this system, whenever it is systematically made in one language or another. The only regularities that can be ignored are those that are found in all languages and attributed to certain constraints imposed by the structure of the human articulatory or perceptual system. For example, it is useless to note the difference between the nasal bilabial consonant at the end of *in* in *in between* and the labiodental nasal which often replaces it in *in fact*.[6] There is no rule that systematically distinguishes these two types of sounds in any language,

---

[4] See *SPE* (306–8) for some of the reasons why the system originally proposed by Jakobson had to be modified.

[5] Of the different phonetic alphabets, the most currently used is that of the *International Phonetic Association*, which has been described in the booklet *The Principles of the International Phonetic Association;* it is periodically reprinted (University College, London). For other alphabets, see Haudricourt and Thomas (1967).

[6] On bilabials and labiodentals, see p. 46 below.

and labiodental nasals only regularly replace bilabial nasals when the latter immediately precede an [f] or a [v̥] (Ladefoged, 1971: 37).

In reality, the phonetic transcriptions in books on linguistics are very rough approximations of the ideal we have just been describing. They are like geographical maps of partially unexplored regions. Besides those features that have not yet attracted the attention of scholars, there are others which are not represented in the phonetic transcriptions, because it has not yet been decided how best to describe them systematically. This is the case, for example, with the variations in the melodic height of the voice, which play an important role in the intonation of all languages.

The degree of precision in phonetic transcriptions also varies according to the needs of the subject matter. For, unless it is precisely this point which is being discussed, it is needless constantly to remind the reader, for example, that in French *r* is pronounced voiceless ([r̥]) when it is next to a voiceless consonant (see p. 47), and voiced ([r]) everywhere else; writing a single sound [r] in every case is sufficient. Such inaccuracies are of no consequence so long as they do not affect the validity of the points at issue.[7]

Still, it must be remembered that in theory a phonetic representation is a finite and exhaustive characterization of the set of all the linguistically relevant properties of the pronunciation of a form. Take, for example, the sentence *vous écriviez* 'you were writing' and its phonetic representation [vuzekr̥ivye]. It is composed of a sequence of ten speech sounds, each one defined by a set of φ specifications that correspond to the universal stock of φ distinctive features. If the specifications characterizing a sound are all placed on the same vertical column, and if the successive specifications of one feature in the different sounds are all placed on a horizontal line, a rectangular table, or matrix, is obtained, in which each column represents one sound and each line one distinctive feature. The matrix in question is in fig. 11b (p. 52 below). The sequence of phonetic symbols enclosed in square brackets, [vuzekr̥ivye], is just a convenient substitute for this matrix, and has no status in linguistic theory.

<hr/>

[7]   Reasons of practical convenience also come into play in the choice of the phonetic symbols. When transcribing a particular language, it is common to replace rare symbols occurring only in the International Phonetic Alphabet by others in common usage. For instance, we have used the letter *r* to stand for the voiced uvular fricative [ʁ] which occurs at the beginning of *route* in Parisian French. So as to simplify the printer's task, we have also used this letter *r* to stand for the voiced coronal sonorant [ɹ] which occurs at the beginning of *root* in most varieties of American English. Since we are in some cases using the same letter with different phonetic values depending on whether it occurs in a transcription of French or English, we have given the values of the phonetic symbols for French and English in separate tables at the beginning of this book.

So far, we only know a part of the universal stock of distinctive features. In *The Sound Pattern of English*, Chomsky and Halle proposed a system of about thirty distinctive features, to be completed and reshuffled as knowledge of the phonology of languages improved. For our part we will only present a fragment of this system, and limit ourselves to what is strictly necessary for the understanding of the general principle of distinctive features and the discussion of several concrete examples. For an account of the system as a whole, we refer the readers to the book by Chomsky and Halle. In what follows, our purpose is therefore not to survey, even rapidly, the whole range of the different articulatory possibilities that can be used to linguistic ends. The articulatory possibilities presented here and their corresponding distinctive features constitute only a limited sub-set of what has been listed up to now. Those readers who wish to have a more general idea of the different branches of phonetics will benefit from reading the general introduction by Denes and Pinson (1963). For more detailed accounts, see Catford (1977), Ladefoged (1964, 1971 and 1975), Malmberg (1968), Smalley (1968), Westermann and Ward (1933). On the subject of acoustic phonetics, see the straightforward introduction by Ladefoged (1962).

When approaching phonology for the first time, it little matters whether the reader can or cannot give a complete definition of the distinctive features of all the speech sounds mentioned in this book. It is sufficient if he gains a clear idea of the general principle of classification by distinctive features and the exact delineation of the most important features, such as [syllabic], [consonantal], [sonorant], [nasal]. The reader must not be put off by the luxuriance of the terminology. At first reading, he should pay special attention to what is being described, mostly quite simple things, without worrying too much about remembering the terms used to designate them. The index at the end and the tables at the front of the book will allow him to familiarize himself progressively with phonetic terminology, as it is repeatedly used in the following chapters. Whenever a term designating a distinctive feature is first mentioned, it is italicized. It alone has any status in linguistic theory. We have also given the most common traditionally established terms, which are employed to enable us to abbreviate. For example, the distinctive feature [fricative] does not exist, but there is no harm in using the term as a convenient abbreviation of 'continuous non-sonorant'.

The energy necessary for speech is provided by the compression of air in the lungs. This air escapes by the trachea in a continuous flow (expiration).

In order to escape, the air column thus set into motion has to pass through the larynx and the vocal tract (fig. 4).

Fig. 4

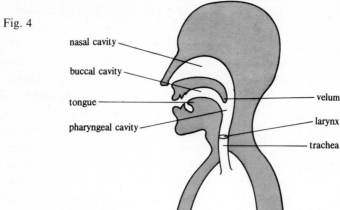

nasal cavity

buccal cavity

tongue

pharyngeal cavity

velum

larynx

trachea

lungs

The larynx and the vocal tract

The larynx is a cartilaginous structure situated at the top of the trachea. Inside the larynx are the vocal cords. These are two lip-shaped folds which function like a valve. The spacing between the cords is adjustable and enables the outlet of air to be controlled. Roughly speaking, vocal cords are like the branches of a V situated in a horizontal plane, the tip of which is turned towards the front of the body (towards the Adam's apple). The glottis is the empty space between the vocal cords. The amount of air that can pass through the glottis at a given moment depends on the space between the vocal cords. The glottis is closed when the vocal cords are tightened up against each other, completely blocking the passage of air. The vocal cords can also be wide apart, thus offering no resistance to the passage of air (as during normal breathing). The glottis is then said to be open.

In certain conditions, the opening and closing of the glottis takes place in rapid succession (several hundred times a second) and the continuous flow of air which comes from the trachea is separated into a series of little puffs of air corresponding to as many successive openings of the glottis.[8] The vocal cords are then said to vibrate, and the sounds produced as a result of the vibration of the vocal cords are said to be *voiced* ([+ voice]), whereas the others, by opposition, are said to be *voiceless* ([− voice]). The successive

[8]   The mechanism underlying the vibration of the vocal cords is clearly and simply described in *SPE:* 301.

puffs of air corresponding to the opening of the glottis follow one another at too rapid a pace for us to perceive them separately. This results in a regular buzzing, the laryngeal sound. The laryngeal sound excites the resonances of the vocal tract.

A simple comparison will lead to a better understanding of the respective roles of the vocal cords and the vocal tract. When one plucks a guitar string, its vibrations are transmitted to the mass of air contained in the sound box, and the nature of the sound we hear depends on two factors: the way in which the string vibrates and the characteristics of the sound box. For a given box, the way in which the string vibrates determines the pitch and loudness of the sound. The quicker the string vibrates (the more it is stretched), the higher the note in the scale, i.e. the higher its pitch; the larger the amplitude of the vibrations (the more forcefully one plays), the louder the sound. On the other hand, the characteristics of the sound box determine the quality (colour) of the sound.

The same string does not have an identical sound when it is stretched over a guitar box or over a banjo box. What happens is that the air in the box takes in the string vibrations and alters them. It enhances some of their aspects and dampens others. In short, it imposes a quality of its own on them and this quality in the end depends on the shape of the box, its volume, the disposition of its openings, etc. The speech apparatus is like a musical instrument whose sound box (vocal tract) can be altered at will.

Complex adjustments in and below the larynx enable us to control the mode of vibration of the vocal cords, on which the pitch and loudness of the sounds produced depend. The quality is regulated by the shape of the different cavities of the vocal tract.

The scope of the present introduction leaves us no room for a discussion of pitch and loudness. This does not mean that they are of secondary importance, or that nothing precise can yet be said about them, but we will simply say here that these properties of sound play an essential role in tone languages,[9] in the manifestations of stress and accent,[10] and in intonation, about which very little is yet known. [11]

---

[9]   Cf. Pike (1948). For discussions within the framework of generative phonology, cf., for example, Goldsmith (1976 a, b), Hyman (1975), Hyman and Schuh (1974), Leben (1971; 1973), Wang (1967), Williams (1976), Woo (1969; 1970).

[10]   In addition to *SPE*, the major part of which is dedicated to the detailed study of stress in English, the following works on stress may be consulted: Bierwisch (1968), Brame (1971), Bresnan (1971; 1972), Browne and McCawley (1965), Halle (1970; 1971; 1973 b; 1975), Halle and Keyser (1971), Kenstowicz (1974), Kiparsky (1973 a), Lehiste (1970), Liberman and Prince (1977), McCawley (1968 a), Ross (1972), Shibatani (1972), Zeps and Halle (1971).

[11]   But see the recent and promising works of Leben (1976) and Liberman (1975).

The nasal cavity and the pharyngobuccal cavity

The vocal tract consists of two cavities: the nasal cavity and the pharyngobuccal cavity (pharynx + mouth). The nasal cavity communicates with the outside by the nostrils. At its other end, it falls into the pharyngobuccal cavity. At the intersection where the two cavities meet there is a mobile muscular tissue, the velum or soft palate, which is a continuation of the bony roof of the mouth (hard palate). The velum acts as a wicket-gate. At rest, it hangs down, thus enabling all or part of the air coming from the pharynx to get out through the nasal cavity. The sounds then produced are said to be *nasal* ([+ nas]).[12] The velum can also be lifted to the horizontal position, thereby preventing any communication between the pharyngobuccal cavity and the nasal cavity. The air from the pharynx then has to pass through the mouth only. Thus *non-nasal* sounds ([− nas]) are obtained (cf. figs. 6, 7, 9, and 10). The shape and volume of the nasal cavity are fairly constant and it can only be closed off in one place, at the back. On the other hand, the pharyngobuccal tube is liable to take various forms and be narrowed or blocked in several places.

Vowel quality

If we keep to essentials, the resonance properties of the pharyngobuccal cavity depend on two factors: the position of the lips and the position of the tongue. The rounding and thrusting forward of the lips results in the total

Fig. 5

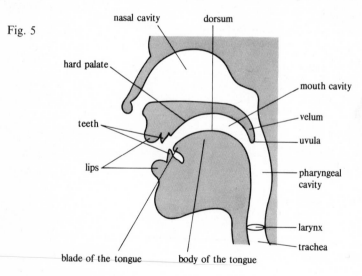

[12]   Cf. figs. 4 and 5, which represent the position of the organs during the production of a nasal vowel, and fig. 8 p. 44.

length of the pharyngobuccal tube being increased and the size of the opening by which it communicates with the outside being reduced. The sounds thus produced are said to be *rounded* ([+ round]) (*u, o, ü*, etc.). The others are said to be *non-rounded* ([− round]) (*i, e, a*, etc.).

Along most of its length, the floor of the pharyngobuccal tube is formed by the upper side of the tongue (see fig. 5). The tongue is a combination of muscles terminated at the front by a tip capable of extremely rapid and precise movements. The anterior part, including the tip and what immediately surrounds it, is called the blade of the tongue. The rest is what we will call the body of the tongue. Similarly, the upper surface of the tongue is divided into two areas: the upper surface of the blade or just 'the blade', and the dorsum, which extends back to the root of the tongue. The blade as a whole can be controlled independently of the body of the tongue.

The body of the tongue can move in two dimensions: up and down with concomitant movement of the lower jaw (vertical axis), and backwards and forwards (horizontal axis). As the body of the tongue moves upwards, the dorsum gets closer to the roof of the mouth, and the diameter of the pharyngobuccal tube is thereby narrowed. But this narrowing does not take place in a uniform manner all the way down the tube. The tightest place forms a kind of narrowing which divides the pharyngobuccal tube into two cavities, each one with its own resonance properties. The position of this narrowing in the tube depends on the location of the body of the tongue along the horizontal axis.

In the system proposed by Chomsky and Halle, the body of the tongue can only take three distinct positions on the vertical axis, and two on the horizontal one. When the body of the tongue is at its lowest point, the sounds produced are *low* ([+ low]) (*ɛ, a, ɔ*, etc.) and when it is at its highest point they are *high* ([+ high]) (*i, ü, u*, etc.). It therefore follows that no sound can be at the same time [+ low] and [+ high]. Sounds that are neither [+ low] nor [+ high], i.e. those which are both [− low] and [− high], are those produced when the tongue is in an intermediary position (*e, ö, o*, etc.). When the body of the tongue is at the back of the

	[− back]	[+ back]
[+ high] [− low]	i ü	u
[− high] [− low]	e ö	o
[− high] [+ low]	ɛ œ	a ɔ

mouth, the sounds are said to be *back* ([+ back]) (*u*, *o*, *a*, etc.) and the others *non-back* ([− back]) (*i*, *e*, *ü*, *ö*, etc.). By combining the possible positions along these two axes, a table can be derived which divides the vowels of French into six boxes. Where two vowels are situated in the same box they are distinguished by the shape of the lips (unrounded or rounded). By adding the specifications [− round] and [+ round], we obtain table I above.[13]

The sounds figuring in this table are all non-nasal; the velum is raised and the glottal vibrations excite only resonances of the pharyngobuccal tube. By lowering the velum, part of the air is let out through the nose and adds the resonances of the nasal cavity to those of the pharyngobuccal tube. Thus, to each different position of the lips and the body of the tongue there correspond two distinct vowels, a nasal and a non-nasal one. A nasal vowel is usually symbolized by the addition of a tilde to the letter which stands for the corresponding non-nasal vowel. Thus the letter [ε] stands for a vowel which is [− nas, − high, + low, − back, − round] and [ε̃] stands for a vowel which is [+ nas, − high, + low, − back, − round].

The consonants: manner of articulation

During the production of the sounds described in the preceding paragraph, the air flows freely through the pharyngobuccal tube without meeting any obstacle. Such sounds are said to be *non-consonantal* ([− cons]). Let us now see the way in which *consonantal sounds* are produced ([+ cons]). To produce such sounds, the pharyngobuccal tube must be totally or partially closed. This closure can be caused by the lips, the blade, or the back of the tongue. Depending on the greater or lesser obstruction to the flow of air, the obstruents or *non-sonorants* ([− son]) can be distinguished from the *sonorants* ([+ son]).[14] Let us first examine the obstruents.[15]

Obstruents can be *continuant* ([+ cont]) *or non-continuant* ([− cont]). During the production of continuant obstruents, the position of the speech organs is such that they produce a strong narrowing at a certain point in the pharyngobuccal tube, as, for example, when the lower lip is next to the sharp edge of the upper teeth (fig. 6). The flow of air through the resulting narrow passage gives rise to a friction noise, whence the name of fricative commonly

---

13   Since the publication of *SPE* several modifications have been proposed, resulting in an important reshuffling of the system of features for vowel quality. Cf. Halle and Stevens (1969), Ladefoged (1971), Perkell (1971), Kiparsky (1974).

14   For a more precise formulation, see *SPE*: 302.

15   This word is related to *obstruct, obstruction*.

given to the continuant obstruents (f, v, s, z, etc.). Fricatives have acoustic properties similar to those of the hissing sound which is heard when air escapes from the valve of a tyre, and they are produced in the same manner. Continuant obstruents are [+ cons, − son, + cont].

When the passage of air is momentarily interrupted by a complete obstruction of the pharyngobuccal tube, the resulting sounds are non-continuant obstruents. Thus, to produce [b] or [p] the pharyngobuccal tube is blocked at its anterior end by tightening the lips, and the velum is raised so that the air cannot escape through the nose (fig. 7). The air shut in behind the lips is compressed, and when the lips finally part, it suddenly escapes with a slight burst. The non-continuant obstruents are [+ cons, − son, − cont]. Traditionally they are called stops. For some phonologists, stops also include nasal consonants and the glottal stop (see below). We will not follow this usage, and in this book the term 'stop' will always be exactly synonymous to 'non-continuant obstruent'. The stops to be found in French are p, b, t, d, k and g. Fricatives are not the only continuant speech sounds. Vowels, nasal consonants, liquids and glides are also continuant (see below).

Before leaving the obstruents, we must mention one type of obstruent that does not exist in French, the affricates (the same root as *friction, fricative*). With affricates, the total obstruction of the beginning is not released all at once, as in p, t, k, etc., but gradually, whence a time lapse in which the obstacle to the passage of air is only partially removed, and we hear a friction noise, as with the fricatives. For example, the sounds $č$ and $ǰ$ at the end of the English words *beach* and *bridge* are affricates; the French tend to interpret them as $t + š$, $d + ž$ sequences, since French has no affricates. The feature *delayed release* enables fricatives and affricates on the one hand, that are all [+ del rel], to be contrasted with all the other obstruents, that are [− del rel].

Let us now go on to the [+ cons, + son] segments. There are two kinds: nasals and liquids, and we will examine each in turn.

Imagine the pharyngobuccal tube completely closed at a certain point, so as to produce a non-continuant obstruent, but without the velum being raised. The air then flows freely out, but only through the nasal cavity (fig. 8). The resulting sounds are consonantal and nasal, in accordance with the definitions given above. Various nasal consonants can be obtained, according to where the pharyngobuccal tube is blocked (m, n, $ñ$, $ŋ$). Nasal consonants are [+ cons, + son, + cont, + nas].

Liquids are sounds such as the French l and r. For l, the tip of the tongue blocks the pharyngobuccal tube in its middle (behind the upper teeth) but the air can easily get round the obstacle and freely pass on each side, for the tongue edges are lowered. In the normal Parisian variety of *r*, the air comes out without any audible turbulence through the free space between the posterior part of the dorsum of the tongue and the uvula, a small appendix at the end of the velum. Liquids are [+ cons, + son, + cont, − nas].

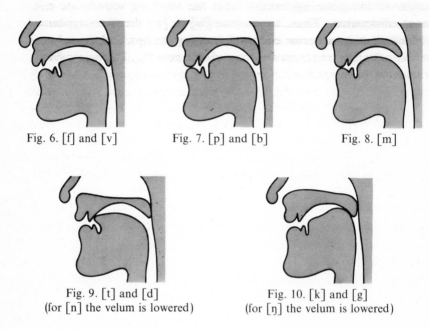

Fig. 6. [f] and [v]   Fig. 7. [p] and [b]   Fig. 8. [m]

Fig. 9. [t] and [d]   Fig. 10. [k] and [g]
(for [n] the velum is lowered)   (for [ŋ] the velum is lowered)

Syllabicity

If all obstruents are necessarily consonantal, the same is not true for sonorants. Besides nasal and liquid consonants, there are also non-consonantal sonorants. Non-consonantal sonorants are divided into two categories, according to whether they are *syllabic* or not. Sounds that can by themselves constitute a syllable are considered as *syllabic* ([+ syll]). The others are *non-syllabic* ([− syll]). Although this distinction poses tricky theoretical problems, its intuitive meaning is clear, and will suffice for this account. The sound with a *u* quality that appears in the pronunciation *troua* [trua] 'made a hole' counts as a syllable, but not that of *trois* [trwa] 'three'.[16] The first, transcribed [u], is a non-consonantal and syllabic sonorant, in other words a vowel. The second, transcribed [w], is a non-

[16] In English, contrast the vowel in the first syllable of *Jewish* to the sound which follows the initial *s* in *swish*.

consonantal and non-syllabic sonorant. In traditional terminology it is called either a semi-vowel or a semi-consonant. In French there are three semi-vowels corresponding to the three high vowels: [w] corresponds to [u], [y] (called yod) corresponds to [i] and [ẅ] corresponds to [ü]. Sonorants which are both consonantal and syllabic, do not exist in French, but are found in many other languages. Thus, English has a syllabic consonant at the end of words such as *bottle* [bɔtl̩], *season* [sizn̩], and *rhythm* [rɪðm̩].

Glides

Besides vowels and semi-vowels, the [– cons] category also includes *h* and *ʔ*. *h* is produced by leaving the glottis open and giving the vocal tract the shape it normally has during the production of a vowel. This sound does not exist in the French spoken in Paris. We can hear it at the beginning of the English words *hat* and *house*. To produce the sound often called glottal stop or glottal catch, *ʔ*, the glottis is tightly closed and suddenly reopened, which gives the following vowel an abrupt onset. Coughing is just a particularly energetic kind of glottal stop. In French and in English, any word beginning with a vowel can be pronounced with an initial glottal stop, as for example when calling: *ʔ Alfred!* or in exclamations such as *ʔout with it!*

Like semi-vowels, *h* and *ʔ* are [+ son, – cons, – syll] and together with the semi-vowels they form a class of sounds called glides. *h* is [+ cont] and *ʔ* [– cont].

The features [son], [cons] and [syll] permit an initial distribution of sounds in the general categories shown in table II above. Opposite each combination of feature values is given the usual name attributed to the category in question in traditional phonetic terminology, as well as a few examples. The opposition between [+ cons] and [– cons] roughly corresponds to the distinction traditionally made between consonants on the one hand, and vowels and semi-vowels on the other.

Consonants: place of articulation

The [+ cons] sounds are produced with a constriction of the pharyngobuccal tube at a certain point traditionally called the point or place of articulation. For non-continuant obstruents and nasal consonants, the obstruction of the air is complete at this point; for continuant obstruents and for liquids, it is only partial. This obstruction can be due to the lips or to various parts of the tongue.

The complete obstruction in the stops *p* and *b* and in the nasal *m* is obtained by pressing the lips together, which is why they are called bilabials (from the Latin word *labia* 'lip'). In the case of the fricatives, *f* and *v*, the lower lip is placed against the edge of the upper teeth, which is why they are called labiodentals. The term 'labial' includes bilabials and labiodentals.

The complete obstruction in the dental stops *t* and *d* and in the dental nasal *n* is obtained by pressing the tip of the tongue against the teeth (fig. 9).[17] For the dental fricatives *s* and *z*, the tightening of the tube consists of the narrow passage left between the interior side and gums of the upper teeth and the blade of the tongue. The constriction of *š* and *ž* takes place slightly further back.

We call *anterior* [+ ant] all those consonants whose place of articulation is the same as that of *s* and *z* or further forward, and we will call *non-anterior* [− ant] all the others, such as *š*, *ž*, *k*, *g* and *ñ*, whose place of articulation is situated further back than that of *s* and *z*. A distinction is also made between *coronals* ([+ cor]), whose articulation involves the blade of the tongue, and *non-coronals* ([− cor]). Labials are anterior and non-coronal, dentals are anterior and coronal, and *š*, *ž*, *č* and *ǰ* are non-anterior and coronal. Finally, there are also consonants that are non-anterior and non-coronal: *ñ*, *k* and *g*.

The obstruction in the nasal consonant *ñ* is obtained by pressing the front part of the dorsum of the tongue against the hard palate, and that of *k* and *g* by pressing the back part of the dorsum of the tongue against the velum or the posterior part of the hard palate (fig. 10). In traditional terminology, *ñ* is a prepalatal, or more simply a palatal, and *k* and *g* are velars. The palatal stops corresponding to *ñ* appear in French only in certain kinds of pronunciations considered vulgar, for example in words such as *cinquième* 'fifth' *fringué* 'dressed' (slang) but they are found in many of the languages of the world. We will transcribe them *ḳ* and *ǧ*. The velar nasal corresponding to *k* and *g*, in transcription *ŋ*, is the consonant written *ng* in English (as in *song* [sɔŋ]). To press the dorsum of the tongue against the hard palate or the velum, the body of the tongue must be raised to its maximum height in the mouth. Palatals and velars are therefore [+ high], like the vowels *i*, *ü* and *u*. Palatals are articulated when the body of the tongue is forward in the mouth, and velars when the body of the tongue is at the back of the mouth. The palatals and velars are therefore respectively [− back] and [+ back]. *š*, *ž*, *č* and *ǰ* are [+ high] and [− back] like the

---

[17]   This is true for French dentals. English dentals are pronounced by pressing the tip of the tongue just behind the upper teeth, against the alveolar ridge.

prepalatals, but [+ cor], whereas the palatals (and the velars) are [− cor], since their articulation does not involve the blade of the tongue.

Most of the consonants discussed in the preceding paragraphs are grouped in table III above. This table only partially summarizes what has been said about these consonants, since it only considers eight of the thirteen features we have described. That is why *t* is in the same box as *c*, and *d* as *ž* : the feature of delayed release is not represented in the table. It is the only one, among the thirteen features presented, whose values distinguish *t* from *c* and *d* from *ž*. Similarly, the semi-vowels and liquids are on the same horizontal line because the feature [cons] is not represented in the table. Compare this with table II, which takes the feature [cons] into account, and where the semi-vowels and liquids are on different lines.

In order to help the reader take in the content of the phonological rules more rapidly, and to avoid as much as possible the accumulation of feature specifications in the text, we will adopt the following conventions: V is equivalent to [+ syll], C to [− syll], N to [+ cons, + nas], O to [− son] (obstruent), L to [+ son, + cons, − nas] (liquid). Note that according to our conventions C includes not only consonantal (non-syllabic) segments but also glides: *w*, *y*, *h*, etc. The word 'consonant' will be given the same meaning throughout the book. Unless the contrary is explicitly stated, this term will be used as an abbreviation of 'non-syllabic segment'. Care must also be taken not to confuse O with the symbol Ø, representing zero.

FROM SURFACE STRUCTURES TO PHONETIC
REPRESENTATIONS

A list of all the speech sounds that appear in the pronunciation of French would include several hundred and probably even several thousand different units, each one able to appear only under very specific phonetic and syntactic conditions. Take, for example, the voiceless sonorant consonants [l̥], [r̥], [n̥] and [m̥], which appear only next to another voiceless consonant, and the corresponding voiced consonants [l], [r] [n] and [m], which appear everywhere else: the initial consonant of the second word is voiceless in *cette latte* [sɛtl̥at] 'this slat', *cette natte* [sɛtn̥at] 'this plait', *cette masse* [sɛtm̥as] 'this mass', *cette rate* [sɛtr̥at] 'this spleen', whereas it is voiced in *des lattes* [delat] 'slats', *des rates* [derat] 'spleens', etc. Similarly, the last consonant of the verbal roots *appel-* 'call' and *sem-* 'sow' is voiceless in *vous appelez* [vuzapl̥e] 'you call', *vous semez* [vusm̥e] 'you sow', whereas it is voiced in *vous appellerez* [vuzapɛlre] 'you will call' and in *vous sèmerez* [vusɛmre] 'you will sow'. French children do not have to learn separately the two variants [l̥at] and [lat] of the morpheme *latte*, or the two variants [n̥at] and [nat] of the morpheme *natte*, etc. In order to pronounce these morphemes correctly in all contexts, all they have to do is remember the fact that *latte* begins with an *l*-type sound, *natte* with an *n*-type sound, etc., together with rule (1):

> (1)   [+ son, − syll] segments are voiceless when adjacent to a
>   [− voice] segment.

Consider the fact that at least two degrees of vowel length can be distinguished in the phonetic representations of French. The vowel of *bouge* 'move' is recognizably longer than that of *bouche* 'mouth', that of *case* 'hut' longer than that of *casse* 'break', that of *vire* 'change direction' longer than that of *ville* 'town', that of *sauve* 'safe' (fem.) longer than that of *sauf* 'safe' (masc.). This is another case of an alternation automatically regulated by the context. When the child learns the words *bouge* and *bouche*, he does not have to remember that the *u* of the first word is longer than the *u* of the second. All he has to remember is that the segment following the vowel is a *ž* in the first word and a *š* in the second, and he has to know a rule which states that in certain conditions a vowel lengthens in front of *ž, z, r* or *v*.

One last example: the stem of the verb *manier* 'to handle' is pronounced [mani] in *il le maniera* [manira] 'he will handle it', *j'en manie un* [mani] 'I handle one', *j'en connais le maniement* [manimã] 'I know how to handle it'. It is pronounced [many] in *vous le maniez* [manye] 'you handle it', *c'est très maniable* [manyabl] 'it can easily be handled'. These pronunciations do not altogether differ; the group [man] remains constant throughout. Only the last segment varies, and even then its variation is minimal, since [i] and [y] are only differentiated by the feature [syll]: [i] is [+ syll] and [y] is [− syll]. The alternation between [+ syll] and [− syll] in the pronunciation of the last segment of *mani-* is a particular case of rule (2):

> (2)   [+ son, + high] segments are pronounced [− syll] when
>   they immediately precede a vowel belonging to the same
>   word.[18]

Rule (2) accounts for the fact that *avou-* is pronounced [avw] in *avouez* [avwe] 'admit', as opposed to [avu] in *il avoue* [avu] 'he admits', *il*

---

[18]   The formulation of this rule has been much simplified for clarity. Indeed we have not considered the case where the segment [+ son, + high] is preceded by an obstruent and a liquid, as in *refluer* [rəflüe] 'to ebb', *trouer* [true] 'to make a hole', cf. Dell (1972) and Morin (1971).

avouera [avura] 'he will admit'. Similarly, note the alternations between [+ syll] and [− syll] in the following: *expédier* [ekspedye] 'to send off', *expédie* [ekspedi] 'sends off', *expéditeur* [ekspeditœr] 'sender'; *contribuable* [kɔ̃tribwabl] 'tax-payer', *contribue* [kɔ̃tribü] 'contributes', *contribution* [kɔ̃tribüsyɔ̃] 'contribution'; *statuette* [statwɛt] 'statuette', *statue* [statü] 'statue', *statufier* [statüfye] 'to erect a statue to'; *échouer* [ešwe] 'to fail', *échoue* [ešu] 'fails'; *génial* [ženyal] 'genial', *génie* [ženi] 'genius', etc. Speakers do not have to memorize separately the two different pronunciations in each case.

Linguists consider the speech sounds which occur in the phonetic representations of a language as manifestations of more abstract underlying entities, the *phonemes* of that language. For example, in French [l̥] and [l] are said to be two realizations of the same phoneme /l/, and it is said that the phoneme /i/ is realized as [i] in *dévie* [devi] 'deviates' and as [y] in *dévier* [devye] 'to deviate'. The hundreds of speech sounds which occur in phonetic representations can thus be reduced to a few dozen phonemes (about thirty for French), so that the various pronunciations of a single morpheme can be considered as phonetic realizations of a unique phoneme sequence stored in the lexicon. For in the lexicon, information concerning the pronunciation of each morpheme is given in terms of phonemes and not in terms of speech sounds. The lexical entry of *petit* 'little', for example, contains the *phonological representation*[19] /pətit/, i.e. the sequence of phonemes /p/, /ə/, /t/, /i/, /t/, and it is the task of the phonological rules to indicate that the phonological representation /pətit/ is actualized as the phonetic representation [pti] in *des petits tas* [deptita] 'little stacks', as [pœti] in *sept petits tas* [sɛtpœtita] 'seven little stacks', as [ptit] in *un petit os* [ɛ̃ptitɔs] 'a little bone', and as [pœtit] in *chaque petit os* [šakpœtitɔs] 'every little bone'.

In the phonetic representation which describes the pronunciation of a given sentence, one should distinguish two kinds of specifications. Some follow from other properties of the morpheme in question or of those surrounding it in the sentence, and can be predicted by a rule. There is, therefore, no need for the speaker–hearer to overcrowd his memory with them. Others, on the contrary, cannot be predicted. They are idiosyncratic – and must be learnt by heart. In *cette latte* [sɛtl̥at] 'this slat', knowing the initial segment of *latte* is [+ son, − syll] and that it is preceded by a [− voice] segment (the preceding *t*), rule (1) predicts that this initial

---

[19] To make things simpler, we will assume, for the time being, that the lexicon contains phonological representations. The distinction between phonological representations and lexical representations will be made later (see p. 83).

segment must itself be [− voice]. On the other hand, it is an idiosyncratic fact that the initial segment of *latte* is non-nasal (contrast with *natte* [nat] 'plait '), sonorant (contrast with *date* [dat] 'date '), anterior (contrast with *rate* [rat] 'spleen '), and so on. When we say that in the lexicon the whole of the information concerning the pronunciation of *latte* is the sequence /latə/, we are in fact summing up all such idiosyncratic facts.

We say that the list of French phonemes has only one phoneme of the /l/ type because a child learning a new French word containing an *l* need not remember whether it is voiced or voiceless. The difference of voicing between [l] and [l̥] is of no use in distinguishing two lexical items. These two speech sounds are actualizations of the same phoneme /l/. This is not the case in Burmese, where a voiced *l* is opposed to a voiceless *l* in the lexicon. The speakers of Burmese distinguish in the same environment between [la] 'moon ' and [l̥a] 'beautiful ' and these must be considered as pronunciations of two different sequences of phonemes /la/ vs. /l̥a/.

Note that rule (1) does not state that the feature specification for voicing is always predictable in French. This rule only applies to segments which are at the same time sonorant and non-syllabic. For example, nothing enables one to predict the voicedness of the obstruent *b* in *cette boule* [sɛtbul] 'this ball ', as opposed to the voicelessness of *p* in *cette poule* [sɛtpul] 'this hen ', and this is what forces us to include in the list of French phonemes two distinct phonemes /p/ and /b/, which only differ in the specification of the feature [voice].

Let us examine the derivation of sentence (3), which has the phonetic representation (4):

(3)   *vous écriviez*   'you wrote'
(4)   [vuzekṛivye]

The syntactic component generates the surface structure: its general features are represented in (5):

(5) $_S[\ _N[vous]_N \ _V[écriv + imperf + 2 \ plur]_V \ ]_S$

imperf is the name given to the morpheme marking the imperfect, and *2 plur* to the morpheme marking the second person plural. By applying the rules for inserting boundaries to (5), we obtain (6):

(6)   *## vous # écriv + imperf + 2 plur ##*

For *vous*, *ecriv-*, *imperf* and *2 plur*, the lexicon gives the following phonological representations, respectively: /vuz/, /ekriv/, /i/ and /ez/. Sentence (3) thus has the phonological representation (7):

(7) / # # vuz # ekriv + i + ez # # /

Strictly speaking, the labelled brackets of (5) should have been included in (6) and (7), but in all the cases examined IN THIS BOOK the only way syntactic structure affects phonology is through distribution of the + and # boundaries. From now on, labelled brackets will therefore be omitted, but the reader should remember that they form as inherent a part of phonological representations as do phonemes or + and # boundaries. Chomsky and Halle (1968), for example, have shown that these brackets play a very important role in the operation of rules predicting the position of stress in English.

It is thanks to the various rules of the phonological component of French that the phonological representation (7) results in the phonetic representation (4). Rule (1) indicates that the /r/ of /ekriv/ is realized as [r̥] since it follows /k/, which is voiceless. Rule (2) indicates that the /i/ of the ending *-iez* is realized as [y] since it precedes /e/, a vowel belonging to the same word. Finally, we will see later that there is a rule in French which indicates that an obstruent preceding ## is realized as zero, that is to say that no sound corresponds to it in the phonetic representation. This rule deletes the final /z/ of representation (7). The succession of operations which we have rapidly described is the derivation of the phonetic representation [vuzekr̥ivye] from the phonological representation / # # vuz # ekriv + i + ez # # /.

The phonological component is a device which associates at least one phonetic representation to each phonological representation. This device can be imagined as a sort of machine producing phonetic representations from phonological representations. The machine has as input the phonological representations and as output the phonetic representations. In order to understand how this mechanism functions, it is necessary first to understand exactly what phonological representations are, and how phonological rules are applied.

Phonemes have so far been represented as phonetic letters enclosed between diagonal slashes for the sake of brevity only. Phonemes are in reality columns of φ specifications corresponding to the φ distinctive features defined by the theory of universal phonetics (see p. 35). In practice, since columns of feature specifications take up too much space and are difficult to read, it is convenient to designate each one by the phonetic letter corresponding to it. When we say that the phonological representation of *vous écriviez* is $/\#\#\mathrm{vuz}\#\mathrm{ekriv}+\mathrm{i}+\mathrm{ez}\#\#/$, and that its phonetic representation is [vuzekṛivye], it is simply a way of using convenient abbreviations for the representations (a) and (b) in fig. 11.[20]

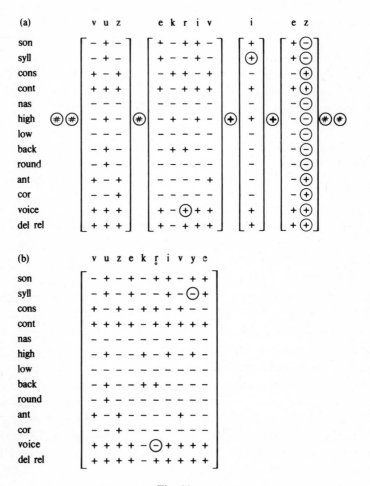

Fig. 11

20 We have circled all the details which differentiate these representations, so that they can be more easily compared. The French phonological representations postulated in this chapter are useful as examples only. We do not imply that they are the representations found at the most abstract level. They are in fact only intermediary representations which we have purposely chosen as quite close to the phonetic representations.

Like speech sounds, the phonemes of a language are characterized by columns of feature specifications, but here the resemblance ends. The set of speech sounds is defined once and for all within the phonetic theory, that is to say by referring only to the articulatory and perceptual possibilities available to human beings for linguistic uses. The phonetic representation of a sentence directly characterizes a certain pronunciation, without taking into consideration any other aspects of the language to which this sentence belongs. On the other hand, a phonological representation is an abstract object which can only be interpreted within the framework of the system of a given language as a consequence of that language's phonological rules. Each language has its own small number of phonemes which combine in various ways in the lexicon to give the phonological representations of the morphemes.

The phonological component of French contains, for example, the following rules:

$$(8) \quad 1 \;\rightarrow\; [-\text{syll}] \quad \Big/ \quad \begin{bmatrix} +\text{son} \\ +\text{high} \end{bmatrix} \quad [+\text{syll}]$$
$$\phantom{(8) \quad 1 \;\rightarrow\; [-\text{syll}] \quad \Big/ \quad }1 \phantom{\begin{bmatrix} +\text{son} \\ \end{bmatrix}} 2$$

$$(9) \quad 2 \;\rightarrow\; [-\text{voice}] \Big/ \quad [-\text{voice}] \quad \begin{bmatrix} +\text{son} \\ -\text{syll} \end{bmatrix}$$
$$\phantom{(9) \quad 2 \;\rightarrow\; [-\text{voice}] \Big/ \quad }1 \phantom{[-\text{voice}]} 2$$

$$(10) \quad 1 \;\rightarrow\; \varnothing \quad \Big/ \quad [-\text{son}] \quad \# \quad \#$$
$$1 \phantom{[-\text{son}]} 2 \quad\;\; 3$$

Rule (8) indicates that any high sonorant preceding a vowel is non-syllabic. Rule (9) indicates that any non-syllabic sonorant following a voiceless segment is itself voiceless. Rule (10) indicates that any obstruent preceding two # boundaries is deleted.

These phonological rules can be interpreted in two different ways. On the one hand, they can be considered as *statements* according to which certain properties of the pronunciation of a French sentence can be deduced from others. For example, rule (8) expresses in formal terms the following generalization: in a sequence of two segments of which the first is sonorant and high, and the second syllabic, the first is non-syllabic. Knowing that at one point of the sentence there is a [+ son, + high] segment immediately followed by a [+ syll] segment, we can automatically deduce that the first segment is pronounced [− syll] (see rule (2), p. 48).

On the other hand, a phonological rule can also be considered as a set of instructions indicating how a certain *operation* is to be carried out. This operation, taking any representation (input) subject to the rule, produces another representation (output) obtained by applying certain modifications: 'from any representation W that has the property K, another representation W' can be made, by modifying W in this or that way'. Phonological rules are all of the form X → Y/ K, 'rewrite X as Y when the condition K is met'. Thus rule (8) gives us the following instructions: for each representation containing a sequence of two segments, the first sonorant and high, and the second syllabic, write a minus sign in front of the feature [syll] of the first sound.

The part of the rule to the right of the diagonal slash indicates the conditions that a representation must meet for it to be affected by the rule. Only representations containing a sequence of two segments of which the first is [+ son, + high] and the second [+ syll] can be subject to rule (8). This part of the rule is called its *structural description*. The part of the rule to the left of the diagonal slash indicates which changes are to be made in a representation meeting the structural description. It is called the *structural change*. The structural change of (8) indicates that the first segment must be replaced by a segment that is identical in all points, except for the specification of the feature [syll], which must be rewritten [− syll]. When a segment of a representation meets the conditions required by the structural description of a rule for it to be modified by this rule, we say that this segment *is subject* to the rule, and when the rule modifies a segment, we say that it *affects* this segment or that it *operates on* this segment.

Suppose representation (7) / # #vuz # ekriv + i + ez # #/ is submitted to rule (8). This input representation is scanned segment by segment in order to spot which ones are subject to the rule. The /v/ of /vuz/ is not subject to (8); it is a [− son] segment, and the rule only affects [+ son] segments. The following /u/ is also not subject to (8); it is indeed a [+ son, + high] segment, but it is followed by /z/, which is [− syll], whereas the rule only affects segments followed by a [+ syll] segment. Segments of the input representation are thus examined one by one. In this particular case, only the /i/ of the morpheme of the imperfect is subject to rule (8). It is [+ son, + high], and followed by /e/, which is [+ syll]. Then, following the instructions of the structural change, the specification [+ syll] in the column corresponding to that /i/ is replaced by [− syll]. In other words, the vowel *i* is replaced by the semi-vowel *y*. The rule leaves all the other segments of representation (7) unchanged, since these are not subject to it. Thus, by applying rule (8), from the input / # #vuz #ekriv + i + ez # #/, we get the output # #vuz #ekriv + y + ez #.

A phonetic representation corresponding to a given phonological representation is derived by successively applying all the rules of the phonological component. Each rule modifies the segments that are subject to it and *leaves the others unchanged*. Here, for example, is the succession of operations by which a grammar containing the rules (8), (9) and (10) associates the phonetic representation (4) to the phonological representation (7):

(11)   phonological repr. $/\#\#\text{vuz}\#\text{ekriv}+\text{i}+\text{ez}\#\#/$

$$\vdots \qquad\qquad\qquad \vdots$$

rule (8) $\#\#\text{vuz}\#\text{ekriv}+\text{y}+\text{ez}\#\#$
rule (9) $\#\#\text{vuz}\#\text{ek}\underset{\circ}{\text{r}}\text{iv}+\text{y}+\text{ez}\#\#$
rule (10) $\#\#\text{vuz}\#\text{ek}\underset{\circ}{\text{r}}\text{iv}+\text{y}+\text{e}\ \#\#$

$$\vdots \qquad\qquad\qquad \vdots$$

phonetic repr. $[\text{vuzek}\underset{\circ}{\text{r}}\text{ivye}]$

Opposite the name of each rule is the representation obtained by applying this rule (the output of the rule). Each rule takes the output of the preceding rule as its input. Thus rule (9) applies to the representation $\#\#\text{vuz}\#\text{ekriv}+\text{y}+\text{ez}\#\#$, obtained by applying rule (8). This representation is the output of (8) and the input of (9). Rule (9) indicates that in French a non-syllabic sonorant is voiceless when it is preceded by a voiceless segment (see rule (1), p. 48). It gives the following instructions: in a sequence of two segments of which the first is [− voice] and the second [+ son, − syll], the second must be rewritten as [− voice].[21] Rule (9) is applied to the output of (8) by rewriting *r* as $\underset{\circ}{r}$, whence the representation $\#\#\text{vuz}\#\text{ek}\underset{\circ}{\text{r}}\text{iv}+\text{y}+\text{ez}\#\#$, which is then submitted to rule (10). This rule indicates that obstruents are not pronounced when they are followed by two word boundaries. It instructs one to rewrite an obstruent as zero in this context, in other words to delete it (Ø means 'zero'). This rule will be justified in chapter 4, p. 157, hard cover edition. Attention should be paid to

---

[21] As it is formulated here, this rule is not general enough. It only operates in cases where the voiceless consonant and the non-syllabic sonorant immediately follow each other without being separated by any word boundary. It accounts for the devoicing of the first *r* but not of the second in *trente # rats* [$\text{tr}\tilde{\text{a}}\text{t}\underset{\circ}{\text{r}}\text{a}$] 'thirty rats'. Furthermore, it does not say anything about cases where the non-syllabic sonorant is not preceded, but followed, by a voiceless segment, as in *carte* [$\text{ka}\underset{\circ}{\text{r}}\text{t}$] 'map'. This is of no importance to the present discussion, aimed at explaining, with the help of some simple examples, how the phonological rules work.

the fact that when a column containing a $[-\text{son}]$ specification is followed by $\#\#$, the entire column is suppressed from the representation, not just the $[-\text{son}]$ specification within the column. Rule (10), therefore, transforms the output of (9) into the new representation $\#\#\text{vuz}\#\text{ekṛiv}+\text{y}+\text{e}\#\#$.

Apart from (8), (9) and (10), the phonological component of French grammar has many other rules that have not been mentioned here. In order to simplify matters, we will suppose that their application does not modify any specification in the derivation which leads from the phonological representation (7) to the phonetic representation (4).[22] The detail of the successive steps corresponding to the application of these rules is replaced in the derivation represented in (11) by a series of dots. Once the last phonological rule of the grammar has been applied, all the $\#$ and $+$ boundaries are automatically erased by virtue of a convention that has been given once and for all in linguistic theory and is valid for all grammars. Accepting this convention amounts to claiming that word and morpheme boundaries do not have any phonetic interpretation or, in other words, that the signal does not contain any boundary-specific markers. These boundaries only have an indirect phonetic effect; they condition, in certain cases, the realization of the surrounding phonemes. It is by applying this convention of boundary suppression that one moves from the output of rule (10) to the phonetic representation [vuzekṛivye]. The ordered set of successive representations figuring in (11) is known as the *derivation* of [vuzekrivye]. The phonological representation $/\#\#\text{vuz}\#\text{ekriv}+\text{i}+\text{ez}\#\#/$ is the input of the derivation, and the phonetic representation [vuzekṛivye] is its output. If we compare these two representations (see p. 52), we notice that the specifications of most of the distinctive features are identical in both. Only those specifications which fall under the scope of a rule are modified during the derivation. In the phonological representation, the /i/ of /ekriv/ and that of the morpheme of the imperfect are two occurrences of the same segment $[+\text{son}, +\text{syll}, +\text{high}...]$ defined beforehand by the grammar as belonging to the phonemes of the French language. In the course of the derivation, the second /i/ is rewritten as $[-\text{syll}]$ by applying rule (8), while the first is not modified by any rule and appears unchanged at the phonetic level. If the second /i/ is phonetically realized as $[-\text{syll}]$, it is because of rule (8); but if the first is phonetically realized as $[+\text{syll}]$, it is because by definition the phoneme /i/ of French is $[+\text{syll}]$ and *no rule has modified this specification in the course of the*

---

[22] In other words, we assume they apply trivially, cf. p. 57.

derivation. In other words, unless a phonological rule explicitly indicates the contrary, the French phoneme /i/ is actualized as the speech sound [i]; this follows automatically from the distinctive feature content of the column which defines the phoneme /i/.

Il all the # and + boundaries occurring in a phonological representation are deleted, we obtain a distinctive features matrix which can be interpreted as a sequence of speech sounds.[23] If this is done, for instance to the phonological representation (7) /# #vuz#ekriv + i + ez# #/, we get a certain feature matrix corresponding to the sound sequence [vuzekriviez], which is how (7) would get phonetically interpreted, if it were not subject to any of the rules of the phonological component of French. In short, the feature specifications of a phonetic representation differ from those of the phonological representation from which they derive only in so far as the differences can be attributed to the phonological rules, and the existence of a phonological rule is only postulated when it throws light on regularities which would otherwise remain unexpressed.[24]

When the application of a rule R to an input W yields an identical output W, R is said to apply trivially to W. For example, R is said to apply trivially to W when W does not satisfy the structural description of the rule, and hence the rule does not operate.[25] Trivial application has in some ways a similar status to that of multiplication by 1, which associates any number to itself. For example, rule (9) trivially applies to #vuz# in the derivation (11) and yields the output #vuz#, identical to the input #vuz#. It would be unnecessarily tedious to write down systematically all the cases of trivial application, as we did for rules (8), (9) and (10) in derivation (11). In fact, when a derivation is given, it is customary to present explicitly only those aspects of the derivation that represent cases of non-trivial application; the rest is implicit. For example, derivation (11) will be presented in the form of (11′);

$$(11′) \qquad\qquad /\# \#vuz\#ekriv + i + ez\# \#/$$

$$\text{rule (8)} \qquad\qquad\qquad y$$

$$\text{rule (9)} \qquad\qquad \underset{\circ}{r}$$

$$\text{rule (10)} \qquad\qquad\qquad \varnothing$$

$$[vuzek\underset{\circ}{r}ivye]$$

[23] Cf. p. 34, n. 3.
[24] Cf. p. 135.
[25] On the cases in which a rule applies 'vacuously', cf. p. 69.

It must be kept in mind that (11′) is only a convenient abbreviation for (11). Let it be clear that a rule simultaneously applies (and when possible operates) at all points of the input submitted to it, and that in a derivation the rules of the phonological component are all successively applied. Strictly speaking, in a grammar that has a phonological component containing *n* rules, each derivation is a sequence of *n* + 2 representations, where the first is a phonological representation, the last a phonetic representation, and the remaining *n* representations are intermediary level representations, each one corresponding to the output of a rule.[26] The reason why the derivations given in the literature generally have only five or six lines, is that all the other steps in the derivation are taken for granted, either because they correspond to cases of trivial application, or because they involve rules which do not concern the subject under discussion. Phonological representations are symbolized by diagonal slashes (/X/) and phonetic representations by square brackets ([X]). As for the intermediary representations, in this book they sometimes appear between diagonal slashes and sometimes not, but no significance should be attached to this wavering, which is only for reasons of typographical convenience.

Let us now come back to rule (8), as it is formulated on page 53. We have seen that the two segments to the right of the oblique bar do not play the same role. Whereas the application of the rule rewrites segment no. 1 as [− syll], it leaves segment no. 2 unchanged. Segment no. 2 simply indicates the environment in which the rule operates. In order to avoid using numbers, rule (8) is written in the form of rule (8a), where the dash indicates the position occupied by the segment to be modified in relation to the environment.

$$\text{(8a)} \quad \begin{bmatrix} + \text{son} \\ + \text{high} \end{bmatrix} \quad \rightarrow \quad [- \text{syll}] \quad / \quad \underline{\hspace{1cm}} [+ \text{syll}]$$

Similarly, rules (9) and (10) on page 53 are written in the forms (9a) and (10a):

$$\text{(9a)} \quad \begin{bmatrix} + \text{son} \\ - \text{syll} \end{bmatrix} \quad \rightarrow \quad [- \text{voice}] \quad / \quad [- \text{voice}] \underline{\hspace{1cm}}$$

$$\text{(10a)} \quad [- \text{son}] \quad \rightarrow \quad \emptyset \quad / \quad \underline{\hspace{1cm}} \# \#$$

Nothing prevents us from considering as part of the environment, both the specifications of the structural description which define the segments

---

[26] We are leaving aside the principle of cyclical application and cases of disjunctive ordering, cf. p. 75, nn. 38 and 39.

adjacent to the one to be modified, and the specifications which define the very segment to be modified.

Rule (8) can, for example, be written as (8b), (8c) or (8d):

$$(8b) \quad [+ \text{son}] \quad \rightarrow \quad [- \text{syll}] \quad \Big/ \left[\begin{array}{c} \underline{\quad\quad} \\ + \text{high} \end{array} \right] [+ \text{syll}]$$

$$(8c) \quad [+ \text{high}] \quad \rightarrow \quad [- \text{syll}] \quad \Big/ \left[\begin{array}{c} \underline{\quad\quad} \\ + \text{son} \end{array} \right] [+ \text{syll}]$$

$$(8d) \quad [\quad] \quad \rightarrow \quad [- \text{syll}] \quad \Big/ \left[\begin{array}{c} \underline{\quad\quad} \\ + \text{son} \\ + \text{high} \end{array} \right] [+ \text{syll}]$$

Rules (8), (8a), (8b), (8c) and (8d) are strictly equivalent notational variants. The essential point is to remember that the structural description of the rule is always the sum of what is on the left of the arrow and on the right of the diagonal slash. As for the structural change, the dash indicates the position of the segment to be rewritten in relation to the environment, and the specifications between the arrow and the diagonal slash indicate how it must be rewritten.

The rules we have seen so far are obligatory rules, that is to say they inevitably operate each time their structural description is satisfied. There are also so-called optional rules, which do not necessarily operate each time their structural description is met. These fluctuations give rise, for each input, to two outputs that are in free variation (see p. 18). Thus, in French, any vowel situated at the beginning of a sentence can be optionally preceded by a glottal stop. Assuming that the beginning and end of a sentence is marked by a § symbol in phonological representations, we will write the following optional rule:

$$(12) \quad \emptyset \quad \rightarrow \quad ? \quad /\S \text{——} [+ \text{syll}]$$

This rule optionally rewrites zero as ? between § and a vowel, in other words, it optionally introduces a glottal stop in front of a vowel situated at the beginning of a sentence. *Annette tombe* 'Annette is falling' can be pronounced [anɛttɔ̃b] or [ʔanɛttɔ̃b]. The single input /§anɛt#tɔ̃b§/ gives rise to the identical output /§anɛt#tɔ̃b§/ when the rule does not operate, and to the output /§ʔanɛt#tɔ̃b§/ when it does operate, whence we finally get two pronunciations in free variation: [anɛttɔ̃b] and [ʔanɛttɔ̃b]. There is another rule in French by which a voiced stop situated at the end of a sentence is optionally nasalized when the preceding segment is a nasal vowel (Morin, 1971: 51):

$$(13) \quad \begin{bmatrix} - \text{cont} \\ + \text{voice} \end{bmatrix} \rightarrow [+ \text{nas}] \quad / \quad \begin{bmatrix} + \text{syll} \\ + \text{nas} \end{bmatrix} \text{---} \S$$

Depending on whether this rule operates or not, the second word of *Annette tombe* is pronounced [tɔ̃m] or [tɔ̃b]. By combining these two possibilities with those allowed by the preceding rule, one can derive from the unique input /ʃanɛt#tɔ̃bʃ/ four phonetic representations in free variation: [anɛttɔ̃b], [ʔanɛttɔ̃b], [anɛttɔ̃m], [ʔanɛttɔ̃m].

In most cases, variations in the pronunciation of a morpheme can be attributed to phonological rules. The morpheme in question then has a unique phonological representation underlying the different phonetic forms through which it manifests itself. The two pronunciations [l̥at] and [lat] are manifestations of the same phonological representation /latə/. But take, for example, the root of the verb *aller* 'to go', a morpheme that we will call *all-*. It is pronounced [al] in *vous allez* [ale] 'you go', and [i] in *vous irez* [ire] 'you will go' (the following *r* is not a part of the root, it is the manifestation of the future morpheme). Contrary to what we noticed in [l̥at] and [lat], the phonological representations [al] and [i] form an isolated pair which do not enter any series of analogous alternations. The future of *pédalez* [pedale] 'you pedal', *emballez* [ãbale] 'you pack', *étalez* [etale] 'you spread', is *pédalerez* [pedalre] 'you will pedal', *emballerez* [ãbalre] 'you will pack', *étalerez* [etalre] 'you will spread', and not **pédirez*, **embirez*, **étirez*. Suppose we wish to derive [al] and [i] from the same phonological representation, let us say /al/. The phonological component will have to contain a rule which rewrites *al* as *i* in a certain environment *K*, and a characterization of this context *K* will have to be included in the formulation of this rule and will have to be sufficiently restrictive to prevent the grammar from generating **pédirez*, **embirez*, etc., so that the rule will in fact only operate in the case of the verb *aller* 'to go'. It is better to take the [al] ~ [i] alternation for what it is: an idiosyncratic property of the morpheme *all-*, and not the consequence of any general structural feature. Rather than burdening the phonological component with a rule which can only be applied to the future of the morpheme *all-*, we will give two distinct phonological representations to this morpheme: /al/ as underlying *allez* 'go', and /i/ as underlying *irez*.

Consider also the word *œil* [œy] 'eye', which becomes *yeux* [yö] 'eyes' in the plural, when we have *deuil* ~ *deuils* [dœy] 'mourning/s' (and not

dieux), écureuil ~ écureuils [eküroey] 'squirrel/s' (and not **écurieux),*
seuil ~ seuils [soey] 'threshold/s' (and not **sieux),* etc. The lexical entry of
œil has on the one hand the phonological representation /œy/ as in *œil,*
œillade [œyad] 'wink', *œillère* [œyɛr] 'blinker', etc., and on the other
hand /iö/ as in *yeux.*[27]

One speaks of suppletion when a morpheme has several phonological
representations, and the phonological representations are said to be
allomorphs of the morpheme in question. *All-* is a suppletive morpheme and
the phonological representations /al/ and /i/ are allomorphs of this
morpheme. We will use the term allomorph here in a broad sense so that it
can also be used to refer to the single phonological representation of
morphemes which are not suppletive (these constitute the vast majority of
the lexicon). We will say, for example, that the phonological representation
/mani/ is the (only) allomorph of the morpheme *mani-* 'to handle'.

We will call 'spelling out' the operation which associates an allomorph to
each morpheme in a surface structure (an operation which spells out each
morpheme as a certain sequence of phonemes). It is this operation which, for
example, makes it possible to go from representation (6) on page 50 to
representation (7). The phonological part of each lexical entry can be
considered as a set of *spelling rules* specific to the lexical item under
consideration, rules of the kind: 'the lexical item I has the phonological
representation /X/ when in the context K'. In most cases, those when a
morpheme only has one allomorph, its lexical entry only has a single
spelling rule: 'I has the phonological representation /X/'. This single rule
does not specify anything about the context K, that is to say it invariably
operates in all the surface structures where the morpheme in question
occurs. For example '*mani-* has the phonological representation /mani/'. In
the case of suppletion, on the other hand, the lexical entry has several spelling
rules, each one related to a given context. Thus the lexical entry of *all-*
indicates that this morpheme is spelt out as /i/ in the future and conditional
(*ir-ez* [ire] 'you will go', *i-r-i-ez* [irye] 'you would go'), as /v/ in the
singular and in the third person plural of the present indicative (*v-ais* [vɛ]
'I go', *v-as* [va] 'you go', *v-a* [va] 'he goes', *v-ont* [võ] 'they go'), as well as
in the singular imperative (*v-a* [va] 'go!'), and finally as /al/ in all its other
forms.

There are also spelling rules which associate a phonological matrix to a
sequence of morphemes. The proposition *de* 'of' and the article *le* 'the' are
normally spelt out /də/ and /lə/. Thus the sequence *de le* 'of the' has the

---

[27] The first segment of /iö/ is rewritten as *y* by the phonological rule (8), whence finally [yö].

phonological representation /də#lə/ in *la valeur de l'or* [lavalœrdələr] 'the value of gold '.[28] On the other hand, this sequence is spelt out /dü/ when the following word begins with a consonant, as in *la valeur du diamant* [lavalœrdüdyamã] 'the value of diamonds', whose surface structure (omitting the labelled brackets) is *la valeur de le diamant*. As this is an isolated fact which cannot be explained by the interaction of general rules, it must be accounted for by introducing a spelling rule into the grammar, which associates the phonological matrix /dü/ to the morpheme sequence *de le* in a —— # C environment.

Thus we have at our disposal two types of mechanisms to account for variations in the pronunciation of morphemes: phonological rules and spelling rules. Attributing a given variation to one or the other system of rules is not simply a matter of convenience. Phonological rules have a general import and reflect structural features characterizing the language as a system. Spelling rules, on the other hand, form a part of the idiosyncratic information contained in the lexical entries. Each one of the cases of suppletion is an irregularity that the speaker has had to memorize separately.

We are now able to describe from beginning to end the sequence of operations by which a grammar generates the set of well-formed phonetic representations of sentences. Each surface structure generated by the syntactic component is the input of #-insertion rules and spelling rules, which associate a specific phonological representation to the surface structure. The phonological representation is subject to the rules of the phonological component, which associate one or more phonetic representations to it (see fig. 12).

Strictly speaking, only those rules which make it possible to go from phonological representations to phonetic representations are called phonological. Rules such as #-insertion or spelling rules, which form, as it were, a bridge between the output of the syntactic component (surface structures) and the input to the phonological component (phonological representations), are called readjustment rules, and their set forms the readjustment component.

Since phonological representations are outputs of the readjustment component and inputs to the phonological component, describing the readjustment component and the phonological component are two tasks that presuppose each other. *Any variation in the pronunciation of a morpheme*

---

[28] The /ə/ in the article /lə/ is dropped in front of the initial vowel of the noun *or*, cf. II, chap. 6.

that is not accounted for by the phonological component must be accounted for by the readjustment component and vice versa. Strictly speaking, describing the phonology of a language is simply describing its phonological rules and the way in which they interact, but one cannot even partially carry out this task without making a number of assumptions about the properties of the readjustment component of that language. We will therefore say that the task of a phonologist describing a language is only at an end when he has specified in detail the part of fig. 12 within the broken lines, and when he has constructed a specific device that generates the set of phonetic representations of well-formed sentences, taking as an input the corresponding set of surface structures. Therefore, the linguist undertaking the phonological description of a language theoretically has the following problem: knowing the infinite set Σ of the surface structures of that language and the infinite set P of the corresponding phonetic representations, he must construct a device which exactly defines the correspondence between Σ and P; this device must take the set Σ as its input and generate the set P as its output.

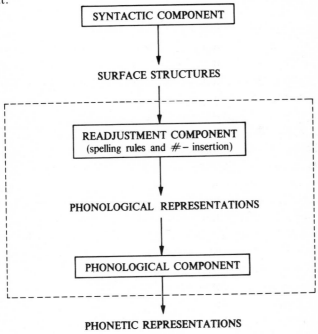

Fig. 12

Since the surface structure of a sentence is not merely raw data that is immediately accessible to observation, but an abstract object generated by the syntactic component, to suppose Σ known is to suppose that the syntactic component of the language in question has already been totally described by previous research, which obviously never happens in reality. Our knowledge of the syntax of even the best described languages is still very fragmentary. Luckily, it is not necessary to know all the aspects of the syntax of a language to describe its phonology, since only some of the syntactic features included in the surface structure are relevant in predicting pronunciation. This is why in the preceding pages we have been content to limit our concrete examples of surface structures of French sentences to roughly schematic representations. More precise representations are not possible, but this is of relatively little importance since we know that the missing details are not relevant in predicting pronunciation, at least where those aspects of French phonology which are already fairly well known are concerned. This last restriction is important, since the study of as yet little known aspects of French phonology such as for example stress or intonation patterns certainly cannot progress without a more detailed study of the surface structures.

To conclude, let us draw a parallel between the formal grammars presented on pages 6–11 and the phonological components, considered as formal grammars of a particular kind. In the case of a phonological component, the formulae to be generated are well-formed phonetic representations. The initial sequences, at the start of the derivations, are the infinite set of phonological representations. A phonological component is, therefore, a formal grammar which has an infinite set of initial sequences, and not a small finite number as in the grammars G_4, G_5, etc. on page 9. The infinite language constituted by these initial sequences is itself generated by another formal grammar, composed of the syntactic and readjustment components. Just as in the derivations of the grammars G_4, G_5, etc., there are auxiliary symbols such as J, K, etc., which never appear in the formulae of the generated language, so in the derivations of a phonological component, there are symbols such as # and + that do not occur in the final output of the derivation, i.e. in the phonetic representation.

Phonological components are organized very differently from the particular grammars G_4, G_5, etc., which we considered when introducing the basic notions concerning formal grammars. In both cases the rules apply sequentially, but here the resemblance ends. In the grammars G_4, G_5, etc., the order in which the rewrite-rules are given is of no importance, and a given rule can be applied several times in the course of the same derivation. On the other hand, in a phonological component the rules are applied in a pre-established order, and each rule is only applied once in the derivation.

Lastly, conditions for ending a derivation are very different. In the first case, a derivation stops when the sequence in question no longer contains any symbol that can be rewritten by any rule. In the other, it stops when the last rule has applied.

THE ORDER OF APPLICATION OF PHONOLOGICAL RULES [29]

On page 58, we explained that in order to derive a phonetic representation from a phonological representation, all the phonological rules are successively applied in an order that has been pre-established once and for all; each rule receives as input the representation resulting from the application of the preceding rule, whence the existence of a succession of intermediate levels between the level of phonological representations and the level of phonetic representations, each level corresponding to the output of one of the phonological rules. There is no *a priori* reason why grammars should be organized in such a way. Consider, for example, the derivation (11') on page 57. The order of application of the rules in no way changes the final result. It little matters whether they are applied in the order (8-9-10) in which they were given or, for example, in the order (10-8-9), in other words by deleting the final *z* before rewriting *i* as *y*, this operation preceding the replacement of *r* by *ŗ*. It could just as well have been decided that all the rules are to be applied to the phonological representation simultaneously, each one operating on the segments subject to it. There would then be no intermediate levels of representation, and the phonetic representation would be obtained by simultaneously carrying out in the phonological representation the modifications prescribed by each rule.[30] The derivation (11') would then have the following form:

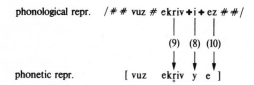

phonological repr. /# # vuz # ekriv ✦i✦ ez # #/

          (9) (8) (10)

phonetic repr.   [vuz   ekŗiv y e]

If this were so, phonological rules would then be statements establishing a direct relationship between the phonemes and the speech sounds

---

[29] Cf. *SPE*: 18-20, 340-50; Chomsky (1964: 70-75; 1967 *b*), Halle (1962), McCawley (1968 *a*: 19-23), Postal (1968: 140-52). For rule ordering according to Bloomfield, see Bloomfield (1933: 213, 222; 1939) and the comments by Chomsky (1964: 70, n. 8.).

[30] And by deleting all the # and + boundaries, cf. p. 56.

corresponding to them in the phonetic representations. Rule (9) would indicate, for example, that each [+ son, − syll] phoneme preceded by a [− voice] phoneme has a corresponding [− voice] speech sound at the phonetic level.

We are thus faced with choosing between two competing modes of organization for the phonological component: simultaneous or sequential application? Of course, this choice is only interesting in so far as it has empirical consequences, i.e. in so far as we can find facts that would be better accounted for by one hypothesis rather than the other. Such facts are not difficult to find, for the languages of the world have an abundant supply of them. We will look at two examples, and in each case it will be clear that a sequential application is necessary.

Our first example is taken from French. Rule (8a) on page 53, which will henceforth be known as SEM ('semivocalization'), rewrites any high vowel immediately followed by another vowel as a semi-vowel. Since all vowels are [+ voice] in phonological representations, the semi-vowels thus obtained are [+ voice]. But consider the following forms (imperative ∼ past participle):

> *dévie* [devi] ∼ *dévié* [devye] 'to deviate'
> *défie* [defɪ] ∼ *défié* [defye̥] 'to challenge'
> *avoue* [avu] ∼ *avoué* [ăvwe] 'to admit'
> *bafoue* [bafu] ∼ *bafoué* [bafwe̥] 'to flout'
> *gradue* [gradü] ∼ *gradué* [gradẅe] 'to graduate'
> *situe* [sitü] ∼ *situé* [sitẅe̥] 'to locate'

These forms show that semi-vowels are [+ voice] after a [+ voice] segment, but [− voice] after a [− voice] segment. The devoicing of semi-vowels after [− voice] immediately reminds us of that of nasal and liquid consonants in the same environment, under the influence of rule (9a), page 58, which we will henceforth call DEV ('devoicing'). The alternation between [y] and [y̥] in *dévié* [devye], *défié* [defye̥] is parallel to that between [l] and [l̥] in *meublé* [mœble] 'furnished', *peuplé* [pœ̥ple̥] 'populated', between [r] and [r̥] in *givré* [živre] 'frosted', *chiffré* [šifr̥e] 'numbered', etc. Similarly, compare the alternation between [y] and [y̥] in *gaviez* [gavye] 'you stuffed', *gaffiez* [gafye̥] 'you blundered' and that of [r] and [r̥] in *gaverez* [gavre] 'you will stuff' and *gafferez* [gafr̥e] 'you will blunder'. How can the fact be expressed that the devoicing of nasal and liquid consonants, and that of semi-vowels arising from high vowels, are two manifestations of the same process? If all the phonological rules are to be applied simultaneously to the phonological representation /defi + e/

(*défié*), we cannot put the voicelessness of [y̥] in *défié* on the same footing with that of [ɹ̥] in *chiffré* and attribute them both to the DEV rule. For as it is formulated so far DEV affects only non-syllabic sonorants, whereas in the phonological representation, the segment /i/ underlying [y̥] is [+ syll]. There can be no question of reformulating DEV so that it can affect all the sonorants, both syllabic and non-syllabic, since it would then devoice any vowel following a voiceless consonant, and our grammar would generate ungrammatical strings, such as *[kafe̥] instead of [kafe] (*café*), etc. In fact in French the only vowels that are regularly realized as [− voice] sounds are high vowels, precisely when they lose their syllabicity as a result of the application of the SEM rule.

Exactly the desired result can be obtained when the SEM rule is applied first, rewriting these vowels as [− syll]. At that point, they satisfy the structural description of DEV, which rewrites them as [− voice]. See the derivation of *défié* below, to which we have added those of *dévié* and *chiffré*, for comparison:

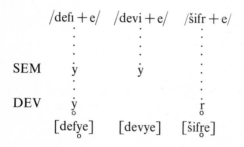

	/defɪ + e/	/devi + e/	/šifr + e/
SEM	y	y	
DEV	y̥		r̥
	[defy̥e]	[devye]	[šifr̥e]

By representing the realization [y̥] of the /i/ of /defɪ + e/ as the product of the rules SEM and DEV successively applied in that order, we claim that the [− syll] and [− voice] characteristics of this [y̥] are related in the following way: /i/ is realized as [− syll] because it precedes a vowel and French has a rule, SEM, which rewrites high vowels preceding a vowel as [− syll]. This /i/ is further realized as [− voice] because it follows a [− voice] segment, and being [− syll] as a result of the SEM rule, it is subject to the DEV rule. The DEV rule affects all the non-syllabic sonorants without distinguishing between those, like the *r* in *chiffré*, that are already non-syllabic in the phonological representation, and those, like the *y* in *défié*, that become so by application of the SEM rule. In order to get a better understanding of the point of applying the rules in a specific order, let us examine the kind of grammar we would have to write if we decided to apply the rules simultaneously. Apart from SEM and DEV, which we will give again for the sake of convenience, such a grammar would have to contain rule (14):

$$(14) \quad \begin{bmatrix} + \text{son} \\ + \text{high} \end{bmatrix} \rightarrow [-\text{voice}] \quad / \quad [-\text{voice}] \underline{\quad\quad} [+\text{syll}]$$

$$\text{SEM} \quad \begin{bmatrix} + \text{son} \\ + \text{high} \end{bmatrix} \rightarrow [-\text{syll}] \quad / \quad \underline{\quad\quad} [+\text{syll}]$$

$$\text{DEV} \quad \begin{bmatrix} + \text{son} \\ - \text{syll} \end{bmatrix} \rightarrow [-\text{voice}] \quad / \quad [-\text{voice}] \underline{\quad\quad}$$

Rule (14) devoices high sonorants followed by vowels and preceded by a voiceless segment. This rule rewrites the /i/ of /defi + e/ as [− voice] at the same time as SEM rewrites it as [− syll], whence the phonetic representation [defye]. As might be expected, (14) bears a strange resemblance to SEM and DEV. The structural description of SEM is contained in that of (14), i.e. any segment which is subject to (14) is also subject to SEM. The resemblance between (14) and DEV is even more striking. Both rules devoice sonorants preceded by a voiceless segment. To write two different rules, (14) and DEV, implies incorrectly that we are dealing with two different processes. As far as we know, all the writers on the subject implicitly acknowledge that the devoicing of liquids and nasals and that of semi-vowels are two aspects of one and the same process, cf., for example, Malmberg (1969: 134) and Martinet (1965a: 106).

We will borrow our second example from Kongo of San Salvador (which we will simply call Kongo from now on), a Bantu language from the north of Angola, described in Bentley (1887). All our data are taken from this book. In the following examples, we have written the forms according to Bentley's spelling (but see n. 33) which is for the most part a phonetic transcription. We have inserted hyphens to show the division of words into morphemes. Kongo has five vocalic phonemes: /i, e, a, o, u/. Most words consist of a root which can be flanked by prefixes or suffixes.

Kongo words are subject to the following phenomenon of vocalic harmony: when there is a [− high, − low] vowel in the root, any other vowel situated to the right of it is [− high]. In other words, when the root contains either the vowel [e] or [o], any vowel situated to its right can be either [a], [e] or [o], but not [i] or [u]. Thus the suffix which is used to form the verbal stem of the middle voice is pronounced *uk* when the root contains the vowels *a, i* and *u*, and *ok* when it contains the vowels *e* or *o*. Similarly,

the suffix of the emphatic forms is pronounced *il* in the first case, and *el* in the
second.

(15)   active   middle   emphatic

bak-a	bak-uk-a	bak-il-a	' to tear '
dik-a	dik-uk-a	dik-il-a	' to feed '
tung-a	tung-uk-a	tung-il-a	' to mend '
kes-a	kes-ok-a	kes-el-a	' to knock down '
somp-a	somp-ok-a	somp-el-a	' to borrow '

The vowels of the prefixes have no effect on the following vowels. For
example, *kumbi* ' engine ' becomes *e-kumbi* in the plural and not **e-kombe; e-
kombe* is the plural for *kombe* ' league '. We will therefore write the vocalic
harmony rule below, in which the labelled bracket $_R[$ symbolizes the left end
of the root and X, Y and Z represent any sequences (which can be empty)
not containing an occurrence of #.

$$\text{HARM:} \quad [+ \text{syll}] \quad \rightarrow \quad [- \text{high}] \quad \Big/ \quad _R\!\left[\quad X \begin{bmatrix} + \text{syll} \\ - \text{high} \\ - \text{low} \end{bmatrix} Y \underline{\quad} Z \ \# \right.$$

This rule rewrites as non-high any vowel preceded by a non-high and non-
low vowel which occurs to the right of the beginning of the root.[31] Thus the
phonological representations of *kes-ok-a* and *kes-el-a* (15) are respectively
/kes + uk + a/ and /kes + il + a/. The HARM rule rewrites the /u/ and /i/
of the suffixes as *o* and *e* respectively. Note, incidentally, that it also applies
to the final /a/ of the two forms. These /a/ are subject to the HARM rule, but
since they are already [− high] in the input, the operation of the rule does
not modify them. We have here a case of trivial application which is different
from the ones we have already met, where the segments under consideration
were left unchanged because the rule did not operate. Here the segments
under consideration are indeed subject to the rule, and its operation merely
confirms a specification present in the input. In such cases, the rule is said to
apply ' vacuously '.

The HARM rule affects sequences of vowels that are as lengthy as the very
rich morphology of Kongo permits. For example, the indirect causative

---

[31] According to this formulation, the vowel *e* or *o* which triggers harmonization can well
belong to a suffix, and not to the root. And it is actually often the case, as for example in
kang-akes-el-a, from /kang + akes + il + a/, where *kang* is the root and *akes* a suffix. We did
not mention this possibility initially to avoid complications.

form of *veng-a* 'to repel' is *veng-om-w-es-es-a* derived from /veng-
+um+w+is+is+a/. Compare it to that of *bang-a* 'to destroy', which is
bang-um-w-iš-is-a,[32] from /bang+um+w+is+is+a/, where HARM
does not operate, since neither *e* nor *o* is present.

There is another rule by which the phoneme [s] is actualized as [š] in
front of /i/.[33] It is realized as [s] everywhere else, and any occurrence of the
sounds [s] and [š] is a realization of the phoneme /s/. See, for example, the
alternations in *twas-a* ~ *twaš-il-a* 'to inflict', *yas-a* ~ *yaš-il-a* 'to open',
vas-a 'to break', *vaš-i* 'fragment', etc. We will therefore write the rule PAL
(for 'palatalization'):

PAL   s   →   š   /——i

Let us now consider *sumb-iš-is-a* and *vond-es-es-a*, which are the indirect
forms of the causative of *sumb-a* 'to buy' and *vond-a* 'to kill'. These forms
derive from /sumb+is+is+a/ and /vond+is+is+a/ respectively, and
the way in which they derive is intuitively clear: in /sumb+is+is+a/,
HARM cannot operate, since there are no *e* or *o* vowels, and the *s* of the
first suffix is rewritten š as it precedes an *i*; in /vond+is+is+a/, on the
other hand, the *o* of the root triggers rewriting *i* as *e*, whence *vond-es-es-a*,
in which the *s* of the first suffix does not need to be palatalized, since it
precedes an *e* and not an *i*. Thus, in order to decide whether an /s/
preceding an /i/ is subject to palatalization or not, we must first know
whether the /i/ is subject to vowel harmony. Only an /s/ preceding an /i/
that is left untouched by vowel harmony can be palatalized. Precisely this
result is obtained by applying the HARM rule before the PAL rule:

	/sumb+is+is+a/	/vond+is+is+a/
HARM		e e
PAL	š	
	[sumbišisa]	[vondesesa]

---

[32] On the sound [š] of the third suffix, see below.

[33] In Bentley's spelling, [š] is written as *x*. In fact /s/ is not the only phoneme to be palatalized
in front of *i*. The phonemes /t/, /l/ and /z/ are realized respectively as [č], [d] and [ž] in
front of *i*, and as [t], [l] and [z] everywhere else (pp. 529 and 619). The discussion below on
the relation between vowel harmony and the palatalization of /s/ is equally valid for /t/, /l/,
/z/.

If the rules were applied in the reverse order, we would get the following derivations, the second of which yields an ill-formed output:

	sumb + is + is + a	/vond + is + is + a/
PAL	š	š
HARM		e e
	[sumbišisa]	*[vondešesa]

Let us examine how we would account for the data if we always applied the phonological rules simultaneously. The HARM rule can be kept in its present form, but the PAL rule has to be reformulated. If we apply the HARM and PAL rules simultaneously to the representation /vond + is + is + a/, we get *[vondešesa]. For, in the light of simultaneous application, PAL in its present form palatalizes any /s/ followed by an /i/. PAL has to be reformulated so that it will only operate in front of an /i/ that is to be spared by HARM. As a first approximation we have PAL′, which we will not try to write in formal terms:

> PAL′:   /s/ is realized as [š] if it is followed by an /i/ and if the condition K is not violated.
>
> K: if /i/ belongs to the root or to a suffix, no vowel situated between it and the beginning of the root is [− high, − low].

In fact, as soon as the field of data to be accounted for by the grammar is widened, the PAL′ rule is unsatisfactory. There is a suffix *-i*, which is added to verb roots to form the corresponding agent nouns. But this suffix is an exception to the HARM rule. The verb *vond-a* 'to kill' which has already been mentioned becomes *vond-i* 'killer' and not **vond-e*, as the HARM rule would lead us to expect, *bong-a* 'to take' becomes *bong-i* and not **bong-e*, etc. Now, *mwes-a* 'to show' becomes *mweš-i* 'show-er'. This suffix /i/ has to be marked with an exception feature, [− HARM rule], thus preventing it from being modified by HARM.[34] If HARM is applied before PAL, the grammar correctly predicts that /mwes + i/ should be pronounced [mweši], for the phonological representation first undergoes the HARM rule, which applies trivially since the feature [− HARM rule] of the suffix prevents it from operating, whence the identical output /mwes + i/ which is then subject to PAL, which rewrites it as /mweš + i/.

Let us now examine the derivation of *mweš-i* under the assumption that

---

[34]   On the subject of exceptions, see pp. 115 ff.

HARM and PAL' are simultaneously applied. The HARM rule applies trivially for the same reasons as before. But rule PAL' cannot operate, since the representation /mwes + i/ violates the condition K: /i/ belongs to a suffix, and the root contains the vowel /e/, which is [− high, − low]. Thus, we finally obtain *[mwesi]. In order to enable PAL' to operate in this case, a second condition must be added, K', to the condition K of rule PAL':

> K': if the vowel /i/ is marked [− HARM rule], the rule still operates even if the condition K is violated.

In order to preserve the principle of simultaneous application, we are obliged to complicate the structural description of the palatalization rule and include the conditions K and K', which have nothing to do with the phenomenon of palatalization as such.

Let us recall what brought us to this point. The problem was to choose between two modes of application of the phonological rules, i.e. between two competing hypotheses about the structure of linguistic theory. Following one hypothesis the phonological rules are applied 'in parallel' to a common input (the phonological representation), each one taking into consideration only the information contained in that particular phonological representation, and each one operating without taking into account the way in which the other rules operate. Following the other hypothesis, they operate 'in series' and each rule has to take into account the modifications brought about by the preceding rules.

Similarly to the notions 'phonological matrix', 'structural description' or 'nasal', the principles governing the application of the phonological rules must be defined once and for all, and identically for all grammars, or else our descriptions of particular languages would have no empirical import whatsoever. For a certain statement on a particular language or all languages to have empirical import (i.e. that in principle it would be conceivable that some data could falsify it), the meanings of the terms must be stable, and fixed independently of their presence in this particular statement. If, for example, we did not decide once and for all on the meaning to be given to 'phoneme' and 'nasal', nothing would prevent us from claiming that all languages have three nasal phonemes. If the meaning of the terms is allowed to vary from one language to another at the convenience of the describer, then the statement 'French has three nasal phonemes' or 'all languages have three nasal phonemes' has no empirical import, *since it is compatible with any state of affairs.* By excluding nothing, it states nothing. The same is true for the manner of application of the phonological rules. If we do not establish universal principles governing the manner of application of phonological rules, and if we give ourselves the right to decide as we wish, for each language, and – why not? – for each form to be derived, the way in which the rules are to be applied, we then have such a broad field of possibilities that, whatever the facts, they can always be given a description which meets any condition given in advance.

In order to make up our minds over these two proposed modes of application, we proceeded in the following manner. Taking a set of data from a particular language, we constructed two competing grammars – or rather fragments of two such grammars – that account for the data. The rules of the first grammar were designed to be applied sequentially, and those of the second simultaneously. Take, for example, the data concerning vowel harmony and palatalization in Kongo, and compare one grammar containing HARM and PAL, designed to be applied 'in series', with the other containing HARM and PAL', to be applied 'in parallel'. Each grammar generates exactly the same set of phonetic representations; it is essential to keep this point in mind. What we are comparing is not the ability of the two grammars to account for the data, which is the same, but the way in which they account for them.[35] For French, as for Kongo, we have seen that a grammar with rules applying simultaneously accounts for the data only at the cost of complications that obscure the generality of the processes at work.

In each case, two phonological processes are at work, A and B, and both operate at the same point in a string. A and B do not have symmetrical roles. A does not depend on B, but B depends on A. In French the SEM rule is applied without taking into account the effects of the DEV rule; the DEV rule, on the other hand, takes into account the effects of the SEM rule, for the application of the SEM rule creates non-syllabic sonorant segments that are devoiced by DEV for the same reason as those already occurring in the phonological representations. Similarly, in Kongo, HARM is applied without taking PAL into account; but PAL takes into account the effects of HARM, which, by transforming certain *is* into *es*, destroys the conditions in which PAL could operate. The existence of such an asymmetrical relation of dependence between the different phonological processes is a structural trait shared by all languages. By deciding once and for all that phonological rules apply sequentially, this trait can be incorporated into the notion 'possible human language', which it is the task of linguistic theory to characterize. By applying rule A before rule B, we are simply using a device which has

---

[35] Cf. Chomsky (1965: 39–40).

precisely the formal properties required to reflect the fact that rule B has to take factors that depend on the action of rule A into consideration, whereas rule A does not take into account the effects of the action of rule B. Concerning the application of rules, the words 'before' and 'precede' indicate priorities of a logical, not chronological, kind.[36]

When stipulating that rules are to be applied simultaneously to the phonological representation, we do not have any natural way of indicating their interdependence, for we are obliged to define the conditions in which each one takes effect (its structural description) in terms of the sole information contained in the phonological representations. In Kongo, for example, palatalization only takes place in front of those /i/s that are not subject to HARM. But in phonological representations, nothing in the list of specifications of an /i/, considered by itself, indicates that it will or will not be affected by HARM. We have, therefore, been obliged to incorporate the conditions K and K' into the structural description of the palatalization rule; they precisely define, at the phonological level, the contexts in which an /i/ is not subject to HARM. Now the structural description of the palatalization rule contains two kinds of conditions which have nothing to do with each other. On the one hand we have the presence of an /i/, and this is directly related to the nature of the palatalization process, and on the other, we have conditions K and K', that merely reflect in a roundabout way the fact that PAL depends on HARM.

This would be even more striking if we looked at a great number of languages that have palatalization rules. In many cases, we would see that once this palatalization rule has been ordered correctly in relation to the other rules, it can be formulated so as to take into account only the nature of the segment which immediately follows the consonant subject to palatalization, without considering the properties of the preceding segments.[37] This gives us a strong argument in favour of successive application. By adopting a linguistic theory that enables phonological rules to be applied in a certain order, we give ourselves the means to construct, for the most diverse languages, grammars in which the palatalization rules would have a family resemblance. We have said that all languages obey

---

[36] The application of rules in a certain order reflects the synchronic structure of a language at a given moment, and this order is in theory independent of the succession in time of sound changes which led to this particular language situation. On the relation between the (synchronic) order of the rules and the relative chronology of sound changes, cf. Derwing (1973: 115–22), Halle (1962), Halle and Keyser (1967), Harris (1969), Keyser (1963), King (1969), Kiparsky (1967; 1968*a*; 1970; 1971), G. H. Matthews (1970), *SPE:* chap. 6.

[37] See below the palatalization rule for Zuni (p. 77), and that for Zoque (p. 96).

certain universal principles of organization, and that linguists have set themselves the task of discovering these principles. In this task, any similarity between the grammars of different languages is a precious clue, for *there is no reason to postulate more differences between the grammars of various languages than is strictly necessary for each of these grammars to be able to generate the set of sound-meaning pairs characteristic of the language being described.* In short, when choosing between several descriptions compatible with the data, linguists have every reason to prefer systematically the description which enables them to introduce a greater unity to the diversity of the phenomena.

All that the preceding discussion shows is that the phonological component has to be organized in such a way that a rule can, in certain cases, be applied at the output of another. But this condition still leaves many possibilities open. One can conceive of a great number of general models of phonological components which all meet this condition equally well, although they differ substantially among themselves. One can conceive, for example, of types of grammars where the same rule could be applied several times during the same derivation, or of a rule which could be applied in certain derivations and not in others, or of two rules which would be applied in the order A-B in some derivations and in the reverse order, B-A, in others, and so on ad lib.

The organization of the phonological component as described on page 58 is based on the following hypothesis: for any grammar whose phonological component contains n rules, these rules can always be ordered in a certain sequence of n terms R_1, R_2 ... R_n, where each rule appears once and only once. This sequence defines an order of application fixed once and for all, the same for all the derivations of the grammar in question. Each phonological representation is first submitted to the rule R_1, the first rule in the sequence. Rule R_1 spots all the segments that are subject to it and then simultaneously modifies them in accordance with the indications of its structural change, leaving the others unchanged. The obtained representation is then submitted to rule R_2 which operates in the same way, and so on until rule R_n. Once rule R_n has been applied and all the # and + boundaries deleted, the derivation comes to an end, and the output obtained is the phonetic representation. Each rule is applied once [38] and only once.[39] The order of application is the same for all derivations. In order to define the

---

[38] Cases of disjunctive ordering are exceptions to this. They are not discussed in this book, see *SPE*: 36, 357.

[39] We have omitted cyclical application, see *SPE*: chaps. 2 and 3.

phonological component of a grammar, a list must be given of the n rules that it contains and the order $R_1 ... R_n$ in which the rules are applied.

It is on the preceding hypothesis that most of the research in generative phonology over the last twenty years has been founded and it has led to a complete renewal of the field. This hypothesis has recently been challenged,[40] and will probably be superseded in the fairly near future; the normal fate for any general hypothesis in a science that is still only in its infancy, as is ours. Nonetheless, we adhere to it without restrictions in what follows, since the modifications which have been proposed are only of secondary importance at an elementary, introductory level like ours; moreover, their implications are far from having been thoroughly explored.

We will take our last example from Zuni, an American Indian language.[41] The forms we will take as examples are all invented. The use of real examples would have forced us to enter into complications that are not relevant to our present purpose.

The Zuni language has five vowels: *a, e, i, o, u*. The last vowel of a word is not pronounced when the next word begins with a vowel. A word pronounced [nisa] in front of a pause, or when the following word is [tewa], is pronounced [nis] when the following word is [elo]. Another word is similarly pronounced [bolu] in front of a pause or of [tewa], but [bol] in front of [elo], etc. In short, the two alternating pronunciations of each word are interrelated in a regular manner. Knowing the pronunciation in front of consonants, one can deduce the pronunciation in front of vowels by dropping the last vowel. Note that conversely one cannot deduce the pronunciation of a word in front of a consonant from its pronunciation in front of a vowel. Simply knowing that a word is pronounced [nis] in front of vowels, it is impossible to know whether the final vowel which appears in front of a consonant is [a] rather than [i] or [o]. If two words are distinguished only by their final vowels when occurring in front of a

---

[40] Since the publication of *SPE*, the order of application of rules is one of the problems which has most interested phonologists. The necessity of applying certain rules to the output of others is not questioned. The problem is, rather, to find out whether the order in which the rules apply is necessarily the same for all derivations, and whether in most cases it cannot be deduced from properties of the rules and from properties of the representations to which these rules apply, cf. for example Chafe (1968), Anderson (1969; 1974), Kenstowicz and Kisseberth (1970), Kisseberth (1972b), Dell (1973b). On the implications of that debate for historical phonology, cf. Kiparsky (1968a; 1971).

[41] The facts presented here were discussed in detail in a controversy which followed the publication of Newman (1965), cf. Davis (1966), Walker (1966), and the replies of Newman (1967), Tedlock (1969), Michael (1971). The disagreement did not bear on the facts, but their interpretation. Here we are following the conclusions of Michael (1971).

consonant, their pronunciations merge in front of a vowel. For example, in front of a word beginning with a consonant such as [tewa], one can distinguish between the words [nisi] and [nisa], but in front of a word beginning with a vowel such as [elo], they are both pronounced [nis]. The final vowel will be indicated in the phonological representation attributed to each word; for example, the phonological representation underlying [nisa] ~ [nis] will be /nisa/, and that underlying [nise] ~ [nis] will be /nise/, etc., and we will state the following phonological rule of elision:

ELIS: $V \rightarrow \emptyset \quad / \underline{\hspace{2em}} \# V$

ELIS indicates that a vowel is to be deleted when it is the first element of a $V \# V$ sequence, that is to say when it is at the end of a word followed by another beginning with a vowel. Taking the representations /nisa#elo/ and /nisi#elo/, the application of this rule yields identical phonetic representations, [niselo] and [niselo].

The phonetic representations of Zuni also contain two sounds of the k type, a velar k ([k]) and a palatal k ([ǩ]). If, for the time being, the ks that precede a vowel subject to deletion are left aside, the distribution of these two sounds is extremely simple; [ǩ] only appears in front of [i], [e] and [a], and [k] appears everywhere else. For example, we have the words [suǩa], [owiǩe], [oǩi], [naku] and [leko]; but there cannot be such words as *[suka], *[owike], *[oki], *[naǩu] and *[leǩo], which violate the restrictions that we have just stated. In short, if we posit a single phoneme /k/, we can always predict if it will be realized as [ǩ] or [k], depending on whether or not it is subject to the following palatalization rule:

PAL: $k \rightarrow \check{k} \quad / \underline{\hspace{2em}} \begin{bmatrix} + \text{syll} \\ - \text{round} \end{bmatrix}$

PAL indicates that k must be rewritten as $\check{k}$ in front of any non-rounded vowel, that is to say in front of i, e and a.

With the linguistic theory we have adopted, it is not enough to formulate precisely the ELIS and PAL rules, their order of application must also be discovered. To decide whether it is ELIS-PAL or PAL-ELIS, cases must be found where a k precedes a final vowel that is subject to elision. For example, the word /suka/ is pronounced [suǩa] in /suka#tewa/ ([suǩatewa]) and [suǩ] in /suka#owi/ ([suǩowi]). This last form, and others that are similar, unequivocally show that the pronunciation of /k/ always depends on the nature of the final vowel, even if it is elided, i.e. PAL must be applied before ELIS causes the final vowel of the word to disappear.

We have given below the correct derivation of [suḵowi], together with the derivation one would obtain if one applied PAL after ELIS:

	/suka # owi/		/suka # owi/
PAL	suka̦ # owi	ELIS	suk # owi
ELIS	suḵ # owi	PAL	
	[suḵowi]		*[sukowi]

This last example illustrates a property of rule ordering which was not apparent in the preceding two examples. By applying a rule A before a rule B, we guarantee two different things:

(i) A cannot take into account the effects of applying B.

(ii) B is obliged to take into account the effects of applying A.

In fact, the examples from French and from Kongo only illustrate point (ii), and we will see that the example from Zuni illustrates point (i).

The example from French shows that DEV has to take the results of SEM into account, and the example from Kongo shows that PAL must take the results of HARM into account (ii). By ordering SEM before DEV and HARM before PAL, we also guarantee the fact that SEM cannot take the result of applying DEV into account, nor HARM that of applying PAL (i). This last point is not clearly apparent, since it so happens that the independence of SEM in relation to DEV and that of HARM in relation to PAL is in any case guaranteed by the very contents of the rules, independently of the order in which they are applied. In French, the SEM rule would apply in any case without taking the effects of DEV into account even if DEV preceded SEM, for DEV modifies certain specifications of the feature [voice], and the structural description of SEM does not include the feature [voice]; that is to say, the way in which SEM is applied at one point of a sequence does not depend on the specification of the feature [voice] at that point. It is the same for Kongo: HARM would in any case apply without taking the effects of PAL into account, even if PAL preceded HARM, for PAL modifies consonants, whereas HARM only affects vowels.

The Zuni example on the other hand illustrates (i). If we order PAL before ELIS, it is essentially to prevent PAL from taking into account the effect of ELIS, i.e. to enable the *k* preceding the final *a* to be palatalized, in spite of the fact that this *a* is elided by ELIS. This example is also interesting for other reasons. Consider the forms /suka # owi/ and /suku # owi/ and their respective pronunciations: [suḵowi], [sukowi]. It is the presence of the vowel *a* in the phonological representation of the first form, and *u* in that of the second, which conditions the alternations between the realizations [ķ] and [k] of the phoneme /k/. Knowing that a consonant is of the type *k*, it is impossible invariably to predict whether it is a [ķ] or a [k], if only the vowels present in the *phonetic* representations are taken into account. There are certain generalizations that cannot be expressed only in terms of the information contained in the phonetic representations. The alternation between [ķ] and [k] is perfectly regular, but this regularity is partially obscured at the surface by the operation of ELIS, which removes some of the vowels responsible for the presence of a preceding [ķ].

	son	syll	cons	cont	nas	high	low	back	round	ant	cor	voice	del rel
a	+	+	−	+	−	−	+	+	−	−	−	+	+
ɔ	+	+	−	+	−	−	+	+	+	−	−	+	+
æ	+	+	−	+	−	−	+	−	+	−	−	+	+
ɛ	+	+	−	+	−	−	+	−	−	−	−	+	+
o	+	+	−	+	−	−	−	+	+	−	−	+	+
ːö	+	+	−	+	−	−	−	−	+	−	−	+	+
e	+	+	−	+	−	−	−	−	−	−	−	+	+
u	+	+	−	+	−	+	−	+	+	−	−	+	+
ːü	+	+	−	+	−	+	−	−	+	−	−	+	+
ï	+	+	−	+	−	+	−	−	−	−	−	+	+
y	+	−	−	+	−	+	−	−	−	−	−	+	+
l	+	−	+	+	−	−	−	−	−	+	+	+	+
r	+	−	+	+	−	−	−	+	−	−	−	+	+
ñ	+	−	+	+	+	+	−	−	−	−	−	+	−
n	+	−	+	+	+	−	−	−	−	+	+	+	−
m	+	−	+	+	+	−	−	−	−	+	−	+	−
ž	−	−	+	+	−	+	−	−	−	−	+	+	+
š	−	−	+	+	−	+	−	−	−	−	+	−	+
z	−	−	+	+	−	−	−	−	−	+	+	+	+
s	−	−	+	+	−	−	−	−	−	+	+	−	+
v	−	−	+	+	−	−	−	−	−	+	−	+	+
f	−	−	+	+	−	−	−	−	−	+	−	−	+
g	−	−	+	−	−	+	−	+	−	−	−	+	−
k	−	−	+	−	−	+	−	+	−	−	−	−	−
d	−	−	+	−	−	−	−	−	−	+	+	+	−
t	−	−	+	−	−	−	−	−	−	+	+	−	−
b	−	−	+	−	−	−	−	−	−	+	−	+	−
p	−	−	+	−	−	−	−	−	−	+	−	−	−
	son	syll	cons	cont	nas	high	low	back	round	ant	cor	voice	del rel

Fig. 13

LEXICAL REDUNDANCY

Let us agree, for the sake of this discussion, that French has 28 phonemes as defined in fig. 13. Any allomorph contained in the lexicon is a sequence of segments taken from this table. Since French has retained as phonemes only 28 combinations amongst the hundreds allowed by the universal stock of features, the specifications of the different features inside the same segment are related by very strict combinatory restrictions that can be stated in the form of rules. Here are some of these rules, that the reader can verify by looking at fig. 13.

R1:   all the phonemes are $[-\text{glott}]$
R2:   any phoneme that is $[+\text{nasal}]$ is also $[-\text{syll}]$
R3:   any phoneme that is $[+\text{son}]$ is also $[+\text{voice}]$

The restriction R1 distinguishes French from a number of other languages of the world that oppose glottalized and non-glottalized phonemes.[42] There are analogous restrictions that indicate that no French phoneme is aspirated, pharyngealized, etc. It is the existence of such restrictions valid for all the phonemes of French that has allowed us to represent only thirteen features on fig. 13 out of the φ distinctive features defined by linguistic theory. Actually, every French phoneme is a column of φ specifications corresponding to these φ features, but for each one of the columns of fig. 13, the φ − 13 specifications that are not represented automatically follow from the other existing 13 as a result of rules specific to French.

Rule R2 excludes nasal syllabic consonants and nasal vowels from the list of French phonemes. Rule R3 excludes voiceless sonorants. Note that these rules are only valid for phonemes, i.e. the segments that appear in phonological representations. Nothing prevents them from being violated at the phonetic level: French has nasal vowels (cf. II p. 164) and voiceless sonorants (cf. p. 47) at the phonetic level.

Apart from restrictions binding together feature values belonging to the same segment, which reflect the fact that any arbitrary combination of plus and minus signs allowed by the universal phonetic combinatory is not a phoneme of French, there also exist sequential restrictions, i.e. restrictions that bind together feature specifications belonging to successive segments of the same matrix. This reflects the fact that any arbitrary sequence of French phonemes is not a possible allomorph. For example, /bafu/, /bafi/ and /parfidre/ are sequences of phonemes allowed by the structure of the

---

[42]   Any sound which requires a momentary closure of the glottis is glottalized. The only sound in French that is glottalized is the glottal stop (cf. p. 45).

language, but not */ngo/, */ifšu/ or */tfakp/. Of the three possible sequences that we have given, only /bafu/ is actually attested. It is the phonological representation of the verb *bafouer* 'to flout'. There is an infinite number of phoneme sequences that do not break any of the combinatory restrictions imposed by the structure of French,[43] but as the lexicon only contains a few thousand allomorphs, most of these possible sequences do not figure in the lexicon; /bafi/ and /parfidre/ are among these. The fact that there is no morpheme whose phonological representation is /bafi/ or /parfidre/ does not arise from any structural constraint, but is only an accidental gap. On the other hand, sequences like */ngo/ or */ifšu/ are not possible allomorphs of French. The former violates the constraint expressed by rule R4, and the latter that expressed by rule R5:

R4: any allomorph which is [+ son, + cons] in its first segment, is [− cons] in its second segment

R5: in any sequence of two [− son, + cont] segments the first is /s/ and the second /f/

Rule R4 excludes from the set of possible allomorphs of French any sequence of phonemes that begin with a nasal or liquid consonant followed by a consonant: */ngo/, */lpa/, */rse/, etc. Rule R5 excludes any sequence of fricatives other than /sf/ (cf. *sphère* 'sphere', *phosphore* 'phosphorus'): */ifšu/, */isža/, */ivza/, etc. The same remarks can be made about sequential constraints as were made above on constraints inside segments: they are defined at the phonological level, but can well be violated at the phonetic level. For example, there are morphemes that have at the phonetic level an initial sonorant consonant followed by another consonant, cf. *renard* which is pronounced [rnar] in *un renard* [ɛ̃rnar] 'a fox'. But we will see later that the phonological representation of *renard* is /rɘnard/ (cf. II, p. 162), a sequence that does not break rule R4.

By constructing a complete system of rules similar to R1–R5, it should be possible to delimit exactly the set of all possible phonological matrices in French. We shall call rules of this type *morpheme structure rules*. A phonological matrix that does not violate any of the morpheme structure rules of French is a possible allomorph of French.

By relating certain feature specifications in the phonological matrices, the morpheme structure rules enable us to predict some specifications on the basis of others. Let us take for example the phonological representation of

---

[43]. But there are languages where the set of possible allomorphs is finite. This is the case of Chinese, for example.

the root of *nourrir* 'fo feed ', i.e. /nur/, which is a certain matrix of φ lines and three columns. In order to distinguish it from all the other φ × 3 possible matrices of French, it is not necessary to give the exhaustive list of the φ × 3 specifications it contains, or even the 13 × 3 = 39 specifications on the phonological matrix (a) in fig. 14: it is sufficient to give the seven feature specifications of matrix (b), which is obtained by deleting from (a) all those specifications that can be predicted from others. Indeed /n/ is the only French phoneme that is [+ nas, + cor]; in other words, knowing only that a phoneme of French contains the specifications [+ nas] and [+ cor], it can be deduced that it necessarily contains the specifications [+ son, − syll, + cons, + cont...], i.e. the set of specifications characteristic of the column /n/. Furthermore, rule R4 guarantees that the second segment is non-consonantal, since it follows a morpheme-initial sonorant consonant. And there is only one phoneme in French that is [− cons, + high, + back], /u/. And so on.

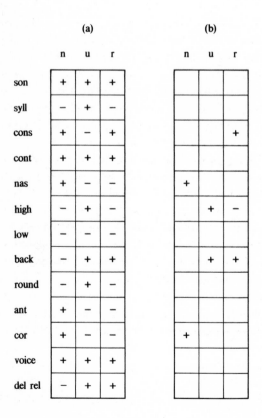

Fig. 14

It goes without saying that knowing these morpheme structure rules considerably lessens the amount that has to be stored in memory while learning new words. Contrary to what we said in the first place (see p. 49), allomorphs are not set out in the lexicon as phonological representations, i.e. as matrices of φ lines in which each box necessarily contains a plus or minus sign. This would indeed be equivalent to assuming that speakers memorize one by one all the specifications contained in the phonological representations, whereas for the most part these specifications are *redundant*, i.e. they automatically follow from other specifications. It is therefore necessary to distinguish between the phonological representation of an allomorph and its lexical representation. Schematically, the lexical representation of an allomorph is what is left of its phonological representation once all its redundant specifications have been put aside. In other words, a specification present in a lexical representation is by definition not predictable on the basis of the others. We will say that these specifications are *distinctive*. Phonological matrices like 14(a) are said to be completely specified. Each box necessarily contains a plus or a minus sign. Lexical matrices like 14(b), on the other hand, are said to be incompletely specified. Only distinctive specifications are represented. The boxes corresponding to redundant specifications are left empty. All the subject has to learn is the information contained in the incompletely specified matrices. From the point of view of phonology, the lexicon is a set of incompletely specified matrices in which only distinctive specifications are represented.

In order to go from a lexical matrix to the corresponding phonological matrix, all the blanks must be replaced by plus or minus signs. This can be done by using the morpheme structure rules. Like phonological rules, these rules can be considered not only as statements characterizing the language, but also as information on how to carry out certain operations on strings of symbols. For example, R2 indicates that in any column containing the specification $[+ \text{nas}]$, the empty box corresponding to the feature $[\text{syll}]$ must be filled by a minus sign. Similarly, R4 indicates that in any matrix in which the first column is $[+ \text{son}]$ and $[+ \text{cons}]$, the empty box on the second column corresponding to the feature $[\text{cons}]$ must be filled by a minus sign. The morpheme structure rules thus enable each (incompletely specified) lexical representation to be transformed into the corresponding (completely specified) phonological representation. Morpheme structure rules belong to the readjustment component, since they contribute to the definition of the phonological representations, which are the input to the phonological component.

There is a fundamental difference between phonological rules and morpheme structure rules. Whereas phonological rules change plus signs into minus signs and vice versa, permutate columns and add or suppress entire columns, morpheme structure rules can only fill in empty boxes. During the transformation of a lexical matrix into the corresponding phonological matrix, the number of columns is the same, and the specifications that were initially present in the lexical matrix remain unchanged. The morpheme structure rules only add new (redundant) specifications to the distinctive specifications, and can never modify the latter. The transformation of a morpheme's lexical matrix into its actual pronunciation in a given sentence is carried out in two steps: transformation of the lexical matrix into the phonological matrix by filling in the empty boxes (morpheme structure rules); then transformation of the phonological matrix into the phonetic matrix by modification of certain specifications, permutations of columns, addition or subtraction of entire columns (see fig. 15).

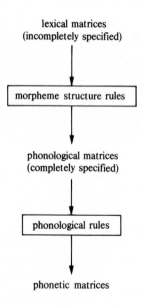

lexical matrices
(incompletely specified)

morpheme structure rules

phonological matrices
(completely specified)

phonological rules

phonetic matrices

Fig. 15

The morpheme structure rules operate on each allomorph taken separately in the lexicon. All the constraints they express bind together feature specifications enclosed within single morphemes. On the other hand, phonological rules operate on sequences of allomorphs and boundaries generated by the syntactic component and the readjustment component. The constraints which they enforce often involve feature specifications which are separated from one another by morpheme or word boundaries.

Once all the morpheme structure rules have applied, the resulting phonological matrices leave no indication by which the distinctive specifications (i.e. those that were already present in the lexical representations) can be distinguished from the redundant specifications (i.e. those that were added). In a derivation, the phonological rules modify the distinctive specifications in the same way as the redundant specifications. In other words, it is only necessary to distinguish between distinctive and redundant when comparing lexical representations to phonological representations, but distinctive specifications and redundant specifications are treated in exactly the same way by phonological rules. This is fundamental. If the features with a distinctive specification were not liable to change signs during the passage through the phonological component, that specification would remain unchanged right through to the phonetic level. But this is not the case.

The existence of morpheme structure rules is just an instance at the phonological level of a more general phenomenon, that of lexical redundancy. The lexicon is a list of lexical entries, and each lexical entry is itself a list of properties that specifically characterize a particular lexical item, i.e. properties that do not follow from rules governing the combination of lexical items into sequences. The lexicon of a language is a finite, but indefinitely extensible list. New lexical items can always be added to it. It is also, however, a structured list. The set of syntactic, semantic and phonological rules do not exhaust all the regularities that define the structure of a language, and the different properties constituting each lexical entry are related among themselves by certain restrictions that are anything but accidental.

To limit oneself to making an exhaustive list of actually attested lexical items would be to assume implicitly that this list is extensible in any direction, and that there are no constraints to limit the field of new lexical items that can be added. But explaining involves, among other things, excluding what is impossible, and a simple list does not exclude anything, it simply records what is there. Lists are in some sense zero degree structures. When we look further than the set of actually attested allomorphs of a language, we try to define the set of all the allomorphs possible in that language; we are aiming beyond the observed data at the structure that enabled them to exist.

Before leaving the subject of lexical redundancy, it is useful to insist on the essential distinction which must be made between the facts of redundancy that are universal and a part of linguistic theory, and those that specifically belong to one or another language and must be explicitly represented in its description. For example, it is a universal fact that there are no speech sounds (and therefore no phonemes) that are [− cont, + syll]. This statement characterizes the notion of language in general, and it need not be repeated each time one begins the description of a new language. It must be integrated once and for all into linguistic theory. On the other hand, the fact that no phonological matrix of French contains the specification [+ glott] is particular to that language and must be explicitly mentioned in its grammar.

We will say no more about morpheme structure rules. Phonological redundancy poses tricky problems which have not yet been satisfactorily answered. In this domain, the development of generative phonology has so far not had much more to add to the little that had already been done within the framework of previous theories. The only important thing that generative phonology has added to the subject is a certain clarification of the problems involved. The morpheme – or rather the allomorph – is the only unit within which constraints on phoneme sequences are to be expressed. By defining these constraints (morpheme structure rules) and by defining the constraints on sequences of allomorphs (syntactic rules and readjustment rules) we *ipso facto* impose certain limitations on the phoneme sequences permitted within the word or the sentence; a grammar does not have to contain special rules to account for these limitations.

The conception of morpheme structure rules presented in the preceding pages is borrowed from an approach which was introduced by Halle (1959), and developed in the important article by Stanley (1967) and in *SPE* (chap. 8).[44] More recently, Chomsky and Halle proposed a different approach to the problem, which considers again and enriches the notion of 'markedness' that was developed by linguists of the Prague school.[45] It still remains to be seen whether this new approach will in time justify the hopes that have been placed in it.

---

[44] On the status of morpheme structure rules, see also the interesting remarks by Lightner (1973) and Sampson (1970).
[45] Cf. *SPE* (chap. 9) and Postal (1968: chap. 8).

3

Two fragments of a phonological component

Now that we have considered the basic notions, it is time to examine the way in which the phonological component functions on the basis of concrete examples. The following two accounts were conceived with the idea of conveying the general approach rather than presenting particular facts, rules or data. Our aim is to get across the feeling that nothing can be taken for granted in a linguistic description, that everything has to be justified, and to give an idea of which considerations are relevant when deciding between two competing grammars.

In each of the two examples described below, we isolated a small number of facts from the rest of the language, chosen because they are organized in a coherent set that can be examined separately without distorting the overall picture of the structure from which they have been extracted. We had to omit certain details which would have led us to digress at greater length than is warranted by the point at issue. Even so the simplifications that result are in fact few in number and concern only points of minor importance: details which have to do with the formulation of this rule or that, and do not affect the general organization of the system.

SOME PHONOLOGICAL RULES OF ZOQUE

Our first example is taken from Zoque, a language from the south of Mexico. The morphology of Zoque has been quite thoroughly described in the articles by Wonderly (1951; 1952). All our data come from these articles.

Consider the following forms:

[tihu]	'he arrived'	[kaʔu]	'he died'
[tihpa]	'he arrives'	[kaʔpa]	'he dies'
[tihkeʔtu]	'he also arrived'	[kaʔkeʔtu]	'he also died'
[tihkeʔtpa]	'he also arrives'	[kaʔkeʔtpa]	'he also dies'

These forms contain the verbal roots /tih/ 'to arrive', /kaʔ/ 'to die', and the suffixes /u/, perfective aspect, /pa/, imperfective aspect, /keʔt/ 'also'.

Consider now the analogous forms of the verb /poy/ 'to run':

[poyu]	'he ran'	(/poy + u/)
[popya]	'he runs'	(/poy + pa/)
[pokye?tu]	'he also ran'	(/poy + ke?t + u/)
[pokye?tpa]	'he also runs'	(/poy + ke?t + pa/)

These forms illustrate the fact that when a morpheme ending in a yod is followed by another morpheme beginning with a consonant, there is permutation – linguists say metathesis – of the yod and the following consonant.

$$\text{META:} \quad y\,C \;\to\; C\,y$$

Thus, the underlying representation of [popya] is /poy + pa/, which becomes /po + pya/ by application of META. This metathesis is not an oddity confined to a few isolated forms. It is a perfectly general process that even affects words recently borrowed from Spanish. Here are a few more examples. There is a suffix /kuy/ that enables nouns to be formed from verbs. Thus, we have the following pairs: [yospa] 'he works', [yoskuy] 'work'; [petpa] 'he sweeps', [petkuy] 'broom'; [hapya] 'he writes' (from /hay + pa/), [hakyuy] 'writing' (from /hay + kuy/). There is also a suffix /kəsi/[1] 'on': [mesa] 'table' gives [mesakəsi] 'on the table', [kuy] 'tree' gives [kukyəsi] 'on the tree'. Similarly the words [yoskuy], [petkuy], [hakyuy] mentioned above respectively give [yoskukyəsi], [petkukyəsi], [hakyukyəsi]. In this last word, the metathesis rule simultaneously operates in two different places of the representation /hay + kuy + kəsi/.

At the same time, there is a rule stating that all non-continuants are voiced when they follow a nasal consonant:

$$\text{VOICE:} \quad [-\text{cont}] \;\to\; [+\text{voice}] \;/\; [+\text{nas}] \underline{\hspace{2em}}$$

It is this rule that explains that alongside the series [tihu] ~ [tihpa] ~ [tihke?tu] mentioned above, one finds the series [kunu] ~ [kunba] ~ [kunge?tu] formed from the verb /kun/ 'to fall'.

---

[1]　The symbol ə here stands for a non-high, non-low, unrounded back vowel.

TABLE 1

	I	II	III	IV
(a)	ki?mu	ki?mba	ki?mge?tu	ki?myahu
(b)	kihpu	kihpa [2]	kipke?tu	kipyahu
(c)	maŋu	maŋba	maŋge?tu	maŋyahu
(d)	hahku	hakpa	hahke?tu [2]	hakyahu
(e)	kunu	kunba	kunge?tu	kuñahu
(f)	?ehcu	?ecpa	?ecke?tu	?ehčahu
(g)	wihtu	witpa	witke?tu	wihḳahu
(h)	sohsu	sospa	soske?tu	sohšahu

Consider now the conjugated forms of table 1 above. The meanings of the forms on line (a) are, from left to right, respectively: 'he went up', 'he is going up', 'he also went up', 'they went up'. The forms of the next lines are constructed on the same model. In this table, and in the following ones, the square brackets indicating that the forms represented are phonetic representations have been omitted.[3] From a morphological point of view, the forms of column iv only differ from those of column i by the presence of the suffix /yah/, third person plural. These forms show that when a coronal consonant is followed by a yod the two articulations merge: $n + y$ gives $\tilde{n}$ (line e), $c + y$ gives $\check{c}$ (line f), $t + y$ give $\underline{k}$ (line g), $s + y$ gives $\check{s}$ (line h). Let us call PAL (for palatalization) the rule that accounts for this process. This rule will be written formally below (p. 96).

Note furthermore that if a root ends in *VhC* when the following suffix begins with a vowel, it loses the *h* in front of a suffix beginning with a consonant. Thus, the verb 'to walk' (line g) is pronounced [wiht] in [wihtu], but [wit] in [witpa] and [witke?tu]. The same is true for the forms in lines (b), (d), (f) and (h). We will suppose that the verbs on lines (b), (d), (f), etc. have the following representations: /kihp/, /hahk/, /?ehc/, etc., and we will propose the rule H-DEL, indicating that *h* is deleted when followed by two consonants (i.e. two non-syllabics):

$$\text{H-DEL:} \quad h \;\rightarrow\; \emptyset \quad / \underline{\hspace{2em}} CC$$

---

[2] One could have expected /kihp + pa/ to yield *[kippa], and /hahk + ke?t + u/ to yield *[hakke?tu]. The forms [kihpa] and [hahke?tu] show that there is a rule which deletes a consonant in certain groups of identical consonants, and that this rule must be ordered before H-DEL (see further below).

[3] The verbs respectively mean: (a) 'to go up', (b) 'to fight', (c) 'to come', (d) 'to cross', (e) 'to fall', (f) 'to dance', (g) 'to walk', (h) 'to cook'.

We still have to order these rules among themselves. Consider, for example, the forms (1)–(4) where we have the prefix /nay/, reciprocal, the suffix /yatəh/, third person plural, and the roots /nehp/, /ken/, /caŋ/ and /sun/, which are also found in [nehpu] 'he kicked', [kenu] 'he looked', [caŋu] 'he hit' and [sunu] 'he was in love':

(1) /nay + nehp + yatəh + pa/   [nañepyatəhpa]   'they   kick   each   other'
(2) /nay + ken + yatəh + pa/   [nakyeñatəhpa]   'they see each other'
(3) /nay + caŋ + yatəh + pa/   [načaŋyatəhpa]   'they hit each other'
(4) /nay + sun + yatəh + pa/   [našuñatəhpa]   'they   love   each   other'

The forms (1), (3) and (4) show that the PAL rule must be applied after the META rule. We can see below what happens in the derivation of form (4), according to whether PAL is ordered before or after META:

	/nay + sun + yatəh + pa/		/nay + sun + yatəh + pa/
META	na + syun + yatəh + pa	PAL	nay + suñ + atəh + pa
PAL	na + šuñ + atəh + pa [4]	META	na + syuñ + atəh + pa
	[našuñatəhpa]		*[nasyuñatəhpa]

The order of application META–PAL reflects the fact that the palatalization rule does not differentiate between [+ cor] *y* sequences arising from the permutation of a *y* [+ cor] sequence, and those that were already present in the phonological representations, i.e. those that come from the juxtaposition of a morpheme terminated by a coronal and one beginning with a yod. All the [+ cor] *y* sequences are subject to palatalization, whatever their origin. If palatalization only affected [+ cor] *y* sequences of the second type, one would have to order PAL before META (see the derivation on the right).

Similarly, it can be seen that the H-DEL rule must be ordered after PAL, which has the effect of merging two [− syll] segments into one. The

---

[4]   The sequence *un + ya* is rewritten *uñ + a* and not *u + ña*. More generally, if we designate a certain coronal consonant as *C*, and the consonant that results from the merging of *C* with *y* as *C′*, and if *W* and *Z* represent any two sequences, the PAL rule (p. 96) and the convention (10) on p.112 guarantee that any sequence *WC + yZ* is rewritten as *WC′ + Z* and not as *W + C′Z*. The importance of this detail will become apparent when we discuss rule H-INS (p. 111, n. 24).

underlying *h* of /kihp + yah + u/ does not appear in the phonetic representation [kipyahu] (table 1, b) because it is followed by *p* + y , which is a *CC* sequence, and it is therefore subject to H-DEL. The *h* of /wiht + yah + u/, however, is retained in the pronunciation [wiḫahu] (line g) for the PAL rule rewrites the sequence of two consonants *t* + *y* as the single consonant *ḳ*, which destroys the conditions necessary for H-DEL to operate. We give below the derivation of /wiht + yah + u/, according to whether PAL is ordered before or after H-DEL:

/wiht + yah + u/   /wiht + yah + u/

PAL	wihḳ + ah + u	H-DEL	wit + yah + u
H-DEL		PAL	wiḳ + ah + u

[wihḳahu]   *[wiḳahu]

If we absolutely wanted to apply H-DEL before PAL, we would have to give H-DEL a less general formulation that would stipulate that *h* be dropped in front of all *CC* sequences except coronals followed by yod. [+ cor] *y* sequences would be mentioned in two points of the grammar: in the PAL rule and in the H-DEL rule, and this would seem like an accident. The grammar would thus not establish any correlation between the fact that the only *CC* sequences in front of which *h* is retained consist of a coronal followed by a yod, and the fact that there is a rule, PAL, that reduces any [+ cor] *y* sequence into a single consonant.

Up till now, we have established the following order: META–PAL–H-DEL. As for the VOICE rule, so far we have no reason to order it one way or another in relation to the three other rules.

All the verb forms [5] cited up to this point are forms of the third person, and the verb is not preceded by any auxiliary, nor by any prefix indicating the person. In Zoque, there are forms similar to those of our 'compound tenses', where the verb is preceded by an auxiliary, in which case a personal prefix is necessarily added to the verb root. Take, for example, the verb /puht/ 'to go out' that gives [putpa] 'he is going out', [puhtu] 'he went out', [nəmbuhtu] 'I am going out', [nəmbyuhtu] 'you are going out', [nəpyuhtu] ' he is going out '. [nəmbuhtu] derives from /nə #n + puht + u/ where /nə/ is the auxiliary marking the progressive aspect ' to be in the process of ', /n/ the prefix of the first person, and where the final suffix /u/

---

[5]   It is only for the sake of convenience that we use verb forms. All the phonological rules presented here are just as applicable for the rest of the language.

has a function similar to that of our infinitive. Any verb preceded by the
auxiliary /nə/ necessarily takes the suffix /u/.⁶ Similarly, [nəmbyuhtu] and
[nəpyuhtu] respectively derive from /nə#ny + puht + u/ and /nə#y +
puht + u/, where /ny/ is the prefix of the second person and /y/ that of the
third. Analogous forms for other verbs, omitting the auxiliary *nə*, are given
in table 2. The forms of the last column are analogous to those in table 1,
column I, and they enable one to bring out the phonological representation
heading each line.⁷

TABLE 2

		I	II	III	IV
		1st pers. progressive /n-/	2nd pers. progressive /ny-/	3rd pers. progressive /y-/	3rd pers. perfective /ɸ/
(a)	/puht/	mbuhtu	mbyuhtu	pyuhtu	puhtu
(b)	/ken/	ŋgenu	ŋgyenu	kyenu	kenu
(c)	/tuh/	nduhu	ñǧuhu	ḳuhu	tuhu
(d)	/ciŋ/	nⱬiŋu	ñǰiŋu	čiŋu	ciŋu

The forms in table 2, column III can easily be explained by assuming that the
third person is marked by the prefix /y/, which is then positioned after the
root-initial consonant by metathesis. Thus [ḳuhu] (form IIIc) derives from
/y + tuh + u/, which gives /tyuh + u/ by application of META and
/ḳuh + u/ by application of PAL. In columns I and II the initial consonant
of the root is preceded by a nasal, which explains why it is voiced (cf. the
VOICE rule above). The point of articulation of this nasal consonant is
totally determined by the following consonant: it emerges as a bilabial in
front of a bilabial (see I(a) [mbuhtu]), as a dental in front of a dental
(see I(c) [nduhu] and I(d) [nⱬiŋu]), as a palato-alveolar in front of a palato-
alveolar (see II(d) [ñǰiŋu]), as a palatal in front of a palatal (see II(c)

---

⁶ This suffix /u/ is different from the one which marks the perfective aspect in [puhtu] 'he
    went out'.
⁷ The meanings of the verbs are as follows: (a) 'to go out', (b) 'to look, see', (c) 'to shoot with
    a bow or a gun', (d) 'to bathe'.

[ñg̊uhu]),[8] and as a velar in front of a velar (see 1(b) [ŋgenu]). We can thus propose the following rules:

R1: [+ nas] → bilabial   / —— bilabial

R2: [+ nas] → dental   / —— dental

R3: [+ nas] → palato-alveolar   / —— palato-alveolar

R4: [+ nas] → palatal   / —— palatal

R5: [+ nas] → velar   / —— velar

This gives the following distinctive features:

$$
\text{R1:} \quad [+\text{nas}] \rightarrow
\begin{bmatrix} +\text{ant} \\ -\text{cor} \\ -\text{high} \\ -\text{back} \end{bmatrix}
\Big/ \underline{\quad}
\begin{bmatrix} +\text{ant} \\ -\text{cor} \\ -\text{high} \\ -\text{back} \\ -\text{syll} \end{bmatrix}
$$

$$
\text{R2:} \quad [+\text{nas}] \rightarrow
\begin{bmatrix} +\text{ant} \\ +\text{cor} \\ -\text{high} \\ -\text{back} \end{bmatrix}
\Big/ \underline{\quad}
\begin{bmatrix} +\text{ant} \\ +\text{cor} \\ -\text{high} \\ -\text{back} \\ -\text{syll} \end{bmatrix}
$$

$$
\text{R3:} \quad [+\text{nas}] \rightarrow
\begin{bmatrix} -\text{ant} \\ +\text{cor} \\ +\text{high} \\ -\text{back} \end{bmatrix}
\Big/ \underline{\quad}
\begin{bmatrix} -\text{ant} \\ +\text{cor} \\ +\text{high} \\ -\text{back} \\ -\text{syll} \end{bmatrix}
$$

$$
\text{R4:} \quad [+\text{nas}] \rightarrow
\begin{bmatrix} -\text{ant} \\ -\text{cor} \\ +\text{high} \\ -\text{back} \end{bmatrix}
\Big/ \underline{\quad}
\begin{bmatrix} -\text{ant} \\ -\text{cor} \\ +\text{high} \\ -\text{back} \\ -\text{syll} \end{bmatrix}
$$

$$
\text{R5:} \quad [+\text{nas}] \rightarrow
\begin{bmatrix} -\text{ant} \\ -\text{cor} \\ +\text{high} \\ +\text{back} \end{bmatrix}
\Big/ \underline{\quad}
\begin{bmatrix} -\text{ant} \\ -\text{cor} \\ +\text{high} \\ +\text{back} \\ -\text{syll} \end{bmatrix}
$$

[8] In accordance with the phonetic alphabets in common usage we do not distinguish in our transcriptions between palato-alveolar nasals and palatal nasals; both are transcribed as *ñ*.

Since the point of articulation of a consonant is defined by the specification of the four features [ant], [cor], [high] and [back], the rules R1–R5 have the global effect of copying onto any nasal situated in an environment ——— C the specifications that define the point of articulation of C. The nasal is specified [+ ant] if it precedes a [+ ant] consonant (rules R1, R2) and [− ant] if it precedes a [− ant] consonant (rules R3, R4, R5); it is specified [+ cor] if it precedes a [+ cor] consonant (rules R2, R3) and [− cor] if it precedes a [− cor] consonant (rules R1, R4, R5) and so on. In short, rules R1–R5 are not five independent entities but different aspects of the same process which makes certain specifications of two adjacent segments agree with each other. Note especially that there is no reason to impose one order rather than another on the application of R1–R5; they all operate in contexts mutually excluding each other. Such sets of rules are common. Given that the Greek letters α, β, γ and δ stand for variables that can take on the values plus (+) and minus (−), we can factor out anything that contributes to the similarity of the rules R1–R5 and conflate them in the rule schema N-ASS (i.e. assimilation of nasals):

$$\text{N-ASS:}\quad [+\text{nas}]\quad\rightarrow\quad\begin{bmatrix}\alpha\ \text{ant}\\\beta\ \text{cor}\\\gamma\ \text{high}\\\delta\ \text{back}\end{bmatrix}\Bigg/\ \underline{\quad\quad}\ \begin{bmatrix}\alpha\ \text{ant}\\\beta\ \text{cor}\\\gamma\ \text{high}\\\delta\ \text{back}\\-\text{syll}\end{bmatrix}$$

The schema N-ASS can be expanded, i.e. by giving the variables α, β, γ and δ the different values they can take, the different rules the schema contains can be made explicit. Each combination of particular values of α, β, γ and δ, yields a rule that is a particular case of N-ASS. For example, when in N-ASS the variables α, β, γ and δ, are replaced by the signs +, −, −, −, respectively, rule R1 is obtained; when they are replaced by +, +, −, −, respectively, rule R2 is obtained, and so on. The schema N-ASS has two specifications of the features [ant], [cor] [high] and [back], one of which is situated on each side of the oblique slash. As these two specifications are equipped with the same Greek letter, this ensures that whatever the combination of plus and minus signs by which we replace α, β, γ and δ, this replacement gives rise to a rule where the two specifications of each of the above mentioned features have the same sign. For more details about this notation we refer the reader to *SPE* (350–7). Within the framework of this basic introduction to generative phonology, we will treat on an equal footing simple rules and the schemata that conflate a set of rules on the basis of their formal similarities.[9] The term 'rule' will be used to refer to the former as well as the latter.[10] Here are some derivations involving the rule N-ASS:

	/ny + puht + u/	/ny + tuh + u/	/ny + ciŋ + u/
META	n + pyuht + u	n + tyuh + u	n + cyiŋ + u
PAL		n + ǩuh + u	n + čiŋ + u
N-ASS	m + pyuht + u	ñ + ǩuh + u	ñ + čiŋ + u
VOICE	m + byuht + u	ñ + g̈uh + u	ñ + jiŋ + u
	[mbyuhtu]	[ñg̈uhu]	[ñjiŋu]

The derivation of [mbyuhtu] shows that N-ASS must be ordered after META. For as long as META has not operated, the nasal of the prefix in /ny + puht + u/ is prevented from being assimilated with the *p* by an intervening yod, which does not enter the structural description of N-ASS. N-ASS brings about the assimilation of a nasal only when nasal immediately precedes the consonant whose point of articulation it adopts. N-ASS must also be ordered after PAL, otherwise /ny + tuh + u/, for example, would yield *[ŋg̈uhu], with a nasal that is not assimilated to the following palatal. Finally, the same reasons that prompt us to order N-ASS after META also incite us to order VOICE after META: for in a form such as /ny + puht + u/, until META has operated the non-continuant to be voiced is separated by *y* from the nasal consonant under the influence of which voicing takes place and this prevents VOICE from operating. If VOICE were applied before META, /n + puht + u/ would indeed yield [mbuhtu] but /ny + puht + u/ would yield *[mpyuhtu].

We have just seen how forms containing the prefix /ny/ oblige us to order VOICE after META. On the other hand, there are no forms that oblige us

---

[9] For other types of rule schemata, see pp. 101, 121 and II, p. 192.

[10] The different rules contained in one schema always have exactly the same ordering relations with the other rules of the grammar. In other words, if two rules A and B belong to a certain schema, the grammar cannot have a rule C which would apply after A and before B and which would not belong to this schema. It is this property of schemata which explains the fact that when we give an ordered list of the rules of a grammar (see, e.g., p. 110), we can represent the schemata as wholes without detailing the rules they contain.

to fix the order of application of VOICE in relation to PAL. Here is the schema PAL; it is an abbreviation of the rules PAL_1 and PAL_2:

$$\text{PAL:} \quad \begin{bmatrix} + \text{cor} \\ \alpha \text{ del rel} \end{bmatrix} \quad y \quad \rightarrow \quad \begin{bmatrix} \alpha \text{ cor} \\ + \text{high} \\ - \text{ant} \end{bmatrix} \quad \emptyset$$
$$\qquad\qquad\quad 1 \qquad\quad 2 \qquad\qquad\quad 1 \qquad\quad 2$$

$$\text{PAL}_1: \quad \begin{bmatrix} + \text{cor} \\ - \text{del rel} \end{bmatrix} \quad y \quad \rightarrow \quad \begin{bmatrix} - \text{cor} \\ + \text{high} \\ - \text{ant} \end{bmatrix} \quad \emptyset$$
$$\qquad\qquad\quad 1 \qquad\quad 2 \qquad\qquad\quad 1 \qquad\quad 2$$

$$\text{PAL}_2: \quad \begin{bmatrix} + \text{cor} \\ + \text{del rel} \end{bmatrix} \quad y \quad \rightarrow \quad \begin{bmatrix} + \text{cor} \\ + \text{high} \\ - \text{ant} \end{bmatrix} \quad \emptyset$$
$$\qquad\qquad\quad 1 \qquad\quad 2 \qquad\qquad\quad 1 \qquad\quad 2$$

PAL_1 rewrites *ty, dy, ny* as *ķ, ǧ, ñ*, and PAL_2 rewrites *cy, ƶy, sy*, as *č, ǰ, š*. Note that the structural description of PAL does not include the feature [voice] of the consonant preceding yod, i.e. PAL is indifferent to the effects of VOICE, and then again, VOICE is indifferent to the effects of PAL, since none of the features [cor], [high] and [ant], the specifications of which are affected by PAL, figures in the structural description of VOICE. It little matters whether VOICE is applied before or after PAL, as shown for example in the following derivations:

	/ny + tuh + u/			/ny + tuh + u/
META	n + tyuh + u		META	n + tyuh + u
VOICE	n + dyuh + u		PAL	n + ķuh + u
PAL	n + ǧuh + u		VOICE	n + ǧuh + u
N-ASS	ñ + ǧuh + u		N-ASS	ñ + ǧuh + u
	[ñǧuhu]			[ñǧuhu]

Similarly, there is no reason to impose a particular ordering on VOICE and N-ASS, VOICE and H-DEL or N-ASS and H-DEL.

For the time being, we can establish the partially ordered list of rules shown in (5). The lines linking two rules in this list indicate that there are

(5)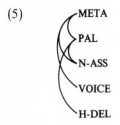

META

PAL

N-ASS

VOICE

H-DEL

forms exemplifying the need to apply the rules in the order given, i.e. forms whose derivation would give an incorrect output if the two rules in question were applied in the reverse order. Such rules are sometimes said to be crucially ordered. Thus META and PAL are crucially ordered, as shown in the derivation of [našuñatəhpa] (p. 90). When two rules are not crucially ordered, two kinds of situations can arise.

In some cases their ordering is nevertheless fixed, since it follows from their ordering in relation to other rules. Thus META is necessarily applied before H-DEL, although in Zoque there is no form that shows the reverse order to be incorrect, since META precedes PAL and PAL precedes H-DEL (see above). Since we have assumed that the order of application of the rules is the same for all the derivations (see p. 75), if META always precedes PAL and PAL always precedes H-DEL, it necessarily follows that META always precedes H-DEL.

In other cases, the order between two rules that are not crucially ordered makes no difference, as, for example, with VOICE and PAL. Our grammar would generate exactly the same set of phonetic representations if instead of applying the rules in the order given in (5), where PAL precedes VOICE, we applied them in a sequence where VOICE preceded PAL, but where the relative ordering indicated by linking lines remained unchanged: META–VOICE–PAL–N-ASS–H-DEL, for example. Nothing in the data examined up to now enables us to choose between these two orders of application.

Returning to the schema N-ASS, its present formulation is too loose, since it predicts, for example, that /kun + pa/ and /kun + keʔt + u/ are to be pronounced *[kumba] and *[kuŋgeʔtu], whereas in table 1 above the forms II(e) and III(e) are [kunba] and [kungeʔtu], where the nasal is not assimilated to the following consonant (see also the analogous forms (a) and (c)). We will reformulate N-ASS as follows:

$$\text{N-ASS:} \quad [+\text{nas}] \;\rightarrow\; \begin{bmatrix} \alpha\ \text{ant} \\ \beta\ \text{cor} \\ \gamma\ \text{high} \\ \delta\ \text{back} \end{bmatrix} \Big/ \quad \# \quad\rule{1.5em}{0.4pt}\quad \begin{bmatrix} \alpha\ \text{ant} \\ \beta\ \text{cor} \\ \gamma\ \text{high} \\ \delta\ \text{back} \\ -\ \text{syll} \end{bmatrix}$$

In its present form, N-ASS indicates that the assimilation of a nasal consonant only takes place at the beginning of a word.[11]

N-ASS poses yet another problem. As it is formulated for the moment, it indicates that the assimilation of place of articulation takes place in front of any non-syllabic segment. It predicts, for example, that at the beginning of a word *ns* yields *ns*, that *nš* yields *ñš*, that *nw* yields *ŋw*, etc. But what actually happens? Note that the forms in table 2 above only illustrate the case where the non-syllabic following an initial nasal is a non-continuant obstruent. Table 3 gives analogous forms illustrating the other cases.[12]

TABLE 3

		I	II	III	IV
		1st pers. progressive /n-/	2nd pers. progressive /ny-/	3rd pers. progressive /y-/	3rd pers. perfective ϕ
(a)	/hahk/	h̃ahku	h̃yahku	hyahku	hahku
(b)	/weh/	w̃ehu	w̃yehu	wyehu	wehu
(c)	/yohs/	ỹohsu	ỹohsu	yohsu	yohsu
(d)	/sohs/	sohsu	šohsu	šohsu	sohsu
(e)	/maŋ/	maŋu	myaŋu	myaŋu	maŋu
(f)	/nihp/	nihpu	ñihpu	ñihpu	nihpu
(g)	/ʔehc/	ʔehcu	ʔyehcu	ʔyehcu	ʔehcu

[11] This formulation is in fact too restrictive. A form like [haŋgyena] 'I have not seen him', from /hay + n + ken + a/ shows that the personal prefixes assimilate their place of articulation even when they are not situated at the beginning of words. Notice also that in this form the final yod of the negative prefix /hay/ does not simply permute with the *n* of the personal prefix, as META predicts, but moves in behind the initial *k* of the root. It would take us too far afield to look into the changes that should be made in N-ASS and META in order to account for these facts. In any case, these changes only concern N-ASS and META and do not affect the rest of the grammar.

[12] The meanings of the verbs are as follows: (a) 'to cross', (b) 'to shout', (c) 'to work', (d) 'to cook', (e) 'to go', (f) 'to plant', (g) 'to dance'.

Before examining what happens to nasals, let us consider what happens to yod in the prefixes in columns II and III. When these are compared with table 2, the yod is seen to occur in the expected place and form. Take column III: /y+hahk+u/, /y+weh+u/, /y+sohs+u/, etc. become, as expected, [hyahku], [wyehu], [šohsu], etc. /y+yohs+u/ becomes [yohsu] (line c). We will not discuss here whether the fusion of the two successive yods into one should be considered a particular case of PAL (which would consequently have to be reformulated) or whether we should attribute this to the rule that reduces certain groups of identical consonants (see p. 89, n. 3). It is sufficient to know that rewriting *yy* as *y* is a perfectly general phenomenon. Thus, along with the forms in table 1, column IV, /poy+yah+u/ 'they ran' yields [poyahu] and not *[poyyahu], /həy+yah+u/ 'they cried' yields [həyahu] and not *[həyyahu], etc.

Let us now consider columns I and II. In table 2, the corresponding forms had an initial nasal consonant. Here the initial consonant is nasalized if it is *h, w* or *y*. The symbols $\tilde{h}$, $\tilde{w}$ and $\tilde{y}$ that appear in the upper half of table 3 stand for nasal glides. These sounds are pronounced as *h, w* and *y* but with a lowered velum. Although Wonderly (1951; 1952) does not discuss this point, one can be fairly sure that the lowering of the velum does not stop immediately at the end of the nasal glide, but is retained during the utterance of the following vowel (and during that of the intervening yod, in the forms of column II). But this is a phonetic adjustment that should not be included in the phonetic representations, since it is universal. Ladefoged (1971: 33) noted that there are no languages in which the position of the velum is independently controlled for a vowel and a glide belonging to the same syllable.

When the initial consonant of the root is neither an obstruent nor an *h, w* or *y*, any trace of the prefix nasal disappears. In the lower half of table 3 the forms of column I are identical to those of column IV and those of column II identical to those of column III. In column II the only evidence of the presence of the prefix /ny-/ is the trace left by its yod.

In order to account for the nasalization of *h, w* and *y*, we will propose the rule NAS (for nasalization):

$$\text{NAS:} \quad \begin{bmatrix} -\text{syll} \\ -\text{cons} \\ +\text{cont} \end{bmatrix} \rightarrow [+\text{nas}] \quad / \quad \# \, [+\text{nas}] + \underline{\qquad}$$

This rule rewrites as a nasal any non-syllabic, non-consonantal, continuant morpheme-initial segment that is preceded by a word-initial nasal. The expression [− syll, − cons, + cont] as represented on the left of the arrow only refers, in Zoque, to the segments *h*, *w* and *y* since in this language there are four non-syllabic and non-consonantal segments, i.e. *h*, *w*, *y* and *ʔ*; the *ʔ* is a non-continuant. The NAS rule accounts for the forms in the upper half of table 3. It rewrites, for examples, /#n + weh + u#/ as #n + w̃eh + u# whence finally [w̃ehu], after the deletion of the initial nasal by N-DEL, a rule which we will discuss below. The reasons that compel us to order NAS after META are of the same kind as those that obliged us to order N-ASS and VOICE after META (see p. 95): if META has not yet operated when NAS is applicable, NAS will be given inputs such as #ny + weh + u# (table 3, ii(b)) in which the word-initial nasal and the morpheme-initial glide to be nasalized are separated by a yod that has not yet been displaced by META. But as we formulated it, NAS only nasalizes morpheme-initial glides that are in direct contact with word-initial nasals. We would therefore have to give it a more complicated formulation that allows for the possibility of an intervening yod; however, such a reformulation is unnecessary if META is applied first.

Finally, we still have to formulate an N-DEL rule that deletes a word-initial nasal consonant in front of any consonant that is not a non-continuant obstruent. We will thus obtain the following derivations:

/#ny + puht + u#/ /#ny + weh + u#/ /#ny + maŋ + u#/

META	#n + pyuht + u#	#n + wyeh + u#	#n + myáŋ + u#
NAS		#n + w̃yeh + u#	
N-DEL		#w̃yeh + u#	#myaŋ + u#
N-ASS	#m + pyuht + u#		
VOICE	#m + byuht + u#		

[mbyuhtu]   [w̃yehu]   [myaŋu]

The formulation of N-DEL poses a slight problem. The set of consonants liable to appear as morpheme-initials at the point where N-DEL is applicable can be divided into two mutually exclusive classes A and B. A is the set { *p, t, č, ḳ, k* } and B is the set { *ʃ, s, š, m, n, ñ, r, l, w, y, h, ʔ* }. A word-initial nasal is subject to N-ASS when it is followed by a consonant of A, and it is dropped when followed by a consonant of B. We want a rule that deletes a nasal in an # —— K environment, where K is a certain combination of feature specifications which is satisfied by any consonant of B and by none of A. But A is the class of [− son, − cont] consonants, i.e. the class of consonants that are *both* [− son] and [− cont]; B is the class of Zoque consonants that are not [− son, − cont], i.e. the class of consonants that are *either* [+ son] *or* [+ cont] *or* both at the same time, as shown in (6). In

(6) the thin continuous line surrounds the class $[- \text{son}, - \text{cont}]$ (class A), the dotted line surrounds the class $[+ \text{son}, + \text{cont}]$, and the thick continuous line surrounds the class of segments that are $[+ \text{son}]$ or $[+ \text{cont}]$ (class B).

(6)

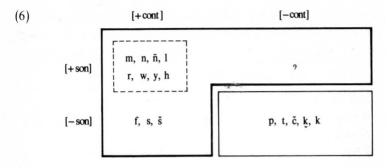

The formalism developed up till now cannot characterize directly class B since, given any two features $[T]$ or $[U]$, the expression $[+ T, + U]$ defines the class of segments that are both $[+ T]$ and $[+ U]$, and not the class of segments that are $[+ T]$ or $[+ U]$.[13] Therefore two rules must be proposed for the deletion of word-initial nasals, one operating in front of $[+ \text{son}]$ segments and the other in front of $[+ \text{cont}]$ segments.

$$\text{N-DEL}_1: \quad [+ \text{nas}] \quad \rightarrow \quad \emptyset \quad / \quad \# \underline{\quad} + [+ \text{son}]$$
$$\text{N-DEL}_2: \quad [+ \text{nas}] \quad \rightarrow \quad \emptyset \quad / \quad \# \underline{\quad} + [+ \text{cont}]$$

If we adopt the general convention that $A\begin{Bmatrix}B\\C\end{Bmatrix}D$ is an abbreviated notation for the two sequences ABD, ACD, taken in that order,[14] the two N-DEL_1 and N-DEL_2 rules can be merged into one equivalent N-DEL schema:

$$\text{N-DEL}: \quad [+ \text{nas}] \quad \rightarrow \quad \emptyset \quad / \quad \# \underline{\quad} + \begin{Bmatrix}[+ \text{son}]\\[+ \text{cont}]\end{Bmatrix}$$

The necessity for N-DEL to be applied after NAS can be ascertained by examining the derivation of $/\# \text{ny} + \text{weh} + \text{u} \#/$ given on p. 100. The reverse order would give the incorrect output *[wyehu]. Since N-DEL is

---

[13] In other words, $[+ T, + U]$ stands for the intersection of the sets $[+ T]$ and $[+ U]$ and not their union.

[14] For more details on bracket notation, see *SPE*: 61–4, 333–4.

applied after NAS and NAS is applied after META, N-DEL must be applied after META. How is N-DEL ordered in relation to PAL? Compare the forms [ỹohsu] (from / #n + yohs + u #/) and [ñihpu] (from / #y + nihp + u #/) (I(c), III(f) in table 3 above). These forms illustrate the fact that words phonologically beginning with / #n + yV/ phonetically begin with [ỹV], whereas words which phonologically begin with / #y + nV/ phonetically begin with [ñV]. Precisely this result is obtained by ordering N-DEL before PAL, as shown in the derivations below:

$$/\#n + yohs + u\#/ \quad /\#y + nihp + u\#/$$

META		#nyihp + u#
NAS	#n + ỹohs + u#	
N-DEL	#ỹohs + u#	
PAL		#ñihp + u#

$$[\text{ỹohsu}] \qquad\qquad [\text{ñihpu}]$$

These derivations merely show that N-DEL can be applied before PAL. To show that N-DEL must be applied before PAL, it must also be shown that the grammar would generate incorrect forms if these rules were applied in the reverse order. Before this question is examined more closely, it should be noted that it is derivations such as those above which show the need for the rules NAS and N-DEL to contain in their structural descriptions a morpheme boundary occurring immediately to the right of the word-initial nasal. The rules in question only concern words where the initial nasal is immediately followed by a morpheme boundary (i.e. it belongs to a prefix) and they cannot operate in derivations such as that of [ñihpu], where the initial *n* belongs to the verb root and is not followed by a morpheme boundary.[15]

Suppose, then, that we order N-DEL after PAL. The first steps in the derivation will be as before, i.e. after the application of META and NAS, the representations #n + ỹohs + u# and #nyihp + u# are obtained. If the PAL rule is then applied, it will palatalize the initial *n* of #n + ỹohs + u#[16] as well as that of #nyihp + u#, whence #ñ + ohs + u# and #ñihp + u# (which finally yields [ñihpu]). Then N-DEL operates and rewrites #ñ + ohs + u# as #ohs + u#, whence finally *[ohsu]. To prevent PAL from wrongly deleting the ỹ of #n + ỹohs + u# as well as all

---

[15] On morpheme boundaries in the application of phonological rules, cf. pp. 111ff.

[16] On the treatment of morpheme boundaries in the application of the PAL, rule, see p. 90, n. 4, p. 111, n. 24.

other similar forms, all that is necessary is to ensure that at the point in the derivation where PAL is applicable, the preceding nasal has already disappeared under the effect of N-DEL, i.e. N-DEL has been applied before PAL.

Since N-DEL must precede PAL and PAL must precede N-ASS (p. 95) N-DEL must precede N-ASS. We drew attention on page 98 to the fact that N-ASS only operates in front of segments which are both non-continuant and non-sonorant, but that nothing in the formulation given on that page indicates this limitation. We now see that this limitation does not need to be explicitly included in the structural description of N-ASS, since it automatically follows from the presence of N-DEL in the grammar. Indeed, once N-DEL has operated, the only initial nasals followed by a consonant that still remain and that are therefore liable to be further affected by N-ASS are those that have not been deleted, i.e. those that are followed by a non-continuant obstruent.

The list in (5) above can now be completed as in (7).

(7)

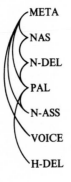

META
NAS
N-DEL
PAL
N-ASS
VOICE
H-DEL

TABLE 4

		I	II	III	IV
		1st pers. progressive /n-/	2nd pers. progressive /ny-/	3rd pers. progressive /y-/	3rd pers. perfective Ø
(a)	/kihp/	ŋgihpu	ŋgihpu	kihpu	kihpu
(b)	/min/	minu	minu	minu	minu
(c)	/ʔiht/	ʔihtu	ʔihtu	ʔihtu	ʔihtu

Consider the forms in table 4.[17] They are analogous to those in tables 2 and 3 above. These forms show that in verbal roots whose first vowel is *i*, there is no trace of the yod of the prefixes. The forms in column III are identical to those of column IV, and those of column II identical to those of column I.[18] This disappearance of a yod when the vowel of the following syllable is *i* is a perfectly general phenomenon in Zoque. Consider also the forms of table 5, where each line has three forms for the same noun, according to whether it is followed by no suffix, a locative suffix /kəsi/ or an instrumental suffix /pit/. The sequence of rules (7) derives *[kyihpu] and *[kupyit] from the phonological representations /y + kihp + u/ (table 4, III(a)) and /kuy + pit/ (table 5, III(b)), whereas the correct outputs are

TABLE 5

		I	II	III
(a)	'stone'	ca?	ca?kəsi	ca?pit
(b)	'tree'	kuy	kukyəsi	kupit
(c)	'leaf'	?ay	?akyəsi	?apit
(d)	'village'	kumguy	kumgukyəsi	kumgupit

[kihpu] and [kupit]. In order to generate these outputs, the superfluous yod has to be eliminated. The formulation of the rule for the deletion of yod depends on its order of application in relation to META. If the deletion of yod is carried out once META has applied and has placed it behind the consonant, where it is in direct contact with the *i*, this rule must be written as Y-DEL. Y-DEL deletes any yod followed by an *i* and preceded by a consonant:[19]

Y-DEL: $y \rightarrow \emptyset \quad / \quad C \text{——} i$

If, on the other hand, the deletion rule is applied at a point in the derivation where META has not yet displaced the *y*, the rule has to be formulated as Y-DEL'. Y-DEL' deletes a yod preceding a consonant that is itself followed by an *i*:

Y-DEL': $y \rightarrow \emptyset \quad / \quad \text{——} C i$

---

[17] (a) 'to fight', (b) 'to come', (c) 'to live'.

[18] In lines (b) and (c), the disappearance of the nasal consonant of the prefix is due to the operation of N-DEL

[19] The left environment of Y-DEL must contain a consonant, for a yod followed by an *i* does not disappear when preceded by a vowel, see, for example, the last syllable of a form like [ha?nhyuyi] 'he does not buy it', which derives from /#ha?n#y + huy + i#/.

Once again we have the choice between two competing grammars that are equally able to generate all the phonetic representations examined up to now: one contains the META and Y-DEL rules, applicable in that order; the other contains the Y-DEL′ and META rules applicable in that order. Here is the derivation of /kuy + pit/ in each grammar:

	/kuy + pit/		/kuy + pit/
META	ku + pyit	Y-DEL′	ku + pit
Y-DEL	ku + pit	META	
	[kupit]		[kupit]

Other data have to be examined in order to decide between the two competing solutions. The forms in table 4 are only representative of cases where the initial consonant of the stem is a non-coronal. Table 6 illustrates the case of initial coronals.[20]

TABLE 6

		I	II	III	IV
		/n-/	/ny-/	/y-/	Ø
(a)	/tih/	ndihu	ñǧihu	ḳihu	tihu
(b)	/siŋ/	siŋu	šiŋu	šiŋu	siŋu

The underlying yod quite normally manifests its presence in columns II and III as a palatalization of the coronal consonant. Compare, for example, the forms of *tih* with those of *tuh* given above in table 2, line (c), and the forms of *siŋ* with those of *sohs* given above in table 3, line (d). Thus, when the root begins with a coronal followed by an *i*, META and PAL operate normally, without the rule for yod deletion intervening in any way. The most direct way of accounting for this is to order the rule for yod deletion after META and PAL. Y-DEL as formulated above is perfectly adequate. This produces derivations such as those presented below, where Y-DEL deletes the yods of all the *Cyi* sequences that remain after PAL has operated.

	/y + tih + u/	/y + kihp + u/
META	tyih + u	kyihp + u
PAL	ḳih + u	
Y-DEL		kihp + u
	[ḳihu]	[kihpu]

[20] (a) 'to arrive', (b) 'to swell'. One can add to the forms in table 6 those given above in table 2, line (d), and table 3, line (f).

On the other hand, if the grammar containing Y-DEL′ and META, applicable in that order, is chosen, it is impossible to order Y-DEL′ after PAL since by hypothesis Y-DEL′ precedes META, and we have shown that META must precede PAL. Thus, the grammar would yield the following derivations:

	/y + tih + u/	/y + kihp + u/
Y-DEL′	tih + u	kihp + u
META		
PAL		
	*[tihu]	[kihpu]

In order to avoid derivations such as the one on the left, Y-DEL′ must be replaced by the less general rule Y-DEL″ that deletes any yod followed by a consonant that is itself followed by an *i*, unless this consonant is a coronal:

$$\text{Y-DEL″:} \quad y \;\rightarrow\; \varnothing \quad \bigg/ \text{———} \begin{bmatrix} C \\ -\text{cor} \end{bmatrix} i$$

This yields the desired result:

	/y + tih + u/	/y + kihp + u/
Y-DEL″		kihp + u
META	tyih + u	
PAL	ḳih + u	
	[ḳihu]	[kihpu]

The rule Y-DEL reflects in a natural way a tendency that can be noticed in the most diverse languages, the avoidance after consonants of sequences containing a semi-vowel followed by the corresponding high vowel: *Cyi*, *Cwu*, *Cẅü*. The deletion takes place whatever the preceding consonant. This fact is not clearly shown in a grammar where the deletion rule is formulated so that it will operate before META, i.e. at a point in the derivation where the *y* to be deleted and the *i* under the influence of which it is deleted do not belong to the same syllable. A grammar that contains Y-DEL′ treats as a coincidence the fact that the *y*s deleted by this rule are precisely those that the application of META would otherwise induce to form *Cyi* sequences. Once Y-DEL′ has been reformulated as the less general rule Y-DEL″, the coincidences become even more suspicious: there is only one case where Y-DEL″ does not delete a yod followed by a *Ci* sequence, thus enabling the META rule to create a *Cyi* sequence, and that is when *C* is a coronal, i.e. in the only case where there is a rule (the PAL rule) that anyway guarantees the elimination of the *Cyi* sequences thus created. We will therefore opt for the grammar that contains the Y-DEL rule ordered after PAL. The order of application of Y-DEL in relation to N-ASS, VOICE and H-DEL makes no difference.

The preceding analysis enables us to attribute to each morpheme a phonological representation on the basis of which we can derive its various phonetic manifestations. Consider, for example, the following forms of the verb *cihc* 'to tear':

(8) (a) [cihcu]   /cihc + u/   'it got torn'
    (b) [cicpa]   /cihc + pa/   'it is getting torn'
    (c) [cihčahu] /cihc + yah + u/ 'they got torn'
    (d) [cihčahpa] /cihc + yah + pa/ 'they are getting torn'

/cihc/ is the only phonological representation that enables us to derive these forms without postulating a suppletion phenomenon or adding new rules to our grammar. If we had taken / cic /, it would have been impossible to account for the presence of an [h] in front of the root's final consonant in (a), (c) and (d), since our grammar does not have any rule that inserts *h*. If we had taken / cihč /, we would not have been able to derive the final [c] of the root in (a) and (b), for whereas our grammar contains a rule allowing the derivation of *č* from *c* in certain contexts (rule PAL) it does not have any rule that allows the derivation of *c* from *č*.

By thus giving each morpheme one or several allomorphs compatible with all the phonetic data, we can make a list of phonological matrices, which constitutes the set of allomorphs contained in the lexicon. Our task does not end there. For we still have to examine this set of allomorphs to bring out the morpheme-internal constraints on feature and segment combinations and make them explicit by giving a system of morpheme structure rules that define the notion of a possible allomorph of Zoque. We will not undertake this task here. We will simply look at one example which gives an idea of the role played by lexical redundancy in the evaluation of a grammar. If a phonological representation compatible with the phonological rules given above is attributed to each morpheme of Zoque, and the list of allomorphs thus obtained is examined, it will be discovered that there are certain restrictions on groups of consonants that can appear after a vowel in morpheme-final position.[21] The groups found in the abundant data given in Wonderly (1951; 1952) are shown in table 7.[22]

TABLE 7

(a)						m	n	ŋ	y	h	ʔ	l	r
(b)	ʔp	ʔt	ʔk	ʔc	ʔs	ʔm	ʔn	ʔŋ	ʔy				
(c)	hp	ht	hk	hc	hs								

Line (a) shows that when a morpheme ends with a single consonant, this consonant is necessarily a sonorant. Lines (b) and (c) show that when a morpheme ends with two consonants the first consonant of the group can only be /ʔ/ or /h/. If it is /ʔ/, the following consonant can be either an obstruent or a sonorant, but if it is /h/, the following consonant is necessarily an obstruent. The restrictions of lines (a) and (c) are complementary. /ken/ is a possible allomorph in Zoque, but not */ket/; on the other hand, */kehn/ is not possible, whereas /keht/ is. Finally, /keʔt/ and /keʔn/ are both possible.

These restrictions necessarily entail a certain complexity in the formulation of morpheme structure rules. We would greatly simplify these if we supposed that the *h* of the groups *hp*, *ht*, etc. is not present in the phonological representations, but is introduced by the phonological rule H-INS, which inserts and *h* between a vowel and a morpheme-final obstruent.

$$\text{H-INS:} \quad \emptyset \;\rightarrow\; h \quad / \; V \text{——} [-\text{son}] +$$

We can rearrange the data in table 7 as shown in table 8, where line (c) has disappeared and completes the empty spaces of line (a).

TABLE 8

(a)	p	t	k	c	s	m	n	ŋ	y	h	ʔ	l	r
(b)	ʔp	ʔt	ʔk	ʔc	ʔs	ʔm	ʔn	ʔŋ	ʔy				

[21] With the exceptions of a few rare grammatical morphemes such as the personal prefixes *n-*, *ny-*, *y-* all the morphemes of Zoque have at least one vowel: *maŋ*, *kiʔn*, *cihc*, etc.

[22] By group of consonants, we mean any sequence with one or more non-syllabic segments. In table 7 the diagonal slashes that indicate sequences of phonemes are omitted. To be exhaustive, the groups /yh/, /ps/, /ks/ and /ʔks/, which are also possible at the end of morphemes, should be added to table 7. Their existence does not run counter to the arguments below.

This new perspective leads to a reconsideration of all the allomorphs of our lexicon ending with obstruents. Where we had previously posited such phonological representations as /kihp/, /wiht/, /puht/, /hahk/, /yohs/, /ʔehc/, etc., we must now propose the representations /kip/, /wit/, /put/, /hak/, /yos/, /ʔec/, etc. The morpheme structure rules are thus greatly simplified: any non-syllabic phoneme of Zoque, sonorant or not, can occur as a unique consonant at the end of a morpheme, or as the second term of a group of consonants of which the first is necessarily /ʔ/.[23]

We have thus been able to simplify our definition of the notion ' possible morpheme of Zoque ', but this simplification has only been gained by adding to the complexity of the phonological component, since we had to include an additional rule (H-INS). It could therefore seem that we have merely transferred the problem. But consider the following derivations of [cihcu] and [cicpa], on the assumption that we accept the changes we have introduced:

	/cic + u/	/cic + pa/
H-INS	cihc + u	cihc + pa
H-DEL		cic + pa
	[cihcu]	[cicpa]

Rather than insert an *h* in front of any morpheme-final obstruent preceded by a vowel, and be forced to delete it later on each time the following morpheme begins with a consonant (see the derivation on the right), we can just as well directly formulate H-INS so that it will operate only when the following morpheme begins with a vowel. This enables us to do without H-DEL. We thus propose to reformulate H-INS as follows:

$$\text{H-INS:}\quad \emptyset \;\rightarrow\; h \quad / \quad V \;\underline{\qquad}\; [-\text{son}] + V$$

/cic + u/ is still subject to this new version of the rule and finally yields [cihcu], whereas /cic + pa/ is no longer subject to it and yields [cicpa]. The V preceding the environment dash in H-INS indicates that the insertion of an *h* only takes place after a vowel. If we had simply specified the context as ——— [− son] + V, the rule would have affected representations such as /kuʔt + u/ ' he ate ', whence the output *[kuʔhtu] instead of [kuʔtu].

To summarize: at the beginning, we had assumed that pairs such as [wihtu] ~ [witpa], [cihcu] ~ [cicpa], etc., were to be accounted for by a

---

[23]   We just have to add a clause prohibiting the groups *\/ʔh/, *\/ʔ ʔ/, *\/ʔl/ and *\/ʔr/, but this clause is in any case necessary even if we opt for the analysis implied by table 7.

rule for the deletion of *h*. But when we took a closer look at the combinatory restrictions inside the phonological matrices that this assumption entailed we discovered that the alternations between zero and *h* can be accounted for just as well by a phonological rule inserting *h*, which enables us to give a much simpler formulation of the morpheme structure rules.

The argument we had given for ordering H-DEL after PAL (p. 91) is also valid for H-INS. The order of H-INS in relation to the other rules makes no difference, as was the case for H-DEL.

By replacing H-DEL by H-INS in the sequence of rules in (7) above, and by adding the rule Y-DEL, we obtain the fragment of a grammar given in (9)(the page numbers in parentheses refer to discussions of the rule; those in bold type to its final formulation). We give below the pages where the relative ordering between the different rules is discussed:

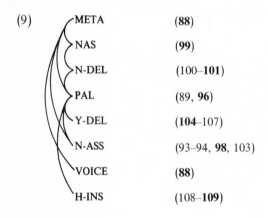

(9)   META   (**88**)

NAS   (**99**)

N-DEL   (100–**101**)

PAL   (89, **96**)

Y-DEL   (**104**–107)

N-ASS   (93–94, **98**, 103)

VOICE   (**88**)

H-INS   (108–**109**)

META–NAS, 100 ; META–PAL, 90 ; META–N-ASS, 95 ;
META–VOICE, 95.
NAS–N-DEL, 101.
N-DEL–PAL, 102–3.
PAL–Y-DEL, 107; PAL–N-ASS, 95; PAL–H-INS, 110.

To conclude our discussion on Zoque, we will examine some points of detail that raise problems of a general nature. Note first that H-INS only inserts *h* in front of obstruents that are at the end of morphemes; this is indicated by the + boundary of the $V \longrightarrow O + V$ environment. The rule affects the sequences $VO + V$, but not the sequences VOV or $V + OV$,[24] where the obstruent and the following vowel belong to the same morpheme.[25] An example of a VOV sequence: the morpheme /yatəh/ (p. 90) is pronounced [yatəh] and not *[yahtəh]. An example of a $V + OV$ sequence: /kama + kəsi/ ('corn-field', plus the locative suffix) is pronounced [kamakəsi] and not *[kamahkəsi]. This leads us to examine the particular status of + boundaries in relation to the application of phonological rules.

The preceding discussion presupposes that, when the structural description of a rule mentions a morpheme boundary, only those representations containing a morpheme boundary in the position required by this structural description are affected. H-INS inserts an *h* in front of the second *c* of *cic + u* because this representation contains the sequence *ic + u* which is of the form $VO + V$ required by the structural description, but not in front of the *t* of *yatəh* because *atə* has the form VOV and not $VO + V$. This is a direct consequence of the way in which we defined the phonological rules and their mode of application in chapter 2. We can thus account for the phonological processes that only operate when the segments involved belong to different morphemes. Such phonological processes are very common among the languages of the world.

Consider now the rule VOICE, that we repeat here:

VOICE: $[- \text{cont}]$ → $[+ \text{voice}]$ / $[+ \text{nas}]$——

If we follow strictly what was said in chapter 2 on the way in which rules are applied, VOICE only voices a stop preceded by a nasal when these two segments belong to the same morpheme. It accounts for the voicing of the stop in [ʔaŋge] 'again', since the corresponding phonological representation /ʔaŋke/ contains the sequence *ŋk*, which is of the form $[+ \text{nas}][- \text{cont}]$ as required by the structural description of the rule. On the other hand, the rule should not be able to account for the voicing of the bilabial in [kunba] 'he runs', since, in the representation /kun + pa/, the sequence *n + p* is of the form $[+ \text{nas}] + [- \text{cont}]$, and not $[+ \text{nas}][- \text{cont}]$ as the rule apparently requires.

[24] It is the fact that H-INS does not affect the sequences $V + OV$ which brings out the importance of the remark made on p. 90, n. 4. Here is the derivation of [wihk̩ahu] (see p. 91), once H-INS has replaced H-DEL: PAL rewrites /wit + yah + u/ as /wik̩ + ah + u/, which is then rewritten as /wihk̩ + ah + u/ by H-INS. If the output of PAL were /wi + k̩ah + u/, H-INS would not be able to operate, for the sequence /i + k̩a/ is not of the form $VO + V$.

[25] Wonderly's data do not contain any examples of a $V + O + V$ sequence.

If we have been able to formulate VOICE as above and still allow it to affect sequences of a nasal followed by a stop with an intervening morpheme boundary, it is because we implicitly accepted (following *SPE*: 364) that the application of phonological rules follows a certain convention that we will now make explicit:

> (10)   If the structural description of a rule requires that the inputs to this rule contain a XYZ sequence, the rule in question also affects the inputs that contain a sequence $X + Y + Z$ or $X + YZ$ or $XY + Z$ (where X, Y and Z are arbitrary sequences, possibly empty ones).

Convention (10) was adopted because it was noticed that in general, when a phonological rule can operate in a XY sequence (whose two terms belong to the same morpheme), it can also operate in the corresponding $X + Y$ sequence (whose two terms are situated on either side of a morpheme boundary). On the other hand, rules are frequently found that affect $X + Y$ sequences and not the corresponding XY sequences; this we indicate by explicitly including a $+$ boundary in their structural description.[26] By virtue of convention (10), when an XY expression occurs in the structural description of a phonological rule, this expression must be interpreted as representing the set of sequences that are either of the XY form or of the $X + Y$ form.

Suppose that we adopt convention (10), and that in addition we prohibit ourselves from using any notation that would permit reference to a set containing all the XY sequences, but none of the corresponding $X + Y$ sequences. We would thus eliminate any means of formulating phonological rules which only affect sequences not containing morpheme boundaries. This brings us to note in passing a general methodological point: when a certain formalism is adopted, it commits us to accept as true certain general statements that restrict our notion of a possible language. If we give ourselves a system of notation that is too poor to permit the formulation of a phonological rule which applies only inside morphemes, and if at the same time we claim that our linguistic theory (of which these notations are an integral part) provides the basis for an adequate description of any language, we have to admit that no language could have a phonological rule that would only operate inside morphemes; in other words, we have to

---

[26]   This is the case, for example, for H-INS.

consider as true for all languages – that is to say as a universal – statement (11):

> (11)   Any phonological rule that can operate within morphemes can also operate across morpheme boundaries.

(11) is an empirical claim that could be falsified by a single example. But, even if not a single counter-example could be produced, it might be objected that we have no right to claim that (11) is true for all languages, considering that linguists only know a ridiculously small sample of all the languages that have existed or that exist today, let alone the ones to come. To surrender to this objection would be to mistake the real import of empirical generalizations such as (11). In order to be able to consider (11) as true, it is not necessary to have examined all languages, and to have shown (11) to be true for each one. This is an impossible task, since most languages that have been spoken have left no trace and we know nothing about those that will be spoken in a thousand years. And even if we imagined that we had supernatural powers enabling us to know all the languages of the past and future, we would not be in a better position, since these would only be a finite number of languages among an infinity of possible ones. In order to have the right to claim that (11) is a true proposition, it is sufficient that (11) be compatible with all the data we have to date,[27] i.e. that up to now we know of no fact invalidating it. The same is true for all empirical generalizations, whether in linguistics or elsewhere.

There is no convention analogous to (10) concerning # boundaries. When the structural description of a rule requires the input to contain an XYZ sequence, it cannot operate on $X\#Y\#Z$, $X\#YZ$ or $XY\#Z$ sequences. One frequently encounters phonological processes that operate only within words. An instance of this is the rule for the formation of semi-vowels in French (SEM, p. 68). This rule rewrites the *i* of *dévier* 'to deviate' [devye] (/devi + e/) as yod, but not that of *joli ami* 'pretty friend' [žɔliami] (/žɔli#ami/), which is separated from the following vowel by a word boundary.

One last comment. It is the result of a negative finding that brought Chomsky and Halle to propose convention (10): they could not find in any language known to them a phonological rule only affecting sequences not

---

[27]   ...and that it not contradict the other general propositions we hold as true. On p. 176, we will find a counter-example to (11). It challenges the validity of proposition (11), but not the validity of the preceding discussion, which only bears on the status of universals in general, as well as the relation between universals and the formalism used in describing languages.

containing morpheme boundaries. In order to obtain a correct characterization of the notion of 'possible language', one must not only consider what is found in all languages, *but also what cannot be found in any of them*. There is here a similarity of approach between the theory of languages – linguistic theory – and the theory of the sentences of a particular language – the grammar of that language. In order to formulate correctly the rule of *liaison* in French, it is equally important to know that *des amis* 'friends' is pronounced [dezami], and that *des tamis* 'sieves' cannot be pronounced *[deztami] (cf. p. 25).

Continuing our discussion of H-INS, we will now turn to certain facts, not mentioned previously, that raise the question of exceptions. Consider, for example, the following pairs: [puhtu] 'he went out', [putə] 'get out', [sohsu] 'it cooked', [sosa] 'cook it!, [kihpu] 'he fought', [kipə] 'fight!'. The second form of each pair is an imperative constructed by adding to the root a suffix consisting of a single vowel the quality of which is sometimes [ə] and sometimes [a], depending on the quality of the vowel of the root. In order to identify the vocalic phoneme that underlies this vowel of varying quality, we would have to examine various phonological rules of Zoque that are not relevant to our present discussion. Let us simply agree to represent this phoneme by /X/ and to know that /X/ is [+ syll]. [putə] [sosa] and [kipə] have the phonological representations /put + X/, /sos + X/, and /kip + X/, but contrary to what H-INS would lead us to expect, the final obstruent of the root is not preceded by an *h*. H-INS in fact predicts that these forms should be pronounced *[puhtə], *[sohsa], and *[kihpə], similarly to [puhtu], [sohsu] and [kihpu].

The suffix *-i* that enables nouns to be derived from certain verbs is in the same situation as *-X*; compare [huhku] 'he smoked' and [huki] 'cigarette', [kihtu] 'it broke' and [kiti] 'piece', [nihpu] 'he planted' and [nipi] 'plantation', etc. Compared with suffixes such as *-u* (completed aspect) that let H-INS operate normally (they constitute the great majority), there are only a dozen suffixes like *-X* and *-i*. A study of the list of these suffixes does not bring out any phonological, syntactic or semantic property which is common to them all and opposes them to the others. If, for example, they all had a front vowel and the others all had a back vowel, it could be concluded that H-INS formulated as it is on page 109 is too general, and that its environment must be reformulated as

$$V\text{---}O+\begin{bmatrix} V \\ + \text{back} \end{bmatrix}.$$ But one does not find any such thing. The only property that these suffixes have in common, is precisely their exceptional behaviour in relation to H-INS. It could of course be supposed that,

although they begin with a vowel at the phonetic level, in the phonological representations these suffixes in fact begin with a consonant which prevents H-INS from operating and is deleted by a rule ordered after H-INS. But which consonant? Apart from their exceptional behaviour in relation to H-INS, these suffixes behave in all other respects like the other suffixes with an initial vowel, and a rule that would delete their assumed initial consonant would not have any general significance.

We are obliged to admit that this exceptional behaviour does not reflect any underlying regularity. All that a grammar can do in such a case, is to record the facts: the Zoque morphemes with an initial vowel are divided into two categories, those on the one hand (the vast majority) that require the insertion of an *h* between a vowel and a final obstruent in a preceding morpheme and on the other hand those in front of which nothing of the sort takes place. It would be rather too hasty simply to get rid of the H-INS rule because it has exceptions. The possibility of exceptions is one of the things that distinguishes *rules* from *laws of nature* (see Miller, 1964: 98). The first can be broken, but not the second. The existence of exceptions weakens the generality of a rule, but does not automatically take away its status as a rule. It is better to have a rule whose scope is reduced by certain exceptions than no rule at all. It would not enter anyone's mind to give up the generalization according to which French verbs take on the ending *-ez* for the second person plural, under the pretext that this generalization is contradicted by a handful of forms such as *êtes* 'you are', *faites* 'you do', *dites* 'you say', etc.[28]

We will, therefore, keep the H-INS rule, and assume that it operates each time the conditions required by its structural description are met, unless one of the segments submitted to the rule contains the specification $[-$ H-INS$]$.

In the lexicon, the suffixes *-X* and *-i* are marked with the specification $[-$ H-INS$]$, but not the suffix *-u*, as a consequence of which H-INS normally operates in front of *-u* but not of *-X* or *-i*. More generally, we associate a feature $[R]$ to each rule R of the grammar, and we indicate that a certain morpheme is an exception to a rule R by including in its lexical entry the specification $[-$ R$]$.[29] Speakers only have to memorize cases in which a morpheme is an exception to a rule, and the occurrence of a $[-$ R$]$ specification in a lexical entry adds to the memory load for this lexical entry. In fact, all other things being equal, the lexical entry of the morpheme *-i* is

---

[28] On exceptions, cf. Chomsky (1962: 244–5; 1965: 103, n. 28; 1967 *b*: 118–19, n. 17); *SPE* (ix, 146, 172–6, 374–6); Postal (1968: chap. 6).

[29] For a more precise formulation, cf. *SPE*: 374–6.

more complex than that of the morpheme -*u*, since it contains an additional idiosyncratic specification, the specification [− H-INS].

What exactly is involved in this discussion will be seen more clearly by examining the way in which the grammar would have to be formulated if we did not allow certain morphemes to be marked as exceptions in the lexicon. The H-INS rule would have to be reformulated by including in it the list of all the morphemes in front of which there is regularly an *h* insertion in the preceding morpheme, when the latter ends in a *VO* sequence:

$$
\text{H-INS}': \quad \emptyset \;\rightarrow\; h \quad \Big/ \quad \text{V} \!\!-\!\!-\!\! \text{O} + \left\{ \begin{array}{c} \text{-}u \\ \vdots \\ \vdots \\ \vdots \\ \vdots \end{array} \right\}
$$

This rule does not express the fact that all the suffixes included in the list between braces begin with a vowel. Furthermore, the longer the list between braces, the more complex the rule will be. The list gets longer as the rule permits fewer exceptions, since the only morphemes not to be included in the list are those in front of which the rule does not operate, such as -*X* and -*i*. In short, if we exclude from linguistic theory devices that formalize the notion of exception, we then have to accept that the existence of numerous exceptions reduces the complexity of our grammars instead of augmenting it.

Take the form [məcihkis] 'toy' (genitive) that derives from /məc + ik + is/, in which /məc/ is the root of the verb 'to play', /ik/ a suffix used to form nouns from verbs, and /is/ the genitive suffix. To generate this form, H-INS must operate normally in front of the final *k* of the suffix -*ik*, but not in front of the final *c* of the root. The fact that H-INS operates normally in [məhcəyu] 'he played' from /məc + əy + u/ shows that the incapacity of H-INS to operate in the first morpheme of /məc + ik + is/ should not be imputed to *məc*, but to *ik*: like -*X* and -*i*, -*ik* is one of those morphemes that prevent H-INS from operating in the preceding morpheme. But this does not prevent it from being itself normally subject to the rule, since an *h* appears in front of its final *k*.

Consider now the form [krusis] 'cross' (genitive) that derives from /krus + is/. Here the fact that H-INS has not operated in front of the *s* is not to be imputed to the suffix -*is* (see above [məcihkis]) but to the morpheme

krus itself, which is never realized as *[kruhs] whatever suffix follows it.[30]
These examples show us that there are two ways for one morpheme to be
an exception in relation to a rule; in cases such as *krus*, it is the segments
contained in the morpheme itself that cannot be affected by the rule; in cases
such as the morpheme *-ik*, the segments contained in the morpheme cannot
serve as environments for the operation of the rule in an adjacent morpheme. Kisseberth (1970*a*) distinguished these two types of exceptions
and proposed to indicate them in the lexical entries with the help of different
idiosyncratic features: morphemes that are exceptions of the *krus* type,
would be marked [− rule R], and those of the *-X*, *-i*, *-ik* type would be
marked [− environment R]. With these notations, the lexical entry of *krus*
will contain the specification [− rule H-INS] and those of *-X*, *-i*, and *-ik*
will contain the specification [− environment H-INS].

The pronunciation of Zoque has sounds that we described from the outset
as [c], [z̴], [č] and [j]. But if we keep strictly to phonetic facts, Wonderly's
(1951) information on the pronunciation of these sounds is too sparse for us
to find out whether they are indeed simple affricates rather than sequences of
a stop followed by a fricative: [t] + [s], [d] + [z], [t] + [š] and [d] + [ž],
respectively. Note first of all that the question would not arise if we had a
system of distinctive features that left no room for affricates, i.e. that would
exclude the possibility of combining into a single segment a complete
closure of the mouth cavity and a narrowing which produces a noise of
friction. Within the framework of such a system, a complete obstruction of
the *t* type immediately followed by a friction of the *s* type, would always
have to be interpreted as belonging to two successive segments, i.e. to be
transcribed [ts]. But such a system is too weak, for we know of certain
languages that systematically make distinctions that are very naturally
accounted for by opposing affricates on the one hand, and sequences of a
stop followed by a fricative on the other.[31]

Nonetheless, why did we decide in favour of the affricates in the case of
Zoque, and how would we reformulate our grammar, if further phonetic
research ultimately revealed that the forms we noted, [cihcu],
[cihčahu], etc., are in fact pronounced [tsihtsu], [tsihtšahu], etc.? For, if
we had taken the latter phonetic representations as a starting point, we
could have been tempted to posit the phonological representations

---

[30] This word clearly comes from the Spanish *cruz* 'cross'. Borrowed words are often
exceptions to various phonological rules.

[31] See for example the description given by Bright (1957: 7) of the contrast between [č] and
[tš] in Karok.

/tsits + u/, /tsits + yah + u/ (instead of /cic + u/, /cic + yah + u/), which would have enabled us to do without the phoneme /c/. But by replacing /c/ by /ts/ in table 8, p. 108, we would upset the table's symmetry: /ts/ is a sequence of consonants of which the first is not /ʔ/, and the /ʔts/ group (that would now replace /ʔc/) contains three phonemes. Thus the /ts/ and /ʔts/ groups should be placed together with the /ks/ and /ʔks/ groups (p. 108 n. 22). Hence these groups /ts/ and /ʔts/ join the ranks of a minority of morpheme-final groups which are not of the (ʔ)C form and this weakens the import of the (ʔ)C formula as a general characterization of possible groups of consonants at the end of morphemes. We would fall into exactly the same kind of difficulties concerning restrictions on consonant clusters occuring at the beginning of morphemes or between two vowels belonging to the same morpheme. In short, the reinterpretation of /c/ as /ts/ compels us to adopt a more complex definition of the notion of 'possible allomorph of Zoque'.

It also compels us to complicate the formulation of various phonological rules. We will only give one example, that of H-INS: in order to derive [tsihtsu] from /tsits + u/ and [tsitšahu] from /tsits + yah + u/ (which yields /tsitš + ah + u/ after application of PAL), H-INS would have to be reformulated so as to insert an *h* not only in the environment $V\text{---}O + V$, but also in the environments $V\text{---}ts + V$ and $V\text{---}tš + V$, these being the only two cases where the insertion of an *h* must be allowed in front of two consonants. Note in particular that we cannot simply reformulate the environment of H-INS as $V\text{---}O(O) + V$,[32] since there would then be an *h* insertion in /poks + u/ 'he sat' and in /kips + u/ 'he thought', whence *[pohksu] and *[kihpsu] instead of the correct forms [poksu] and [kipsu]. The rule would therefore have to stipulate explicitly that the insertion of *h* takes place in front of a group of two obstruents only if the first is coronal.

The preceding discussion shows that both the morpheme structure rules and the phonological rules require the affricates of Zoque to be treated as single consonants[33] rather than as groups of two consonants, and be considered as such until a very late stage in the derivations (since H-INS is

---

[32] I.e reformulate H·INS as $\emptyset \to h/V\text{---}O(O) + V$. By convention, the expression A(B)C is an abbreviated notation of the two sequences *ABC* and *AC*, in that order. The above reformulation is thus an abbreviated notation for the two following rules:
$\emptyset \to h/V\text{---}OO + V$
$\emptyset \to h/V\text{---}O + V$
See below, p. 192.

[33] Of course we are not talking of genuine *ts* groups which could result from the juxtaposition of a morpheme ending in a *t* in front of one beginning with an /s/, in sequences like /pat + sep/. Wonderly unfortunately gives us no information about such groups.

one of the last rules in the phonological component).[34] Even if tomorrow a more precise description of Zoque, based on a more elaborate phonetic theory, tells us that what we had taken to be single affricates should in fact be interpreted phonetically as clusters of a stop followed by a fricative, this would only be of consequence at the level of the phonetic representations. In other words, it would only be important at the last stage of the derivations, and would in no way lessen the strength of the arguments given above, concerning the previous stages of the derivations. In short, it is here a question of superficial phonetic facts, with no great structural significance, which will then be accounted for by simply adding a rule at the end of the phonological component to indicate that the affricates must be rewritten as the corresponding stop plus fricative sequences: $c \rightarrow ts$, $\dot{z} \rightarrow dz$, $\check{c} \rightarrow t\check{s}$, $\check{j} \rightarrow d\check{z}$.

The preceding discussion throws light on the role played in certain cases by phonological considerations in the choice of a system of distinctive features. Even in the absence of a very detailed phonetic description of the consonantal articulations of Zoque, the facts that we have set out show that the system of distinctive features must include affricates. For we have shown that a single underlying segment must correspond in the phonological representations to complex articulations like that noted by the second c of [cihcu]. However the segments composing the phonological representations are not entities without phonetic content. They are feature specification columns which are allowed by linguistic theory. By defining the set of possible columns of specifications, linguistic theory also contributes to the definition of the universal stock from which each language draws the list of its phonemes.

By availing ourselves of a linguistic theory that allows for the possibility of combining in one segment a complete stoppage of the mouth cavity and a narrowing which produces a noise of friction we can write much simpler grammars for Zoque and for a great number of other languages spoken all over the world. It is interesting to note that to the best of our knowledge no phonetician has ever proposed to interpret an articulatory sequence such as [ft] as one sound, and also, as far as we know, there are no languages where what is phonetically realized as [ft] behaves throughout the derivations as a single consonant.

---

[34] The problem of 'one or two phonemes?' has been much discussed by the structuralists. See, among others, Troubetzkoy (1939: 57–68), Martinet (1949: 1965a: chap. 4), Harris (1951: chaps. 7–9), Ebeling (1960: chap. 2), and the references in these books.

THE VOWELS OF YAWELMANI

Our second example is borrowed from the Yawelmani dialect of Yokuts, an American Indian language of California. Newman's (1944) grammar of Yawelmani served as a basis for the phonological discussions on this language, in the generative perspective, of Kuroda (1967) and Kisseberth (1969*a, b*; 1970*b, c*). In what follows, we are merely borrowing from a very careful discussion by Kisseberth (1969*a, b*), though points too technical for the present book have been omitted. It is to be hoped that this adaptation has not detracted from the rigour of the original.

Both at the phonological and at the phonetic level, Yawelmani distinguishes between long and short vowels. In our transcription, the vowels followed by a colon are long ([+ long]) and the others are short ([− long]). Leaving aside differences in length, the phonetic representations of Yawelmani contain only five vowels: the high vowels *i* and *u* and the low ɛ, *a* and ɔ. They are no non-high and non-low vowels such as *e* and *o*. Since the low vowels are non-high by definition, the set of non-high vowels and the set of low vowels coincide in Yawelmani. In transcription the letters followed by an apostrophe stand for glottalized consonants, and those with a dot underneath, alveolar dentals. *x* is a voiceless velar fricative similar to that in the German word *Nacht* [naxt] 'night'. In what follows, we will limit ourselves to verb forms, but it should be understood that the rules we will present also apply to the other forms of the language. The forms we cite here do not represent isolated cases but are part of large sets of forms that show identical alternations.

The verbs of Yawelmani are composed of a root followed by one or several suffixes. These suffixes present alternations in vowel quality that depend on the nature of the last vowel of the root, as shown in the examples in table 9.[35]

TABLE 9

	I future passive	II passive aorist	III precative gerundial	IV dubitative
(a)	xilnit	xilit	xilʔas	xilal
(b)	hudnut	hudut	hudʔas	hudal
(c)	gɔpnit	gɔpit	gɔpʔɔs	gɔpɔl
(d)	maxnit	maxit	maxʔas	maxal

[35] (a) 'to tangle', (b) 'to recognize', (c) 'to take care of an infant', (d) 'to procure'.

The roots show no variation throughout table 9 and we will posit the phonological representations /xil/, /hud/, /gɔp/ and /max/. The suffixes -*nit* and -*it* always have the vowel [i], except when the vowel of the root is *u* (line b), in which case they have the vowel [u]; the suffixes -*ʔas* and -*al* always have the vowel [a] except when the vowel of the radical is ɔ, in which case they have the vowel [ɔ] (line c). The vowel quality alternations to which the suffixes are subject involve the features [back] and [round], but not the features [high] and [low]. If we give these suffixes the phonological representations /nit/, /it/, /ʔas/ and /al/ respectively, i.e. if we suppose that the suffixes with high vowels have an underlying vowel /i/ and those with a low vowel have an underlying vowel /a/, we can account for the facts summarized in table 9 by positing the following two rules:

(12)   i   →   u   / u C$_0$ ——

(13)   a   →   ɔ   / ɔ C$_0$ ——

i is rewritten as *u* when the vowel of the preceding syllable is *u*, and *a* is rewritten as ɔ when the vowel of the preceding syllable is ɔ. C$_0$ means any sequence of zero consonants or more. More generally, we adopt the following convention:[36] for any X, the symbol X_n represents the set of sequences formed by repeating X at least n times. For example, X_3 is the set { XXX, XXXX, XXXXX ... }. Thus (12) is an abbreviation for the infinite set of rules given in (14):

(14)   i   →   u   / u ——

        i   →   u   / u C ——

        i   →   u   / u CC ——

        i   →   u   / u CCC ——

Why such a notation is useful is easy to understand. Suppose that instead of writing rule (12) we had written the rule (12′):

(12′)   i   →   u   / u C ——

Rule (12′) operates in /hud + it/ (IIb), in which *u* and *i* are separated by a single consonant, but not in /hut + nit/ (Ib), in which *u* and *i* are separated by two consonants. A grammar containing only rule (12′) would indicate that the vowel of a suffix is only harmonized when this vowel and the preceding vowel are separated by a single consonant. But in Yawelmani, harmonization takes place whatever the number of intervening consonants.

---

[36] Cf. *SPE:* 343–4.

It is frequently necessary to write rules affecting an *X* segment when this segment is in the neighbourhood of a *Y* segment but where *X* and *Y* do not necessarily touch and can be separated by an indefinite number of segments of type *Z* (usually consonants).[37]

Let us come back to rules (12) and (13), which are in fact convenient abbreviations of (15) and (16):

$$(15) \quad \begin{bmatrix} + \text{syll} \\ + \text{high} \end{bmatrix} \rightarrow \begin{bmatrix} + \text{round} \\ + \text{back} \end{bmatrix} \Bigg/ \begin{bmatrix} + \text{syll} \\ + \text{round} \\ + \text{high} \end{bmatrix} C_0 \underline{\quad\quad}$$

$$(16) \quad \begin{bmatrix} + \text{syll} \\ - \text{high} \end{bmatrix} \rightarrow \begin{bmatrix} + \text{round} \\ + \text{back} \end{bmatrix} \Bigg/ \begin{bmatrix} + \text{syll} \\ + \text{round} \\ - \text{high} \end{bmatrix} C_0 \underline{\quad\quad}$$

Owing to the notation by variables introduced on page 94, we can conflate rules (15) and (16) into a single schema:

$$\text{HARM:} \quad \begin{bmatrix} + \text{syll} \\ \alpha \text{ high} \end{bmatrix} \rightarrow \begin{bmatrix} + \text{round} \\ + \text{back} \end{bmatrix} \Bigg/ \begin{bmatrix} + \text{syll} \\ + \text{round} \\ \alpha \text{ high} \end{bmatrix} C_0 \underline{\quad\quad}$$

HARM indicates that a vowel is rewritten as rounded and back when the vowel of the preceding syllable is itself rounded and has the same height (α high). The variable notation enables us to express in a natural way the fact that vowel harmony only takes place between vowels that have the same specification for the feature [high].

Let us now go on to the verbal roots with long vowels. The facts are summarized in table 10,[38] which presents forms analogous to those in

TABLE 10

	I	II	III	IV
	future passive	passive aorist	precative gerundial	dubitative
(a)	mɛk'nit	mɛːk'it	mɛk'ʔas	mɛːk'al
(b)	ṣognut	ṣɔːgut	ṣogʔas	ṣɔːgal
(c)	dɔsnit	dɔːsit	dɔsʔɔs	dɔːsɔl
(d)	tannit	taːnit	tanʔas	taːnal

[37] The rule for vowel harmony in Kongo (p. 69) can be formulated by using this notation.
[38] (a) 'to swallow', (b) 'to unwrap', (c) 'to report' (d) 'to go'.

table 9. The root of the verb has a long vowel when the suffix begins with a vowel (columns II and IV), and a short vowel when the suffix begins with a consonant (columns I and III). In fact, in Yawelmani a vowel is always short when it is followed by two consonants (or by one consonant at the end of words, cf. p. 132). A contrast between long and short vowels at the phonetic level occurs only when what follows is a *CV* sequence. We will write the following rule, that shortens any vowel followed by two consonants:

BREV: V → [− long]   / —— C C

The root of the verb in (d) has the phonological representation /taːn/, where the colon following the *a* indicates that in the corresponding phonological matrix, this vowel is specified as [+ long]. BREV operates on /taːn + nit/ (Id), whence the output [tannit], but not on /taːn + it/ (IId), whence the output [taːnit], where the underlying length is preserved.

It may be wondered why we choose to interpret length alternations in table 10 as reflecting the existence of BREV, which shortens any vowel followed by two consonants, rather than positing the reverse rule, which would lengthen any vowel followed by a *CV* sequence:

(17)   V → [+ long]   / ——CV

In this case the verb in (d) would have the phonological representation /tan/, with a short underlying vowel. Rule (17) would operate in /tan + it/ whence [taːnit], but not in /tan + nit/, whence [tannit]. But in this case we would have to consider all the verbs of table 9 as exceptions to rule (17). Consider, for example, line (d) in table 9. The forms (IId) and (IVd) are pronounced [maxit] and [maxal], not *[maːxit] and *[maːxal] as rule (17) would lead us to expect. Since the morphemes that always have a short vowel (table 9) are at least as numerous as those possessing a vowel that is sometimes long and sometimes short (table 10), the forms marked as exceptions to (17) would be at least equal in number to regular forms, which would much reduce the generality of (17). This problem does not arise if we adopt BREV.

For the time being, we will therefore posit the following phonological representations: table 9, (a) /xil/, (b) /hud/, (c) /gɔp/, (d) /max/; table 10, (a) /mɛːk'/, (b) /ṣɔːg/, (c) /dɔːs/, (d) /taːn/. Tables 9 and 10 summarize all the relevant data concerning verbs with roots that have a *CVC* structure; i.e. by giving all Yawelmani verbs with a *CVC* structure phonological representations like those above, and by systematically examining the list of allomorphs thus obtained, we find that the only underlying short vowels that appear in this list are /i/, /u/, /ɔ/, /a/ and the only long ones, /ɛ:/, /ɔ:/ and /a:/. It is never necessary to postulate underlying short /ɛ/ vowels since all the short [ɛ] vowels that appear at the phonetic level alternate with the corresponding long ones under conditions defined by BREV, and must therefore be considered as arising from /ɛ:/. Furthermore, there are no forms that require an underlying /i:/ or /u:/. The [i:] and [u:] vowels do indeed appear at the phonetic level in Yawelmani, but only in a very marginal way and through the operation of rules that have nothing to do with our present discussion (cf. Kuroda, 1967: 12, n. 3). We are, therefore, prompted to postulate the underlying vowel system represented in (18).

(18)

		– round		+ round
		– back	+ back	
+ high	– long	i		u
– high			a	ɔ
	+ long	ɛ:	a:	ɔ:

This lay-out suggests that the system of long vowels is obtained from that of short vowels by an operation which would, as it were, consist of flattening the latter by abolishing all the height distinctions. Long vowels are the [+ low] equivalents of short vowels: /ɛ:/ corresponds to /i/, /a:/ corresponds to /a/; and the same low vowel /ɔ:/ corresponds to the two vowels /u/ and /ɔ/, which are contrasted only in their specifications of the features [high] and [low]. Compared with the vowel system of other languages, the system represented by (18) is slightly peculiar, for in general vowel systems that distinguish between long and short tend to possess a certain symmetry; in most cases the long and short series contrast with each other term for term. But let us first examine the facts on vowel harmony in table 10.

The forms of lines (a), (c) and (d) confirm our formulation of HARM. In lines (a) and (d), the vowel of the suffix is never rounded since the vowel of the root (ε: and a:) is unrounded; in line (c) the vowel of the suffix is rounded when it is *a*, which is non-high like the ɔ*:* of the root, but not when it is *i*, which is high (cf. table 9 (c)). On the other hand, line (b) poses a problem: if the underlying root vowel were /ɔ:/ as we have supposed, we would expect to have forms exactly parallel to those of (c). The underlying forms /ṣɔ:g + nit/, /ṣɔ:g + it/, /ṣɔ:g + ʔas/ and /ṣɔ:g + al/ should yield the pronunciations *[ṣɔgnit], *[ṣɔ:git], *[ṣɔgʔɔs] and *[ṣɔ:gɔl]. But what in fact happens is the exact reverse of what HARM predicts: the low vowels of the suffixes -*ʔas* and -*al* remain unrounded when in fact they are subject to the rule, and the high vowels of the suffixes -*nit* and -*it* are pronounced rounded, when in fact the rule should not affect them.

If we now wish to maintain the hypothesis that the underlying vowel of the verbs in line (b) is /ɔ:/, as it is for those in line (c), the grammar must allow for two classes of verbs that have /ɔ:/ as a root vowel: regular verbs on the one hand (c), and irregular verbs on the other (b). But the fact that a form is irregular is no excuse not to account for it in exact terms as we do for regular forms. A grammar must generate all well-formed phonetic representations, whether or not they are regular. How are we going to account for the irregular verbs in line (b)?

Their lexical entry must indicate that though it is non-high and rounded as required by (16) above, the vowel of these verbs does not cause the following non-high vowel to be rounded, i.e. a specification [− environment (16)] has to be included in the lexical entry of each of these verbs. This accounts for the forms (iiib) and (ivb), where HARM (part (16)) does not operate although the conditions of its structural description are met. (ib) and (iib) still have to be accounted for; they suggest that part (15) of HARM has been formulated in too restrictive a way. This rule only predicts the rounding of a high vowel in cases where the vowel of the preceding syllable is itself high (and rounded). But forms (ib) and (iib) show that rounding can also take place in certain cases where the vowel of the preceding syllable is non-high. This is so each time this vowel belongs to an irregular ɔ*:* verb (marked [− environment (16)]). One must, therefore, reformulate rule (15) so that it will state the following: a high vowel is rewritten as rounded and back when the preceding syllable contains a rounded vowel that is either high or [− environment (16)]. We will not write out this rule formally, but it is obvious that this reformulation of (15) destroys the similarity that existed between (15) and (16), a similarity which was due, among other things, to the fact that harmonization took place only between vowels of the same height. Let us note in passing that only long vowels are liable to have the specification [− environment (16)]. In table 9, there are no /ɔ/ verbs that behave in the same way as the irregular /ɔ:/ verbs of (10b). In the light of the present analysis, this fact is considered as purely accidental.

In Yawelmani, the form of the root does not depend just on the phonological properties of suffixes. Each suffix is characterized not only by its phonological representation, but also by the fact that it calls for a certain 'grade' of the root. Each root is liable to take on a certain number of different forms or 'grades' depending on the category to which the following suffix belongs. For example, the suffixes *-it, -nit, -ʔas* and *-al* of tables 9 and 10 all call for the same grade of the root, called its 'reduced grade'. Other suffixes call for a different form called 'zero grade'. The phonetic representations of the reduced form and zero form for each of the verbs of tables 9 and 10 are given in table 11. In column A' the colons in parentheses are a reminder that the vowels concerned are sometimes short and sometimes long, according to the number of consonants that follow them (BREV). The zero forms always have a short vowel. For the verbs on

TABLE 11

	A reduced grade	B zero grade	A' reduced grade	B' zero grade
(a)	xil-	xil-	mɛ(:)k'-	mik'-
(b)	hud-	hud-	ṣɔ(:)g-	ṣug-
(c)	gɔp-	gɔp-	dɔ(:)s-	dɔs-
(d)	max-	max-	ta(:)n-	tan-

the left of table 11, i.e. those of table 9, the zero form and the reduced form are identical. For those on the right (verbs from table 10), the vowel of the reduced form and of the zero form have the same specifications for the features [round] and [back]. There is a systematic relationship between the reduced form and the zero form, and it is necessary to postulate a rule enabling the one to be predicted from the other.

If we try to deduce the reduced form from the zero form the forms in lines (c) and (d) pose serious difficulties. The zero forms in line (d), for example, both have a short *a*, and nothing allows us to decide in which cases the vowel of the corresponding reduced forms must be short ([max-] ~ [max-]) and in which cases it must be long ([tan-] ~ [taːn-]). On the other hand, look at what happens when we try to deduce the zero form from the reduced form. The rule which predicts one on the basis of the other seems to be basically a shortening rule: one obtains the zero form by replacing the vowel of the reduced form by the corresponding short vowel (which is the same in the case of the left side of table 11). We will therefore write the following rule, in which Z is an arbitrarily chosen symbol indicating that the following suffix belongs to the class of suffixes that call for a zero form:

$$\text{ZERO:} \quad V \rightarrow [-\text{long}] \quad / \quad \underline{\quad\quad} C_0 + Z$$

In the case of certain long vowels the passage to a zero form is further accompanied by an adjustment of the feature [high]. The short analogue of ε: is the high vowel i, and the short analogue of certain $\mathfrak{o}$:s is the high vowel u (line b). This time the problem is to distinguish between the $\mathfrak{o}$:s on line (b), which are subject to this adjustment, and those on line (c), which remain [+ low] in the zero form. The $\mathfrak{o}$: vowels subject to this adjustment in height are precisely those we had to mark as [− environment (16)].

All the difficulties we have met so far have the same origin: our hypothesis that the $\mathfrak{o}$:s of the verbs in line (b) and those of the verbs in line (c) in table 10 derive from the same phoneme $/\mathfrak{o}$:/. These difficulties disappear if we make the following hypothesis, in accordance with Kuroda and Kisseberth: the vowel system of Yawelmani is $/i, u, a, \mathfrak{o}, i:, u:, a:, \mathfrak{o}:/$, in which the long and the short series correspond term for term, and there is a phonological rule by which any long vowel is necessarily rewritten as low. The operation of that rule has the effect of realizing the phonemes $/i:/$ and $/u:/$ as $[\varepsilon:]$ and $[\mathfrak{o}:]$:

$$\text{LOW:} \quad \begin{bmatrix} +\text{syll} \\ +\text{long} \end{bmatrix} \rightarrow \begin{bmatrix} -\text{high} \\ +\text{low} \end{bmatrix}$$

The verbs in table 9 and those in table 10, (c) and (d), have as before (cf. p. 123) the phonological representations $/\text{xil}/$, $/\text{hud}/$, $/\text{gop}/$, $/\text{max}/$, $/\text{do:s}/$ and $/\text{ta:n}/$. On the other hand, those in table 10, (a) and (b), have the phonological representations $/\text{mi:k'}/$ and $/\text{ṣu:g}/$. The forms (IIIa), (IIIb) and (IIId) in table 10 have, for example, the following derivations:

	$/\text{mi:k'}+\text{?as}/$	$/\text{ṣu:g}+\text{?as}/$	$/\text{ta:n}+\text{?as}/$
LOW	mɛ:k'+?as	ṣɔ:g+?as	
BREV	mɛk'+?as	ṣɔg+?as	tan+?as
	[mɛk'?as]	[ṣɔg?as]	[tan?as]

The LOW rule must be applied before the BREV rule. LOW only affects long vowels. But once BREV has been applied, all the vowels that remain in front of two consonants are short and LOW can no longer operate. If LOW were applied after BREV we would obtain *[mik'ʔas] and *[ṣugʔas].

The derivation of the zero forms no longer poses a problem. It is sufficient to order ZERO before LOW:

	/mi:k' + Z/	/ṣu:g + Z/	/dɔ:s + Z/	/ta:n + Z/
ZERO	mik' + Z	ṣug + Z	dɔs + Z	tan + Z
LOW				
	[mik'-]	[ṣug-]	[dɔs-]	[tan-]

In the analysis we propose, the vowels that show up as ɔ(:) at the surface derive from two sources: some come from the phoneme /u:/ and others from the phoneme /ɔ:/. By ordering HARM and LOW adequately we can account in a very simple manner for the difference in behaviour between the verbs in line (b) and those in line (c) of table 10 in relation to vowel harmony. This difference is similar to that between the corresponding verbs of table 9:

	10, ɪɪ(b)	10, ɪɪ(c)	10, ɪv(b)	10, ɪv(c)
	/ṣu:g + it/	/dɔ:s + it/	/ṣu:g + al/	/dɔ:s + al/
HARM	ṣu:g + ut			dɔ:s + ɔl
LOW	ṣɔ:g + ut		ṣɔ:g + al	
	[ṣɔ:gut]	[dɔ:sit]	[ṣɔ:gal]	[dɔ:sɔl]

	9, ɪɪ(b)	9, ɪɪ(c)	9, ɪv(b)	9, ɪv(c)
	/hud + it/	/gɔp + it/	/hud + al/	/gɔp + al/
HARM	hud + ut			gɔp + ɔl
	[hudut]	[gɔpit]	[hudal]	[gɔpɔl]

The difference in vowel quality between the suffixes in [ṣɔ:gut] and [dɔ:sit] is the same as that between those of [hudut] and [gɔpit], and the difference in vowel quality between the suffixes in [ṣɔ:gal] and [dɔ:sɔl] is the same as that between those of [hudal] and [gɔpɔl]. With each pair, the underlying vowel of the root is of type u ([+ high]) in the first form, whereas it is of type ɔ ([− high]) in the second. But LOW, applied after HARM, eradicates the difference between u: and ɔ: so that /ṣu:g/ and /dɔ:s/ have phonetically the same vowel [ɔ:]. The forms of (b) no longer need to be lexically marked as exceptions to part (16) of HARM, and it is no longer necessary to complicate the formulation of HARM in a way that would entail considering the harmonization of suffixes with high vowels and that of suffixes with low vowels as two distinct processes (cf. p. 125). Consider also the fact (cf. p. 125) that only the roots with a long ɔ condition the harmony of suffixes in two different ways (according to whether they belong to (b) or to (c) of table 10), whereas there is no similar division among the roots with a short ɔ. This fact appeared to be accidental in our preceding analysis, in the sense that we would have had to add to the grammar a special rule whose sole purpose would have been to express it: a rule of lexical redundancy stipulating that only roots with an ɔː vowel can be marked [− environment (16)]. On the contrary, this fact is explained in the analysis now proposed: it automatically follows from the fact that the ɔ(ː) vowels derive in certain forms from a high vowel and in others from a low vowel, whence the difference in behaviour of the suffixes that follow, whereas the root vowels that are always realized as [ɔ] whatever the number of following consonants can only derive from /ɔ/, whence the uniform behaviour of suffixes after these vowels.

In summary, the proposed analysis presents the following advantages: (i) it enables us to postulate a vowel system that possesses the symmetry generally expected in systems that distinguish between long and short vowels; (ii) it enables us to characterize the harmonization of high-vowelled suffixes and that of low-vowelled suffixes as two instances of a single process, and relieves us from having to mark certain roots as exceptions;[39] (iii) the rule that goes from reduced forms to zero forms is very simple (ZERO), and the vowel quality adjustments that are found in such cases can be imputed to LOW. A certain price has had to be paid to obtain such simplifications: LOW has had to be added to the grammar. But note that in any case we would have had to pay such a price. For if we had chosen the analysis that is implied by the system of underlying vowels in (18), we would have needed morpheme structure rules to account for the particular structure of that system, and one of these rules would have stipulated that any [+ long] vocalic phoneme in Yawelmani is necessarily also [− high, + low]; in short, our grammar would have also contained LOW. It is just that LOW would have been a morpheme structure rule instead of a phonological rule ordered after HARM.

[39] Exception features must only be used as a last resort, since to mark a lexical item as an exception is to state that some particularities of its behaviour cannot be accounted for by any rule. Exception features which are represented in a lexical entry are idiosyncratic properties which have to be especially memorized and thus increase the memory load of the person learning the language.

We have not yet mentioned all the facts that must be taken into consideration in order to decide between the two analyses. Consider the dissyllabic roots given in table 12.[40] The roots considered are all of the form

TABLE 12

	I	II	III	IV
	future passive	passive aorist	precative gerundial	dubitative
(a)	hiwεtnit	hiwε:tit	hiwεt?as	hiwε:tal
(b)	ṣudɔk'nut	ṣudɔ:k'ut	ṣudɔk'?as	ṣudɔ:k'al
(c)	?ɔpɔtnit	?ɔpɔ:tit	?ɔpɔt?ɔs	?ɔpɔ:tɔl
(d)	yawalnit	yawa:lit	yawal?as	yawa:lal

CVCVC. The first vowel is always short and we can derive it from the corresponding short underlying vowel. The second vowel derives from an underlying long vowel, as shown by the alternations in length between columns I and II, and between III and IV. These alternations are governed by BREV (cf. table 10). Within the framework of the analysis we have proposed, *ε(:)* represents the phoneme /i:/ and *a(:)* the phoneme /a:/. As for *ɔ(:)*, the behaviour of the suffixes leads to the conclusion that it represents /u:/ in line (b) and /ɔ:/ in line (c) (cf. table 10, (b) and (c)). The respective phonological representations of the roots of the verbs in table 12 are therefore (a) /hiwi:t/, (b) /ṣudu:k'/, (c) /?ɔpɔ:t/ and (d) /yawa:l/.

These forms illustrate the fact that in a verbal root of a /CVCV:C/ structure, the two underlying vowels are of the same quality. This generalization is a particular consequence of a very general morpheme structure rule stipulating that in any morpheme beginning with a /CVCV:/ sequence the two vowels must be identical apart from their length. This rule accounts in an illuminating way for the constraints on vowel combinations that are found in the verbal roots in table 12. Phonetically there are four short vowels (*i, u, ɔ, a*) and three long vowels (*ε:, ɔ:, a:*). If they could freely combine in *CVCV:* sequences, we would expect to find twelve (4 × 3) distinct types of roots; but in fact, only the four represented in table 12 are possible. If the first vowel is *i*, the second is necessarily *ε:*; if it is *u* or *ɔ*, the second is necessarily *ɔ:*; finally, if it is *a*, the second is necessarily *a:*. This correspondence is strictly identical to the one we found between the long

[40]   (a) 'to walk', (b) 'to remove', (c) 'to arise from bed', (d) 'to follow'.

vowels of reduced forms and the short vowels of zero forms (table 11, columns A' and B').

Let us pause to consider the case of ɔ(:), which corresponds in certain cases to *u* and in others to ɔ. We have seen that our analysis accounted in a very natural way for the correlation we found between the facts of vowel harmony and 'grade' alternations: the rounding of the high-vowelled suffixes is triggered off only by those ɔ(:) vowels which have an *u* reflex in the zero form (line (b) in tables 10 and 11), and the rounding of the low-vowelled suffixes is triggered off only by the ɔ(:) vowels which have an ɔ reflex in the zero form (line (c) in tables 10 and 11). Table 12 presents exactly the same correlation: in the forms in line (b) the first vowel of the root is *u*, and it is the high-vowelled suffixes that are rounded; in those of line (c) the first vowel of the root is ɔ, and it is the low-vowelled suffixes that are rounded. Here are the derivations of the forms (IIb), (IIc), (IVb) and (IVc) of table 12, which should be compared with the similar derivations given on page 128.

	/ṣudu:k'+it/	/ʔɔpɔːt+it/	/ṣudu:k'+al/	/ʔɔpɔːt+al/
HARM	ṣudu:k'+ut			ʔɔpɔːt+ɔl
LOW	ṣudɔ:k'+ut		ṣudɔ:k'+al	
	[ṣudɔ:k'ut]	[ʔɔpɔːtit]	[ṣudɔ:k'al]	[ʔɔpɔːtɔl]

Finally, before examining the behaviour of the suffixes with long underlying vowels, it is necessary to add to what we have said about BREV. Consider the forms in table 13,[41] which are analogous to the corresponding forms in tables 9, 10 and 12. The roots, all of the form /CVCV:/, are / ili:/, /c'uyu:/, /hɔyɔ:/ and /pana:/, respectively. The suffixes of columns II and IV,

TABLE 13

	I	II	III	IV
	future passive	passive aorist	precative gerundial	dubitative
(a)	ʔilɛːnit	ʔilɛt	ʔilɛːʔas	ʔilɛl
(b)	c'uyɔːnut	c'uyɔt	c'uyɔːʔas	c'uyɔl
(c)	hɔyɔːnit	hɔyɔt	hɔyɔːʔɔs	hɔyɔl
(d)	pana:nit	panat	pana:ʔas	panal

[41] (a) 'to fan', (b) 'to urinate', (c) 'to name', (d) 'to arrive'.

-*it* and -*al* respectively, lose their initial vowel by the effect of a truncation rule that does not concern us here, and phonetically they only appear as final consonants. The short vowel preceding the final consonant derives from the final vowel of the root, which is long at a phonological level. These forms illustrate the fact that in Yawelmani any vowel preceding a word-final consonant is necessarily short. Taking advantage of the brace notation introduced on page 101, we can rewrite BREV as follows:

$$\text{BREV:}\quad V \rightarrow [-\text{long}] \quad / \quad \underline{\quad} C \left\{ \begin{array}{c} \# \\ C \end{array} \right\}$$

Let us recapitulate, in (19) below, the phonological rules we have given so far (the page numbers in parentheses refer to discussions of the rule; those in bold type to definitive formulations). The order of applications is justified on the following pages: p. 128 for ZERO and LOW, p. 128 for HARM and LOW, p. 127 for LOW and BREV.

(19)　　ZERO　　　　　(126-**7**)

　　　　HARM　　　　　(121-**2**)

　　　　LOW　　　　　　(**127**)

　　　　BREV　　　　　(123, **132**)

Columns A, B and C of table 14 give the forms of the future middle passive of the verbs in tables 9, 10 and 12 respectively. These forms are composed of the root followed by the middle passive suffix $/n/$[42] and the future suffix $/Vn/$ in which $/V/$ is a vocalic phoneme whose exact identity will be examined now. This phoneme phonetically manifests itself as $[\varepsilon]$ in lines (a), (c) and (d) and as $[\mathfrak{d}]$ in line (b). $[\varepsilon]$ can only come from $/i:/$ by application of LOW and BREV (and the vowel concerned does indeed fulfil the necessary conditions for BREV to operate, since it precedes a consonant (n),

TABLE 14

	A	B	C
(a)	xilnɛn	mɛk'nɛn	hiwɛtnɛn
(b)	hudnɔn	ṣɔgnɔn	sudɔk'nɔn
(c)	gɔpnɛn	dɔsnɛn	ʔɔpɔtnɛn
(d)	maxnɛn	tannɛn	yawalnɛn

[42] The phonological representation of this suffix is in fact $/in/$ (cf. Kisseberth, 1969a : 40), but this has no bearing on the points discussed below.

occurring at the end of a word). Let us, therefore, suppose that the phonological representation of the future suffix is /iːn/. The rules we have given so far and the order of application attributed to them lead us to expect precisely the phonetic representations presented in table 14. Here, for example, are the derivations of the forms in columns A and B:

	(a) /xil + n + iːn/	(b) /hud + n + iːn/	(c) /gɔp + n + iːn/	(d) /max + n + iːn/
HARM		uː		
LOW	ɛː	ɔː	ɛː	ɛː
BREV	ɛ	ɔ	ɛ	ɛ
	[xilnɛn]	[hudnɔn]	[gɔpnɛn]	[maxnɛn]

	/miːk' + n + iːn/	/ṣuːg + n + iːn/	/dɔːs + n + iːn/	/taːn + n + iːn/
HARM			uː				
LOW	ɛː	ɛː	ɔː	ɔː		ɛː		ɛː
BREV	ɛ	ɛ	ɔ	ɔ	ɔ	ɛ	a	ɛ
	[mɛk'nɛn]		[ṣognɔn]		[dɔsnɛn]		[tannɛn]	

Let us take, for example, the derivations of the forms of column A. At the point in the derivation where HARM is applicable, LOW has not yet operated, so that the vowel of the suffix is still [+ high] as in the phonological representation. It therefore harmonizes in (b) where the vowel of the root is itself [+ high], but not in (c) where this vowel is [− high]. LOW then operates and rewrites the vowel of the suffix as [+ low]. If we take into account only what we see in the phonetic representations, it could seem that the future suffix behaves in a deviant way with respect to HARM, or that HARM is incorrectly formulated, since the vowel of the suffix is [− high] but nonetheless behaves like a [+ high] vowel: it is realized as rounded in the presence of high rounded vowels (cf. [hudnon]) and as unrounded in the presence of low vowels (cf. [gɔpnɛn]).

After the forms of table 14, which illustrate the behaviour of the suffixes with underlying long high vowels, let us see, in conclusion, those of (20) that illustrate the behaviour of suffixes with underlying long low vowels:

(20)

(a) bilɛṣʔaːnit   'to finish'
(b) ʔukɔc'ʔaːnit   'to depend on'
(c) k'ɔʔɔːʔɔːnit   'to throw'
(d) p'axat'ʔaːnit   'to mourn'

These forms are in the future durative passive (see Newman, 1944: 102) and are composed of the roots /bili:ṣ/, /ʔuku:c'/, /k'ɔʔɔ:/ and /p'axa:t'/ followed by the suffixes /ʔa:/ and /nit/. They have the following derivations:

/bili:ṣ + ʔa: + nit/   /ʔuku:c' + ʔa: + nit/

HARM		
LOW	ɛ:	ɔ:
BREV	ɛ	ɔ
	[bilɛṣʔa:nit]	[ʔukɔc'ʔa:nit]

/k'ɔʔɔ: + ʔa: + nit/   /p'axa:t' + ʔa: + nit/

HARM	ɔ:	
LOW		
BREV		a
	[k'ɔʔɔ:ʔɔ:nit]	[p'axat'ʔa:nit]

The fragment of grammar of (19) was formulated by taking into account only the suffixes with underlying short vowels (see tables 9, 10, 12 and 13). But when it came to accounting for the behaviour of suffixes with long underlying vowels (see table 14 and (20)) we were able to use it again, without having to change anything in it. In other words, the phonetic alternations in suffixes with short vowels and those in suffixes with long vowels are ruled by exactly the same principles. In particular, our analysis gives the same explanation of two facts that, at first sight, do not seem to have anything in common: the fact that *some* ɔ(:)s behave in the same way as *u* when they function as *environments* for the operation of HARM (compare line (b) in tables 10 and 12 with line (b) in table 9), and the fact that *all* the ɛ(:)s behave in the same way as *i* when they are *inputs* of HARM (compare columns A, B and C in table 14 with column I of tables 9, 10 and 12). These two facts are due to the existence of a LOW rule ordered after HARM. We will leave the reader the task of examining the additional complications that have to be introduced into the analysis implied by the underlying vowel system of (18) (p. 124), when attempting to account for the facts in table 14 and in (20).

This discussion will close with a few general remarks. The first concerns the abstract nature of phonological representations and the demand for generality and simplicity. In all the discussions preceding those on Yawelmani, the phonological representations that we gave were abstract in the sense that often the specifications at the phonological level were different from their reflexes at the corresponding phonetic level. For example, the specification [+ syll] in the /i/ of /defi + e/ *défié* ' defied ' has as its phonetic reflex the specification [− syll] in the [y̥] of [defy̥e] (see p. 67). All the same, in general, the phonological rules only operate in certain environments, and in those environments where they do not operate the underlying specifications are transmitted unchanged to the phonetic level. Thus the specification [+ syll] of the last segment of /defi/ *défi* ' challenge ' is kept intact in the phonetic representation [defi]. The [+ syll] nature of the last segment of the underlying representation /defi/ is therefore directly manifested at the phonetic level for some occurrences of this morpheme. Things are different when some specifications are affected by a phonological rule that operates in all environments, like LOW in Yawelmani. This rule enables us to postulate underlying long, high vowels (*i:*, *u:*), which are never realized phonetically as such. At the phonetic level, the future suffix sometimes appears as [ɛn] and sometimes as [ɔn], i.e. always with a low vowel; and yet this does not prevent us from attributing to it a phonological representation /i:n/, with a high vowel. In short, the fact that at the phonetic level all occurrences of a morpheme contain a certain specification does not necessarily guarantee that this specification also appears in the phonological representation of that morpheme.

It could seem that, by allowing for such important discrepancies between the phonological representations and the phonetic representations, we are leaving the field open for the most arbitrary manipulations.[43] But let us remember that the gap between the two levels of representation is to be bridged in a perfectly explicit manner by the operation of the phonological rules and that the wider the gap, the more complex the phonological component has to be. This considerably limits our field of action. *For the addition of each new phonological rule must be justified by showing that the resulting complexity added to the grammar is largely compensated for by the simplifications that the rule produces for various other points in the grammar.* What reason have we to claim that the final underlying vowel of *défi* [defi] ' challenge ', *joli* [ʒɔli] ' pretty ', *pari* [pari] ' bet ', etc., is [− back], if it is not the wish to obtain the simplest possible grammar? Suppose that we give these morphemes the phonological representations /defɯ/, ʒɔlɯ/, /parɯ/, etc., in which /ɯ/ is a [+ high, − round, − nas ...] vowel like /i/, but is

---

[43] This very important question has been the subject of a long, and as yet unfinished discussion, cf. Kiparsky (1968*b*; 1973*b*), Kisseberth (1969*b*), Hyman (1970; 1973), Brame (1972).

[+ back], whereas /i/ is [− back]. In order to go from these phonological representations to the phonetic representations [defi], [žɔli], [pari], etc., which have a final [− back] vowel, the grammar must have a phonological rule that rewrites all the [+ high, − round] segments as [− back]. But there is no justification for this rule. It does not simplify either the lexical entries or any of the other rules. It is the underlying vowel /i/ that enables us to establish the most direct relation between the phonological representations of these morphemes and their phonetic representations, and we have no reason not to prefer it (that is to say, we have every reason to prefer it).

For the same reason, our first impulse was to attribute to the phonemes /ɛ:/ and /ɔ:/ all the occurrences of the vowels [ɛ:] and [ɔ:] that are found in Yawelmani. But we soon had to acknowledge that the ɛːs and certain ɔːs behave like high vowels, and that it was on the basis of their phonetic realization only that we wished to derive them from low underlying vowels. By making them derive from high underlying vowels, by including in the grammar the LOW rule, which rewrites them as low vowels, we can fruitfully explain the gap between their phonetic quality and their behaviour with respect to certain rules. It would not, of course, be impossible to construct a grammar that would account for the same data and derive these vowels from the phonemes /ɛ:/ and /ɔ:/. We took the first steps in that direction on pages 123–6.[44] But compared with the grammar we have adopted it would necessarily entail a number of complications that could hardly be justified by any argument except simply the desire to stick to the hypothesis that all ɛːs derive from /ɛ:/ and all ɔːs[45] from /ɔ:/. However this hypothesis must be justified like any other. And the only way to do this is to show that it enables us to account for the data with a maximum of generality – which is not the case here.

We should now turn to an examination of the status of generality and simplicity considerations, which we have been continually appealing to in the preceding discussions. Let us first remember that linguists have a dual task: one is concerned with linguistic theory, and the other with particular grammars (cf. pp. 28ff).

From the point of view of linguistic theory – the theory of languages in general – the problem is to give a definition of the notion 'possible language'. Linguistic theory states a certain number of conditions that any

[44] Iverson (1975) recently proposed an analysis which on certain points is an improvement on the analysis we sketched on pp. 123–6, but which is nonetheless still open to criticisms of a similar kind.

[45] ... leaving aside the ɔː which appears in the ending -ʔɔːnit of (c) in (20) above.

grammar must fulfil. For example, any grammar must contain a phonological component that is an ordered set of rules applying sequentially. Or again, if we take the lexicon, the information about the pronunciation of morphemes must be represented in the form of distinctive feature matrices, etc. When, for instance, we compared the merits of simultaneous and sequential application of the phonological rules at the end of chapter 2, we were concerned with linguistic theory.

From the point of view of the grammar of a particular language – the theory of the sentences of that language – the problem is to give a definition of the notion ' well-formed sentence ' for the language in question. The data consist of native speakers' intuitions concerning the sentences of this language: some sound–meaning pairs are well-formed, others not. The system of hypotheses – the theory – proposed by linguists in order to account for these data is a grammar. In order to be a possible candidate, a grammar must simultaneously satisfy the two following demands: it must fulfil the general conditions that linguistic theory imposes on all grammars, and it must generate the infinite set of well-formed sound–meaning pairs of the language under study. But in the present state of linguistic theory it is possible to propose for a given language many different grammars that fulfil these two conditions. Is it really necessary to choose between these different grammars, and if so, what criteria are to be used in marking the choice?

By finding a grammar that makes predictions that are never contradicted by the native speakers' intuitions, the linguist fulfils the programme we set out in chapter 1, when we said (p. 5) ' to describe a language is to construct the grammar of that language ', i.e. 'a device which gives an explicit definition of the set of well-formed sound–meaning pairs of that language ' (cf. also p. 13). If it were, as this quotation would lead us to believe, just a question of proposing a perfectly explicit definition of a certain infinite set of objects, all the grammars generating this set would be strictly equivalent, and the choice of one rather than another would simply be a matter of personal taste. But linguists have greater ambitions. Those who know a language, say English, acquired during the first years of their life a certain system of knowledge enabling them to pronounce and understand an infinity of sentences and to have intuitions that linguists can use as data. What linguists propose to discover when they describe English, is *the* grammar of English; i.e. an adequate representation of the system of knowledge stored in the native speakers' brains. Among all the grammars that generate the set of descriptions of well-formed sound–meaning pairs of English, how may we decide which is the most adequate representation of this system of knowledge?

In linguistics, as in other sciences, when there are several competing theories covering the same set of data, the theory which requires the fewest and most general hypotheses is to be preferred. Between two grammars that generate the same set of descriptions of sound–meaning pairs, the one containing the smallest number of rules, and the rules that have the most general scope, is chosen; in other words, the simplest grammar. This is an absolutely fundamental point. All linguists proceed in this manner, whatever school they belong to, and if they are often not aware of it, it is generally because they are not aware that for any set of data, their theoretical presuppositions (whether they are explicit or not) allow for a great number of competing descriptions. All grammarians, for example, will say that in French adjectives agree in number and gender with the noun they modify. This is the same as saying that the grammar of French contains a syntactic rule that predicts the gender and number of adjectives from that of the nouns they modify. From the knowledge that the adjective *vieux* 'old' modifies *armures* 'armours' and that *armures* is feminine plural, this rule predicts that the adjective itself is feminine plural, i.e. *de vieilles armures* [vyɛyzarmür] 'old armours' and not *de vieux armures [vyözarmür]. And yet it is nonetheless perfectly possible to claim that it is the noun that agrees with the adjective and not the reverse, in other words to propose a rule predicting the gender and number of nouns from that of the adjectives. But it is easy to demonstrate that a grammar containing such a rule would be inextricably complicated, and that is the reason why no one has ever held such a point of view. Another example: it is commonly stated that the adjectives *readable, eatable, foreseeable*, etc., are formed by adding the suffix *-able* to the verbs *read, eat, foresee*, etc. But there is no *a priori* reason why one could not claim the reverse, i.e. that there is a rule that forms verbs by dropping *-able* from adjectives of the form *X-able*. No one has ever defended such a position, and with good reason. We have shown (in Dell, 1970) that if one takes a similar stand for the *-able* adjectives in French, one inevitably gets caught up in extremely complex word-formation rules that leave certain essential generalizations unexpressed.

We have appealed constantly to considerations of simplicity in order to justify our preference for this or that analysis in our discussions of Zoque and Yawelmani. In the preceding discussions take any argument aimed at showing that rule A should be ordered before rule B, and you will see that ultimately it rests on considerations of overall simplicity in the grammar. It is nearly always possible to construct a competing grammar in which B precedes A, but in that case it is necessary to introduce into the formulation of either A or B (or both) complications that increase the grammar's overall complexity.[46] More generally, to state that a certain grammar G is *the* grammar of the language L is to state that, amongst all the grammars meeting the conditions imposed by linguistic theory and generating all and only the well-formed sound–meaning pairs of L, G is the simplest grammar.[47]

Simplicity of formulation is not a goal in itself. Constructing grammars of the greatest simplicity only interests us in as far as the greatest *simplicity* equals the greatest *generality*. Consider, for example, the LOW rule in Yawelmani; we give it again below for the sake of convenience. If, in the grammar (19) above, we replaced this rule by rules LOW_1 and LOW_2, we would obtain a grammar that would generate exactly the same sound–meaning pairs:

$$\text{LOW:} \quad \begin{bmatrix} + \text{syll} \\ + \text{long} \end{bmatrix} \rightarrow \begin{bmatrix} + \text{low} \\ - \text{high} \end{bmatrix}$$

$$LOW_1: \quad \begin{bmatrix} + \text{syll} \\ + \text{long} \\ - \text{back} \end{bmatrix} \rightarrow \begin{bmatrix} + \text{low} \\ - \text{high} \end{bmatrix}$$

$$LOW_2: \quad \begin{bmatrix} + \text{syll} \\ + \text{long} \\ + \text{back} \end{bmatrix} \rightarrow \begin{bmatrix} + \text{low} \\ - \text{high} \end{bmatrix}$$

Whereas LOW affects all the long vowels, whether they are front or back, LOW_1 only affects long front vowels and LOW_2 only affects long back vowels. Together they have exactly the same effect as LOW. There is no reason to order LOW_1 before LOW_2 or the reverse, and LOW_1 and LOW_2 have exactly the same ordering relationships with the other rules. Both must be applied after ZERO and HARM, and before BREV. The grammar containing LOW_1 and LOW_2 does indeed express the fact that *i:* is rewritten as *ɛ:*, and *u:* as *ɔ:*, but it considers these two facts as utterly unrelated. It also treats as a coincidence the fact that these two rules must be applied at the same stage in the derivation, at a moment when ZERO and HARM but not BREV have already applied. On the other hand, (19) encompasses all these facts in the same generalization expressed by LOW.

---

[46] Cf., for example, the order of application of PAL and H-DEL (p. 90) and that of META and Y-DEL (pp. 104–7).

[47] It will be seen below that we define 'the simplest grammar' as that containing the fewest symbols.

As Chomsky says (1965: 42) 'We have a generalization when a set of rules about distinct items can be replaced by a single rule (or more generally, partially identical rules) about the whole set... ' A grammar must express the fact that the existence of linguistic regularities is not fortuitous, but follows from certain properties of languages as structured systems. It must pack the facts in as tight as possible a network of generalizations.

Each grammar contains a finite number of symbols. As a first approximation, the 'simplicity' of grammars can be defined in the following way: between two grammars formulated within the framework of the same linguistic theory, the simplest (or, equivalently, the least complex) is that which contains the smallest number of symbols.[48] In order to formulate each rule and to specify the content of each lexical entry, it is necessary to write out a certain number of symbols, and each symbol adds to the overall complexity of the grammar.

If an adequate formalism is chosen for the writing of grammars, the more a rule is general, the simpler it is (the lowest number of symbols it has). The LOW rule, for example, is simpler than LOW_1 (its structural description contains one specification fewer) and this reflects the fact that it is more general. The set of segments that are $[+ \text{syll}, + \text{long}]$ contains the set of symbols that are $[+ \text{syll}, + \text{long}, - \text{back}]$. LOW_1 is a special case of LOW. Similarly, compare rule (21) to the hypothetical rule (22):

(21) $[+ \text{syll}]$ → $[- \text{long}]$ /   —— $[- \text{syll}]$ $[- \text{syll}]$

$$(22) \quad \begin{bmatrix} + \text{syll} \\ + \text{round} \end{bmatrix} \rightarrow [- \text{long}] \bigg/ \text{——} \begin{bmatrix} - \text{syll} \\ - \text{cons} \\ + \text{high} \\ - \text{back} \end{bmatrix} [- \text{syll}]$$

Rule (21) rewrites as short any vowel followed by two non-syllabic segments. It is the same as BREV (p. 123). Rule (22) rewrites as short any rounded vowel followed by two non-syllabic segments, the first of which is a yod. The representations /paːy + nit/, /pɔːt + nit/, and /pɔːy + nit/ are all subject to rule (21) but only the third is subject to rule (22) since the *aː* of the first is non-round and the *ɔː* of the second is not followed by a yod. Any representation that is subject to (22) is also subject to (21) but the converse

---

[48] Each distinctive feature specification counts as a single symbol.

is not true. The conditions required by the structural description of (22) are more restrictive (less general) than those required by the structural description of (21) and this is reflected by the fact that the formulation of (22) requires four more specifications than that of (21).

The complexity of a linguistic description (the number of symbols that it contains) evidently depends on the symbolism used in writing grammars or, in other words, on the linguistic theory which is being used as a framework. It is, for example, easy to imagine a system of distinctive features in which the formulation of rule (22) would require fewer symbols than that of (21). But such a system would not account for the fact that (21) is more general than (22). The system of distinctive features proposed by Chomsky and Halle is designed precisely to establish the best possible correlation between the degree of generality of the phonological rules and their 'simplicity', as measured by counting feature specifications.[49] The same is true for the abbreviatory devices which conflate several partially similar rules into one rule schema. These devices allow one to factor out and to represent only once in the grammar the specifications that are common to all the rules.[50] It is by no means a simple task to design a notational system such that, given any two grammars formulated within the framework of the system and generating the same set of sound–meaning pairs, the one which contains the fewest specifications is also the one which leaves no significant generalization unexpressed, for this entails making explicit what is meant by 'significant generalization' in linguistics. For further discussion on this fundamental problem of the construction of a linguistic theory, we refer the reader to Chomsky (1965: 34–47; 1967*b*: 107–9), Chomsky and Halle (1965: 106ff.), Halle (1962; 1969), *SPE* (chap. 8) and to the objections raised by Botha (1971), Derwing (1973: 135–43) and McCawley (1968*b*: 559–60).

Note that it is again our wish for the greatest generality that several times induced us to consider facts drawn from languages other than the ones for which we were constructing a grammar.[51] In as far as we possibly can, we wish to account for similar facts from one language to another by ascribing them to formally similar rules, in the hope that we will one day be able to show that these similitudes from one language to another are not totally fortuitous, but spring (at least partially) from general properties of grammars.

---

[49] For an idea of the kind of considerations which are relevant in choosing distinctive features, cf., for example, McCawley (1967; 1968*a*: 26, n. 15), Kiparsky (1968*a*: 185–9; 1974), Postal (1968: 75–6), Contreras (1969), Anderson (1971).

[50] Cf. Chomsky (1965: 43–4), Kiparsky (1968*a*: 171–83), Bach (1968). McCawley (1971).

[51] Cf., for example, pp. 106 and 124. See also p. 74.

Thus, the problem of knowing which is the grammar of a given language has in principle a unique solution.[52] This does not mean that there is a recipe for reaching that solution. Until recently, one of the tasks that many linguists attributed to general linguistics was the elaboration of discovery procedures for grammars, or at least of justification procedures. By discovery procedures, is meant a set of instructions indicating the steps to be followed by the linguist in order to go from the raw data (the sentences pronounced by his informant) to the description of the language (its grammar). The operations to be carried out on the data are fixed once and for all, are valid for any language, and are rigorously defined so that nothing is left to the judgement of the describers. They guarantee in principle that two people independently working on the same language will give it two descriptions which will be identical, point for point. All the attempts that have been made to design such procedures have failed. A less ambitious task would be that of defining justification procedures for grammars.[53] Then it would no longer be a question of giving a procedure exactly stating the steps that lead from raw data to the completed description, but only a question of setting tests which, given a language and a certain grammar, would lead to a decision as to whether this grammar was in fact the grammar of the language under study.[54]

The attempts to design justification procedures did not succeed any better than those to design discovery procedures. One of the reasons for these failures should be obvious: in order to be able to elaborate discovery or justification procedures, one has to have a precise idea of the properties that any grammar of a natural language must necessarily have, in other words, one has to have a very specific linguistic theory. But we are still far from the mark.

In order to find out the grammar of a language and justify it, linguists cannot depend on a set of precepts and recipes that would guarantee the 'correct' result each time they were scrupulously applied. Of course they must make use of rigour and method, but also of astuteness and

---

[52] ... apart from those cases where the order of application of two rules is indeterminate (cf. p. 97).

[53] Chomsky (1957) calls them 'decision procedures'. On the difference between the discovery, justification (or decision) and evaluation of grammars, cf. Chomsky (1957: chap. 6), Ruwet (1967: sec. 6.2).

[54] Procedures given as discovery procedures are often in fact justification procedures. This is the case, for example, with the seven 'rules for determining phonemes' in Troubetzkoy (1939: 47–66) and with the set of segmentation and classification operations organized around the 'commutation' test in Martinet (1956: secs. 3.14–3.16; 1960: secs. 3.7–3.12, 3.22–3.23; 1965a: 63–8, 111).

imagination. Linguists know that the grammar they are looking for must fulfil three conditions: (i) answer the general conditions imposed by linguistic theory, (ii) be compatible with all the data of the language under study, and (iii) be the simplest of the grammars which fulfil conditions (i) and (ii). It is therefore a question of thinking up grammars and then verifying whether they fulfil the above conditions. The way a linguist gets to the grammars he is testing is not important. All means are fair, even premonitions and consulting fortune tellers, for those who believe in them.

Once it is accepted that the linguist envisages as a hypothesis only those grammars that satisfy condition (i), we explained on pages 13–15 how he proceeds to make sure that condition (ii) is met: each grammar he imagines makes an infinity of predictions that go beyond the finite sample of the data (positive and negative) taken into account in order to construct that grammar. He tests these predictions with speakers and some of the predictions are in contradiction with their intuitions about what is well- or ill-formed. This compels him to think up another grammar compatible with this new data. In the end, he obtains a grammar whose predictions are never contradicted by his informants: each time he presents them with a sound–meaning pair that is generated by this grammar, they accept it as well-formed, and each time he presents them with one that the grammar excludes, they reject it as ill-formed; he can test as many predictions as he likes without ever finding a contradiction.[55]

So here we have our linguist in possession of a grammar that meets conditions (i) and (ii). How does he manage to make sure that it also meets condition (iii)? Theoretically, he would have to construct for the language under study all the grammars that meet conditions (i) and (ii), and then find out which is the simplest. But since at present linguistic theory is not yet very specific and allows for the construction of an infinity of distinct grammars for each language, he would find himself faced with an unlimited task. In fact, in the vast majority of cases, these grammars lack generality in such a striking manner that one can eliminate them without taking the trouble of constructing them in detail. For example, this would be the case with a grammar of Yawelmani in which rule BREV would be replaced by as many distinct rules as there are groups of two consonants preceded by a vowel in Yawelmani.

$$\text{BREV}_1 \quad V \rightarrow [-\text{long}] \quad / \quad \text{——tn}$$
$$\text{BREV}_2 \quad V \rightarrow [-\text{long}] \quad / \quad \text{——kp}$$
$$\vdots \qquad\qquad \vdots \qquad\qquad\qquad \vdots$$

---

[55] Cf. n. 56.

Once all the grammars of that kind have been tacitly eliminated, there usually only remains a small number of plausible ones, and a choice can be made between them by using arguments such as those we have used in our discussion on Zoque and Yawelmani. *To justify a grammar is to envisage all the competing grammars and systematically eliminate them.*

Strictly speaking, the linguist can never prove that the grammar he proposes is the simplest, since it is always possible that there is an even simpler grammar which he has not thought of. And the only way to show him that the grammar he is defending is not the simplest one, is to present him with another even simpler one. A linguist who claims that a certain grammar is the simplest is in a situation encountered in all the empirical sciences. He cannot prove that he is right, but he can be proved to be wrong, if such is the case. As long as this has not been done, his claim must be considered to be true.[56]

A concluding word on the relations between phonology and morphology. In general, traditional grammars ascribe to morphology all the facts concerning the sequential positioning of morphemes inside words, as well as alternations between the allomorphs of a same morpheme in the presence of certain 'grammatical morphemes'. In the linguistic theory sketched here, facts of the former type belong to the syntactic component, whereas those of the latter belong to the readjustment component (spelling rules) and no distinction is made such as the one usually made between 'lexical morphemes' (*spring, knight, sleep*, etc.) and 'grammatical morphemes' (*to, who, your, -ed*, etc.). This is, in fact, because of broad simplifications adopted for reasons of convenience. A general and detailed theory of morphological facts is still to be formulated,[57] but it cannot be doubted that grammars will have to have a morphological component, situated in an area that will encompass part of the syntactic component as it is conceived today as well as part of the readjustment component. Whatever the exact form and status of the rules of the morphological component, it goes without saying

---

[56]   This also holds for the proposition 'grammar G generates descriptions of all the well-formed sound–meaning pairs of language L, and of those only'. Since linguists only check a finite set of predictions made by their grammars, it is always conceivable that some of the unchecked predictions are in fact incorrect. Linguists can therefore never be absolutely certain that their grammars are compatible with all the data that could be collected. On the other hand, it can be proved that a grammar is not, by simply providing a sound–meaning pair about which that grammar makes incorrect predictions. As long as this has not been done, the above proposition must be accepted as true.

[57]   For attempts in this direction within the framework of generative grammar, cf. Aronoff (1976), Bierwisch (1967), Dell (1970), Halle (1973*a*), Kiefer (1970; 1971; 1973) and Wurzel (1970). For a short summary and references, see P. H. Matthews (1970) for the American structuralists, and Vachek (1966) for the Prague School.

that their complexity contributes to the global complexity of grammars. An extremely forceful argument in favour of a phonological analysis is when it can be shown that it entails a very simple account of the morphology of the language described, i.e. when it reduces facts of suppletion to a minimum and postulates inflectional paradigms constructed on a uniform model.

Consider table 15: lines (a), (b), (c) and (d) take up the phonetic representations given in the Zoque tables 2(a) p. 92, 4(a) p. 103, 3(e) p. 98, and 4(b) p. 103 respectively. Each phonetic representation is accompanied by its underlying phonological representation:

TABLE 15

	I	II	III	IV
	1st pers. progressive	2nd pers. progressive	3rd pers. progressive	3rd pers. perfective
(a)	[mbuhtu] /n + put + u/	[mbyuhtu] /ny + put + u/	[pyuhtu] /y + put + u/	[puhtu] /put + u/
(b)	[ŋgihpu] /n + kip + u/	[ŋgihpu] /ny + kip + u/	[kihpu] /y + kip + u/	[kihpu] /kip + u/
(c)	[maŋu] /n + maŋ + u/	[myaŋu] /ny + maŋ + u/	[myaŋu] /y + maŋ + u/	[maŋu] /maŋ + u/
(d)	[minu] /n + min + u/	[minu] /ny + min + u/	[minu] /y + min + u/	[minu] /min + u/

Keeping to what is apparent at the phonetic level, person marking in Zoque verbs would appear to be regulated by rather complex morphological mechanisms.[58] In line (a) the first person is indicated by a nasal prefix, the third person by an infix *y*,[59] and the second person by simultaneous prefixation and infixation. In line (b) only the nasal prefix is apparent, whence the homophony of I with II and III with IV. In line (c) only

---

[58] Lack of space forces us to limit these remarks to the inflection of verbs, but the inflection of nouns has exactly the same variations. Thus *pən* 'man' yields *mbən* in *ha?nəh mbən* 'I am not a man', *mbyən* in *ha?nmih mbyən* 'you are not a man', *pyən* in *ha?n pyən* 'he is not a man', etc.

[59] Whereas prefixes and suffixes are morphemes which are added before or after another morpheme (*un*-kind, kind-*ness*), infixes are morphemes which are inserted inside other morphemes. Thus in Tagalog (a language of the Philippines) from the root *basa* 'to read' can be constructed inflectional forms such as *bumasa* 'to have read' and *binasa* 'to have been read', by infixing ·*um*- and ·*in*-.

the infix *y* is apparent, whence the homophony of ɪ with ɪv and ɪɪ with ɪɪɪ. In line (d), finally, there are no prefixes or infixes, so that we get the impression that here we have an invariable verb. In fact, we have treated the differences from one line to the other as mere surface variations with a single underlying inflectional paradigm, the same for all verbs. All the forms have the prefix /n/ in the third person, the prefix /ny/ in the second person and the prefix /y/ in the third person. It is worth going back rapidly over the reasons which enabled us to hypothesize a single underlying inflectional paradigm.

First, a word on the underlying forms that we chose for the three prefixes. The forms ɪ(a) and ɪɪ(a) require the postulation of a prefixed /n/,[60] and those of ɪɪ(a) and ɪɪɪ(a) that of a yod. By considering this yod as prefixed (i.e. by considering that in the phonological representations it is situated in front of the initial consonant of the root), we can account for the position of the three person markers with the help of a single morphological rule: 'the person markers are immediately prefixed to the verb root'. And as other data that has nothing to do with person marking (p. 88) compels us in any case to include the phonological rule META in the grammar, we already have at our disposal a mechanism which can account for the position of the yod following the initial consonant of the root. If we treated this yod as an infix, by attributing, for instance, the phonological representation /n + p + y + ut + u / to [mbyuhtu], we then would have to complicate the morphological rule given above: 'in a person marker, the nasal element (if there is one) is immediately prefixed to the verb root, and the yod (if there is one) is infixed behind the first consonant of the root'. But nothing justifies such a complication. To adopt this formulation would be to claim that in Zoque there is one case of genuine infixation, that of the yod of person markers behind the initial consonant of the root, and that this has nothing to do with the existence of the phonological rule META, whose effect is precisely to displace a yod behind the initial consonant of the following morpheme.

Thus, the forms of line (a) induce us to postulate, for *certain* verbs, the conjugation pattern $n + X$, $ny + X$, $y + X$. If this paradigm cannot be extended to *all* the verbs of Zoque and these have to be distributed into several classes, each one characterized by a particular conjugation paradigm, the complexity of the grammar will have to be increased by including other morphological rules destined to account for the spelling out

---

[60] We did not justify our choice of the coronal /n/ rather than /m/, /ŋ/ or /ñ/ as an underlying nasal consonant for the first and second person prefixes. The reasons for this choice involve the notion of markedness, which we have not discussed in this introduction, see *SPE*: chap. 9.

of person markers in the different conjugation paradigms. Consider line (b), in which forms II and III do not present any phonetic trace of a prefixed yod: this has not prevented us from postulating one in the underlying representations, so that the same pronunciation [kihpu] derives in column III from /y + kip + u/ and in column IV from /kip + u/. Why did we not postulate /kip + u/ in both columns? Tacitly, we reasoned in the following way: if all the verbs are conjugated in the same way, the phonological representation of form III(b) must be /y + kip + u/ and that of form IV(b) must be /kip + u/, like /y + put + u/ and /put + u/ in line (a). Now certain forms, where it is not a question of person markers (cf. table 5) compel us in any case to posit the phonological rule Y-DEL, and a grammar containing this rule will precisely associate the same phonetic representation [kihpu] with the two phonological representations /y + kip + u/ and /kip + u/. We therefore find ourselves in the following position: our grammar must in any case contain certain morphological rules destined to account for the conjugation on line (a), and it must also in any case contain the phonological rule Y-DEL, and all these rules taken together enable us to account just as well for the forms on line (b). We have therefore no reason to get into unnecessary complications by supposing that the verbs of the (b) type have a different conjugation paradigm from those of the (a) type. Nothing prevents us from supposing that they have the same conjugation, and not doing so would lead to complicating the morphological rules without getting anything in return. A similar argument enables us to extend the inflectional paradigm of line (a) to all the other verbs of Zoque.

The superficial variations resulting from the operation of the phonological rules present the observer with a screen which distorts certain features of the morphological structure of the language. It is precisely one of the functions of a phonological description to break through this screen, and to sort out those phonetic variations that can be attributed to phonological rules of general import and those that belong to morphology. The description of the phonology of a language cannot be considered as an isolated task and as an end in itself. It goes hand in hand with the description of other sub-systems (and more particularly with that of morphology), which all fit together to constitute the grammar of the language described.

PART II

Problems in the phonology of French

4

Schwa in underlying representations

Under the heading 'The formation of the feminine gender in oral and written language', Marguerite Durand (1936: 25) writes: 'the question is seen in a very different light depending on whether the written or spoken language is under study... Apart from a few details consisting of the doubling of final consonants, or the adding of accents to the vowel of the final syllable, the rule for spelling the feminine forms is as follows: the feminine in French is formed by adding a mute *e* to the end of the masculine form of the word.

'This rule, taught in schools from the primary grade onwards, is the only one which we are conscious of as far as the difference between the genders is concerned, and there is no attempt to make pupils aware of the rules inherent in the spoken language. If the laws of our language had not been a topic of study for grammarians, and if an explorer restated the grammatical rules according to the spoken language, it would certainly never occur to him to say, on the basis of what he heard, that the feminine was formed by adding a mute *e* to the end of a word in the masculine form.' She then goes on to say: 'the feminine is formed by adding a phoneme to the masculine form and this phoneme is a consonant, which gives us our first result: in written French... the feminine is characterized by a vocalic ending, whereas in the spoken language it is characterized by a consonantal ending' (p. 32).

In order to illustrate Durand's thesis, the pronunciations [pla] and [plat] should be compared with the corresponding spellings *plat* 'flat' (masc.) and *plate* 'flat' (fem.). Whereas in pronunciation the transition from the masculine [pla] to the feminine [plat] is made by adding a final [t], in writing the spelling *plat* changes to the spelling *plate* by adding the letter *e*.

We propose to show that the discrepancy between pronunciation and writing is apparent rather than real,[1] and that in order to account in the most general terms for gender alternations, the phonetic representations of

[1]   This chapter takes up some of the arguments developed by Schane (1968*b*) and Dell (1973*a*).

feminine adjectives must be derived from phonological representations ending in a certain vowel phoneme that we will denote with an upside-down *e* or 'schwa'. /ə/ has the peculiarity of not generally being realized by any sound at the phonetic level. It is this phoneme /ə/ that traditional spelling represents as the *e muet*.[2] At the end of a word, the mute *e* (an accentless *e*) is in general not pronounced, and simply indicates that it is the consonant represented by the preceding letter which must be pronounced. We will show that when the range of data considered is gradually broadened, Durand's analysis (or others, identical in principle[3]) can only be maintained at the price of ever-increasing complications that obscure certain regularities.

Durand (1936: 73–104) has compiled a list of some 5,600 words liable to gender alternations (nouns and noun determiners), from which an exhaustive list can be drawn up of the different phonetic alternations by which French marks genders. As nouns and noun determiners show the same range of phonetic alternations, and as gender alternations occur only sporadically in nouns, we will simplify the discussion by limiting it to noun determiners, principally to adjectives.

Certain adjectives do not have the same phonetic representation, according to whether they modify a masculine or a feminine noun. For example, *creux* 'hollow' is pronounced [krö] in *un plat creux* 'a hollow dish' and [kröz] in *une tasse creuse* 'a hollow cup'. *Creux* is said to agree in gender with the noun it modifies and there is thus said to be a masculine form [krö] and a feminine form [kröz]. On the contrary, other adjectives have the same phonetic representation whatever the gender of the nouns they modify: *bleu* 'blue' is pronounced [blö] in both *un plat bleu* 'a blue dish' and *une tasse bleue* 'a blue cup'. Rather than distinguish two classes of adjectives: those like *creux* that would agree in gender and would have a masculine and a feminine form, and those like *bleu*, which would not agree and would have a single form, we will suppose that all adjectives are subject to rules of agreement and that they all have a masculine and a feminine form, but that these two forms are not always phonetically distinct.[4] Like

---

2   This analysis is not new. For example, it was put forward, with a few differences in detail, by Hjelmslev (1948) and by Togeby (1951), also in De Felice (1950), Schane (1967; 1968a; 1968b) and Valdman (1970). We are following Schane's variant. On latent consonants, see also Bloomfield (1933: 217) and Harris (1951: 168–9).

3   For two particularly clear examples, see Nyrop (1903: Foreword), and Blanche-Benveniste and Chervel (1969: 131, 139, 180).

4   See p. 160. Compare with the fact that some verbs like *savoir* 'to know' and *être* 'to be' have different forms in the present indicative and the present subjunctive (*savent* ~ *sachent*, *sont* ~ *soient*) and others do not, such as *laver* 'to wash' (*lavent* ~ *lavent*).

Durand, we will take phonetic representations as our only starting point:
what an anthropologist who knew nothing about French spelling
would hear. We will therefore distinguish between the 'invariable' adjectives (those that have the same phonetic representation in both genders) and
the others; the masculine form precedes the feminine in the following list:[5]

(1) 'Invariable' adjectives

    (a) $v \sim v$[6] : *flou* ~ *floue* [flu] 'blurred'
                 Other examples: *carré* ~ *carrée* [kare] 'square';
                 joli ~ *jolie* [žɔli] 'pretty'; *poilu* ~ *poilue* [pwalü]
                 'hairy'

    (b) $O \sim O$: *vide* ~ *vide* [vid] 'empty'
                 Other examples: *atroce* [atrɔs] 'atrocious'; *unique*
                 [ünik] 'unique'; *triste* [trist] 'sad'; *courbe* [kurb]
                 'curved'

    (c) $N \sim N$: *jaune* ~ *jaune* [žon] 'yellow'
                 Other examples: *sublime* [süblim] 'sublime'; *digne*
                 [diñ] 'worthy'; *terne* [tɛrn] 'dull'; *calme* [kalm]
                 'quiet'; *borgne* [bɔrñ] 'one-eyed'

    (d) Others : *seul* ~ *seule* [sœl] 'alone'
                 Other examples: *pareil* ~ *pareille* [parɛy] 'alike';
                 rare [rar] 'rare'; *souple* [supl] 'flexible'; *pauvre*
                 [povr] 'poor'

(2) 'Variable' adjectives

    (e) $v \sim vO$: *plat* ~ *plate* [pla] ~ [plat] 'flat'
                 Other examples: *froid* ~ *froide* [frwa] ~ [frwad]
                 'cold'; *laid* ~ *laide* [lɛ] ~ [lɛd] 'ugly'; *gros* ~
                 grosse [gro] ~ [gros] 'fat'; *jaloux* ~ *jalouse* [žalu]
                 ~ [žaluz] 'jealous'

---

[5] In this chapter, v represents non-nasal vowels, $\tilde{v}$ nasal vowels and V all vowels, whatever
the specification of the feature [nas]. For the other abbreviations see page 47. We have
ignored a few sporadic alternations that are not central to our discussion, such as that of
neuf [nœf] ~ *neuve* [nœv] 'new', *sec* [sɛk] ~ *sèche* [sɛš] 'dry', *beau* [bo] ~ *belle* [bɛl]
'beautiful', etc. We have also ignored the alternations $V \sim VOO$, as in *suspect* [süspɛ] ~
suspecte [süspɛkt] 'suspicious', *distinct* [distɛ̃] ~ *distincte* [distɛ̃kt] 'distinct'. Concerning
the latter, cf. Dell (1970: 66–7) and Selkirk (1972: 313–15).

[6] Invariable forms ending in a nasal vowel are extremely rare. Durand only mentions *marron*
[marɔ̃] 'brown', *grognon* [grɔnyɔ̃] 'grumpy', *ronchon* [rɔ̃šɔ̃] 'grumpy', *gnangnan*
[nyãnyã] 'namby-pamby'.

(f) $Vr \sim VrO$:   *court ~ courte* [kur] ~ [kurt] 'short'
Other examples: *fort ~ forte* [fɔr] ~ [fɔrt] 'strong';
divers ~ diverse [divɛr] ~ [divɛrs] 'diverse'; *lourd*
~ *lourde* [lur] ~ [lurd] 'heavy'

(g) $\tilde{v} \sim \tilde{v}O$:   *grand ~ grande* [grã] ~ [grãd] 'big'
Other examples: *long ~ longue* [lõ] ~ [lõg] 'long';
saint ~ sainte [sɛ̃] ~ [sɛ̃t] 'saint'; *blanc ~ blanche*
[blã] ~ [blãš] 'white'; *profond ~ profonde* [prɔfõ]
~ [prɔfõd] 'deep'

(h) $\tilde{v} \sim vN$:   *plan ~ plane* [plã] ~ [plan] 'even'
Other examples: *plein ~ pleine* [plɛ̃] ~ [plɛn]
'full'; *fin ~ fine* [fɛ̃] ~ [fin] 'delicate'; *brun ~*
brune [brɛ̃] ~ [brün] 'brown'; *bon ~ bonne* [bõ]
~ [bɔn] ' good'

If the case of nasal consonants, to which we will return further on, is set aside, the only consonants that can act as feminine inflectional endings are obstruents. Adjectives ending in a liquid or a semi-vowel are in general invariable.[7]

Taking a form such as [dus] *douce* 'soft' (fem.), Durand proposes that the final *s* is the inflectional ending of the feminine. In other words, she proposes that the phonological representations of [du] *doux* (masc.) and [dus] *douce* (fem.) derive from something like /du/ and /du + s/, in which /du/ is the phonological representation of the morpheme *doux*, and /s/ that of the *Feminine* morpheme. Similarly, [tut] *toute* 'every' (fem.) would derive from /tu + t/ where /tu/ is the phonological representation of the morpheme *tout* (which appears without any inflectional ending in the masculine [tu] *tout*), and /t/ another phonological representation of the *Feminine* morpheme. One should therefore consider the *Feminine* morpheme as a suppletive morpheme that manifests itself with the allomorph /s/ after the morphemes *doux*, *gras*, *pervers*, etc., with the allomorph /t/ after *tout*, *mort*, *lent*, etc., with the allomorph /z/ after *curieux*, *mauvais*, *ras*, etc.[8] According to this view, French adjectives would be divided into a certain number of inflectional classes, a given inflectional

---

[7]   There are exceptions, the most salient of which are the adjectives ending in *ier* [ye] ~ *ière* [yɛr], such as *premier* 'first', *droitier* 'right-handed', etc.; see Selkirk (1972: 343–5).

[8]   The other adjectives besides *doux* and *tout* are: *gras* [gra] ~ *grasse* [gras] 'fat', *pervers* [pɛrvɛr] ~ *perverse* [pɛrvɛrs] 'perverse', *mort* [mɔr] ~ *morte* [mɔrt] 'dead', *lent* [lã] ~ *lente* [lãt] 'slow', *curieux* [küryö] ~ *curieuse* [küryöz] 'curious', *mauvais* [mɔvɛ] ~ *mauvaise* [mɔvɛz] 'bad', *ras* [rà] ~ *rase* [raz] 'level'.

class being defined by the fact that all the adjectives belonging to it call for the same consonant as a feminine marker. There would be as many inflectional classes as there are different consonants that can be used as feminine endings, with in addition the class of 'invariable' adjectives.

Thus, in the same way as French verbs are divided into 'conjugations' (the 'first conjugation ': *graver* 'to engrave', *jouer* 'to play', *trancher* 'to cut', etc., 'second conjugation': *gravir* 'to climb', *jouir* 'to enjoy', *franchir* 'to cross'), adjectives would also be divided into several 'declensions': the *s* declension, the *t* declension, etc. This analysis shows the morphology of French adjectives in a rather unusual light, but it has the advantage of starting from phonetic reality rather than conventional spelling and of being constructed methodically. But let us slightly expand the scope of the data we are examining.

In words derived from adjectives, it is nearly always the feminine form that appears in front of the derivational suffix:[9]

> *étroit* [etrwa] ~ *étroite* [etrwat] ~ *étroitesse* [etrwatɛs]
>   'narrow'   'narrowness'
> *jaloux* [žalu] ~ *jalouse* [žaluz] ~ *jalousie* [žaluzi]
>   'jealous'   'jealousy'
> *gros* [gro] ~ *grosse* [gros] ~ *grossir* [grosir]
>   'fat'   'to put on weight'

A feminine form also appears when a masculine adjective immediately precedes a noun beginning with a vowel:[10] *petit écrou* 'small screw' is pronounced [pœtitekru] and not *[pœtiekru]; *petit ami* (masc.) and *petite amie* (fem.) 'little friend' are homophonous: [pœtitami].[11]

By calling the final consonant of [pœtit] *petite* a feminine inflectional ending, it might look as if one were suggesting that it was a specialized indicator of the feminine. But the facts that have just been discussed show that this is not the case: the same consonant appears in *petitesse* 'smallness', where the problem of the gender of *petit* does not arise, and in *petit écrou*, in which the adjective is masculine, since it agrees with the masculine noun *écrou*. Rather than talk of masculine and feminine forms it would be better

---

[9] There are a few exceptions, such as *noir* (masc.) [nwar] ~ *noire* (fem.) [nwar] 'black' ~ *noircir* [nwarsir] (not *[nwarir]) 'to blacken', *nu* (masc.) [nü] ~ *nue* (fém.) [nü] 'naked' ~ *nudité* [nüdite] (not *[nüite]) 'nakedness', etc.

[10] On *liaison*, see p. 25 above.

[11] We leave aside certain voicing alternations: [s] in [fos] *fausse* (fem.) 'false' vs. [z] in [fozami] *faux ami* (masc.) 'false friend', [d] in [grãd] *grande* (fem.) 'big' vs. [t] in [grãtami] *grand ami* (masc.) 'great friend', cf. Schane (1967: 42; 1968b: 127).

to speak of a short and a long form,[12] for example, especially as the appearance of an additional consonant in derivational morphology and *liaison* is just as common in words that have nothing to do with gender alternations. Here are a few examples, (1) from derivational morphology: *débarras* [debara] 'riddance', *débarrasser* [debarase] 'to get rid of'; *mât* [ma] 'mast', *mâture* [matür] 'masts on a ship'; *tard* [tar] 'late', *tarder* [tarde] 'to be long'; (2) from *liaison*: *chez* 'at someone's home' is pronounced [še] in *chez lui* 'at his home' and [šez] in *chez eux* 'at their home'. As in the case of the adjectives, the additional consonant that appears in the above forms and in all other similar forms is necessarily an obstruent. Note finally that when the same word can appear alternatively as a derivational base or in a *liaison* environment, it is the same additional obstruent that appears in each case. For example, *trois* [trwa] takes the consonant *z* in both cases: *trois fils* [trwafis] 'three sons', *troisième* [trwazyɛm] 'third', *trois ans* [trwazã] 'three years'.

Thus, independently of gender alternations, a number of morphemes oscillate between two different realizations whose appearance is conditioned by the context: a short form and a long form, distinguished by an additional final obstruent, called a 'latent consonant'. For all morphemes, whether they are liable to gender alternations or not, we can postulate a single underlying representation corresponding to the long form, and from which the short form is obtained by taking away the final segment, if this segment is an obstruent. Thus the morpheme *plat* 'flat' has the underlying representation /plat/, whence the pronunciation [plat] in the feminine form *plate* and in the derived verb *aplatir* 'to flatten' where the final *t* is maintained, and the pronunciation [pla] in the masculine form *plat* where it is deleted; *rare* 'rare' and *flou* 'blurred' will similarly have the underlying representations /rar/ and /flu/, but as /r/ and /u/ are not obstruents they never disappear, and thus the long and short forms are identical. The pronunciation of these two morphemes is therefore the same in all environments: [flu] and [rar].

The rule responsible for the deletion of final obstruents has still to be formulated. Once it is noticed that almost all the derivational suffixes of French begin with a vowel, the similarity between the retention of the latent consonant in *liaison* and its retention in derivational morphology is striking: in each case, the following morpheme begins with a vowel and is closely connected to the preceding morpheme, i.e. it is separated by a morpheme boundary (*petit + esse*) or by a single word boundary (*petit # ecrou*). If we

[12] We have borrowed these terms from Blanche-Benveniste and Chervel (1969: 131).

leave aside the feminine forms for the time being, we can say that a morpheme-final obstruent is deleted in all environments other than——$+$ V and ——$\#$ V, i.e. in the following environments:

——$+$ C :   *petit $+$ s $\#$ ami $+$ s*   [ptizami]/*[ptitzami]
            'little friends'

——$\#$ C :   *petit $\#$ clou*   [ptiklu]/*[ptitklu]
            'little nail'

——$\#$ $\#$:   *c'est trop petit $\#$ $\#$*   [pti]/*[ptit]
            'it is too small'

We will thus postulate the following truncation rules: $TRUNC_a$, $TRUNC_b$, and $TRUNC_c$, and they can be conflated into the TRUNC schema.[13]

$$TRUNC_a: \quad [-son] \quad \rightarrow \quad \emptyset \quad / \quad ——+C$$
$$TRUNC_b: \quad [-son] \quad \rightarrow \quad \emptyset \quad / \quad ——\#C$$
$$TRUNC_c: \quad [-son] \quad \rightarrow \quad \emptyset \quad / \quad —— \# \#$$

$$TRUNC: \quad [-son] \quad \rightarrow \quad \emptyset \quad / \quad ——\left\{ \begin{array}{l} \left\{ \begin{array}{l} + \\ \# \end{array} \right\} C \\ \# \# \end{array} \right\}$$

This analysis accounts in a particularly simple manner for the way in which the plural is marked in nouns and noun determiners. Apart from special cases such as *mon ~ mes* [mɔ̃] ~ [me(z)] 'my' (masc. sing. ~ plur.),[14] *votre ~ vos* [vɔtr] ~ [vo(z)] 'your' (sing. ~ plur.), *principal ~ principaux* [prɛ̃sipal] ~ [prɛ̃sipo(z)] 'principal' (masc. sing. ~ masc. plur.), *œil ~ yeux* [œy] ~ [yö(z)] 'eye' (sing. ~ plur.), which require the use of additional mechanisms, it is only necessary to suppose that to form the plural of a noun or a noun determiner /z/ is added to the underlying representation of the corresponding singular form. As /z/ is an obstruent, it is deleted by TRUNC each time it is in the appropriate environment, and it occurs phonetically (as [z]) only in the environment ——$\#$ V, i.e. when the syntactic conditions allow *liaison* with the following word, and when this word begins with a vowel. Take, for example, *un petit écrou* 'a little screw' and *des petits écrous* 'little screws'; in the singular /$\#$ pətit $\#$ ekru $\#$ $\#$/[15] the

---

[13] This is only a first approximation. Schane (1967; 1968*a*) proposed an ingenious analysis which enabled $TRUNC_a$ and $TRUNC_b$ to be conflated with the elision rule responsible for the dropping of the vowel of the article (marked by an apostrophe in writing) in *l'étoile* [letwal] 'the star', *l'ami* [lami] 'the friend', but it appears that this solution is in the end untenable, cf. Milner (1967), Dell (1970) and Selkirk (1972).

[14] From now on we will give between parentheses the consonant which appears in the phonetic representations when all the conditions for *liaison* are met. For example, we write [me(z)] to indicate that one pronounces [mez] in *liaison* and [me] elsewhere.

[15] The schwa which occurs in the underlying representation of *petit* will be explained below.

final *t* of *petit* is not subject to TRUNC, whence [ptitekru]. In the plural $/\#$pətit$+$z$\#$ekru$+$z$\#$ $\#/$, this *t* is deleted by the application of TRUNC$_a$, for it is separated from the initial vowel of *écrous* by the plural *z*. This *z* is retained, for it is not subject to TRUNC. Lastly, the final *z* of /ekru$+$z$\#$ $\#/$ is deleted by application of TRUNC$_c$, whence finally [ptizekru]. Contrary to the difference between [ptitekru] and [ptizekru], one pronounces [ptiklu] both in *un petit clou* 'a small nail' and in *des petits clous* 'small nails'. In the singular $/\#$ pətit $\#$ klu $\#$ $\#/$ the final *t* of *petit* is deleted by TRUNC$_b$. In the plural $/\#$ pətit $+$ z $\#$ klu $+$ z $\#$ $\#/$ it is deleted by TRUNC$_a$ in front of the following *z* which is, in turn, deleted by TRUNC$_b$. Lastly, the final *z* of $/\#$ klu $+$ z $\#$ $\#/$ is deleted by TRUNC$_c$. We therefore see that if the contrast between the singular and the plural manifests itself as a difference in pronunciation in the case of *petit écrou* ~ *petits écrous* but not in the case of *petit clou* ~ *petits clous*, this is due simply to the existence of the phonological rule TRUNC, which allows the allomorph /z/ of the plural morpheme to manifest itself phonetically in certain environments and deletes all trace of it in others.

We give below the surface structures,[16] phonological and phonetic representations of *petits écrous* and *petits clous*.

(a) $\#$ *petit* $+$ *plur* $\#$ *écrou* $+$ *plur* $\#\#$ $\#$ *petit* $+$ *plur* $\#$ *clou* $+$ *plur* $\#\#$

(b) $/\#$ pətit $+$ z $\#$ ekru $+$ z $\#\#$ / $/\#$ pətit $+$ z $\#$ klu $+$ z $\#\#/$

(c)   [ptizekru]   [ptiklu]

The similarity between the surface structures in line (a) is due to the fact that the syntactic component of French has a completely general agreement rule that introduces the morpheme *plur* ('plural') after all the determiners of a noun which is itself followed by the morpheme *plur*. This rule affects the adjective *petit* in front of the plural noun *clous* as well as in front of the plural noun *écrous*. The similarity between the phonological representations in line (b) is due to the fact that there is a single spelling rule that associates the same phonological representation /z/ to all the occurrences of the morpheme *plur* present in surface structures. The similarity disappears only on moving from line (b) to line (c), i.e. by the effect of the phonological rules; *écrous* begins with a vowel, whereas *clous* begins with a consonant, whence the presence of the plural *z* in one case and its absence in the other. The phonological rule TRUNC, which must in any case belong to the phonological component of French if we wish to account for the alternations between the long and short forms previously discussed, therefore allows us both to account for the complex distribution of the

---

[16]   On the omission of labelled brackets, see p. 51.

plural *z* at the phonetic level, and at the same time to handle number agreement itself by positing a syntactic mechanism (agreement rule) and a morphological mechanism (spelling rule) each of a very simple kind. This is of course not possible unless sufficiently abstract phonological representations are postulated, i.e. representations that are sufficiently different from their corresponding phonetic representations. If our phonological representations only contained occurrences of the phoneme /z/ at the points where a [z] is actually pronounced, we would be obliged to consider that it is the agreement rule or the spelling rule which is responsible for the appearance of a [z] in [ptizekru] and its absence in [ptiklu]. If, for example, we assumed that the presence of [z] in [ptizekru] and its absence in [ptiklu] are due to the fact that the syntactic rule of number agreement has operated in the first case but not in the second; in other words, if we supposed that the adjective *petit* were followed by the morpheme *plur* in the surface structure of *petits écrous* but not in that of *petits clous*, we would have to formulate the syntactic rule of agreement in a more restrictive way: 'a noun determiner agrees in the plural with the noun it modifies if this noun is itself in the plural *and furthermore, if the noun determiner in question immediately precedes a word beginning with a vowel, under conditions that allow* liaison. Taking into account the fact that the allomorph of the morpheme *plur* is an obstruent (/z/), the condition in italics that we have just included in the formulation of the number agreement rule (a rule belonging to the syntactic component) has oddly enough the same effect as the TRUNC rule (a phonological rule). This condition characterizes precisely those environments in which a word-final obstruent is not subject to TRUNC. To formulate the rule of number agreement in this way is to deny the obvious: the alternation between [z] and Ø found in *petits écrous* ~ *petits clous* does not reflect any property of the number agreement rule itself. It comes from a completely general mechanism, the same as that responsible for the alternations between [t] and Ø in *petit écrou* ~ *petit clou* and between [z] and Ø in *chez elle* 'at her home' ~ *chez lui* 'at his home'.

If the TRUNC rule correctly predicts the behaviour of latent consonants in the cases of *liaison* and derivational morphology examined above, there is apparently one case where this is not so, i.e. the feminine forms. Consider, for example, *petite clef* [ptitkle] 'small key' and *petites étoiles* [ptitzetwal] 'small stars'. If we consider only what is apparent at a phonetic level, the final *t* of *petite* in [ptitkle] is immediately followed by the initial *k* of the following word and should be deleted by TRUNC$_b$, as it is in *petit clou*. Similarly, in [ptitzetwal], where it immediately precedes the plural *z*, it should be deleted by TRUNC$_a$, as it is in *petits écrous*. It would therefore seem necessary systematically to mark the feminine forms as exceptions to TRUNC–unless their exceptionality is only apparent and their behaviour really follows from some property of their phonological representation which is not immediately perceptible at the phonetic level.

Imagine that in order to form the feminine of any noun determiner, an ending consisting of a certain *vowel* /ə/ is added, and that this vowel is phonetically realized as zero in most cases. *Petite* 'small' (fem. sing.), for example, has the phonological representation / # pətit + ə # / and *petites* (fem. plur.) has the phonological representation / # pətit + ə + z # /. Thus the final *t* of the adjective *petite* cannot be deleted by TRUNC since it is immediately followed by a vowel, and it appears intact at the phonetic level, just as it does in front of the derivational suffix *-esse* in *petitesse*. In this hypothesis, the phonetic contrast between [pti] *petit* and [ptit] *petite* is a surface manifestation of an underlying contrast between the representations / # pətit # / and / # pətit + ə # /. Since the vowel /ə/ leaves no direct trace at the phonetic level, its presence is only indirectly marked by the presence of the final consonant characteristic of the long form. In the case of adjectives without a latent consonant such as *flou*, the contrast between the masculine form / # flu # / and the feminine form / # flu + ə # / is not indicated by any difference at the phonetic level. Both are pronounced [flu]. Since the long and short forms are identical, no trace is left at the surface level, even an indirect one, of the presence of the ending /ə/. The invariability of this kind of adjective is in the end rather a superficial phenomenon. Like all other adjectives, they are subject to the syntactic rule stating that adjectives agree in gender with the noun they modify and like them they take a feminine ending phonologically represented by /ə/. It is simply because of a particular set of circumstances that this ending does not leave any material mark in the spoken chain. It is rather like when two equal and opposing forces are exerted on a body at rest; the effects of these forces cancel each other out and the body remains static, as if it were not submitted to any force.

An attempt to attribute the surface invariability of these adjectives to deeper causes, for example by supposing that they are not subject to the syntactic rule of gender agreement, would lead to difficulties similar to those described above concerning number agreement.[17]

---

[17] Such a hypothesis would also imply that the adjectives ending in *-al* ~ *-aux* are liable to gender agreement only in the plural. For these adjectives the masculine and feminine forms are phonetically distinct in the plural, but homophonous in the singular: *égal* 'equal', for instance, has the following forms: masc. sing. *égal* [egal], fem. sing. *égale* [egal], masc. plur. *égaux* [ego], fem. plur. *égales* [egal].

All we know for the time being about the phoneme /ə/, whose presence we have postulated in the feminine ending, is that it is a vowel. But we know nothing of the quality of this vowel and it would be difficult to know more if it were always realized as Ø. Luckily for us, it sometimes occurs as a vowel in pronunciation. When a feminine adjective immediately precedes a word with an 'aspirated *h*',[18] /ə/ is realized as the vowel [œ]. We have, for example, *grosse outre* [grosutr] 'big water skin', *grosse poutre* [grosputr] 'big beam', but *grosse housse* 'big cover' is pronounced [grosœus] and not *[grosus]. The vowel [œ] that appears in such cases does correspond to an underlying segment, and is not simply a vowel that would be automatically inserted by a phonological rule each time a word with a final consonant immediately preceded another with an aspirated *h*; otherwise, it would be hard to understand why an [œ] appears in *quelle housse* [kɛlœus] 'which dust-sheet' and not in *quel hêtre* 'which beech' pronounced [kɛlɛtr] (homophonous with *quel être* 'which being') or [kɛlʔɛtr], but in any case not *[kɛlœɛtr].

If French has an underlying segment which is sometimes realized as Ø and sometimes as [œ] it would be very surprising if this segment never appeared except in the feminine ending. In fact there are other environments where the vowel [œ] alternates with Ø. Consider, for example, the verbs *secouer* 'to shake' and *skier* 'to ski'. When the preceding word ends in a vowel, the *s* and the *k* can be pronounced one after the other: [marisku] *Marie secoue* 'Marie shakes' and [mariski] *Marie skie* 'Marie skis'. When the preceding word ends in a consonant, an [œ] appears between the *s* and the *k* of *secouer* but not of *skier*: [žaksœku] *Jacques secoue*, but [žakski] *Jacques skie* (never *[žaksœki]). The same difference can be seen between *pelouse* and *place*. The *l* follows the *p* in [lapluz] *la pelouse* 'the lawn' and [laplas] *la place* 'the square', but in [sɛtpœluz] *cette pelouse* 'this lawn', there is an intervening [œ], whereas there is none in [sɛtplas] *cette place* 'this square'. The pronunciation *[sɛtpœlas] is never permitted.

In order to account for alternations such as that between [sku] and [sœku] there are two possibilities: the first consists of positing the underlying representation /sku/ where no vowel appears between /s/ and /k/, and to assume that there exists a phonological rule of epenthesis[19] that

---

¹⁸ On aspirated *h*, see pp. 237–8.

¹⁹ Epenthesis is the name given to a phonological process which introduces a segment not present in the phonological representation. The segment thus introduced is said to be epenthetic.

inserts a vowel *œ* between two consonants at the beginning of a word when the preceding word ends in a consonant. This rule, when applied to the representation /žak # #sku/ would yield /žak # #sœku/, whence finally [žaksœku]. But *skier* would have to be considered an exception to the rule of epenthesis so as to prevent it from operating in /žak # #ski/ *Jacques skie*. More generally, the words whose phonological representation begins with a group of consonants would need to be divided into two classes: those that are regularly subject to the rule of epenthesis (*secouer, pelouse, ferais* 'would do', etc.) and those that are exceptions to that rule (*skier, place, frais* 'fresh', etc.) The second possibility is preferable: the vowel [œ] that appears in *Jacques secoue* is the realization of an underlying vowel /ə/ which can be deleted in certain cases. We will posit the VCE$_1$ rule,[20] which deletes any /ə/ preceded by a single word-initial consonant when the preceding word ends in a vowel.

$$\text{VCE}_1: \quad \text{ə} \rightarrow \emptyset \ / \ \text{V} \#_1 \text{C} \text{——}$$

The underlying representation of *secoue* is /səku/. VCE$_1$ deletes schwa in /mari # #səku/, giving [marisku]. When schwa is not deleted, as in /žak # #səku/, where the rule cannot operate, it is rewritten later on as *œ*, giving finally [žaksœku]. *Skie*, on the other hand, has the underlying representation /ski/, without anything intervening between the /s/ and the /k/, and is therefore always realized as [ski].

To account for the deletion of the schwa of the feminine ending in such forms as *petite clef* /#pətit +ə #kle # #/ 'small key', where it immediately precedes the word boundary, and in *petites épaules* /#pətit +ə +z #epol +z # #/ 'small shoulders' where it is separated from the word boundary by the *z* of the plural, we will posit the E-FIN rule.[21]

$$\text{E-FIN:} \quad \text{ə} \rightarrow \emptyset \quad / \text{——} \text{C}_0 \#$$

This rule deletes any schwa which immediately precedes a word boundary or which is separated from it only by a consonant sequence. In order to show how the TRUNC, E-FIN and VCE$_1$ rules operate we have given

[20] The initials VCE stand for 'vowel–consonant–schwa'. This rule will be examined in more detail below. In accordance with the convention adopted (p. 121), $\#_1$ stands for a sequence of an undetermined number of # boundaries. The rule operates however many word boundaries separate the two words.

[21] The initials E-FIN stand for 'schwa-final'. This rule is only a first approximation. On the deletion of final schwas, see chapter 6.

below the derivations of *deux petits trous* 'two small holes' and *deux petites roues* 'two small wheels', both pronounced [döptitru].

$$/\text{döz} \# \text{pətit} + z \# \text{tru} + z \# \# /$$

TRUNC	dö	# pəti	# tru	# #
E-FIN				
VCE₁	dö	# p ti	# tru	# #

[döptitru]

$$/\text{döz} \# \text{pətit} + \text{ə} + z \# \text{ru} + z \# \# /$$

TRUNC	dö	# pətit + ə	# ru	# #
E-FIN	dö	# pətit	# ru	# #
VCE₁	dö	# p tit	# ru	# #

[döptitru]

TRUNC must be ordered before E-FIN. For if E-FIN were applied before TRUNC, the final schwa of $/\text{pətit} + \text{ə} + z \# /$ would first be deleted by E-FIN, giving $/\text{pətit} + z \# /$, a form in which the final *t* is no longer protected from truncation in front of the *z* of the plural. TRUNC must also precede VCE₁ so that at the point of the derivation where VCE₁ is applicable, the final *z* of $/\text{döz}/$ has disappeared and is no obstacle to the deletion of the schwa of $/\text{pətit}/$. Finally, E-FIN must precede VCE₁. *Petite mesure* 'small measurement' is pronounced [pœtitmœzür], never *[pœtitmzür]. In $/\text{pətit} + \text{ə} \# \text{məzür}/$ the retention of the schwa of *mesure* is explained by assuming that E-FIN begins by deleting the final schwa of *petite* so that when VCE₁ is applicable, the schwa in *mesure* is preceded by the sequence $/t \# m/$, an environment in which VCE₁ does not operate.

There is nothing paradoxical about considering that on the one hand the representation of *petite* ends in a vowel at the point of the derivation where TRUNC is applicable (whence the retention of the final *t*), and on the other hand this representation ends in a consonant at the point of the derivation where VCE₁ is applicable (whence the retention of schwa in *mesure*). This naturally follows from the fact that the rules are applied in the order TRUNC, E-FIN, VCE₁.

The possibility of postulating final schwas that are deleted by E-FIN leads us to account in the following way for 'invariable' adjectives with final obstruents, such as *lisse* [lis] 'smooth', *moite* [mwat] 'moist', *vide* [vid] 'empty', etc. Consider, for example, *lisse*, always pronounced [lis]. If the phonological representation were $/\text{lis}/$, the *s* would be dropped in the masculine and we would have the alternation [li] ~ [lis] parallel to *las* [la] ~ *lasse* [las] 'weary' (from $/\text{las}/$ ~ $/\text{las} + \text{ə}/$). It would be better to give *lisse* the phonological representation $/\text{lisə}/$, with a final schwa which forms an integral part of the stem. At the phonological level, therefore, *lisse* has a /CVCV/ structure and its *s* has no more reason to be dropped than that of *lasso* /laso/ 'lasso'. Thus, all the morphemes whose phonetic representation ends in an obstruent which never drops actually have a final schwa at the phonological level.[22] Contrast /ešardə/ [ešard] (*écharde* 'splinter') and /bavard/ (*bavard* [bavar] ~ *bavarde* [bavard] 'talkative, masc. ~ fem.'); /pəluzə/ [pœluz] (*pelouse* 'lawn') and /žaluz/ (*jaloux* [žalu] ~ *jalouse* [žaluz] 'jealous, masc. ~ fem.'); /rešə/ [reš] (*rèche* 'harsh') and /freš/ (*frais* [fre] ~ *fraîche* [freš] 'fresh, masc. ~ fem.'), etc. Like the others, adjectives of this type take the ending /ə/ in the feminine. *Lisse* therefore has a masculine from /#lisə#/ and a feminine form /#lisə + ə#/.

The analysis we have just sketched the main outline of is corroborated by the behaviour of nasal vowels.[23] Up till now, we have left aside the words whose long form ends in a nasal consonant and whose short form ends in a nasal vowel, such as *plane* [plan] ~ *plan* [plã] 'even (surface)', *plafonner* [plafɔne] 'to reach a maximum' ~ *plafond* [plafɔ̃] 'ceiling', *baigne* [bɛñ] 'bathes' ~ *bain* [bɛ̃] 'bath', etc. Here the deletion of the final consonant always goes along with the nasalization of the preceding vowel. Following the logic of the analysis we put forward, the feminine *plane* has the phonological representation /#plan + ə#/ from which [plan] derives by applying rule E-FIN. The masculine *plan* must have a phonological representation similar to that of *plane*, except for the absence of a feminine ending, namely /#plan#/. In order to derive the phonetic representation [plã], a rule must be postulated which nasalizes any vowel preceding a word-final nasal consonant and which deletes this consonant:

$$\text{NAS:} \quad \underset{1}{[+\text{syll}]} \; \underset{2}{[+\text{nas}]} \; \underset{3}{\#} \;\; \rightarrow \;\; \underset{1}{[+\text{nas}]} \; \underset{2}{\varnothing} \; \underset{3}{\#}$$

---

[22] Certain forms such as *sept* [sɛt] 'seven' are to be treated as an exception. If *sept* had the representation /sɛtə/, retention of the final schwa would be expected in front of an aspirated *h*. But *sept housses* is pronounced [sɛtus] or [sɛtʔus], but not *[sɛtœus].We have therefore to admit that some obstruents are exceptions to the TRUNC rule. A general distinction has to be made between those obstruents which are never dropped because they are protected by a final schwa and those which are exceptions to TRUNC. For a preliminary discussion of this question, cf. Schane (1967: 46–9; 1968a: 8–9), Dell (1970: 59–64), Selkirk (1972: 326–33).

[23] On the particular problems posed by nasals in *liaison*, see the detailed discussions of Selkirk (1972) and Dell (1973b). Concerning words with reduplication like *bonbon, cancan*, see Morin (1972).

In /#plan#/, this rule rewrites the sequence *an#* as *ã#*, whence finally [plã]. The presence of a final schwa in the representation /#plan + ə#/ underlying *plane* prevents NAS from operating, since the *n* at the end of *plan* is followed by a vowel. Although it has no direct phonetic manifestation, the schwa of the feminine has exactly the same effect as the vowel *i* in /a + plan + ir/ (*aplanir* [aplanir] 'to even out').

The NAS rule enables us to reduce the alternations [plã] ~ [plan] and [pla] ~ [plat] (*plat* ~ *plate* 'flat') to the single formula /X/ ~ /X + ə/, i.e. it enables us to preserve the generality of the rule that spells out the ending of the feminine as /ə/. It also enables us to explain why there are not (and could not be) any adjectives that have the feminine form [plan] and the masculine form [pla], parallel to [plat] ~ [pla]; for NAS guarantees that a final nasal consonant cannot be dropped without first nasalizing the preceding vowel.

If we had adopted an analysis where long forms were obtained from short ones by adding a final consonant, for example by deriving [plan] *plane* from the representation /#plã + n#/, we would have had to include a special clause in the grammar, stipulating that only short forms ending in a nasal vowel can receive a nasal consonant. We would also have had to postulate the rule NAS':

$$\text{NAS':} \quad [+ \text{syll}] \quad \rightarrow \quad [- \text{nas}] \quad / \underline{\hspace{1cm}} [+ \text{nas}] \#$$

Whereas NAS nasalizes vowels followed by a word-final nasal consonant, NAS' denasalizes them. Whereas NAS describes a phenomenon of assimilation that is widely attested in the languages of the world, cases of dissimilation similar to NAS' are, to say the least, extremely rare.

Such an analysis would also come up against difficulties due to the fact that the operation of NAS is accompanied by adjustments in vowel quality that sometimes bring about the phonetic merger of several underlying vowels. For example, [i] has as its nasal counterpart not [ĩ] but [ɛ̃]: *fine* [fin] ~ *fin* [fɛ̃] 'delicate' (fem. ~ masc.), *latine* [latin] ~ *latin* [latɛ̃], 'Latin' (fem. ~ masc.), etc. But in certain cases [ɛ] corresponds to [i], in others to [ɛ] (*plein* [plɛ̃] ~ *pleine* [plɛn] 'full', masc. ~ fem.), and it can also correspond to [ü] (*un* [ɛ̃] ~ *une* [ün] 'one', masc. ~ fem.). Thus, given a non-nasal vowel occurring in a long form, the nasal vowel of the corresponding short form can always be deduced, but the reverse is not true: the same nasal vowel can correspond to several non-nasal vowels in long forms. If the representation of *fine* were /#fɛ̃ + n#/ and that of *saine* [sɛn] 'healthy' (fem.) were /#sɛ̃ + n#/,[24] there would be no formal difference

---

[24] The masculine form is *sain* [sɛ̃].

between these two representations to indicate that the result of the denasalization of /ɛ/ must be [i] in the first form and [ɛ] in the second. Our analysis avoids all these difficulties. *Fine* and *saine* directly derive from /#fin + ə#/ and /#sɛn + ə#/ by the application of E-FIN. *Fin* and *sain* derive from /#fin#/ and /#sɛn#/ by the application of NAS, whence the intermediary representations /#fĩ#/ and /#sɛ̃#/. From /#fĩ#/ the final output [fɛ̃] is reached by the application of certain phonological rules that readjust the quality of certain nasal vowels, and one of their effects is to rewrite ĩ as ɛ̃.[25]

By writing the NAS rule, we are claiming that *some* nasal vowels derive from underlying /VN/ sequences: those that alternate at the end of words with [vN] in the phonetic representations. But what about those that do not show such alternations, for example, *hareng* [arã] 'herring', *selon* [sœlɔ̃] 'according to', *lent* [lã] ~ *lente* [lãt] 'slow', etc.? Since in these cases nothing suggests the presence of a nasal consonant, we have at first sight no reason not to derive these vowels from underlying /ã/ and /ɔ̃/. According to this hypothesis [marɔ̃] derives from /#marɔ̃ + ə#/ when it modifies a feminine noun, as in *jupe marron* 'brown skirt', and from /#marɔ̃#/ when it modifies a masculine noun, as in *chapeau marron* 'brown hat', just as [blö] derives from /#blö + ə#/ in *jupe bleue* 'blue skirt' and from /#blö#/ in *chapeau bleu* 'blue hat'. It is curious to note how rare the 'invariable' adjectives ending in a nasal vowel are,[26] whereas those ending in a non-nasal vowel are extremely common.

Let us suppose, on the contrary, that the list of French phonemes contains only non-nasal vowels, and that *all* the nasal vowels that appear at the phonetic level derive from underlying /VN/ sequences.[27] /VN/ sequences are realized as [ṽ] not only in front of a word boundary, but also in front of a consonant. NAS has to be reformulated.[28]

$$\text{NAS:}\quad [+\text{syll}]\ [+\text{nas}]\ \left\{\begin{matrix} C \\ \# \end{matrix}\right\}\ \rightarrow\ [+\text{nas}]\ \varnothing\ \left\{\begin{matrix} C \\ \# \end{matrix}\right\}$$
$$\quad\quad\quad\ 1\quad\quad\ 2\quad\quad\ 3\quad\quad\quad\ 1\quad\ 2\quad\ 3$$

The phonological representation of *lent* 'slow' is /#lant#/ where *an* is rewritten ã in front of the following *t* through application of NAS. This *t* is

---

[25] On these rules, see Schane (1968a: 45–50).

[26] See pp. 153, n. 6.

[27] See Schane (1968a: 142-3).

[28] Morin (1971: 168) has noted that this rule has a few exceptions, all of them slang words or borrowings: *clamse* [klams] 'he dies', *binse* [bins] 'thing', *round* [rund] 'round (in boxing) , etc.

deleted by TRUNC, whence finally the phonetic representation [lã]. Apart from the handful of exceptions mentioned in note 28, any [NC] sequence occurring in a phonetic representation derives from a /NəC/ sequence. Had the nasal consonant been in contact with the following consonant from the phonological level onwards, it would have dropped after nasalizing the preceding vowel. Thus, the lexical representation of *caneton* [kantɔ̃] 'duckling' is /kanətɔn/, whereas that of *canton* [kãtɔ̃] 'canton' is /kantɔn/.

Since adjectives normally take the ending /ə/ in the feminine, there cannot be any feminine forms ending in a nasal vowel at the phonetic level, because any nasal vowel derives from a /VN/ sequence, and /VN/ cannot be realized as [ṽ] when followed by a vowel. The phonological representation of *marron* must be /#marɔn#/ in *jupe marron* as well as in *chapeau marron*. If *bleu* and *marron* are both 'invariable' adjectives, this is not so for the same reasons. *Bleu* is invariable because the phonological rules associate the same phonetic representation to the phonological representations /#blö+ə#/ and /#blö#/. *Marron* is invariable because, contrary to the general rule, it does not take the ending /ə/ in the feminine, and consequently it has the same phonological representation /#marɔn#/ in both genders. The invariability of *bleu* is only a result of the normal operation of the morphological and phonological rules. That of *marron* is an oddity from a syntactic or a morphological point of view.[29]

The impossibility of having adjectives that regularly take the ending /ə/ and whose phonetic representation ends in a nasal vowel in the feminine should be related to the following fact: at the phonetic level, French does not accept word-internal sequences of two vowels, where the first is nasal. There are sequences such as [ea] (*béat* 'blissful') and [eã] (*séance* 'seance'), but there are no sequences such as *[ɛ̃a] or *[ɛ̃ã]. Indeed, if within a word any nasal vowel [ṽ] derives from a /VN/ sequence preceding a consonant, a [ṽV] sequence can only derive from a /VNCV/ sequence, in which the C is dropped after the nasalization of the first vowel and the deletion of N. But in French the only case where one can plausibly argue for the existence of an underlying consonant liable to be deleted between two vowels is that of the 'aspirated *h*',[30] and there are very few forms where aspirated *h* occurs word-internally, e.g. *enhardir* [ãardir] 'to embolden', *Panhard* [pãar] (a proper name). Apart from these, French words do not have [ṽV] sequences.

---

[29] One often hears children say **jupe marronne*, where *marron* is treated like a regular adjective.

[30] See pp. 237–8.

As a conclusion to this chapter, we will just mention a fact that takes us back to where we began. As Schane remarks (1967: 58; 1968*a*: 16–17) traditional spelling is very close to our phonological representations as far as the treatment of latent consonants and final schwas is concerned. As we have not at any point based arguments in support of our analysis on the facts of writing, this remark is not a logical necessity: it is an empirical finding. There is nothing puzzling about it if one shares the commonly held opinion that, in general, the principle of alphabetic writing is to match the phonological representations phoneme by phoneme. Of course, an agreement must first be reached on what is meant by a 'phonological representation' of French. When discussing spellings such as *plate* ([plat]) and *plat* ([pla]), Blanche-Benveniste and Chervel (1969: 139) are puzzled by 'this paradoxical practice of writing a vowel so that people will pronounce a consonant... [a practice which] creates a fictitious situation where the consonant is treated as if it occurred intervocalically, inside the word, and not finally...'. Their puzzlement is understandable, since they assume that *plate* [plat] and *plat* [pla] have the phonological representations $/\#\text{plat}\#/$ and $/\#\text{pla}\#/$. By generalizing the *t* of the long form, which allows the same invariant letter sequence P-L-A-T to be associated with all the occurrences of the morpheme *plat*, French spelling, according to Blanche-Benveniste and Chervel, would be using a device characteristic of ideographic writings, which transcribe all the occurrences of a given morpheme with the help of a single graphic unit and do not take into account the variations in pronunciation from one occurrence to another. But we have shown that the representations $/\#\text{plat}\#/$ and $/\#\text{pla}\#/$ are only an intermediate stage, and derive from more abstract representations $/\#\text{plat}+\text{ə}\#/$ and $/\#\text{plat}\#/$ by application of TRUNC and E-FIN. The invariability of the written representation of the morpheme *plat* reflects the invariability of its phonological representation.[31] The defects of the present French writing system are countless, but it must be admitted that on this point at least it offers a faithful reflection of linguistic reality.

---

[31] Our analysis predicts that school children should have no difficulty in mastering the writing conventions which stipulate that *plate* 'flat' (fem.) is read [plat], and *plat* 'flat' (masc.), [pla], since these conventions are the exact counterparts of the phonological rules E·FIN and TRUNC.

5

Schwa in closed syllables

First a word about the dialect of French described here. It is the author's.[1] The behaviour of schwa is one of the areas of French phonology where variations between one speaker and another are very frequent, even between people who have very similar pronunciations. It is therefore to be expected that many readers, even Parisian academics of the same generation, will be in disagreement over one point or another in the data that are used as the basis of our discussion. There are probably no two individuals who have an identical pronunciation, which implies that there are no two individuals who have exactly the same grammar in their heads. Of course, similarities between individual grammars largely override the differences, otherwise communication would be impossible. But the differences are too considerable to be ignored or treated as accidental vagaries around a fictitious 'average pronunciation'.[2] The grammar internalized by each individual is unique when it is taken as a whole, but this whole is specific to the individual concerned more in the way its basic parts are put together than in these parts themselves, which are usually also found in the grammars of other individuals, but combined in a slightly different way. Thus, though strictly speaking the grammar we are about to construct is only trying to account for our own pronunciation, our goal in constructing it is above all to provide a system of reference useful to the study of other pronunciations found in France.

---

[1] Born in 1943, he lived in a small village of the Yonne until 1949, since when he has been living in Paris.

[2] It has been known for a long time that some variations within a linguistic community can be correlated to sociological variables, such as belonging to a certain social category, or a specific age group. But it has only been discovered recently how precise and systematic these correlations are. The rigorous study of variation is undoubtedly an important advance in recent linguistics. Some examples of variation and a discussion of their theoretical and methodological implications can be found in Fasold (1970) and Labov (1971, 1972). On the role of variation in linguistic evolution, see Weinreich, Labov and Herzog (1968).

Most of the phonological rules concerning schwa are rather 'late' ones. We mean by this that they are ordered after most of the other phonological rules, and as a consequence, the representations submitted to them are fairly similar to the final phonetic representations. It is useful to introduce the following difference in meaning between the expressions 'phonological representations' and 'underlying representations', which we have so far used as synonyms: we will continue to call 'phonological representations' the representations that are inputs to the first phonological rule, whereas the expression 'underlying representation' will include not only phonological representations but also all the intermediate levels of representation that appear throughout a derivation. The underlying representations that we will examine will in general be the inputs to the late phonological rules that account for the behaviour of schwa, and not the phonological representations. In order not to bring in any unnecessary complications, the underlying representations we will posit will differ from the final phonetic representations only in those features relevant to the rules mentioned. For example, if we are studying the outcome of schwa in *patienterez* 'you will be patient', whose phonological representation is something like /pasiant $+ \vartheta + r + ez$/, we will take as a starting point a simplified intermediate representation such as /pasyãt $+ \vartheta + r + e$/, as, for the purposes of studying schwa, we are not concerned that the *y* of [pasyãtre] derives from *i* by application of SEM, that *ã* derives from *an* by application of NAS and that the final *z* is deleted by TRUNC.

SCHWA AND Œ

In the dialect described here, schwa is always realized as [œ].[3] For example, *quel genêt* 'which broom (shrub)' and *quel jeunet* 'which youngster' are absolutely homophonous ([kɛlžœnɛ]), as are *jeune vaurien* 'young scamp' and *je ne vaux rien* 'I'm worthless' ([žœnvoryɛ̃]).

These examples are timely reminders that not all the [œ] vowels that appear in the phonetic representations are derived from underlying schwas. The [œ] in *genêt* alternates with zero (*des genêts* [dežnɛ]), whereas that of *jeunet* is pronounced whatever the context: *des jeunets* 'youngsters' is always pronounced [dežœnɛ] and never *[dežnɛ]. If we attributed the same underlying representation /œ/ to the first vowel of *genêt*, *neveu*

---

[3]   The only exception is when schwa is retained in front of a pause as in *sur ce* 'this being said', *prends-le* 'take it', where it oscillates between [œ] and a vowel which is very close if not identical to that in *peu* [pö] 'little'.

[nœvö] ~ [nvö] 'nephew' and *geler* [žœle] ~ [žle] 'to freeze', and to that of *jeunet, neuvième* [nœvyɛm] ~ *[nvyɛm] 'ninth' and *gueuler* [gœle] ~ *[gle] 'to shout' (slang), it would be impossible to distinguish between the *œ*s that can alternate with zero and those that cannot at the level of the underlying representations. For this reason we will posit the underlying vowel /œ/ for the second type of *œ* only. For the first, we postulate an underlying vowel /ə/. For the time being, the column of feature specifications represented by this symbol *ə* cannot be exactly defined. We will simply say that it is a vowel which is different from all the others present in the derivations in that it alone is subject to such rules as E-FIN or VCE_1. We will add that, once all the phonological rules deleting or inserting schwa have been applied, the grammar has a rule which rewrites *ə* as *œ*. We therefore obtain the following derivations:

	les genêts	*les jeunets*	*quels genêts*
	/le # žənɛ/	/le # žœnɛ/	/kɛl # žənɛ/
VCE_1	le # ž nɛ		
ə → œ			kɛl # žœnɛ
	[ležnɛ]	[ležœnɛ]	[kɛlžœnɛ]

Seen in this light, differences in the pronunciation of *ə* from one speaker to another are a superficial phenomenon.[4] They arise from very late phonological rules.

We think it convenient to keep the letter *ə* in our phonetic representations as a means of representing those phonetic [œ]s that are derived from underlying schwas. But let it be clear that this is simply a notational device. When, in the following, we note [žənɛ], [žəle] for *genêt* and *gelé*, it is simply a way of indicating the pronunciation [žœnɛ], [žœle] and at the same time of drawing attention to the fact that the first vowel derives from /ə/.

E-ADJUSTMENT

The possibility of alternating with zero is not the only property that distinguishes the [œ] derived from /ə/ from those derived from /œ/. In conditions which we will try to define, [œ] or zero deriving from /ə/ alternate with [ɛ], as can be seen, for example, in the following alternations:

[4] On these differences, see e.g. Martinet (1945: 63–70), Pleasants (1956), Zwanenburg (1968).

appeliez [apœlye]^a ~ *appellera* [apɛlra]^b ~ *appel* [apɛl]^c; *hôtelier*
[otœlye]^d ~ *hôtellerie* [otɛlri]^e ~ *hôtel* [otɛl]^f; *achevez* [ašve]^g
~ *achèvement* [ašɛvmã]^h ~ *achève* [ašɛv]^i; *crevez* [krœve]^j
~ *crèvera* [krɛvra]^k ~ *crève* [krɛv]^{l,5} etc. At first sight, the principle
governing the alternations between ə and ɛ seems very simple; ə occurs in
open syllables, and ɛ in closed syllables.^{6} Knowing that a vowel is realized
as ɛ in closed syllables,^{7} one cannot predict for sure how it will be realized in
open syllables, as is shown by differences in alternation in *halète*
[alɛt]^m ~ *halètement* [alɛtmã]^n ~ *haletant* [altã]^o, and *alaite*
[alɛt]^p ~ *alaitement* [alɛtmã]^q ~ *alaitant* [alɛtã]^r. Contrast also *mener* with
gêner, *lever* with *rêver*, etc.^{8} On the other hand, a vowel that is realized as
schwa in open syllables is almost always realized as ɛ in closed syllables.^{9} It
is, therefore, the vowel ə and not the vowel ɛ that underlies the alternations
[ə] ~ [ɛ]. We therefore posit the rules ə-ADJ$_a$ and ə-ADJ$_b$, which will be
examined in turn:^{10}

$$\text{ə-ADJ}_a: \quad \text{ə} \rightarrow \text{ɛ} \quad / \quad \text{——C\#}$$
$$\text{ə-ADJ}_b: \quad \text{ə} \rightarrow \text{ɛ} \quad / \quad \text{——CC}$$

Let us first of all look at the forms that ə-ADJ$_a$ is supposed to account for.
These are forms where the ɛ deriving from schwa is the last pronounced
vowel, as is *appelle* [apɛl]^s, *appel* [apɛl]^t, *hôtel* [otɛl], *achève* [ašɛv], etc.
Note in particular the alternations which a certain number of forms

---

5   From /krəv/. Contrast with *abreuvez* [abrœve] ~ *abreuve* [abrœv] 'you ~ I water
    (cattle)', with no vowel alternation, from underlying /abrœv/.
6   On open and closed syllables, see p. 186.
7   The dialect described here does not distinguish between *maître* 'master' and *mettre* 'to put'
    [mɛtr], *bêle* 'bleats' and *belle* (fem.) 'beautiful' [bɛl], *fête* 'festival' and *faites* 'do'
    (imperative) [fɛt]. On these distinctions, see e.g. Grammont (1914: 38).
8   *en menant* [ãmnã] 'by leading', *on mène* [ɔ̃mɛn] 'one leads';
    en gênant [ãžɛnã] 'by hindering', *on gêne* [ɔ̃žɛn] 'one hinders',
    en levant [ãlvã] 'by raising', *on lève* [ɔ̃lɛv] 'one raises';
    en rêvant [ãrɛvã] 'by dreaming', *on rêve* [ɔ̃rɛv] 'one dreams'.
9   We leave the alternations ə ~ wa and ə ~ yɛ aside. Apart from the alternation between the
    weak and strong forms of pronouns (*que* ~ *quoi*, *me* ~ *moi*) and the conjugation of a few
    common verbs (*devons* ~ *doivent*, *venons* ~ *viennent*), these alternations only appear very
    sporadically and certainly do not play the central role in contemporary French phonology
    which Schane (1968a) has attributed to them.
10 ə-ADJ stands for 'schwa adjustment'.

^{a}'you were calling'. ^{b}'he will call'. ^{c}'call' (noun). ^{d}'innkeeper'. ^{e}'inn'. ^{f}'hotel'. ^{g}'you
complete'. ^{h}'completion'. ^{i}'he completes'. ^{j}'you die' (slang). ^{k}'he will die'. ^{l}'he dies'. ^{m}'he
pants'. ^{n}'panting' (n.). ^{o}'panting'. ^{p}'suckles'. ^{q}'suckling' (n.). ^{r}'suckling'. ^{s}'he calls'.
^{t}'call' (n.).

orthographically terminated by -*et* are subject to: *cachet* [kašɛ]ᵃ ~ *cacheter* [kašte]ᵇ, and similarly *paquet* [pakɛ]ᶜ ~ *empaqueter* [ãpakte]ᵈ, *jet* [žɛ]ᵉ ~ *jeter* [žəte]ᶠ, *soufflet* [suflɛ]ᵍ ~ *soufleter* [suflǝte]ʰ, *feuillet* [fœyɛ]ⁱ ~ *feuilleter* [fœyte]ʲ, etc. Following our analysis, *cachet* must have the underlying representation /#kašǝt#/, whence /#kašɛt#/ by application of ǝ-ADJₐ, and finally [kašɛ] by truncation of the final *t*.

If it is necessary to order ǝ-ADJₐ before TRUNC so as to enable it to derive the ɛ of *cachet* and of other forms whose last vowel is no longer in the environment ——C# once TRUNC has been applied, we can no longer use ǝ-ADJₐ to derive the ɛ in forms such as *(il) achève* [ašɛv] 'he completes' or *(il) cachette* [kašɛt] 'he seals', whose last pronounced vowel is not yet in the environment ——C# before the application of TRUNC. For before TRUNC is applied, the schwa that protects the final obstruent of the root from deletion is still present, and these forms have the representations /#ašǝv+ǝ+t#/, /#kašǝt+ǝ+t#/.[11] If the same ǝ-ADJₐ rule is responsible both for the ɛ of *cachet* and for that of *(il) cachette*, we are faced with an ordering paradox, since this rule must be applied before TRUNC in order to derive *cachet*, but after E-FIN – and therefore after TRUNC – in order to derive *cachette*, which is contrary to our general hypothesis that the order of application of the rules is the same for all derivations.[12] Before questioning this hypothesis, let us see if it is possible to account for the ɛ of *cachette* by a rule other than ǝ-ADJₐ, a rule which we would need in any case for other reasons. To do so, we shall examine the forms that ǝ-ADJ_b is supposed to account for.

This is quickly done. This rule always concerns the last vowel of morphemes that are followed by one of three suffixes; -*ement*, -*erie* and -*er*- (future).[13] These suffixes are, with a few others,[14] the only ones that

---

[11] The final *t* is the ending of the third person, which appears in the phonetic representation when it precedes a clitic pronoun beginning with a vowel: *l'achève-t-il?* [lašɛvtil] 'does he finish it?', *l'achève-t-on?* [lašɛvtɔ̃] 'does one finish it?'. The preceding schwa is a thematic vowel characteristic of the 'first conjugation' (cf. p. 187). On verbal endings, see De Felice (1950) and Schane (1968a; ch. 3).

[12] Cf. p. 75.

[13] -*er*- is broken down into /+ǝ+r+/, where /+ǝ+/ is the thematic vowel characteristic of the -*er* conjugation (cf. p. 187) and /+r+/ the future morpheme. But where this point plays no role in our discussion, we write the single suffix /+ǝr+/ so as to avoid overburdening the representations.

[14] These other suffixes are: -*eté*, as in *ancienn-eté* 'oldness'; the -*t* ending of the past participle, as in *écri-t-e* (fem.) 'written'; and the buffer morphemes written -*el*-, -*er*-, -*(e)t*- which appear between the root and a derivational suffix in some lexical items, as in *goutt-el-ette* 'droplet', *mouch-er-on* 'gnat', *can-et-on* 'duckling', *destruct-eur* 'destroyer'.

ᵃ'seal' (n.). ᵇ'to seal'. ᶜ'parcel'. ᵈ'to wrap up'. ᵉ'throw' (n.). ᶠ'to throw'. ᵍ'slap' (n.). ʰ'to slap'. ⁱ'leaf' (n.). ʲ'to leaf through'.

phonetically begin with a consonantal segment in certain contexts. In fact, at a more abstract level of representation, all three are separated from the preceding morpheme by a schwa.[15] The behaviour of this schwa is governed by the rules which delete schwa inside words, mainly rule VCE_2 which will be discussed in detail further on:

$$VCE_2: \quad \partial \rightarrow \emptyset \quad / \quad VC\text{——}$$

Schwa is dropped when it is preceded by VC and is retained when preceded by CC. Thus, the underlying schwa preceding the initial consonant of *-erie*, *-ement* is dropped in *hôtellerie* [otɛlri], *achèvement* [ašɛvmã], but is kept in *ébénisterie* [ebenistəri] 'cabinet-work', *raccordement* [rakɔrdəmã] 'junction'. As for the future suffix, /ər/, its initial schwa phonetically appears not only after CC (*écarterez* [ekartəre] 'you will set aside')[16] but also when it is followed by *-ions, -iez*:[17] *appelleriez* [apɛlərye] 'you would call'.

In such forms as *achèvement* /ašəvə + mã/, *hôtellerie* /otələ + ri/ it could be assumed that the VCE_2 rule first deletes the second schwa, whence /ašəv + mã/, /otəl + ri/, giving rise to a CC group that then enables ə-ADJ_b to rewrite the first schwa as ɛ. This hypothesis is untenable for the following reason: we will see later that when VCE_2 operates in a $VCəCə$ sequence, it deletes either the first or the second schwa as for example in *redevenir* 'to become again', which can be pronounced either [rədvənir] or [rədəvnir]. But if VCE_2 deleted the first schwa of /ašəvə + mã/ and /otələ + ri/ one would obtain *[ašvəmã] and *[otləri]. This can be avoided by assuming that at the step in the derivation where VCE_2 is applicable, the first schwa has already been rewritten as ɛ and is therefore no longer subject to VCE_2. But in that case one has to postulate the rule ə-ADJ_c, ordered before VCE_2. ə-ADJ_c rewrites schwa as ɛ when the vowel of the following syllable is itself a schwa. The alternation *sevrez* [səvre] 'you wean' ~ *sèvrera* [sɛvrəra] 'she will wean' (from /səvr + e/ ~ /səvr + ər + a/) shows that the two schwas can be separated by more than one consonant:

$$\text{ə-}ADJ_c: \quad \partial \rightarrow \quad \varepsilon \quad / \quad \text{——}C_1\partial$$

---

[15] It has been shown in detail (Dell, 1978*a*) that in the case of ·*ement* and ·*erie* this schwa is an epenthetic one inserted by a very early rule which operates only in front of derivational suffixes. The schwa of ·*er*·, on the other hand, is not epenthetic (see pp.187–8).

[16] See p. 208.

[17] See p. 239.

This rule is in any case necessary to account for such forms as *appelleriez* /apəl+ər+i+e/ [apɛlərye] 'you would call', in which ə-ADJ_b is of no use, since the second schwa is not deleted, and consequently the first schwa is at no point in the derivation in front of a *CC* group. We shall also use ə-ADJ_c to derive *achève* and other similar forms.

As it is so far formulated, ə-ADJ_c rewrites the first schwa of any əC_1ə sequence, without bothering about the distribution of morpheme boundaries. It is too general. Schwa is never rewritten as ɛ when it is at the end of a morpheme, see for example the first schwa of /də+vən+e/ *devenez* [dəvne] 'you become' or /rə+səməl+e/ *ressemelez* [rəsəmle] 'you re-sole' (shoes). Nor is it rewritten as ɛ when the schwa of the following syllable belongs to the same morpheme but is not morpheme-final, as can be seen in the pronunciation [ə] of the first schwa of *semel-* in *semelle* [səmɛl] 'sole' ~ *ressemeler* [rəsəmle] 'to re-sole', or of *genev-* in *Genève* [ʒənɛv] 'Geneva' ~ *genevois* [ʒənvwa] 'Genevan'. In fact, schwa never alternates with ɛ except in the environment / + X——C_1ə +/, i.e. when it is the last vowel of a morpheme ending in one consonant or more (a morpheme of the / + XəC_1 +/ type) or when it is the last vowel but one of a morpheme terminated by a vowel which is itself a schwa (a morpheme of the / + XəC_1ə +/ type). All the morphemes we have so far examined are of the / + XəC_1 +/ type: /otəl/, /kašət/, /səvr/, etc. But consider, for example, *etiquette* [etikɛt] 'label' or *Genève*, where the last pronounced vowel has a schwa as its underlying representation; witness its phonetic realization as Ø in *etiqueter* [etikte] 'to label' and *genevois*. These two morphemes must have underlying representations which end in a schwa, without which the final obstruent would be truncated for the same reasons as that of *paquet* [pakɛ], 'parcel', *nerf* [nɛr] 'nerve', (cf. *empaqueter* [ãpakte] 'to wrap up', *énerver* [enɛrve] 'to irritate'). These representations are therefore /etikətə/ and /ʒənəvə/. Rule ə-ADJ_c should be as follows:

ə-ADJ_c: ə → ɛ   / ——$\widehat{C_1}$ ə [− seg]

This rule rewrites schwa as ɛ when it is followed by one or several consonants that belong to the same morpheme, and when the following syllable has a schwa that precedes a word or morpheme boundary.[18] Let us agree that when the structural description of a rule contains the expression $\widehat{XY}$, this means that the rule in question affects all the XY sequences in which X and Y are not separated by a morpheme boundary, but the rule does not affect the corresponding $X + Y$ sequences. It is necessary to introduce this notation, for ∂-ADJ_c must be able to affect $\partial C_1 \partial$ $[- \text{seg}]$ sequences (as in $/\#\text{etik}\partial\text{t}\partial\#/$) or $\partial C_1 + \partial$ $[- \text{seg}]$ sequences (as in $/\#\text{aš}\partial\text{v} + \partial + \text{t}\#/$), but not $\partial + C_1\partial$ $[- \text{seg}]$ sequences[19] (as $\partial + d\partial +$ in $/\text{r}\partial + d\partial + \text{v}\partial\text{n} + \text{e}/$), i.e. it is essential that the first schwa and the following consonant belong to the same morpheme. We therefore have a counter-example to proposition (11), p. 113, which we had envisaged as a possible linguistic universal. Rather than simply abandon (11), it may be possible to substitute for it a less general proposition that would not completely exclude the possibility of phonological rules exclusively operating within morphemes, but that would limit it to the narrowest possible class of cases. We will leave the question open.[20]

Finally, we can account for all the facts of schwa adjustment by writing the following schema, ordered before TRUNC:

$$\partial\text{-ADJ:} \quad \partial \;\rightarrow\; \varepsilon \quad \Big/ \quad -\!\!-\widehat{}C_1 \left\{ \begin{array}{l} \# \\ C \\ \partial\,[-\text{seg}] \end{array} \right\} \quad \begin{array}{l} \text{(a)} \\ \text{(b)} \\ \text{(c)} \end{array}$$

Thanks to the $\widehat{XY}$ notation, ∂-ADJ_a rewrites schwa as ε in $/\#\text{kaš}\varepsilon\#/$ *cachet* [kašɛ] 'seal', but not in $/\#\text{kaš} + \partial + \text{t}\#/$ *(il) cache* [kaš] 'he hides' or in $/\#\text{kɛlk}\partial + \text{z}\#/$ *quelques* [kɛlk] 'few, some'. ∂-ADJ_b accounts for such forms as *cachets* $/\#\text{kaš}\partial\text{t} + \text{z}\#/$ [kašɛ] 'seals' (n.), *appels* $/\#\text{ap}\partial\text{l} + \text{z}\#/$ [apɛl] 'calls' (n.), etc. Thus, the only case in which the schwa of a morpheme of the form $/\#X\partial C_1\partial_0 +/$ is not rewritten as ε is when the morpheme is followed by a vowel other than schwa, as for example in *cachetez* [kašte] 'you seal', whose representation at the point where ∂-ADJ can operate, is $/\#\text{kaš}\partial\text{t} + \text{ez}\#/$.

We will turn aside from the ∂-ADJ rule for a moment in order to consider the elision of schwa in front of a vowel. This will enable us to bring in a notion that we will need several times in the following discussions: the notion of 'induced restriction'.

---

[19] There are no words containing $\partial + C_1 + \partial$ sequences.

[20] Of course we continue to accept convention (10) on page 112. This convention can indeed be adopted without the necessity of considering (11) to be universally true. Adopting (10) entails considering (11) as a universal only if any notation of the $\widehat{XY}$ type is also excluded. Once such a notation is used, to adopt convention (10) is to state that rules affecting both XY sequences and $X + Y$ sequences add less to the complexity of grammars than those which affect only $X + Y$ sequences, or those which affect only XY sequences. Indeed, formulating rules of the latter type requires the use of an additional ($+$ or $\widehat{}$) symbol.

The final schwa of a morpheme is always dropped when the following morpheme begins with a vowel, and this does not seem to depend on the number or the nature of the boundaries separating the two morphemes.[21] Elision takes place before an intervening morpheme boundary, as in *rouvrir* [ruvrir] 'to open again' (from /rǝ + uvrir/, contrast with *refermer* [rǝfɛrme] 'to close again', from /rǝ + fɛrme/). It also takes place before an intervening word boundary, as in *l'air* [lɛr] 'the air' (from /lǝ # ɛr/, contrast with *le fer* [lǝfɛr] 'the iron', from /lǝ # fɛr/), or as in *d'une autre* [dünotr] 'of another' (fem.) (from / # dǝ # ün + ǝ # otr + ǝ/), which is homophonous with *du notre* [dünotr] 'of ours' (masc.) (from /dü # notr/).[22] We will therefore posit the following elision rule:

ELIS: ǝ → $\emptyset$ / ——[$-$ seg]₁ V

This rule is obligatory and does not allow any exceptions. We have already said that in certain forms of the conjugation of *-er* verbs, the stem of the verb is separated from the ending by a thematic vowel, schwa, whose presence is necessary to prevent the deletion of the final obstruent of the root, as for example in *(il) cachette* [kašɛt] '(he) seals'. At first sight, a thematic vowel need not be postulated in such forms as *cachetez* [kašte] 'you seal', since the initial *e* of the suffix *-ez* already accounts for the retention of the preceding *t*. But in this case, the morphological rules governing the conjugation of the *-er* verbs would have to indicate which endings require a thematic vowel and which do not. It is much simpler to assume that all the conjugated forms of *-er* verbs contain the thematic vowel schwa in their phonological representations[23] and that like all the other schwas preceding a vowel, this thematic vowel is deleted by ELIS when the following ending begins with a vowel. *Cachetez* has the phonological representation /kašǝt + ǝ + ez/, which becomes /kašǝt + ez/ by the application of ELIS. Similarly, ELIS rewrites /etikǝtǝ + ǝ + ez/ (*étiquetez* [etikte] 'you label') as /etikǝt + ez/ and this must evidently be done before the application of ǝ-ADJ.

As it has been formulated, ELIS only concerns the schwas that are separated from the following vowel by one or several boundaries. What of the schwas that immediately precede a vowel belonging to the same morpheme? It is impossible to find the answer directly, for whereas French usually allows *VV* sequences within morphemes (see *cruel* [krüɛl] 'cruel', *pays* [pei] 'country', *chahut* [šaü] 'uproar', etc.), there are no morphemes

[21] But cf. p. 233.
[22] Cf. Delattre (1966: 145).
[23] Cf. Schane (1968a: 72).

where it would be necessary to give a phonological representation
containing a sequence /əV/. But this should not prevent us from
reformulating ELIS so that it deletes schwa even in front of a vowel
belonging to the same morpheme:

ELIS: ə → ∅   / ——[− seg]$_0$ V

This new formulation is more general than the preceding one, but it
remains compatible with all the data. Imagine that /əV/ sequences are
possible in the phonological representations, and that beside the morpheme
vélo [velo] 'bicycle' that has the allomorph /velo/, there is another that has
the allomorph /vəelo/. Both representations would merge as /velo/ after the
application of ELIS, and they would finally yield [velo]. We have already
met many cases in which two phonological representations lead to the same
phonetic representation. Thus, certain occurrences of [sɛ̃] derive from
/ #sɛn # / (*sain* 'healthy') and others from / #sɛnt # / (*saint* 'holy')
according to whether it is the adjective pronounced [sɛn] *saine* in the
feminine, or that pronounced [sɛt] *sainte* in the feminine. But in the case of
[velo] nothing enables us to clarify the ambiguity. Since ELIS is an
obligatory rule that does not allow for any exceptions, our grammar
predicts that /velo/ and /vəelo/ will always have the same phonological
representation [velo] *whatever the environment*.[24] Such cases of systematic
ambiguity in all environments are frequent. Take, for example, the
morpheme *saint*, to which we have just attributed the allomorph /sɛnt/. We
could just as well have attributed to it the allomorph /sint/ since the
grammar has phonological rules which enable [ɛ̃] to be derived from /in/.[25]
No alternation permits us to choose, since the phonetic sequence [sɛ̃-]
remains invariant throughout the occurrences of the morpheme *saint*.

In cases such as these, the decision once again hinges on considerations
concerning the global complexity of grammar: among all the
representations that are compatible at the same time with the morpheme
structure rules and with the phonetic data, the most 'simple' representation
is chosen as allomorph, that is to say, the one which least augments the
global complexity of the grammar. For the sake of convenience, we will
name this 'the principle of the simplest representation'. The principle of the
simplest representation is nothing more than a particular case of the general
principle by which the simplest of two grammars that generate the same set
of sound–meaning pairs is chosen. It is not necessary to enter into details

---

[24]   This is not the case for *sain* and *saint*, which are phonetically merged only in environments
      where TRUNC can operate.
[25]   Cf. p. 166.

here on the factors contributing to the complexity of lexical representations. Let us say simply that the complexity of a phonological matrix depends, among other things, on the distance that separates it from corresponding phonetic representations;[26] in the case where several phonological representations of the same morpheme are possible, all things being equal, the one closest to the phonetic representations of the morpheme in question is chosen. This is the principle to which we implicitly conformed when we attributed the allomorph /velo/ to *vélo* from the outset. *A priori*, /velɔt/, /velɔt/ or /velɔp/ could just as well have done the job, since the grammar must in any case contain rules enabling us to derive [so] from / #sot #/ *saut* 'jump' (n.), [sɔ̀] from / #sɔt #/ *sot* 'idiot', and [galo] from / #galɔp #/ 'gallop' (n.), and since these rules necessarily associate the phonetic representation [velo] to /velot/, /velɔt/, and /velɔp/ in any environment in which the morpheme *vélo* is liable to appear. But we do not know of any fact that would lead us to think that the phonological representation of *vélo* ends in a consonant. To prefer /velot/ and the others like it to /velo/ would be to complicate the lexicon uselessly. For the same reasons, assuming that /vəelo/, /veləo/, and /vəeləo/ are possible phonological representations, i.e. that they are allowed by the morpheme structure rules, they could not be retained as allomorphs of the morpheme *vélo*, for /velo/ accounts for the same data at less cost.

More generally, it is impossible *in principle* for a phonological representation of the form /XəVY/ to be included in the lexical entry of a morpheme, since dropping the schwa gives a representation /XVY/ which is shorter, and the organization of the phonological component guarantees that these two representations will always yield the same output whatever the environment. This means that it is quite superfluous to include in the grammar a morpheme structure rule specially designed to prevent / əV/ sequences in phonological representations. The impossibility of such sequences in the lexicon is a particular consequence of the principle of the simplest representation, since the phonological component includes the ELIS rule, which is obligatory and does not allow for any exceptions.

Amongst all the restrictions to be found at the level of phonological representations, we thus propose to treat separately what we will call 'restrictions induced in phonological representations by the phonological component', or more briefly 'induced restrictions'. Once the principle of the simplest representation has been accepted, these restrictions automatically follow from the existence of certain phonological rules that

---

[26] Here we are following Zimmer (1969).

operate within morphemes as well as across morpheme boundaries. Induced restrictions do not need to be explicitly stated in the grammar. The only ones that need explicit formulation (in the form of morpheme structure rules) are the restrictions that are not induced, such as the restrictions (R4) and (R5) on page 81. In other words, the set of possible allomorphs is the logical product of two sets: set A of representations compatible with the morpheme structure rules, and set B of representations compatible with the induced restrictions. Consider, for example, the matrices /lã/, /lɔan/, /lan/ and /lant/ in French. The representation /lã/ does not belong to set A, since there is a morpheme structure rule that excludes nasal vowels from the phonological representations,[27] but it does belong to set B. The representation /lɔan/ belongs to set A since there is no morpheme structure rule that excludes the sequence /ɔV/, but it does not belong to set B. Finally, /lan/ and /lant/ belong both to set A and to set B, and are two possible allomorphs of French; only /lant/ is actually attested (cf. *lente* [lãt] 'slow' (fem.)).

By recognizing the existence of induced restrictions, we avoid having to represent the same generalization in two different parts of the grammar: first in the form of a phonological rule and secondly in the form of a morpheme structure rule.[28] We thus differ from the commonly held viewpoint which in fact implies that the class of possible inputs to the phonological component is defined by rules that fall completely outside the functioning of this component: the syntactic rules and the readjustment rules, the morpheme structure rules being included amongst the latter. By introducing the notion of induced restriction, we imply, on the contrary, that these rules as a whole do not completely define the class of possible inputs of the phonological component, and that some constraints to which these inputs are subject are the result of properties belonging to the phonological component itself.

Let us now come back to the ə-ADJ rule. In forms such as *achetiez* [aštye] · 'you were buying' and *cabaretier* [kabartye] 'cabaret keeper', schwa is not rewritten as ε in front of a phonetic *Cy* sequence. Either we keep ə-ADJ$_b$ in its present formulation, in which case it must be applied before the SEM rule, that rewrites *i* as *y*, or else we reshape the environment of ə-ADJ$_b$ by replacing by [+ cons] the symbol *C* at the right of the brace; then the

---

[27] Cf. rule (R2) p. 80.

[28] We are referring to a classic problem which has been clearly stated in Stanley (1967: 402). The existence of induced restrictions explains, for example, the distribution of specifications of the feature [voice] within sequences of obstruents belonging to the same morpheme in Russian (cf. Halle, 1959: 61, 63–5), or that of the feature [back] in the different vowels of a single morpheme in Finnish (cf. Kiparsky, 1968*b*; Rardin, 1969).

order of application of SEM and ə-ADJ does not matter. We have no reason to prefer one solution to the other.

In morphemes which have, according to us, underlying representations of the form $/+X\partial C_1\partial_0+/$, the presence of schwa cannot always be predicted from the environment and cannot therefore be explained by the action of a phonological rule of epenthesis. This is illustrated by the opposition between *il triple* ([tripl], *[tripɛl] 'he triples') and *il appelle* ([apɛl], *[apl] 'he calls'), and similarly between *il exalte* ([egzalt], *[egzalɛt] 'he exalts') and *il halete* ([alɛt], *[alt] 'he pants'), *il riposte* ([ripɔst], *[ripɔsɛt] 'he answers') and *il époussette* ([epusɛt], *[epust] 'he dusts'), *il contacte* ([kɔ̃takt], *[kɔ̃takɛt] 'he contacts') and *il empaquette* ([ãpakɛt], *[ãpakt] 'he wraps up'), etc. Note also that in this position the phoneme schwa is losing ground. Schwa, in fact, never occurs in new morphemes which enter the lexicon. Since it has no means of renewing itself, the stock of morphemes that have an occurrence of schwa can only diminish in time. It is worth noticing the mechanism of this progressive disappearance, since it illustrates a kind of process that is frequently seen in linguistic evolution. The morphemes of the form $/+X\partial C_1\partial_0+/$ and those of the form $/+X\varepsilon C_1\partial_0+/$ cannot be distinguished phonetically when they are in an environment where ə-ADJ operates: the pronunciation [desɛl] represents *il décèle* 'he detects' (from /de+səl+ə+t/) and *il déselle* 'he unsaddles' (from /de+sɛl+ə+t/). We can clarify the ambiguity only by looking at related forms such as the participles *décelant* [deslã] and *désellant* [desɛlã], in which the morphemes in question are followed by a vowel other than schwa. But ask someone who has never met them to form adjectives from the names of the towns *La Rochelle* [larɔšɛl] and *Sartène* [sartɛn]. He will propose [rɔšelɛ] and [sartɛnɛ].[29] This shows that he attributes the phonological representations /rɔšɛl/ and /sartɛnə/ to [rɔšɛl] and [sartɛn], rather than the representations /rɔšəl/ and /sartənə/ implied by the forms *rochelais* [rɔšlɛ] and *sartenais* [sartənɛ] that are given in Robert (1967). More generally, when a morpheme is pronounced [XɛC₁] and the speakers are not compelled by any alternation to derive the [ɛ] from an underlying schwa, they will derive it from /ɛ/. Thus, as the ties between the different words of the same etymological family become looser, or as some words become obsolete, some schwas get reinterpreted as /ɛ/.[30]

---

[29] ... or [rɔšɛlwa] and [sartɛnwa]; the choice of the suffix *-ais* or *-ois* is irrelevant here.
[30] Here too, the lexical representations chosen are those which contribute the least complexity to the grammar. The fact that speakers prefer /ɛ/ is in accordance with the hypothesis put forward above, by virtue of which, all things being otherwise equal, the closer a lexical representation is to phonetic representations, the less it adds to the complexity of the grammar.

Should *chandelier* [šãdəlye] 'candlestick' disappear, *chandelle* [šãdɛl] 'candle' will have its present allomorph /šãndəl/ replaced by /šandɛl/.

Another process, complementary to the preceding one and founded on the same principle, weakens the position of schwa in the lexicon even more. Because of the VCE$_2$ rule, the morphemes of the type / + XVCəC$ə_0$ + / and / + XVCCə$_0$ + / merge phonetically when they are found in a context in which ə-ADJ does not operate. The pronunciations [krakle] *craqueler* 'to crack' (from /krakəl + e/) and [rakle] *râcler* 'to scrape' (from /rakl + e/) are identical except for their initial consonants, and it is the existence of the related forms [krakɛl] *craquèle* 'it cracks' and [rakl] *râcle* 'he scrapes' that teaches us that the /k/ and the /l/ are separated by a schwa in the phonological representation of the first verb, but not in that of the second. The verb *(se) craqueler* is already quite rarely used. Should it disappear, the only forms left will be *craquelé* [krakle] 'crackled' (adj.) and *craquelure* [kraklür] 'crack' (n.), and *craquel-* will be reinterpreted as /krakl/. Similarly, Martinon (1913: 174) remarked that the verb *décolleter* [dekɔlte] 'to bare the neck and shoulders' is conjugated more and more frequently like *récolter* [rekɔlte] 'to reap', i.e. as if there was no underlying schwa between the /l/ and the /t/. The stem *décollet-* is hardly used except in the adjective and the noun *décolleté* [dekɔlte] 'low-neck(ed)', where it always appears in the form [dekɔlt-], and the noun *collet* [kɔlɛ] 'collar', the root of this form, is no longer in current use except in idioms suchs as *collet monté* [kɔlɛmɔ̃te] 'strait-laced (person)' or *prendre au collet* [prãdrokɔlɛ] 'to take by the scruff of the neck'. Since the etymological relation is no longer felt, nothing prevents *décollet-* from being reinterpreted as /dekɔlt/.

Selkirk (1972: 396–8) accounts for the alternation between schwa and ɛ by supposing that the underlying vowel is not ə but ɛ, and by positing a phonological rule that rewrites ɛ as ə when the following syllable carries the word stress. This rule affects the second ɛ in /arsɛl + ɛr + y + e/ *harcèleriez* [arsɛlərye] 'you would harass', but not the first, whence [arsɛlərye].

But if we ask someone to form from *empaquetable*[31] derivatives ending in *-iser, -isation* analogous to the series *rentable* [rãtabl] 'profitable', *rentabiliser* [rãtabilize] 'to make profitable', *rentabilisation* [rãtabilizasyɔ̃] 'making profitable', the forms given are always [ãpaktabilize], [ãpaktabilizasyɔ̃] and not, as Selkirk's rule predicts, *[ãpakɛtabilize], *[ãpakɛtabilizasyɔ̃]. Similarly, when people are asked to construct an *-isme*

---

[31] [ãpaktabl]. This adjective, meaning 'that can be wrapped up', is derived from the verb *empaqueter* [ãpakte] 'to wrap up', itself derived from the noun *paquet* [pakɛ] 'parcel'.

derivative of *hôtelier* [otəlye] 'innkeeper' (from *hôtel*) [otɛl] 'hotel'), by analogy with the pair *ouvrier* [uvriye] 'worker' ~ *ouvriérisme* [uvriyɛrism] 'trade unionism', the form given is [otəlyɛrism] and not *[otɛlyɛrism]. Selkirk's analysis also leaves aside the fact that the ə ~ ɛ alternations only concern morphemes of the form $/ + \text{X}ə\text{C}_1ə_0 + /$. Finally, if the schwas that alternate with ɛ are derived from the underlying vowel /ɛ/, it is hard to see how we are to distinguish in the underlying representations the alternating ɛ vowels (as in *lève* [lɛv], 'he raises' ~ *levons* [ləvɔ̃] 'we raise') from those that always remain ɛ (as in *rêve* [rɛv] 'he dreams' ~ *rêvons* [rɛvɔ̃] 'we dream').

The schema ə-ADJ does not account for the change from schwa to ɛ or *e* in *congélation*[a] (cf. *congeler*[b]), *interpellation*[c] (cf. *interpeler*[d]), *appellation*[e] (cf. *appeler*[f]), *dénivellation*[g] (cf. *dénivelé*[h]), *angélique*[i] (cf. *angelot*[j]), *modéliste*[k] (cf. *modeler*[l]). This phenomenon is not peculiar to morphemes of the form $/ + \text{X}ə\text{C}_1ə_0 + /$ since it can be found in *secréter*[m] ~ *sécrétion*[n], *rebelle*[o] ~ *rébellion*[n], *tenace*[q] ~ *ténacité*[r], *reprocher*[s] ~ *irréprochable*[t], *remédier*[u] ~ *irrémédiable*[v]. It has to be accounted for by a special rule of a limited generality, restricted to certain 'learned' derivatives. We will not attempt to formulate it here.

Except for its structural change, the rule for schwa adjustment that we have been discussing is in all points similar to that which lowers *e* into ɛ in morphemes of the form $/ + \text{XeC}_1ə_0 + /$:[32]

$$\text{e-ADJ:} \quad e \rightarrow \varepsilon \quad / \underline{\quad} \, \widehat{\,} C_1 \left\{ \begin{array}{l} \# \\ C \\ ə\,[-\text{seg}] \end{array} \right. \quad \begin{array}{l} \text{(a)} \\ \text{(b)} \\ \text{(c)} \end{array}$$

[32] This rule corresponds to the rule which Selkirk (1972: 367–75) calls 'closed syllabe adjustment'. Although we have been using the data assembled by Selkirk and her remarks concerning this rule, we have come to different conclusions. Selkirk's rule rewrites as ɛ any *e* preceding *CC*, *C#* or *Cə#*. We leave it to the reader to find out that this rule does not account for all the data that motivate our own formulation of e-ADJ. See also p. 191, n. 50.

[a][kɔ̃ʒɛlasyɔ̃] 'deep-freezing' (n.). [b][kɔ̃ʒle] 'to deep-freeze'. [c][ɛ̃tɛrpɛlasyɔ̃] 'interpellation'. [d][ɛ̃tɛrpəle] 'to interpellate'. [e][apɛlasyɔ̃] 'naming'. [f][aple] 'to call'. [g][denivɛlasyɔ̃] 'change of level'. [h][denivle] 'change of level' (n.). [i][ãʒelik] 'angelic'. [j][ãʒlo] 'little angel'. [k][mɔdelist] 'designer (dress)'. [l][mɔdle] 'to design'. [m][səkrete] 'to secrete'. [n][sekresyɔ̃] 'secretion'. [o][rəbɛl] 'rebel'. [p][rebɛlyɔ̃] 'rebellion'. [q][tənas] 'tenacious'. [r][tenasite] 'tenacity'. [s][rəprɔše] 'to reproach'. [t][irepɔšabl] 'irreproachable'. [u][rəmedye] 'to make better'. [v][iremedyabl] 'irremediable'.

This schema is also ordered after ELIS and before TRUNC. e-ADJ$_a$ accounts for alternations such as that of *completer* [kɔ̃plete]^a ∼ *complet* [kɔ̃plɛ]^b, *péter* [pete]^c ∼ *pet* [pɛ]^d, *décréter* [dekrete]^e ∼ *décret* [dekrɛ]^f. *Pet*, for example, has the underlying representation /#pet#/, whence /#pɛt#/ by application of e-ADJ$_a$, and finally [pɛ] after deletion of the final *t* by TRUNC.[33] e-ADJ$_b$ accounts for alternations such as that of *insérer* [ɛ̃sere]^g ∼ *insertion* [ɛ̃sɛrsyɔ̃]^h, *protéger* [prɔteže]^i ∼ *protection* [prɔtɛksyɔ̃]^j, *gérer* [žere]^k ∼ *gestion* [žɛstyɔ̃]^l. Finally, e-ADJ$_c$ is necessary to account for *célébrer* [selebre]^m ∼ *célébrerez* [selɛbrəre]^n, *céder* [sɛd]^o (from /#sed+ə+·t#/), *cèdera* [sɛdra]^q (from /#sed+ə+r phonetic representation unchanged. This rule equally accounts for *cède* [sɛd]^o (from /#sed+ə+t#/), *cèdera* [sɛdra]^q (from /#sed+ə+r +at#/), forms from which schwa is later on deleted by rules ordered after TRUNC.

ə-ADJ and e-ADJ operate in identical environments and have the same ordering relations with the other rules. They are in fact one and the same process which merges together the three underlying vowels ə, *e* and ɛ into ɛ. Let us assume[34] that the underlying vowel that we note ə is [− high, − low, − round, + back]. This assumption enables us to collapse ə-ADJ and e-ADJ into the schema E-ADJ:

$$\text{E-ADJ:} \quad \begin{bmatrix} +\text{syll} \\ -\text{high} \\ -\text{low} \\ -\text{round} \end{bmatrix} \rightarrow \begin{bmatrix} +\text{low} \\ -\text{back} \end{bmatrix} \bigg/ \underline{\quad} \frown C_1 \left\{ \begin{array}{l} \# \\ C \\ \text{ə} \left[-\text{seg} \right] \end{array} \right. \begin{array}{l} (a) \\ (b) \\ (c) \end{array}$$

Condition on E-ADJ$_b$: $C_1 C \neq OL$[35]

Note that within a single morpheme, ɛ is the only one among the three vowels, ə, *e* and ɛ that can be followed by a *CC* cluster that is not an *OL* cluster. In front of an *OL* cluster one finds ə (as in *sevrer* [səvre]) and *e* (as in *célébrer* [selebre]) as well as ɛ (as in *empêtrer* [ãpɛtre] 'to entangle'). But in front of another *CC* cluster only ɛ can be found:[36] *mercure* [mɛrkür]

---

[33] e-ADJ$_a$ admits certain exceptions, such as *chez* and the ending *-ez*.

[34] As proposed in Dell and Selkirk (1978: 6-7).

[35] The reason for this condition will be given below.

[36] We are leaving aside complications arising from vowel harmony; these will be discussed later.

^{a}'to complete'. ^{b}'complete' (adj.). ^{c}'to fart'. ^{d}'fart' (n.). ^{e}'to decree'. ^{f}'decree' (n.). ^{g}'to insert'. ^{h}'insertion'. ^{i}'to protect'. ^{j}'protection'. ^{k}'to manage'. ^{l}'management'. ^{m}'to celebrate'. ^{n}'you will celebrate'. ^{o}'to give in'. ^{p}'you would give in'. ^{q}'he will give in'.

'mercury', *texte* [tɛkst] 'text', etc. For such morphemes, there is no alternation to indicate whether this ε derives from /ɛ/, /ə/ or /e/. *A priori*, [mɛrkür] can just as well derive from /mɛrkür/, /mərkür/ or /merkür/, since E-ADJ$_b$ guarantees in any case that the vowel of the first syllable will be rewritten as ε. In such cases we will systematically choose /ɛ/ as the underlying vowel. As for the resulting impossibility of allomorphs such as /mərkur/ and /merkur/, where /ə/ and /e/ immediately precede a *CC* cluster that is not an *OL* cluster, we will attribute it to an induced restriction which arises from the presence of E-ADJ in the phonological component. For this analysis to be possible, it must be shown that E-ADJ$_b$ operates in front of all *CC* clusters except *OL* ones; for if it operated also in front of *OL* clusters it would be impossible to oppose /ə/ and /e/ to /ɛ/ in front of *OL* clusters in the phonological representations.

We have no data indicating how *e* behaves in front of an *O* + *L* sequence, since there are no words for which a phonological representation containing an /eO + L/ sequence need be postulated.[37] There are data concerning ə, but they are very limited. The only forms in which an /əO + L/ sequence appears are the forms of the future of *devoir* [dəvwar] 'to owe' and verbs in *-cevoir*. Il E-ADJ were allowed to operate in front of all the *CC* clusters without exception, one would expect the pronunciations *[dɛvre] for *devrez* [dəvre] 'you will owe' /dəv + r + e/ and *[rəsɛvre] for *recevrez* [rəsəvre] 'you will receive' /rə + səv + r + e/. Rather than consider *devrez, recevrez*, etc. as exceptions to E-ADJ$_b$, we will formulate E-ADJ$_b$ so that it will not operate in front of *OL* clusters.[38] We can thus explain the systematic gaps in the distribution of /e/ and /ə/ in the phonological representations as a natural consequence of E-ADJ$_b$. Thus, E-ADJ$_b$ prevents *e* and ə from appearing in front of any *CC* cluster which is not an *OL* cluster, whether both consonants belong to the same morpheme or whether the cluster arises from stringing morphemes together.[39]

Let us remind the reader how the notions 'closed syllable' and 'open syllable' are traditionally defined for French (and for other Romance

---

[37] The only sequences *O* + *L* existing in French can be found in the future of certain verbs, where a root ending in an obstruent is immediately followed by the *r* of the future (*battrez* /bat + r + e/ 'you will beat'). There is no verb of this type whose root is of the form / + XeO + /.

[38] This is expressed by the condition $C_1 C \neq OL$ which we appended to the structural description of E-ADJ$_h$.

[39] ... unless the *CC* group in question wholly belongs to the following morpheme. See *restructurer* 'to restructure' and *déstructurer* 'to destructuralize' where *re*- and *dé*- are pronounced [rə] and [de], as predicted by E-ADJ$_b$, since the sequence ə +*st* and *e*+*st* are not subject to this rule.

languages): any vowel preceding a $C_1 \#$ sequence or a sequence of consonantal segments that is not of the OL type is in a closed syllable. The other vowels are said to be in an open syllable. Vowels in open syllables are therefore followed by V, $\#$, CV, OLV, or by a sequence of a consonant plus a semi-vowel. Once we have these definitions, we can see that the content of the E-ADJ schema can be described in the following way: *ə* and *e*, followed by a consonant that belongs to the same morpheme, are rewritten as *ɛ* when they are in a closed syllable *or when the following syllable contains a morpheme-final schwa*.[40] This rule would be more general if we could eliminate the clause in italics, which accounts only for the case where *ə* and *e* are rewritten as *ɛ* even though they are situated in an open syllable. It is worth making sure that E-ADJ$_c$ is not just an artefact of our analysis.

We have given two reasons to justify E-ADJ$_c$. The first is that we had to account for such forms as *il cachette* [ikašɛt] 'he seals' $/\#$kašət + ə + t$\#/$ and *complète* [kɔ̃plɛt] 'complete' (fem.) $/\#$kɔ̃plet + ə$\#/$, whose surface ɛ cannot be attributed to the operation of E-ADJ$_a$, unless the hypothesis that the order of application of rules is the same in all derivations is abandoned.[41] But since, in any case, there are now reasons to doubt the validity of this hypothesis,[42] these forms do not give us a decisive argument in favour of E-ADJ$_c$. The second argument in favour of E-ADJ$_c$ carries more weight. It is the need to account for *appelleriez* [apɛlərye] 'you would call', *sèvrerez* [sɛvrəre] 'you will wean', *cèderiez* [sɛdərye] 'you would give in', *célébrerez* [selɛbrəre] 'you will celebrate' and all the analogous forms in which a schwa phonetically manifests itself in front of the *r* of the future. But this argument is only valid if it is assumed that the schwa is already present in the representations submitted to E-ADJ, which is precisely what we have done (see p. 175). It could also be imagined that this schwa does not yet exist in the phonological representations and that it is introduced at some point in the derivation by an ə-INS rule, which inserts a schwa in the context $C + \text{---} CV$. If this rule is ordered after E-ADJ$_b$, one obtains derivations such as the following.[43]

---

[40] There is no doubt that linguistic theory will have to be enriched so as to give a theoretical status to the notion of syllable. On this topic, see the difficulties encountered in *SPE*: 241, nn. 2 and 3, and the suggestions of Hooper (1972) and Kahn (1976). Concerning the data covered by our E-ADJ rule, Basbøll (1975) and Cornulier (1977) propose analyses which bring in syllabic structure.

[41] Cf. p. 173.

[42] Cf. p. 76, n. 40.

[43] The phonological representations between diagonal slashes omit certain details which do not concern the present discussion, such as the final *z* of the ending *-ez*; cf. p. 170.

	appellerez	*sèvrerez*	*appelez*	*crevez*
	/apəl + r + e/	/səvr + r + e/	/apəl + e/	/krəv + e/
E-ADJ$_b$	apɛl + r + e	sɛvr + r + e		
ə-INS	apɛl + ər + e	sɛvr + ər + e		
VCE$_2$	apɛl + r + e		apl + e	
	[apɛlre]	[sɛvrəre]	[aple]	[krəve]

The two derivations on the left show that at the time when E-ADJ$_b$ is applicable, the schwa of the root precedes a $C_1 + C$ sequence and is therefore subject to E-ADJ$_b$. ə-INS then introduces a schwa that is subject later on to the same deletion rules as the schwas already present at the phonological level, as shown by the similarity between the two derivations on the left and the two on the right.

We can therefore get rid of E-ADJ$_c$ on two conditions: (1) if we abandon the hypothesis that the order of application of the rules is the same for all derivations, and thus the E-ADJ$_a$ rule could account for the ɛ of *cachette* as well as for that of *cachet*; (2) if we assume that the schwas that appear in *sèvrerez*, *appelleriez*, etc. do not derive from any vowel already present in the phonological representations, but from a vowel introduced by an epenthesis rule ordered after E-ADJ$_b$.

Point (2) seems to us difficult to defend, for not all verbs phonetically have a schwa in front of the *r* of the future, and it so happens that those that do have one are precisely the ones which retain their root-final obstruents in the three persons of the singular of the indicative, and in the imperative singular. We are speaking of the first conjugation verbs.[44] Compare, for example, *border* (root /bɔrd/) 'to border' and *tordre* (root /tɔrd/) 'to twist': *borderez* [bɔrdəre] 'you will border', *tordrez* [tɔrdre] 'you will twist', *borderiez* [bɔrdərye] 'you would border', *tordriez* [tɔrdriye] 'you would twist', *il borde* [bɔrd] 'he borders', *il tord* [tɔr] 'he twists'. This can be explained naturally by supposing that in the phonological representations of all the forms of the first conjugation, the final segment of the root is separated from the ending by a thematic vowel /ə/.[45] This thematic vowel protects a preceding consonant from truncation and manifests itself as [ə] when it is not subject to any one of the rules for schwa deletion which we will discuss further on. Thus the final obstruent of /bɔrd/ is deleted in the noun *bord* / # bɔrd # / 'edge', but is retained in *il borde* / #bɔrd + ə + t # /. A thematic

---

[44] In the 'first conjugation' we include all the *-er* verbs; in the second, all the *-ir ~ iss-* verbs (*finir, blanchir*, etc.); and in the third, all the remaining verbs (*perdre, servir, devoir*, etc.).
[45] Cf. p. 177.

vowel also underlies the schwa of *borderez* (from /bɔrd + ə + r + e/). On the contrary, the phonological representation of verbs such as *tordre* does not contain any thematic vowel, and the ending is directly in contact with the root. Nothing prevents the *d* of the root from being deleted in *il tord* /#tɔrd + t#/, and there is no schwa in the pronunciation of *tordrez* /tɔrd + r + e/.[46] By assuming that the *-er* verbs differ from all the others in that they have a thematic vowel /ə/ in the phonological representations of all their conjugated forms, we bring out both the impossibility of deleting the final obstruent from the root and the appearance of a schwa in front of the future *r* as two necessary consequences of a single morphological property. On the other hand, if we attribute the schwa of forms such as *borderez* to the operation of a ə-INS rule, all the verbs other than those ending in *-er* must be marked as exceptions to ə-INS. And if it furthermore happens that, in the singular of the present indicative, all the verbs marked [− rule ə-INS] have phonological representations that do not contain /ə/ between the root and the ending, this is by no means a necessary result; it does not automatically follow from the other properties of the grammar, and must be specially stated in the grammar.

If we accept hypothesis (2), we also have to give up attributing the gaps in the distribution of /ə/ and /e/ in the phonological representations to a restriction induced by E-ADJ$_b$. For to derive [lɛvre] from /ləv + r + e/ (*lèverez* 'you will raise') and [sɛdre] from /sed + r + e/ (*céderez* 'you will give in'), it must be accepted that e-ADJ$_b$ operates even in front of $O + L$ sequences. Furthermore, before ə-INS operates, the underlying representations of *lèverez* and *devrez* [dəvre] 'you will owe' are identical except for the initial consonant: /ləv + r + e/ and /dəv + r + e/. The only way to prevent E-ADJ$_b$ from operating in the latter representation would be to mark as exceptions to E-ADJ$_b$ *devoir* and the *-cevoir* verbs, which would have been already marked as exceptions to ə-INS.

For all these reasons, we think that E-ADJ$_c$ must belong to the grammar of French. For the time being, we will not try to explain why E-ADJ treats *ə* and *e* as if they were in a closed syllable when they are in an open syllable and the following syllable contains a schwa followed by a boundary.

VOWEL HARMONY

In the dialect described here, the regularity of the alternations due to E-ADJ is made less apparent at the surface by the operation of the following

---

[46] On the difference between *borderiez* and *tordriez*, see pp. 217–18.

vowel harmony rule:

$$\text{HARM:} \quad \begin{bmatrix} + \text{syll} \\ - \text{round} \\ - \text{high} \\ - \text{back} \end{bmatrix} \rightarrow [\alpha \text{ low}] \Bigg/ \underline{\quad\quad} C_1 + C_0 \begin{bmatrix} + \text{syll} \\ \alpha \text{ low} \end{bmatrix}$$

This rule is optional. It operates all the more easily in casual speech. It rewrites *e* as *ε* when the following syllable contains a low vowel that does not belong to the same morpheme, and it rewrites *ε* as *e* when the following syllable contains a non-low vowel that does not belong to the same morpheme. Thus *cédant* 'giving in' /sed + ã/ is pronounced [sedã] when the rule does not operate, and [sεdã] when it does; *aider* 'to help' /εd + e/ is pronounced [εde] when it does not operate and [ede] when it does. Whenever HARM operates, it cancels the distinction between the underlying vowels *e* and *ε* in front of morpheme-final consonants. The

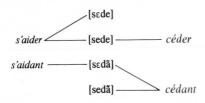

pronunciation [sεdã] can represent *cédant* /sed + ã/ as well as *s'aidant* 'helping (oneself)' /s # εd + ã/, and the pronunciation [sede] can represent *s'aider* 'to help oneself' /s # εd + e/ as well as *céder* 'to give in' /sed + e/. The distinction between *e* and *ε* must nonetheless be maintained in the phonological representations, to account for the fact that the speakers can have a more formal diction, where HARM only operates rather sporadically. It is a fact that the pronunciation [sedã] can only represent *cédant*, and the pronunciation [sεde] can only represent *s'aider*. The data are summarized in the diagram above. Our grammar accounts for this data, since it does not have any rules that can rewrite *ε* as *e* in /s # εd + ã/ (*s'aidant*) or *e* as *ε* in /sed + e/ (*céder*). As the formulation given above indicates, HARM must take into account the morphological make-up of words: *récolte* [rekɔlt] 'harvest' and *détail* [detay] 'detail' are never pronounced *[rεkɔlt], *[dεtay], and *prétend* [pretã] 'he claims' (/pre + tã/) is never homophonous with *prétant* [prεtã] 'lending' (/prεt + ã/).

From the point of view of HARM, the *ε* vowels originating from *e* or *ə* by the application of E-ADJ behave in exactly the same way as the vowels that were already ε in the phonological representations. *Céderez* and *lèvrez* are pronounced [sɛdre], [lɛvre] (when HARM does not operate), or [sedre], [levre] (when HARM does operate). *Cédera* 'he will give in' and *lèvera* 'he will raise' are only pronounced [sɛdra] and [lɛvra], never *[sedra], *[levra]. These facts are accounted for by ordering HARM after E-ADJ.

Whereas E-ADJ is the same in the grammar of all Parisians, (and this can be related to the fact that it is an obligatory rule applicable early on in the derivations), a systematic inquiry would most probably show quite important differences from one speaker to another concerning HARM, which is optional and late.[47] We have given below the derivation of *aiderez*, *céderez*, *lèverez* and *lèvera*, to illustrate the functioning of E-ADJ, VCE$_2$ and HARM. The first three forms have two different pronunciations, according to whether HARM operates or not. These derivations show that HARM must be ordered after VCE$_2$.

	aiderez	*céderez*	*lèverez*	*lèvera*
	/ɛd + ər + e/	/sed + ər + e/	/ləv + ər + e/	/ləv + ər + a/
E-ADJ		sɛd + ər + e	lɛv + ər + e	lɛv + ər + a
VCE$_2$	ɛd + r + e	sɛd + r + e	lɛv + r + e	lɛv + r + a
HARM	(ed + r + e)	(sed + r + e)	(lev + r + e)	
	[ɛdre]	[sɛdre]	[lɛvre]	[lɛvra]
	or [edre]	or [sedre]	or [levre]	

To conclude our discussion of E-ADJ, just a word about pronunciations like [ɛlve] and [prɛvne], that appear as alternates to [elve] *élevé* 'raised/brought up' and [prevne] *prévenez* 'you warn'. The realization [ε] of the /e/ in the first syllable of these words cannot be due to HARM, since the vowel of the second syllable is non-low. Neither can it be attributed to E-ADJ; for in /e + ləv + e/ *élevé*, for example, the sequence /e + C$_1$ə/ occurs, and not the sequence /e͡C$_1$ə/, as required by the structural description of E-ADJ$_c$. Whereas the lowering of *e* to *ε* is obligatory in /e͡C$_1$ə/ (cf. *cédera* [sɛdra] *[sedra]), it is optional in /e + C$_1$ə/, as shown by the fact that

---

[47] The existence of such variations is reflected in the literature. Grammont (1914) and Fouché (1956), on which Selkirk (1972) bases her treatment of vowel harmony, only mention the transformation of *ε* to *e* in front of a non-low vowel. On the other hand, Malmberg (1969) and Morin (1971) also discuss *e* becoming *ε* in front of a low vowel. Furthermore Fouché (p. 71) and Malmberg (p. 32) describe dialects where harmony does not affect *ε* in closed syllables, whereas ours does not have this restriction: *rester* and *perdrez* can be pronounced [reste] and [perdre]. Lastly, Morin (p. 98) describes a dialect where the harmony operates without taking morpheme boundaries into account.

élevant can be pronounced [elvã] as well as [ɛlvã]. In short, we are dealing with a different rule from E-ADJ$_c$. The comparison between *céderiez* [sɛdərye]/*[sedərye] 'you would give in ' and *dételiez* [detəlye]/*[dɛtəlye] 'you unharnessed' (as compared with *dételez* [detle]/[dɛtle] 'you unharness'), shows that whereas in $/\widehat{eC_1}ə/$ the lowering of *e* takes place whatever the fate of the following schwa, in $/e + C_1ə/$, this lowering can take place only if the schwa is deleted. We will therefore posit the following optional rule, ordered after VCE$_2$ which is responsible for the deletion of word-internal schwas:[48]

e-LOW: e → ɛ / ⎯⎯ CC

This is only a first approximation. The structural description must include restrictions which prevent the rule from affecting *eCC* sequences where the *CC* cluster comes straight from the phonological representations,[49] as in *pénétrer* 'to penetrate' and *déstructurer* 'to destructurize' which cannot be pronounced *[penɛtre] or *[dɛstrüktüre]. Whatever the exact formulation of e-LOW it is out of the question to conflate it with E-ADJ$_b$, since E-ADJ$_b$ is ordered before VCE$_2$, and e-LOW is ordered after VCE$_2$. The coexistence of E-ADJ$_b$ and e-LOW in the same grammar is certainly not fortuitous, but the formalism developed here does not enable us to throw light on the deep ties that unite them;[50] for the abbreviatory conventions of rule schemata enable us to take advantage of formal similarities between rules only when these rules are adjacent.

WORD STRESS

To conclude this chapter, let us say a few words on the rules governing the positioning of word stress in French; we have to have an idea of them, in order to understand certain developments in the following chapter. They can be described as follows:

STR$_1$: in words that have more than one vowel, and where the last vowel is a schwa, the stress falls on the penultimate vowel.

STR$_2$: in all words that are not subject to the preceding rule, the stress falls on the last vowel.

[48] e-LOW stands for 'lowering of *e*'.
[49] In such sequences, *CC* is necessarily a morpheme-initial cluster (cf. p. 185, n. 39) or an *OL* cluster, or both, since all the other *eCC* sequences are eliminated by E-ADJ$_b$.
[50] Selkirk (1972) has a single rule schema to account for the ɛ of [ɛlve] *élever* 'to bring up' and that of [kɔ̃plɛ] *complet* 'complete'. She has to order it after VCE$_2$ in order to account for the first form (p. 407) and before TRUNC in order to account for the second (p. 371), which is impossible since TRUNC precedes VCE$_2$.

By virtue of STR_1, the stress falls on the penultimate vowel of the first word in, for example, *cette   housse* [sɛtəús] 'this dust-sheet',[51] *énorme hache* [enɔ́rməáš] 'enormous axe', *quelques amis* [kɛ́lkəzamí] 'a few friends'. This rule is formally written as follows:

$$STR_1: \qquad V \;\rightarrow\; \acute{V} \quad / \quad \text{——} C_0 \partial C_0 \#$$

STR_2 concerns any word that is not subject to STR_1, i.e. words with only one vowel (this vowel can be a schwa) and words whose last vowel is not a schwa: *cé tás* 'this pile', *quél tracás* 'what a bother', *tracassér* 'to bother', *tracasseréz* 'you will bother', *plús bavárd qué Marcél* 'more talkative than Marcel'. Let it be quite clear that we are only dealing with *word* stress here, and not with *phrase* stress. In a sentence such as *rends-les-moi ce soir* 'give them back to me tonight', STR_2 places a word stress on each of the five monosyllables. These five equally stressed syllables are not what is heard, however, but something more like *rénds-les-mói ce sóir*. Besides word stress rules, a complete grammar of French must contain stress rules for groups of words and for whole sentences. In the same way as word stress rules give preeminence to a specific syllable over all the others in the same word, the rules for phrase stress establish a hierarchy between the various word stresses within a phrase. For French, these rules have yet to be discovered. Note that monosyllables of the form $\# C \partial \#$ must be given a word stress, since some of them can bear the main stress of a phrase: *sur ce* [sürsö] 'this being said', *attrape-le* [atraplö] 'catch it', *parce que* [paskö] 'because'.[52] It is true that such cases are fairly rare. But this is due to the fact that rules for phrase stress give preeminence to the stress of the last word in a phrase and the syntactic properties of $\# C \partial \#$ monosyllables generally prevent them from being the last word of a phrase.

If STR_2 only takes into account forms that are not subject to STR_1, it can be written as follows:

$$STR_2: \qquad V \;\rightarrow\; \acute{V} \quad / \quad \text{——} C_0 \#$$

Let us agree that, in general, the expression X(Y)Z is an abbreviated notation for the expressions XYZ and XZ, taken in that order. We can then conflate the two rules STR_1 and STR_2 into the schema STR:[53]

$$STR: \qquad V \;\rightarrow\; \acute{V} \quad / \quad \text{——} C_0(\partial C_0)\#$$

---

[51] We put an acute accent above a vowel to indicate that the syllable to which the vowel belongs carries the word stress.

[52] When this word is pronounced alone (as in an evasive or peremptory reply).

[53] The complete definition of parenthesis notation not only implies that STR_1 precedes STR_2 but also that any form which is subject to STR_1 is not subject to STR_2. Rules conflated with the help of this notation are said to be disjunctively ordered. We merely mention disjunctive ordering, since in this book it only plays a role in the stress rule. Detailed explanations of parenthesis notation and disjunctive ordering can be found in *SPE*: 30, 36, 61–4, 71, n. 16.

As it is formulated, STR must be ordered after E-ADJ. The representation /otel/ (*hôtel*) becomes /otɛl/ by application of E-ADJ, a form that is then stressed on the second syllable by STR$_2$. If STR were applied first, /otəl/ would receive the stress on the first syllable because of STR$_1$ (as in *quelques*), whence final *[ótɛl] instead of the grammatical form [otɛ́l].

For the time being, STR can be ordered either before or after the rule that deletes schwa at the end of words. Take, for example, a feminine form such as [žaluz] *jalouse* 'jealous' (fem.), that has the phonological representation /#žaluz + ə#/. If the stress rule is ordered before the rule for the deletion of final schwas, this form will be stressed on the *u* because of STR$_1$. If, on the contrary, the stress rule is ordered after E-FIN, the representation submitted to STR will be /#žaluz#/, and again *u* will receive the stress, but this time because of STR$_2$. Note that even if we ordered STR after E-FIN, we still could not dispense with STR$_1$, since some final schwas (a very small number) are not deleted, and are present from one end of the derivation to the other. This is for instance the case of the final schwa of *cette* in *cette housse* [sɛ́təús] 'this dust-sheet'; forms like this one require a rule that places the stress on the penultimate vowel when the last one is a schwa.

To conclude: in French, the phoneme /ə/ is realized sometimes as [ɛ],[54] sometimes as [œ] and sometimes as zero. We have assumed that in its underlying form it is [− high, − low, − round, + back], but it must be borne in mind that it never surfaces with these specifications in the phonetic representations. Leaving aside cases where schwa is at the end of words (*le*, *quelques*), its phonetic manifestation is always confused with that of another phoneme which can appear in the same context; nothing at the surface distinguishes the [œ] of *abreuvons* [abrœvõ] 'we give water to', which derives from /œ/, from that of *crevons* [krœvõ] 'we die' (slang), which derives from /ə/, and nothing distinguishes the [ɛ] of *rêve* [rɛv] 'he dreams', which derives from /ɛ/, from that of *crève* [krɛv] 'he dies' (slang), which derives from /ə/. What distinguishes schwa from other underlying vowels is therefore less the quality of its phonetic realizations than the particular network of alternations which it undergoes.

We will leave it to the reader to see for himself that the joint operation of ə-ADJ and STR guarantees, at the level of phonetic representations, that schwa – or more exactly [œ] originating from /ə/ – does have the following properties, which have already been noticed by many linguists: (a) apart from the case of #Cə# monosyllables, schwa never appears with word

---

[54]   ... or as [e] by vowel harmony.

stress; (b) within words, the only sequences of consonantal segments that can appear after schwa are *OL* clusters or morpheme-initial clusters. Strictly speaking, this last assertion is not true of the phonetic representations, but of the intermediate representations which are inputs to VCE_2; for example, it is true for the representation /žənəv + wa/ (*Genevois* ' Genevan '), input to VCE_2, but not for [žənvwa] where the application of VCE_2 has created an *nv* cluster that immediately follows the first schwa.

6

Rules for the deletion of schwa

The principles governing the deletion and retention of schwa have already been much written about.[1] To our knowledge, the first attempt to treat the subject systematically dates from the book by Mende (1880). But the real start was given by Grammont (1894; 1914), whose works were the beginning of a series of more and more exhaustive descriptions: Martinon (1913), Leray (1930), Fouché (1956), and Delattre (1966: 17–36), to cite only the most important.[2] These authors have attempted to give as complete a catalogue of the facts as possible, but the absence of any linguistic theory prevented them from giving a description organized as a structured whole. Attempts in this direction were made by Weinrich (1958: 248–60) and Pulgram (1961), but the attentive reader will be easily convinced that they only account for a small part of the data presented here.

We will adopt the following conventions. When we wish to indicate that a schwa is obligatorily pronounced, the letter ə or the e corresponding to it in the orthography will be underlined. For example, we will write [krəve] or cre̲vez 'you die' (slang) to indicate that this word is obligatorily pronounced [krəve], never *[krve]. Parentheses will indicate that the pronunciation of a schwa is optional. We will write, for example, [vɛst(ə)marɔ̃] or vest(e) marron 'brown jacket' to indicate that the pronunciations [vɛstəmarɔ̃] and [vɛstmarɔ̃] are equally possible. A letter with a slash through it will indicate that schwa is obligatorily dropped: for example, we will write [grosⱥtɛtⱥ] or grossⱥ têtⱥ 'fat head' to indicate that the only possible pronunciation is [grostɛt].

---

[1] The present chapter is an expanded version of the first chapter of a PhD thesis written under the direction of Morris Halle (Dell, 1970).

[2] Other references can be found in Martinet (1945) and Zwanenburg (1968). For references to work done after the publication of this book in French, cf. *Studies in French Linguistics* I-2 (1978), which is devoted to French phonology.

DELETION AFTER A VOWEL AND DELETION AFTER A PAUSE

Schwa is obligatorily deleted when it follows a vowel. [3] *Je li¢rai* [lirɛ] 'I
will tie' (from *lier*, to tie) and *je lirai* 'I will read' (from *lire*, to read) are
pronounced in the same way. Compare also *remerci¢ment* [rəmɛrsimã]
'thanks' and *débarqu̲e̲ment* [debarkəmã] 'disembarkation', *vous jou¢riez*
[žurye] 'you would play' and *vous parl̲e̲riez* [parlərye] 'you would speak',
elle est parti¢ trop tôt [ɛlɛpartitroto] 'she left too soon' and *elle est mort(e)
trop tôt* [ɛlɛmɔrt(ə)troto] 'she died too soon'. We will therefore write the
following rule:[4]

V-E: ə → Ø   /   V——

V-E must be applied before rule SEM, that rewrites a high vowel
followed by a vowel as a semi-vowel.[5] Thus when SEM is applicable, V-E
has already deleted the schwa from the sequences $u + ə$, $ü + ə$ and $i + ə$, see,
for example, [avwe] *avouez* 'you admit' and [avu] *avoue* 'he admits', that
respectively derive from /avu + ez/ and /avu + ə + t/. More generally, the
order of application of V-E and SEM accounts for the fact that there are no
*[wə] or *[ẅə] sequences in phonetic representations, nor any [yə]
sequences where the [y] derives from /i/. There are no *[wə] or *[ẅə]
sequences because the only source of [w] and [ẅ] is /u/ and /ü/ (by the
application of SEM), and the order of V-E and SEM guarantees that the
sequences /u + ə/ and /ü + ə/ phonetically manifest themselves as [u]
and [ü]. Similarly, the sequences /i + ə/ necessarily manifest themselves as
[i]. There are [yə] sequences, as for example in *vieille housse* [vyɛyəus]
'old dust-sheet', *fouilleriez* [fuyərye] 'you would search' but the [y] that
occurs there does not derive from an /i/.[6]

There are no morphemes whose phonological representation has a /Və/
sequence. We can conclude, by using an argument in all points similar to
the one given for ELIS (p. 179), that it is not necessary to write a special
morpheme structure rule to exclude the /Və/ sequences from the phonological representations. Given two phonological matrices /XVəY/ and

---

[3] The existence of a schwa in the following examples has been justified in the preceding
chapters. Concerning the underlying schwa in *lierai, joueriez, parleriez*, cf. p. 188; for the
schwa preceding the suffix *-ment* in *remerciement, débarquement*, cf. p. 174; lastly, on the
feminine ending in *partie* and *morte*, cf. chapter 4.
[4] The initials V-E stand for 'vowel-schwa'.
[5] Cf. p. 68.
[6] Postvocalic yods, written *-il(l-)* as in *rail* [ray] 'track', *dérailler* [deraye] 'to go off the
tracks' or *-y-* as in *balayer* [baleye] 'to sweep', *royal* [rwayal] 'royal', never derive from
/i/. On the deep origin of the former, see the suggestions of Schane (1968a: 58). We will
simply denote them as *y* in the underlying representations.

/XVY/ where the second is identical to the first (except for schwa), the phonological component would necessarily give them the same phonetic representation in all contexts. This is due to the existence of the V-E rule, which is obligatory and does not allow for any exceptions. The phonological matrices of the form /XVəY/ are not prohibited by any morpheme structure rule, but they are systematically excluded from the lexical representations owing to the principle of the simplest representation, which necessitates the choice of the corresponding /XVY/ representations, since they add less to the complexity of the lexicon.

It is important to notice that the existence of the V-E rule in the phonological component is not sufficient to guarantee that the phonological representations /XVəY/ and /XVY/ will always be phonetically identical, whatever the context. Suppose that V-E is ordered after E-ADJ, and imagine that besides forms like *fil, filé* ('thread, threaded', root /fil/), there are analogous forms built on a hypothetical root /fiəl/. Here are their derivations:

	/ # fil + e # /	/ # fiəl + e # /	/ # fil # /	/ # fiəl # /
E-ADJ				# fiɛl #
V-E		# fil + e #		
SEM				# fyɛl #
	[file]	[file]	[fil]	[fyɛl]

The derivation of / # fiəl # / shows that if E-ADJ is ordered before V-E it rewrites as ɛ certain schwas preceded by a vowel, thus enabling them to escape deletion by V-E and to appear phonetically as [ɛ]. For our grammar to guarantee that the /Və/ sequences will always be merged with the corresponding /V/ vowels, and so that the impossibility of having any allomorphs containing such sequences can consequently be attributed to an induced restriction, V-E must be ordered before E-ADJ;[7] this we will do since we know of no data that require the reverse order.

The preceding account shows that induced restrictions are not simply due to the presence of a specific rule in the phonological component, but also to the way in which this rule is ordered in relation to the others; in short, induced restrictions depend on the overall structure of the phonological component. This is why we speak of restrictions induced 'by the phonological component' rather than by one or another particular phonological rule.

[7]   The reader can easily check that with this order of application the two derivations on the right yield the same output.

Schwa is obligatorily dropped in front of a pause when it is not the only vowel in the word: *elle est trop petit¢* [ɛlɛtroptit] 'she is too small', *elle est pervers¢* [ɛlɛpɛrvɛrs] 'she is perverse', but *bats-le̲* [balö] 'beat him', *sur ce̲* [sürsö] 'upon this...'. If we use the symbol § to represent a pause, we can write:

$$\text{PAUS:} \quad \text{ə} \;\rightarrow\; \emptyset \quad / \quad VC_0 \;\text{——}\; \S$$

Like ELIS and V-E, PAUS is obligatory and does not allow for any exceptions. From now on, each time we write a new rule, its name will be followed by the sign (OBL) or (OPT), according to whether that rule is obligatory or optional.

We will now examine the behaviour of schwas which occur at the end of polysyllables and which are not subject to either ELIS, V-E or PAUS.

DELETION AT THE END OF POLYSYLLABLES

Schwa is obligatorily dropped when it is preceded by a single non-syllabic segment:[8] *un¢ vieill¢ courtisan¢* 'an old courtesan'. *Petite roue* 'small wheel' and *petit trou* [pətitru] 'small hole', *grande rame* 'big oar' and *grand drame* [grãdram] 'big drama' are pronounced in the same way. We will therefore posit the following rule:

$$\text{FIN-DEL}_1: \quad \text{ə} \;\rightarrow\; \emptyset \quad / \quad VC \;\text{——}\; \#$$
(OBL)

When a schwa occurring in the final syllable of a polysyllable is immediately preceded by two or more consonants, its deletion is optional. It is always possible to pronounce it, but the frequency of the deletion tends to rise in proportion to the speaker's lack of care in pronouncing or his speed in speaking: *il box(e) souvent* [ibɔks(ə)suvã] 'he often boxes', *le text(e) du discours* [lətɛkst(ə)düdiskur] 'the text of the speech', *une énorm(e) pancarte* [enɔrm(ə)pãkart] 'an enormous signboard'. Although we have not examined this point in detail, it cannot be doubted that the frequency of this deletion also depends on the number of surrounding consonants.[9] Thus, all other things being equal, the final schwa of *texte* is more easily dropped in *text(e) tout à fait confidentiel* [tɛkst(ə)tutafɛ...] 'an

---

[8] We have set aside cases in which the following word begins with an aspirated *h* (cf. p. 238), and also the unique case of the word *rien* [ryɛ̃] 'nothing', in front of which the schwa is optionally retained: compare *il mang¢ tout* 'he eats everything' with *il ne mang(e) rien* 'he doesn't eat anything'.

[9] Dell (1977) has shown that in this environment schwa tends to be dropped with increasing ease when the group of preceding consonants begins with an *r*, when the syntactic relation with the following word is rather loose and when the preceding word is strongly stressed.

absolutely confidential text' than in *text(e) strictement confidentiel* [tɛkst(ə)striktəmã...]. We will write the following optional rule:

FIN-DEL$_2$:   ə → Ø   /   CC ⎯⎯ #
(OPT)

As in French there are no monosyllables of the form #CCə#, this rule in fact only concerns final schwas of polysyllables. For the time being we will not examine the relationship between FIN-DEL$_1$ and FIN-DEL$_2$. By systematically looking at all the words in Juilland (1965), it appears that apart from words ending in an *OL* group in which the liquid is never dropped (cf. p. 214 below), all the words that can be pronounced [XCCə] in front of a #$_1$C sequence can also be pronounced [XCC] in the same context. There is only one exception, the word *quelque(s)*. This word behaves regularly in front of a ##C sequence, but is necessarily pronounced with a final schwa in front of #C; contrast *il en a mis vingt et quelqu(e)s sous son chapeau* [...vɛ̃ekɛlk(ə)su...] 'he put about twenty under his hat' and *quelques sous-officiers* [kɛlkəsuzɔfisye] 'a few warrant officers'. *Quelques* is separated from the following word by two # boundaries in the first example, and by a single # boundary in the second.[10]

Just as its structural description predicts, FIN-DEL$_2$ operates among other things inside compound words (combinations of words that themselves count as one word). But here it is subject to an interesting restriction. Léon (1966) noted that the schwa is always retained in words like *porte-plume* [pɔrtəplüm] 'penholder', *porte-voix* [pɔrtəvwa] 'megaphone', *ouvre-boîte* [uvrəbwat] 'tin-opener', where the second term of the compound word only has one syllable phonetically, whereas it is optionally dropped in words such as *port(e)-drapeau* [pɔrt(ə)drapo] 'colour bearer', *gard(e)-malade* [gard(ə)malad] 'sick-nurse', *gard(e)-barrière* [gard(ə)baryɛr] 'gate-keeper' and *ouv(re)-bouteille* [uv(rə)butɛy] 'bottle-opener'. A similar phenomenon can be found inside phrases that immediately precede a strong syntactic break or that are pronounced in isolation (which comes to the same). Even though this time one cannot speak of an obligatory retention, the final schwa of *parle* is dropped much less in *il parl(e) bas* [iparl(ə)ba] 'he speaks softly' than in *il parl(e) plus bas* [iparl(ə)plüba] 'he

---

[10]   As *quelque(s)* is the only word ending in · *lk* whose syntactic properties enable it to appear in front of a single # boundary, it is impossible to compare it with other words to determine whether its behaviour is due to a lexical idiosyncrasy or whether one would find the same impossibility of deleting schwa in any · *lkə* #C sequence. *Quelque* behaves regularly with regard to PAUS and ELIS: *il en a vingt et quelqu*∉*s* 'he's got about twenty', *à quelqu*∉ *organisation qu'il appartienne...* 'whatever organization he belongs to'.

speaks more softly', *il parl(e) beaucoup* [iparl(ə)boku] 'he talks a lot'. Similarly, it is dropped much less in *mets ta vest(e) rouge* [mɛtavɛst(ə)ruž] 'put on your red jacket' than it is in *mets ta vest(e) rouge et blanche* [mɛtavɛst(ə)ružebláš] 'put on your red and white jacket', and less in *gard(e)s-en* [gard(ə)zã] 'keep some of them' than in *gard(e)s-en deux* [gard(ə)zãdö] 'keep two of them'.[11]

Final schwas that are immediately preceded by two consonants belonging to the same word are not dropped when the following syllable carries the main stress of a compound word, and they are rather reluctant to drop when the following syllable carries the main stress of a pre-pausal phrase. These two restrictions are probably a manifestation of the same restriction to the application of FIN-DEL$_2$, but we do not yet know how to formalize this restriction or how to integrate it in the structural description of FIN-DEL$_2$.

In our speech, the phrase *livre d'art chinois* is ambiguous when it is pronounced [livrədaršinwa], where the final schwa of *livre* is pronounced, but not when it is pronounced [livdaršinwa]. In the first case, it can be (a) a book about Chinese art and (b) an artbook that is of Chinese origin. In the second case, on the other hand, interpretation (b) is impossible. This is explained by the fact that the phrase *livre d'art* has become lexicalized as a compound noun, 'art book'. As the second term of this compound noun is monosyllabic,[12] the final schwa of *livre* is always retained, in accordance with the rule posited above, just as it is retained in the compound nouns *Livre Blanc* [livrəblã] 'White Book', *Livre d'Or* [livrədɔr] 'Golden Book', *œuvre d'art* [œvrədar] 'work of art'.[13]

When a schwa occurring in the final syllable of a word is preceded by an *OL* cluster and the following word begins with a consonant, there are two possibilities: either schwa is retained along with the preceding liquid, or it is dropped and takes the liquid with it. *Pauvre vieillard* 'poor old man' is pronounced either [povrəvyɛyar] or [povvyɛyar], never *[povrvyɛyar] or *[povəvyɛyar]. Similarly, one pronounces [prãd(rə)sõtã] *prendre son temps* 'to take one's time', [kapab(lə)dənaže] *capable de nager* 'able to swim'.

---

[11] It had already been noticed by Leray (1930: 172) that the pronunciation [uvvitsɛtpɔrt] is possible instead of [uvrəvitsɛtpɔrt] for *ouvre vite cette porte!* 'open this door quickly!' but not *[uvvit] for *ouvre vite!* ([uvrəvit] 'open up quickly!').

[12] ... once rule ELIS has deleted the schwa of the preposition *de* (cf. p. 232).

[13] The final schwa of *œuvre* is always retained in the compound word *œuvre d'art* but is optionally dropped in free combinations such as *œuv(re) de jeunesse* 'work of youth', *l'œuv(re) de Sally Mara* 'the work of Sally Mara'.

We propose to account for these facts in the following way: words that have in their last syllable a schwa preceded by an *OL* cluster are, like the others, subject to the optional rule FIN-DEL$_2$, and there is an obligatory rule ordered after FIN-DEL$_2$ deleting any word-final liquid when this liquid is preceded by an obstruent and the following word begins with a consonant. Thus dropping the liquid is an automatic consequence of the deletion of the final schwa by FIN-DEL$_2$.

The liquid of a final *OL* cluster can also be optionally dropped in front of a pause (in our dialect this is still a rather sporadic occurrence even in relaxed speech): *ils sont assez pauvres* [isɔ̃asepov(r)] 'they are quite poor', *tu vas la perdre* [tüvalapɛrd(r)] 'you're going to lose her', *il en est capable* [ilãnɛkapab(l)] 'he is capable of doing it'. We will therefore posit the following schema, in which the first sub-rule is obligatory, and the second optional:

$$\text{LIQUEF:} \quad \text{L} \;\rightarrow\; \emptyset \;\; / \;\; \text{O} \;\underline{\hspace{1.5em}}\; \left\{ \begin{matrix} \#_1 \text{C} \\ \S \end{matrix} \right\} \qquad \begin{matrix} \text{(a)} \\ \text{(b)} \end{matrix}$$

INTERNAL SCHWAS

By 'internal schwas' we mean all those that are not subject to any of the rules presented since the beginning of this chapter.

In a word-initial syllable after a pause, schwa is never dropped when it is preceded by two or more consonants (*prenez tout* [prənetu] 'take everything'). It can be optionally dropped when it is preceded by a single consonant, except if it is both preceded and followed by a non-continuant obstruent;[14] this is valid for monosyllables as well as for the initial syllable

---

[14] *Petit* is an exception to this restriction: *p(ə)tit salaud!* 'you little bastard!'. In front of a word with an initial consonant, sentence-initial *ne* and sentence-initial exclamative and interrogative *que* never lose their schwas: *que c'est joli!* 'how pretty it is!', *que va-t-il faire?* 'what will he do?', *ne pars pas trop tard* 'don't leave too late'. E. Selkirk has suggested to us that this is not due to any lexical exception feature, and that exclamative and interrogative *que* always retain their schwa because they usually carry a heavy stress when they are sentence-initial. This fits well with the fact that the complementizer *que*, which is usually not stressed at the beginning of an embedded clause, even sentence-initially, can lose its schwa in that context: *qu(e) Jean vienne ou pas, je m'en fous* 'whether John comes or not, I don't give a damn'. There is also a stylistic factor at work; except for a few rote expressions, exclamative and interrogative *que* are nowadays felt to have a strongly bookish flavour, and schwas which meet the conditions of INI (cf. main text below) drop much less often in more formal styles of speech. Only these stylistic factors can be invoked in the case of sentence-initial *ne* (on the optional nature of *ne*, see p. 237), for it can very well be pronounced unstressed.

Ne, exclamative *que*, and interrogative *que*, are regularly subject to ELIS, in sentence-initial position as elsewhere: *n'écoute pas* 'do not listen', *qu'Anne est jolie!* 'how pretty Ann is!', *qu'attend-il?* 'what is he waiting for?'

of polysyllables:

> *r(e)venez tous* [r(ə)vənetus], [rəvnetus] 'all come back'
> *m(e)sure-moi cette planche* [m(ə)zürmwasɛtplãš] 'measure this plank for me'
> *v(e)nez ici* [v(ə)neisi] 'come here'
> *j(e) stérilise cette seringue* [ž(ə)sterilizsɛtsərɛ̃g] 'I'm sterilizing this syringe'
> *c(e)la ne fait rien* [s(ə)lanfɛryɛ̃] 'it doesn't matter'
> *d(e) mon côté* [d(ə)mɔ̃kote] 'on my side'
> *d(e)vant chez moi* [d(ə)vãšemwa] 'in front of my house'
> *t(e) fais pas de bile* [t(ə)fɛpadbil] 'don't worry' (slang)
> *r(e)trouvez-moi cet argent* [r(ə)truvemwasɛtaržã] 'find me that money'
> *j(e)tez-y un coup d'œil* [ž(ə)teziɛ̃kudœy] 'have a look at it'
> *c(e) travail est trop dur* [s(ə)travayɛtrodür] 'this work is too hard'
> *debout sur une table* [dəbusürüntabl] 'standing on a table'
> *te casse pas la tête* [tɔkaspalatɛt] 'don't overdo it!'
> *de quoi tu te plains?* [dekwatütplɛ̃] 'what are you complaining about?'

We will write the optional rule INI, whose application is immediately preceded by that of the obligatory rule INI-EX:[15]

$$
\text{INI-EX:} \quad \text{ə} \rightarrow [-\text{rule INI}] \Big/ \begin{bmatrix} -\text{son} \\ -\text{cont} \end{bmatrix} \underline{\quad} \#_0 \begin{bmatrix} -\text{son} \\ -\text{cont} \end{bmatrix}
$$
(OBL)

$$
\text{INI:} \quad \text{ə} \rightarrow \varnothing \Big/ \S\ \text{C}\underline{\quad}
$$
(OPT)

Before the application of rule INI, that optionally deletes any schwa preceded by a single initial consonant itself preceded by a pause, the rule INI-EX marks as exceptions to INI any schwa that is both preceded and followed by a non-continuant obstruent.[16]

INI-EX could be dispensed with by integrating the restriction it expresses into the structural description of INI, i.e. by directly formulating INI so that it will optionally delete all the schwas that are at the same time preceded by a single consonant after a pause and surrounded by two consonants of

---

[15] INI stands for 'initial' and EX for 'exception'.
[16] On exception rules like INI-EX, cf. *SPE:* 374–5.

which at least one is something other than a non-continuant obstruent:

$$\text{INI}': \quad \text{ə} \rightarrow \emptyset \quad \bigg/ \quad \S \left\{ \begin{array}{l} \text{C} \!-\!\!-\! \#_0 \left\{ \begin{array}{l} [+\text{son}] \\ [+\text{cont}] \end{array} \right\} \\[2ex] \left\{ \begin{array}{l} [+\text{son}] \\ [+\text{cont}] \end{array} \right\} \quad \underline{\hspace{1.5em}} \end{array} \right\}$$

(OPT)

The presence in the second syllable after a pause of a schwa liable to be deleted by the rules VCE[17] has no influence on the way in which INI operates: the first schwa of *je repartirai* 'I shall leave again' is optionally dropped ([žər(ə)partirɛ] or [žrəpartirɛ]) as is that of *j(e) rattraperai* 'I shall catch up'. This last statement calls for an important remark. By writing the rules INI or INI', we are only claiming that the set of all the occurrences of schwa in initial syllables behind a pause can be divided into two complementary sets: those that do not meet the conditions of the structural description of the rule and that are never deleted, and those that do meet these conditions and that can therefore be deleted. Rules INI and INI' state no more than that. But in fact all the schwas that meet their structural description are not deleted with the same facility, and some syncopes of schwa in initial syllables behind a pause are felt to be more natural than others.[18] It seems to us that the first schwa is less easily dropped in *je repartirai* ([žrəpartirɛ]) than in *je rattraperai* ([žratraprɛ]). Among the other things that influence the frequency with which INI operates, the characteristics of the surrounding consonants have to be taken into account,[19] as well as facts of stress: the longer a phrase, i.e. the further to the right its main stress, the more likely a schwa occurring in the first syllable of that phrase is to be dropped. For example, it is dropped with increasing facility in the following three sentences: *venez* [v(ə)ne] 'come!', *venez ici* [v(ə)neisi] 'come here!', *venez boire un verre* [v(ə)nebwarɛ̃vɛr] 'come and have a drink'. The initial syllable after a pause is one of the contexts where the behaviour of schwa varies most from one speaker to another, which explains that intuitions about what is well or ill-formed are not as clear as they are elsewhere. In any case, there is no doubt that the deletion of schwa

---

[17] On these rules, see below.
[18] It has recently been shown that the dichotomy between obligatory and optional rules which we use here is too rough a tool for observation, and that the factors which inhibit or on the contrary facilitate the operation of optional rules are very refined. On this subject, see the references on p. 170, n. 2.
[19] Cf. Delattre (1966: 28–35).

in this position is subject to particular restrictions. Variations in the formulation of these restrictions will not have any consequence on the organization of the rest of the grammar.

A schwa preceded by two consonants belonging to the same word is never dropped:[20]

> *malmener* [malmǝne] 'to ill-treat'
> *surgelé* [süržǝle] 'deep-frozen'
> *exactement* [egzaktǝmã] 'exactly'
> *Angleterre* [ãglǝtɛr] 'England'
> *satisfaisant* [satisfǝzã] 'satisfactory'
> *harceler* [arsǝle] 'to harass'
> *fermeture* [fɛrmǝtür] 'closing'
> *gouvernemental* [guvɛrnǝmãtal] 'governmental'
> *crevaison* [krǝvɛzõ] 'puncture'
> *squelette* [skǝlɛt] 'skeleton'
> *breton* [brǝtõ] 'Breton', etc.

When an internal schwa is preceded by a single consonant, two cases must be distinguished, according to whether this consonant is word-initial or not.

When the single consonant preceding schwa is not word-initial, schwa is obligatorily dropped, even in slow speech:

> *feuilletez* [fœyte] 'to leaf through'
> *guillemet* [giymɛ] 'inverted comma'
> *acheteur* [aštœr] 'buyer'
> *clavecin* [klavsɛ̃] 'harpsichord'
> *paquebot* [pakbo] 'steam-ship'
> *bandelette* [bãdlɛt] 'strip'
> *promener* [prɔmne] 'to take (someone) for a walk'
> *Danemark* [danmark] 'Denmark'
> *centenaire* [sãtnɛr] 'centenary'
> *souvenir* [suvnir] 'memory', etc.

There are a few exceptions, generally words that are fairly rarely used:

> *Champenois* [šãpǝnwa] 'inhabitant of Champagne'
> *attenant* [atǝnã] 'contiguous'
> *enchevêtrer* [ãšǝvɛtre] 'to entangle'
> *dépecer* [depǝse] 'to skin'

---

[20] ... except if it is the thematic vowel of the future, see below. On certain exceptions which sporadically appear in rapid speech, see Malécot (1955).

Schwa is also dropped when it is followed by more than one consonant: *Fontaineฺbleau* [fɔ̃tɛnblo], *Picheฺgru* [pišgrü] (proper names).[21] We will write the following rule:

$$VCE_2: \quad ə \rightarrow \emptyset \quad / \quad VC \text{———}$$
(OBL)

When the single consonant preceding schwa is word-initial, schwa is always retained if the preceding word ends in a consonant[22] and it is optionally dropped if this word ends in a vowel. (It is dropped all the more easily when the speaker speaks fast and pays little attention to his elocution.) We have the pronunciation *vieฺilles tenailles*[a] but *des t(e)nailles*[b], *quel neveu*[c] but *mon n(e)veu*[d]. Similarly, note the contrast between *j'arriveฺ demain*[e] and *j'arriverai d(e)main*[f], *ils veuleฺnt repartir*[g] and *il veut r(e)partir*[h], *uneฺ secrétaire*[i] and *la s(e)crétaire*[j]. *Jacqueฺs devrait partir*[k] and *Henri d(e)vrait partir*[l]. The last two examples illustrate the fact that schwa is dropped as well when it is followed by more than one consonant.

The schwa of #*Cə*# monosyllables behaves exactly like that of the first syllable of polysyllabic words beginning with #*C*—:[23] we have the pronunciation *feuille de chou* [fœydǝšu][m] but *pied de chou* [pyed(ə)šu][n], *mange le gâteau* [mãžlǝgato][o] but *mangez le gâteau* [mãžel(ə)gato][p]. Nothing changes when this schwa is followed by more than one consonant, as shown by the following examples: *une espèceฺ de scrupule*[q], *pas d(e) scrupules*[r], *costumeฺ de sport*[s], *terrain d(e) sport*[t]. We will write the following rule:[24]

$$VCE_1: \quad ə \rightarrow \emptyset \quad / \quad V \#_1 C \text{———}$$
(OPT)

---

[21] Because of the rule E-ADJ, the following consonant cluster can only be an *OL* cluster. Words where schwa occurs in the environment *VC———OLV* are very rare. Besides the two proper names given in the text, we have been able to find only a few forms which must all be marked as exceptions to VCE₂: *Fontevrault* (proper name) and the future forms of the *-cevoir* verbs (*décevrez* 'you will disappoint', *recevrez* 'you will receive').

[22] But cf. pp. 207 and 209.

[23] ... and not as a final schwa in a polysyllable; this schwa is neither subject to E-FIN₁ nor to E-FIN₂.

[24] This has already been mentioned (p. 162).

[a][vyɛytǝnay] 'old pincers'. [b][det(ə)nay] 'which nephew'. [c][kɛlnǝvö] 'which nephew'. [d][mɔ̃n(ə)vö] 'my nephew'. [e][žarivdǝmɛ̃] 'I arrive tomorrow'. [f][žarivrɛd(ə)mɛ̃] 'I shall arrive tomorrow'. [g][ivœlrǝpartir] 'they want to leave again'. [h][ivör(ə)partir] 'he wants to leave again'. [i][ünsǝkrɛtɛr] 'a secretary'. [j][las(ə)krɛtɛr] 'the secretary'. [k][žakdǝvrɛpartir] 'Jack should leave'. [l][ãrid(ə)vrɛpartir] 'Henry should leave'. [m]'cabbage leaf'. [n]'a head of cabbage'. [o]'eat the cake'. [p]'eat the cake'. [q][ünɛspɛsdǝskrüpül] 'a kind of scruple'. [r][pad(ə)skrüpül] 'no scruples'. [s][kɔstümdǝspɔr] 'sportswear'. [t][tɛrɛ̃d(ə)spɔr] 'sports ground'.

In Delattre (1966), there are systematic lists abundantly illustrating the functioning of VCE_1 and VCE_2 in the different possible cases. Most proper names are exceptions to VCE_1. Haden (1965) noticed such oppositions as that between *j'ai vu l(e) sage*[a], and *j'ai vu Lesage*[b], *sans ch(e)valier*[c] and *sans Chevalier*[d]. Similarly, *René, Seguin, Nemours, Besançon, Ledru-Rollin, Geneviève* (proper names), etc. Exceptions to VCE_1 in fact are not limited to proper names: *femelle*[e], *guenon*[f], *peser*[g], *vedette*[h]. We made a list of all the words beginning with $\# C\partial \#$ contained in Robert (1967) and known by us, and we divided them into those that in our dialect could lose their schwa when the preceding word ends in a vowel and those that could not. The study of this list does not reveal any simple regularity which would enable one to predict, on the basis of the surrounding consonants, whether a schwa in an initial syllable is subject to VCE_1 or not. However, this list does show that it is words and not morphemes which must be marked in the lexicon as exceptions to VCE_1. For a morpheme can be an exception in one word but not in the other. Our speech opposes, for example, *m(e)ner*[i] and *meneur*[j], *s(e)mer*[k] and *semailles*[l], *ch(e)min*[m] and *cheminer*[n]. In general, it is words that are either rarely used or literary which tend to be exceptions to VCE_1.[25] We have shown (p. 163) that VCE_1 must be applied after $FIN-DEL_1$.

VCE_1 and VCE_2 operate normally when the vowel of the preceding syllable is a schwa that cannot be dropped: *entretenir* [atrətnir][o], *breveter* [brəvte][p], *patte de renard* [patdər(ə)nar][q], *elle te demande* [ɛltəd(ə)mãd][r], *laissez-le debout* [leseləd(ə)bu][s], *je pense que ce devant quoi il faut s'incliner* [... səd(ə)vã...][t].[26] Rule VCE_1 can also use, as an environment, schwas which obligatorily appear at the end of the words *quelque(s)*[u],[27] *double*[v],[28] *simple*[w], etc., when they precede a $\# C$ sequence: *quelques s(e)condes*[x], *simple ch(e)mise*[y], *double f(e)nêtre*[z], *entre G(e)nève et Paris*[a'], *contre l(e) mur*[b'].

---

[25] For a similar tendency in English in the case of vowel reduction, cf. Fidelholtz (1975).
[26] On the reasons for which the first schwa is not dropped in the last two forms, cf. p. 235.
[27] On *quelque(s)* before a sequence $\# C$, cf. p. 199.
[28] On this word and the following, cf. p. 216.

[a][ževül(ə)saž] 'I saw the sage'. [b][ževüləsaž] 'I saw Lesage'. [c][sãš(ə)valye] 'without a knight'. [d][sãšəvalye] 'without Chevalier'. [e][fəmɛl] 'female'. [f][gənõ] 'female monkey'. [g][pəze] 'to weigh'. [h][vədɛt] 'filmstar'. [i][m(ə)ne] 'to lead'. [j][mənœr] 'leader'. [k][s(ə)me] 'to sow'. [l][səmay] 'seeding'. [m][š(ə)mɛ̃] 'way'. [n][šəmine] 'to trudge'. [o]'to keep up'. [p]'to patent'. [q]'fox's paw'. [r]'she is asking for you'. [s]'leave him standing'. [t]'I think that what one must yield to...'. [u][kɛlk] 'a few'. [v][dubl] 'double'. [w][sɛ̃pl] 'simple'. [x][kɛlkəs(ə)gõd] 'a few seconds'. [y][sɛ̃pləš(ə)miz] 'a simple shirt'. [z][dubləf(ə)nɛtr] 'double window'. [a'][ãtraž(ə)nɛv...] 'between Geneva and Paris'. [b'][kõtrəl(ə)mür] 'against the wall'.

Contrary to what we said above, in very rapid speech the schwa of a small number of words beginning with $\#C$ — can be dropped even if the preceding word ends in a consonant: *quelle semaine*[a] is sometimes pronounced [kɛlsmɛn]. In rapid speech, also, the schwa of *semaine* is sometimes dropped even when the schwa of the preceding monosyllable has also been dropped; *fin de semaine*[b] is not only pronounced [fɛ̃dəsmɛn] and [fɛ̃dsəmɛn] as predicted by rule VCE_1,[29] but also [fɛ̃dsmɛn]. The other words that have this property in our speech are *je*[c],[30] *semelle*[d], *cerise*[e], *chemise*[f], *fenêtre*[g] and *petit*[h]. In all these words except *petit*, schwa is preceded by a fricative and followed by a sonorant. But there are other similar words which always behave according to VCE_1: *semestre* [s(ə)mɛstr] 'semester', *seringue* [s(ə)rɛ̃g] 'syringe', *chenille* [š(ə)niy] 'caterpillar'.

The facts concerning this point vary from one speaker to another. Some speakers seem to always strictly keep to VCE_1, even when they talk very rapidly. Those that move away from it, do not always do so for the same words. The system of rules that we propose does not account for the facts discussed in the preceding paragraph – it does not generate either [kɛlsmɛn] or [fɛ̃dsmɛn]. It generates the set of well-formed phonetic representations that are common to all speakers whose pronunciations only differ with respect to VCE_1. In this way we have a system which can be used as a frame of reference for a more detailed study of individual differences.

Another area where certain speakers stray more or less from our formulation of VCE_1 is concerning the possibility of deleting the schwa of words beginning with $\#C$ — when the preceding word ends in an *r* (cf. Delattre, 1966: 24; Morin, 1974). In our dialect, this deletion of schwa is still rather sporadic, and subject to special restrictions which are not found when the preceding word ends in a vowel. The following syllable must not be stressed; the schwa of *se* can be deleted in *la terre s(e) vend bien* [latɛrs(ə)vãbyɛ̃] 'the land sells well' but not in *la terre se̱ vend* [latɛrsəvã] 'the land sells'. A preceding continuant in general makes the deletion of schwa more acceptable than a preceding stop: the deletion of schwa sounds much better in *pour s(e) peigner* [purs(ə)penye] 'to comb one's hair' than in *pour t(e) peigner* [purt(ə)penye] 'to comb your hair'.

---

[29] On the way in which VCE_1 affects schwas occurring in adjacent syllables, cf. pp. 224ff.

[30] As can be seen in the pronunciation [fokžmãnay] of *faut que je m'en aille* 'I must go'. VCE_1 only allows [fokžəmãnay] and [fokəžmãnay].

[a] 'which week'. [b] 'end of the week'. [c] [ž(ə)] 'I'. [d] [s(ə)mɛl] 'sole'. [e] [s(ə)riz] 'cherry'. [f] [š(ə)miz] 'shirt'. [g] [f(ə)nɛtr] 'window'. [h] [p(ə)ti] 'little'.

In the future and conditional forms of the *-er* verbs, the schwa preceding the future ending *r* is not only dropped when it is preceded by a single consonant, in accordance with VCE$_2$ (*vol*e*ras* [vɔlra] 'you will fly', *mang*e*ras* [mãžra] 'you will eat'), but it is also optionally dropped when preceded by a cluster of two consonants or more:[31] *parl(e)ras* [parl(ə)ra] 'you will talk', *fix(e)ras* [fiks(ə)ra] 'you will fix', *prétext(e)ras* [pretɛkst(ə)ra] 'you will make a pretext'. The optional deletion of schwa is indeed a specific property of these verbal forms, since elsewhere in the same phonological surroundings, schwa is always retained, as predicted by VCE$_2$; this can be seen in the following pairs:

largu(e)ra [larg(ə)ra] 'he will let go' / *margu*e*rite* [margərit] 'daisy'
calm(e)ra [kalm(ə)ra] 'he will calm' / *palm*e*raie* [palmərɛ] 'palm-grove'
forg(e)ront [fɔrž(ə)rɔ̃] 'they will forge' / *forg*e*ron* [fɔržərɔ̃] 'blacksmith'
insist(e)ra [ɛ̃sist(ə)ra] 'he will insist' / *fumist*e*rie* [fümistəri] 'hoax'

How can these data be accounted for? It is tempting to assimilate the future and conditional schwas to final schwas: the schwa of *fum*e*ra* [fümera] 'he will smoke' is obligatorily dropped like that of *un*e *roue* [ünru] 'a wheel', and that of *prétext(e)ra* [pretɛkst(ə)ra] 'he will make a pretext' is optionally dropped, as that of *text(e) rare* [tɛkst(ə)rar] 'rare text'. It would therefore be enough to postulate the representations *fume#ra* and *prétexte#ra*. In principle nothing opposes the adoption of this analysis, which gives the future and conditional forms a particular morphological status, as long as a number of arguments independently concur to support this. But the only thing which militates in its favour is the behaviour of schwa; and even then the parallel between future schwas and final schwas is not complete: in verbs whose stem ends in *OL*, the schwa and the liquid are never dropped. Whereas *manœuvre rapide* 'fast manœuvre' is alternatively pronounced [manœvrərapid] or [manœvrapid], *manœuvrera* 'he will manœuvre' is only pronounced [manœvrera], never *[manœvra]. Another fact that renders this analysis questionable is the retention of schwa in *hésit*e*riez* [ezitərye] 'you would hesitate', *vol*e*rions* [vɔləryɔ̃] 'we would fly', etc. Later on, we will see that schwa is retained in front of an *Ly* group belonging to the same word (*hôt*e*lier* [otəlye] 'innkeeper') but not to the following word (*petit*e *lionne* [pətitlyɔn] 'small lioness'). On analysing *hésite#riez*, it is hard to see why the schwa is retained none the less, whereas it is dropped in *petite#lionne*.

---

[31] Except if it is an *OL* cluster, in which case schwa is obligatorily retained: *rentr*e*ras* 'you will go in', *souffl*e*ras* 'you will blow'.

It is better to attribute the deletion of schwa in *mang¢ra* [mãžra] 'he will eat', *vol¢ra* [vɔlra] 'he will fly' to the action of the obligatory rule VCE$_2$, and that of schwa in *vals(e)ra* [vals(ə)ra] 'he will waltz', *prétext(e)ra* [pretɛkst(ə)ra] 'he will make the pretext', to the action of a special optional rule that deletes schwa in front of the future morpheme, except when it follows an *OL* cluster:[32]

FUT-DEL: ə → Ø   / ——+r+
(OPT)
    Condition: except behind OL

Although it is not subject to VCE$_1$, schwa is optionally dropped in *Jacques s(e)ra là* [žaks(ə)rala] 'Jack will be there', *Ernest f(e)ra la cuisine* [ɛrnɛstf(ə)ralakwizin] 'Ernest will do the cooking' (compare with *chaque seringue* [šaksərɛ̃g] 'each syringe'). This does not necessarily bring in an additional argument in favour of rule FUT-DEL, however, for there is also the possibility of putting these forms in the same class as *cerise* [səriz] 'cherry', *fenêtre* [fənɛtr] 'window', etc. (see p. 207).

If linguistic theory contained a device enabling the structural description of a rule to distinguish between inflectional suffixes and derivational ones, FUT-DEL could simply be restated as optionally deleting schwa in front of an inflectional ending, since at the time FUT-DEL becomes applicable, the schwas which precede the verbal ending *-r-* are the only 'internal' schwas which precede an inflectional suffix. We have argued (Dell, 1978a) that at least three other phonological rules of French are sensitive to the difference between derivational and inflectional suffixes.

We will review some of the rules we have arrived at:

PAUS: ə → Ø   / VC$_0$——§
(OBL)

FIN-DEL$_1$: ə → Ø   / VC——#
(OBL)

FIN-DEL$_2$: ə → Ø   / CC——#
(OPT)

VCE$_1$:   ə → Ø   / V#$_1$ C——
(OPT)

VCE$_2$:   ə → Ø   / VC——
(OBL)

---

[32] It will be shown (p. 215) that this special restriction concerning *OL* clusters is in fact superfluous.

Rules FIN-DEL$_1$ and VCE$_2$ are intriguingly similar. It could be asked whether having VCE$_2$ does not enable us completely to dispense with FIN-DEL$_1$, which apparently is only a particular case of VCE$_2$. But FIN-DEL$_1$ and VCE$_2$ are in fact two distinct rules. For we have shown (p. 163) that FIN-DEL$_1$ must be applied before VCE$_1$ and we show below that VCE$_1$ must be applied before VCE$_2$. If FIN-DEL$_1$ and VCE$_2$ were one and the same rule, it would have to be applied sometimes before and sometimes after VCE$_1$, which is impossible in the theoretical framework adopted here. Let us show that VCE$_2$ must be applied after VCE$_1$. It is sufficient to compare the derivation of *tu devenais* 'you were becoming' according to whether VCE$_1$ is ordered before or after VCE$_2$:[33]

	/tü ǂ dəvənɛ/	/tü ǂ dəvənɛ/		/tü ǂ dəvənɛ/
VCE$_1$	tü ǂ d vənɛ		VCE$_2$	tü ǂ dəv nɛ
VCE$_2$		tü ǂ dəv nɛ	VCE$_1$	tü ǂ d v nɛ
	[tüdvənɛ]	[tüdəvnɛ]		*[tüdvnɛ]

When VCE$_1$ precedes VCE$_2$, there are two possible derivations according to whether the optional rule VCE$_1$ deletes or does not delete the schwa on the left. If it deletes it, the following schwa is then situated after two consonants, and VCE$_2$ cannot operate. If it does not delete it, the schwa on the right remains preceded by a single consonant and is obligatorily deleted by VCE$_2$. The operation of VCE$_1$ in a $V ǂ_1 CəCə$ sequence thus prevents that of VCE$_2$, and VCE$_2$ operates if and only if VCE$_1$ has not operated before. In other words, VCE$_1$ and VCE$_2$ cannot be applied one after the other to delete two schwas belonging to contiguous syllables, and this perfectly agrees with the data. On the other hand, the reverse order enables the two rules to operate in contiguous syllables, and the result is an ill-formed representation *[tüdvnɛ]. VCE$_2$ must be applied after VCE$_1$, and consequently VCE$_2$ and FIN-DEL$_1$ are different processes.

With FIN-DEL$_1$ preceding VCE$_1$, and VCE$_1$ preceding VCE$_2$, it follows that FIN-DEL$_1$ must precede VCE$_2$. Note that no forms enable us to establish directly this result. For FIN-DEL$_1$ and VCE$_2$ can never affect two contiguous syllables, since there cannot be any words in French where the last and the penultimate syllables both have a schwa (at the point in the derivation where these rules are applicable). In words that have a phonological representation of the type $/ ǂ XəCə(+ C) ǂ /$, the schwa of the penultimate syllable is always rewritten as ɛ by rule E-ADJ, and this takes place before the application of FIN-DEL$_1$ and VCE$_2$.

---

[33] In these derivations and the following, we have omitted the morpheme boundaries, since they are not relevant to the present discussion.

INI must be applied before VCE_1: *je repars* 'I'm leaving again' is pronounced [žrəpar], [žərpar] or [žərəpar]. The last pronunciation is obtained when neither INI nor VCE_1, which are both optional, operate. We give below the derivations of the first two pronunciations, and opposite them one of the derivations that would be obtained if INI were applied after VCE_1.

	/§žə#rəpar/	/§žə#rəpar/			/§žə#rəpar/
INI	§ž #rəpar		VCE_1		§žə#r par
VCE_1		§žə#r par	INI		/§ž #r par
	[žrəpar]	[žərpar]			*[žrpar]

Similarly, INI must be applied before VCE_2 if we want to prevent the grammar from generating *[dvne] from /§dəvəne/ in *devenez riche* [dəvneriš], [dvəneriš] 'become rich'. As there is no rule that has to be ordered between INI and VCE_1 or between VCE_1 and VCE_2, one can merge these three rules into the following schema:

$$ \text{ə} \rightarrow \emptyset \quad / \quad \left\{ \begin{array}{c} \S \\ V(\#_1) \end{array} \right\} C \text{——} $$

Remember that, contrary to VCE_1 and VCE_2, INI has to take into consideration some of the characteristics of those consonants that surround the schwa. Notice, on the other hand, that any word that is an exception to VCE_1 is also an exception to INI and vice versa.[34] This suggests a close relation between INI and VCE_1 which is completely obscured by the formal complexity of the formulation INI' (see p. 203). One would like to be able to say that INI and VCE_1 are two aspects of basically one process; the optional deletion of a schwa after a consonant not preceded by another consonant, this process being subject to particular restrictions after a pause.

EPENTHETIC   SCHWAS

In the list of rules given on page 209, there are three rules which delete schwa at the end of polysyllables: PAUS, FIN-DEL₁ and FIN-DEL₂. If we take a closer look, it turns out that the only final schwas of polysyllables that can be retained in phonetic representations are those preceded by two consonants when the following word begins with a consonant:[35]

---

[34] Exclamative *que* and *ne* are affected by VCE_1 in a regular manner: *Oh qu(e) c'est joli!* 'Oh how pretty!', *demain, n(e) pars pas trop tard* 'tomorrow, don't leave too late'. For interrogative *que*, our intuitions are somewhat fuzzy. On these three words, see p. 201, n. 14.

[35] This generalization does not include the cases mentioned on p. 198 n. 8.

un∉ femme [ünfam] 'a woman', *l'aut(re) femme* [lot(rə)fam]
'the other woman'
un∉ amie [ünami] 'a friend' (fem.), *l'autr∉ amie* [lotrami]
j'en vois un∉ [žãvwaün] 'I can see one', *j'ai vu l'autr∉* [žɛvülotr]
'I have seen the other'

Instead of PAUS, $FIN\text{-}DEL_1$ and $FIN\text{-}DEL_2$, we could simply write the two rules below, which must be disjunctively ordered:[36]

$FIN\text{-}DEL_a$: (OPT) $\text{ə} \rightarrow \emptyset \quad / \quad VC_2 \text{——} \#_1 C$

$FIN\text{-}DEL_b$: (OBL) $\text{ə} \rightarrow \emptyset \quad / \quad VC_0 \text{——} \#$

$FIN\text{-}DEL_a$ optionally deletes any polysyllable-final schwa preceded by two consonants when the next word begins with a consonant. $FIN\text{-}DEL_b$ obligatorily deletes all the polysyllable-final schwas which do not meet the conditions of rule $FIN\text{-}DEL_a$. Call this 'the VC_2-deletion analysis'.

Alternatively, we can first delete *all* the polysyllable-final schwas however many consonants precede them, and then optionally reinsert a schwa when a word ending in two consonants or more is followed by another beginning with a consonant:[37]

$FIN\text{-}DEL_b$: (OBL) $\text{ə} \rightarrow \emptyset \quad / \quad VC_0 \text{——} \#$

EPEN: (OPT) $\emptyset \rightarrow \text{ə} \quad / \quad VC_2 \text{——} \#_1 C$

The environment of $FIN\text{-}DEL_b$ is $VC_0\text{——}\#$ rather than simply $\text{——}\#$ to prevent schwas in monosyllables from being deleted. The EPEN rule, which is usually optional, must however obligatorily operate in stress environments where our previous rule $FIN\text{-}DEL_2$ was not to operate.[38] Call this 'the VC_2-epenthesis analysis'.

We much prefer the VC_2-epenthesis analysis, although we must admit that at present we know of no totally decisive argument in its favour. Let us simply mention the following empirical generalization, which is central

[36] On the reasons why these two rules are allowed to apply disjunctively, see Kiparsky (1973c).
[37] EPEN stands for 'epenthesis'.
[38] Cf. p. 200.

when evaluating the respective merits of the two solutions: any word which shows up phonetically as [XCC] when in front of a word beginning with a vowel, can show up phonetically as [XCCə] before a word beginning with a consonant. In normal, everyday speech there are no exceptions to this generalization. It holds for all *XCC* words alike, whatever their conventional spelling. For instance *mettre* 'to put' shows up as [mɛtr] in *mettre un gant* [mɛtrɛ̃gɑ̃] 'to put on a glove', and it can show up as [mɛtrə] in *mettre des gants* [mɛt(rə)degɑ̃] 'to put on gloves'; *film* shows up as [film] in *film anglais* [filmɑ̃glɛ] 'English film', and it can show up as [filmə] in *film danois* [film(ə)danwa] 'Danish film'. We intend to examine elsewhere the implications of this generalization for a comparison between the VC_2-deletion analysis and the VC_2-epenthesis analysis.

In which order are EPEN and LIQUEF applied? Take, for example, *arbre pourri* 'rotten tree', pronounced [arbrəpuri] or [arbpuri] but not *[arbəpuri]. If LIQUEF is applied before EPEN, one obtains *[arbəpuri] in the case where EPEN operates, as shown by the derivation below, opposite which we have set that of *serp(e) rouillée* 'rusty billhook' for comparison:

	/arbrə # # puri/	/sɛrpə # # ruye/
FIN-DEL$_b$	arbr # # puri	sɛrp # # ruye
LIQUEF	arb # # puri	
EPEN	arbə # # puri	sɛrpə # # ruye
	*[arbəpuri]	[sɛrpəruye]

This difficulty disappears if the reverse order is adopted; the liquid is only deleted if EPEN does not place a schwa between it and the following consonant:[39]

	/arbrə # # puri/	/arbrə # # puri/
FIN-DEL$_b$	arbr # # puri	arbr # # puri
EPEN	arbrə # # puri	
LIQUEF		arb # # puri
	[arbrəpuri]	[arbpuri]

According to our rules, words like *arbre* [arbr] 'tree' have three phonetic variants: one variant [XOLə] can appear in front of a consonant, another variant [XOL] can appear in front of a vowel and a pause, and a third variant [XO] can appear in front of a consonant and a pause. There are,

---

[39] The reader can work out that within the framework of the VC_2-deletion analysis, the data examined here require LIQUEF to be ordered after FIN-DEL.

however, certain words which can never lose their final liquid either before a consonant or before a pause. Before a consonant, these words only have the variant [XOLə], as for example the word *astre* [astr] 'star'. *Astre nouveau* 'new star' can only be pronounced [astrənuvo], not *[astnuvo], and *interrogez les astres* 'consult the stars' can only be pronounced [ε̃tɛrɔželezastr], not *[ε̃tɛrɔželezast]. See also:

> *pègre parisienne* [pɛgrəparisyɛn]/*[pɛgparisyɛn] 'Parisian under-world'
> *c'est le roi de la pègre* [sɛlrwadlapɛgr]/*[sɛlrwadlapɛg] 'he's the king of the underworld'
> *les buffles d'Asie* [lebüflədazi]/*[lebüfdazi] 'Asiatic buffaloes'
> *regarde les buffles* [rəgardlebüfl]/*[rəgardlebüf] 'look at the buffaloes'

The words *astre*, *pègre* and *buffle* must be marked in the lexicon as exceptions to rule LIQUEF.[40] But this is not enough to account for the behaviour of these words before a consonant. In the case of *astre nouveau*, for example, the grammar gives the following two derivations:

	/astrə # # nuvo/	/astrə # # nuvo/
FIN-DEL$_b$	astr # # nuvo	astr # # nuvo
EPEN	astrə # # nuvo	
LIQUEF		
	[astrənuvo]	*[astrnuvo]

The derivation on the left poses no problems. It corresponds to the case in which the optional rule EPEN operates, and it is in all points similar to the derivation given above of [arbrəpuri]. The derivation on the right corresponds to the case in which the optional rule EPEN does not operate.[41] The input to LIQUEF is the intermediate representation *astr # # nuvo*, and as *astre* is marked [− LIQUEF] in the lexicon, this rule cannot delete the final *r*, whence the final output [astrnuvo], which, contrary to what our grammar predicts, is actually ill-formed.

Apparently we are faced with a paradox. On the one hand the agrammaticality of *[astrnuvo] seems to suggest that EPEN, which is usually an optional rule, must operate obligatorily in order to break up the sequences $OL\#_1 C$ which are still intact at the output of LIQUEF. On the other hand, EPEN cannot have access to the information contained in the

---

[40] It is rather literary or rare words that have a tendency to be exceptions to LIQUEF.
[41] Compare with the derivation given above for [arbpuri].

output of LIQUEF, since we have shown for *arbre pourri* that EPEN must precede LIQUEF.[42]

There are other cases where the *OL* clusters demand the presence of a schwa even though schwa alternates freely with zero after the other consonant clusters occurring in the same context; these are the forms of the future (see above p. 208). We have tried to show elsewhere (see n. 44) that to account for all these facts, it is necessary to introduce an output constraint[43] at the end of the grammar. This constraint rejects as ill-formed any phonetic representation which contains a sequence where an obstruent is followed by a liquid, itself followed by a consonantal segment:

$$\text{OBLICONS:} \quad *[-\text{son}] \begin{bmatrix} +\text{son} \\ +\text{cons} \\ -\text{nas} \end{bmatrix} [+\text{cons}]$$

OBLICONS will exclude from the grammar the derivation leading to *[astrnuvo] as well as any similar derivation. Using OBLICONS also allows us to dispense with the special condition preventing rule FUT-DEL from operating after *OL* clusters. If we allow this rule to operate freely without taking into account the nature of the group of consonants preceding the thematic vowel, it will produce the same alternation between schwa and zero after the *OL* clusters as it does after other clusters. Similarly to [fiksərə]/[fiksra] (*fixera* 'he will fix'), [parlərə]/[parlra] (*parlera* 'he will talk') FUT-DEL will yield [siflərə]/[siflra] for *sifflera* 'he will whistle', and the output constraint OBLICONS will eliminate the representation [siflra], which is ill-formed.

Thus by postulating the output constraint OBLICONS, we can avoid an ordering paradox and relate two facts: the fact that FUT-DEL cannot delete schwa after an *OL* group, and the fact that EPEN necessarily inserts a schwa at the end of a word ending in an *OL* cluster which cannot lose its liquid, when the following word begins with a consonant.[44]

[42] The problem remains unchanged if instead of attributing the phonological representations /arbrə/, /astrə/ to *arbre* and *astre* as we did in the text for the sake of convenience, we had attributed to them the phonological representations /arbr/, /astr/. In that case, FIN-DEL$_b$ would apply vacuously. For the time being, we cannot decide whether the morphemes which are phonetically actualized as [XOL] (i.e. *arbre*, *astre*, etc.) have a final schwa in their phonological representations or not.

[43] On the output constraints which have been proposed with regard to syntax, see Ross (1967: chap. 3) and Perlmutter (1971: chap. 2).

[44] For a detailed discussion of OBLICONS, see Dell (1976). We have shown there that the problem raised by the behaviour of words such as *astre* subsists *mutatis mutandis* if instead of choosing the VC$_2$·epenthesis analysis, one chooses the VC$_2$·deletion analysis. We also argued against replacing the output constraint OBLICONS by a late epenthesis rule which would obligatorily insert schwa between an *OL* cluster and a following *C*.

Notice, to conclude, a type of data for which we have not been able to find any really satisfactory treatment. The analysis presented above implies that the behaviour of a word of the XOL type in front of a word beginning with a consonant does not depend on the number of # boundaries separating the two words. Thus the word *autre* 'other' has the two phonetic variants [otrə], [ot] in both *aut(re) poulie* [ot(rə)puli] 'other pulley', where the two words are separated by a single # boundary, and *l'aut(re) pourrira* [lot(rə)purira] 'the other will rot', where they are separated by two # boundaries. But our dialect has a (relatively limited) category of words which can lose their final liquid before a sequence ##C but not before a sequence #C. For example, the words *double* [dubl] 'double', *simple* [sɛ̃pl] 'simple', *entre* [ãtr] 'between', *contre* [kɔ̃tr] 'against' belong to this category, as can be seen from the examples below. In each example (a), one of these words is separated from the following word by a single # boundary, whereas in the corresponding (b) example, it is separated by two # boundaries:

(i) (a) *il veut une double portion de purée*
          [...dubl<u>ə</u>pɔrsyɔ̃...] 'he wants a double helping of mashed potatoes'
     (b) *ceux qui voient doub(le) peuvent rien y faire*
          [...dub(lə)pœv...] 'those who see double can do nothing about it'

(ii) (a) *il suffit d'une simple carte d'identité*
          [...sɛ̃pl<u>ə</u>kart...] 'a mere identity card is enough'
     (b) *c'est bien plus simp(le) comme ça*
          [...sɛ̃p(lə)kɔm...] 'it's much simpler like that'

(iii)(a) *ça se trouve entre Paris et Calais*
          [...ãtr<u>ə</u>pari...] 'it is situated between Paris and Calais'
     (b) *il faut s'asseoir ent(re) pour être à l'aise*
          [...ãt(rə)pur...] 'you have to sit in between to be comfortable'

(iv) (a) *pose-le contre la table*
          [...kɔ̃tr<u>ə</u>la...] 'put it down against the table'
     (b) *ceux qui sont cont(re) lèvent la main*
          [...kɔ̃t(rə)lɛv...] 'those against raise their hands'

At this point, it is worth returning to the hypothesis we discussed briefly on page 162, according to which internal schwas[45] do not derive from

---

[45] The following discussion only concerns 'internal' schwas as we defined them on page 201.

vowels already present in the phonological representations, but from vowels introduced by epenthesis in the course of the derivation. This in fact is what André Martinet[46] has always claimed. He thinks it necessary to postulate a phoneme /ə/ only to account for certain oppositions before 'aspirated *h*', such as those in *l'être*[a] vs. *le hêtre*[b], *dors*[c] vs. *dehors*[d]. Otherwise, the presence or absence of /ə/ would in his view always be mechanically determined by the nature of the context. Any consonantal phoneme /C/ of French would be realized as [Cə] when it occurred between two consonants, and as [C] everywhere else. Thus, according to Martinet (1969: 217) 'the phoneme /d/ has the variant [d] in front of a vowel as in *dans*[e], for example, or after a vowel and in front of a single consonant, as in *là-dessus* [ladsy][f], but a variant [də] between consonants, as in *pardessus* /pardsy/[g], realized as [pardəsy]'. Martinet quite rightly remarks that this analysis has the advantage of explaining in a natural way the fact that, unlike other vowels, schwa never appears in word-initial position.[47] But we know of no other argument in favour of this analysis. The problem we have already mentioned (p. 162) concerning pairs such as *secoue*[h]/*skie*[i], *pelouse*[j]/*place*[k], can be found elsewhere than just after word initial consonants: *perdrix*[l] is pronounced [pɛrdri] and never *[pɛrdəri], whereas *bordereau*[m] is pronounced [bɔrdəro] and never *[bɔrdro]. See also the pairs *portrait*[n]/*forteresse*[o], *marbré*[p]/*Barberot*[q], *Harfleur*[r]/*farfelu*[s], *escrime*[t]/*brusquerie*[u], *sclérose*[v]/*squelette*[w].

Notice also the opposition between the future and conditional forms of the first conjugation, where schwa appears in certain cases, and analogous forms of some verbs of the third conjugation, where it never appears: *borderez* [bɔrd(ə)re][x] but *tordrez* [tɔrdre][y], *fonderiez* [fɔ̃dərye][z] (from *fonder*[a]) but *fondriez* [fɔ̃driye][b'] (from *fondre*[c']). In accordance with the analysis we have defended (p. 188), the above forms have the following

---

[46]   1960: secs. 3–22; 1962: 11–25; 1965a: 125; 1969: 209–19.

[47]   Within the framework of our analysis, the only way to account for this fact is to postulate a morpheme-structure rule preventing any lexical morpheme or any prefix from beginning with a /ə/. The generality of this rule does not go beyond the particular fact justifying its inclusion in the grammar. In this sense our analysis does not explain this fact: it merely acknowledges it.

[a][lɛtr] 'the being'. [b][lɑɛtr] 'the beech'. [c][dɔr] 'sleep!'. [d][dɔ̯ɔr] 'outside'. [e][dɑ̃] 'in'. [f][ladsü] 'upon this'. [g][pardəsü] 'above'. [h][s(ə)ku] 'he shakes'. [i][ski] 'he skis'. [j][p(ə)luz] 'lawn'. [k][plas] 'place'. [l]'partridge. [m]'memorandum'. [n][pɔrtrɛ] 'portrait'. [o][fɔrtərɛs] 'fortress'. [p][marbre] 'marbled'. [q][barbəro] (proper name). [r][arflœr] (proper name). [s][farfəlü] 'extravagant, crazy'. [t][ɛskrim] 'fencing'. [u][brüskəri] 'bluntness'. [v][skleroz] 'sclerosis'. [w][skəlɛt] 'skeleton'. [x]'you will border'. [y]'you will twist'. [z]'you would found'. [a']'to found'. [b']'you would melt'. [c']'to melt'.

underlying representations: /bɔrd + ə + r + e/, /tɔrd + r + e/, /fõd + ə + r + i + e/, /fõd + r + i + e/. The optional deletion of schwa in *borderez* is due to rule FUT-DEL. As to the fact that /i + e/ is realized as [iye] in *fondriez* but as [ye] in *fonderiez*, it is an instance of a widespread regularity that can be approximately described as follows: /iV/ is realized as [iyV] after an *OL* group and as [yV] everywhere else:- *oublier* [ubliye][a], *étudier* [etüdye][b]; *quatrième* [katriyɛm][c], *troisième* [trwazyɛm][d]; *poudrière* [pudriyɛr][e], *glacière* [glasyɛr][f], etc. The grammar will in any case have to contain phonological rules which are formulated to guarantee this result.[48] If we wish at all costs to show that the schwa of *fonderiez* does not derive from an underlying vowel, but is predictable from the environment, we have to suppose that the ending *-iez* of *fonderiez* and that of *fondriez* derive from different phonological representations, but this cannot be independently justified.

Conscious of these difficulties, Blanche-Benveniste and Chervel (1969: 127–30) proposed an analysis where schwa represents a phoneme in certain contexts and is the result of an epenthesis process in others. The analysis uses a fact that we will first present from the point of view of our own analysis: not all groups of consonants are allowed in phonological representations. Consider, for example, what takes place at the beginning of morphemes. The existence of *plisse* [plis] 'he creases', vs. *pelisse* [pəlis] 'pelisse' and *police* [pɔlis] 'police', shows that, at the level of the phonological representations, morphemes beginning with /pl/ can be opposed to others beginning with /pVl/; /pl/ is a possible morpheme-initial consonant cluster at the level of the phonological representations. On the other hand, French cannot oppose morphemes beginning with the sequence /mz/ to morphemes beginning with /mVz/, such as *mesure* [m(ə)zür] 'measure' and *masure* [mazür] 'hovel'; /mz/ is not a possible morpheme-initial consonant cluster at the level of the phonological representations. It can be said that the presence of a vowel between [m] and [z] is predictable in [šakməzur] *chaque mesure* 'each measure', in the sense that the sequence *[šakmzür] is not well-formed in French.[49] Apart from a certain number of exceptions, such as *pneu* [pnö] 'tyre', *psychose* [psikoz] 'psychosis', etc.,

---

[48] On the detail of these rules, see references on p. 48, n. 18.

[49] Strictly speaking what is needed in the environment *k —— mz* is simply the presence *of any vowel*, not necessarily that of the specific vowel schwa. Nevertheless, the reason why people choose to treat schwa (rather than *a* or *o*) as an epenthentic vowel is obvious, even if it has never been explicitly given in the works on this subject: the presence of *a* in *masure* [mazür] 'hovel', is a permanent property of this morpheme, whereas that of schwa in *mesure* depends on the environment.

[a] 'to forget'. [b] 'to study'. [c] 'fourth'. [d] 'third'. [e] 'powder-flask'. [f] 'ice-box'.

there are only two kinds of groups of two consonants that are possible at the beginning of morphemes: *s* followed by a non-continuant (*ski* [ski] 'ski', *scribe* [skrib] 'scribe '),[50] or certain *OL* groups (*place* [plas] 'place ', *crête* [krɛt] 'crest ').[51] As an expository device, we will use the expression WZ as an arbitrarily chosen symbol representing the characterization in distinctive features of the set of clusters of two consonants allowed at the beginning of morphemes, and the expression W'Z' to represent the characterization in distinctive features of the complement of this class (groups of two consonants that cannot occur at the beginning of morphemes). The solution proposed by Blanche-Benveniste and Chervel consists of considering all the schwas that appear at the phonetic level between two consonants WZ as realizations of a phoneme /ə/, and those that appear between two consonants W'Z' as introduced by epenthesis. Thus *secoue* 'he shakes ', *pelote* 'ball' (of wool), *ski*, *place* will be phonologically represented as /səku/, /pələt/, /ski/, /plas/, whereas *mesure*, *genou* 'knee' will be phonologically represented as /mzür/, /žnu/.

Blanche-Benveniste and Chervel were content with sketching the main outlines of their analysis and did not enter into the details, but it is interesting to try to develop it to its ultimate consequences. Note that it implies, at the phonological level, that any sequence of consonants is possible at the beginning of morphemes and it therefore enables one to dispense with the morpheme structure rule necessary in our own analysis to express the fact that only WZ sequences are allowed in that position. The grammar of Blanche-Benveniste and Chervel must contain, as does ours, the optional rule VCE_1 in order to account for the fact that the phoneme schwa can be phonetically realized as zero after $V\#_1C$ (*la pelote* [lap(ə)lɔt]). Let us now look at the epenthesis rule which, in their analysis, is responsible for the presence of schwas such as that of [šakžənu] *chaque genou* (from /šak#žnu/) 'each knee '. It cannot simply be a rule that obligatorily inserts schwa in any environment $C\#_1C$——C. Such a rule would be too general, since it would derive not only [šakžənu] from /šak#žnu/ but also *[šakpəlas] from /šak#plas/ *chaque place* 'each place '. The structural description of the epenthesis rule must indicate that at the beginning of words, the only *CC* sequences subject to the insertion of schwa are W'Z' sequences:

INS$_1$:[52] $\emptyset \rightarrow$ ə   / $C\#_1W'$——Z'
(OBL)

---

[50] As opposed to *secouer* 'to shake', *secret* 'secret'.
[51] As opposed to *pelote* 'ball' (wool), *querelle* 'quarrel'.
[52] INS stands for 'insertion '.

But INS_1 still does not account for the fact that [mežnu] optionally alternates with [mežənu] for *mes genoux* 'my knees'. It is therefore necessary to add an optional rule that inserts schwa in the same groups of consonants as INS_1 when a vowel precedes:

$$INS_2: \quad \varnothing \;\rightarrow\; \text{ə} \quad / \quad V \#_1 W' \text{——} Z'$$
$$(\text{OPT})$$

Thus, instead of our single rule VCE_1, the grammar implied by the analysis of Blanche-Benveniste and Chervel has three: VCE_1, INS_1 and INS_2. These three rules all converge, as if by chance, in the same result; words pronounced [CəCX] when preceded by a consonant can be pronounced either [CəCX] or [CCX] when preceded by a vowel and this is true *whatever the nature of the consonants surrounding schwa*. The grammar in question completely obscures this generalization, since it attributes the alternations between schwa and zero to the action of different rules, according to whether these alternations take place in an environment $\#W'$——Z' (INS_1 and INS_2) or in an environment $\#W$——Z (VCE_1).

Note, in conclusion, that in the perspective adopted by Blanche-Benveniste and Chervel, the pronunciations of forms such as *geler* [ž(ə)le] 'to freeze', *mener* [m(ə)ne] 'to lead', etc. derive from the phonological representations /žl + e/, /mn + e/, where /žl/ and /mn/ do not have any vowels. But apart from these cases, it is a fact that in French the phonological representations of lexical morphemes always have at least one vowel.[53] Finally, we will leave to the reader the task of examining the complications following from the analysis of Blanche-Benveniste and Chervel in the treatment of exceptions, and in that of alternations between schwa and ɛ.

The formulations of LIQUEF, FIN-DEL$_b$ and EPEN given on pages 201 and 212 were designed to account for those cases where schwa is the final vowel of a word which is followed by another word beginning with a consonant, but they have nothing to say about cases where schwa in a final syllable is followed by a consonant[54] that acts as a *liaison* consonant with

---

[53] The only exceptions consist of a few irregular verb forms like *sont* 'they are', *font* 'they do', *ont* 'they have' where the root is /s/, /f/ and zero, respectively.

[54] Owing to the morphological structure of French, this consonant can only be a *t* or a *z* preceded by a boundary. *t* is the ending of the third person (*travers(e)·t·on?* 'does one cross?', *perd(e)nt-ils?* 'are they losing?'); *z* can be the plural ending of nouns and adjectives (*larg(e)s ouvertures* 'wide openings'), or it can be the ending of the second person, which is not subject to truncation when a verb in the imperative is followed by the clitic pronouns *y* and *en*, because of their initial vowel (*résist(e)s·y* 'resist it', *parl(e)s·en* 'speak of it').

the initial vowel of the following word. In such cases, nothing changes; compare *énormes anneaux* [enɔrm(ə)zano] 'huge rings' with *énorme zéro* [enɔrm(ə)zero] 'huge zero' *d'autres anneaux* [dot(rə)zano] 'other rings' with *l'autre zero* [lot(rə)zero] 'the other zero'. To account for these facts, various solutions come to mind.

The first solution would consist in keeping FIN-DEL$_b$, EPEN and LIQUEF with their original formulations and in supposing that, in phonological representations, the *z* of the plural and of the second person, and the *t* of the third person, are separated from the rest of the word by a # boundary. *Autres anneaux*, for example, would have the underlying representation /otrə#z#ano#z/, which enables the rules to operate exactly as in *autre zero* /otrə#zero/. This modification of the phonological representations changes the rest of our analysis very little. Simply, instead of being attributed to rule TRUNC$_a$,[55] the truncation of the final obstruent of the root in *petits* /#pətit#z#/ [p(ə)ti] 'little' (pl.) and in *il tord* /#tɔrd#t#/ [itɔr] 'he twists' would now have to be attributed to TRUNC$_b$.[56]

But Selkirk (1972: 307–9) has argued, in our opinion convincingly, that the endings *z* and *t* should not be separated from what precedes by a # boundary. She gives the following reason: AL-O is a rule which rewrites *al* as *o* in front of a consonant belonging to the same word[57] and this rule operates in particular in front of the endings *z* and *t*: the plural of *canal* [kanal] 'canal' is *canaux* [kano], and the third person of the singular of the present indicative of *valoir* [valwar] 'to be worth' is *vaut* [vo]. If these endings are preceded by a # boundary, the phonological representations of *canaux* and *vaut* are /kanal#z/ and /val#t/ and the rule AL-O must be formulated so as to operate in the environment ——#C. But in this case, the rule will also operate in front of the initial consonant of a following word preceded by a single # boundary, which would lead to non-grammatical

---

[55] Cf. p. 157.

[56] But TRUNC$_a$ is still needed to account for deletions such as that of the final *z* of the root in front of the future *r* in *lirez* /liz+r+ez/ 'you will read'. This rule is much less general than TRUNC$_b$ and its exceptions much more numerous. For example, it operates in *écrirez* /ekriv+r+ez/ 'you will write' but not in *suivrez* /süiv+r+ez/ 'you will follow'. In front of the *r* of the future, it never deletes non-continuants: *battrez* 'you will beat', *tordrez* 'you will twist', *convaincrez* 'you will convince', etc. Schane (1968a: 100–1) explains these forms by supposing that the final consonant of the root is separated from the *r* by a thematic vowel. We cannot go into the reasons which lead us to reject this analysis since this would necessitate a re-examination of much of Schane's conception on the system of vowel alternations in French. For such a discussion, cf. Dell (forthcoming).

[57] Cf. Schane (1968a: 51).

forms. /prɛ̃sipal # defo/ (*principal défaut* 'main defect') would yield, for instance, *[prɛ̃sipodefo] instead of the correct pronunciation [prɛ̃sipalde-fo]. It is better to suppose that the endings z and t are preceded by a $+$ boundary, and thus to limit the operation of rule AL-O to the environment ——C.

If one takes into account that the endings z and t are preceded by a morpheme boundary, FIN-DEL$_b$ and LIQUEF can be reformulated as follows:

$$\text{FIN-DEL}_b\text{:} \quad V \;\rightarrow\; \emptyset \quad / \quad \acute{V}C_0\text{——}$$

$$\text{LIQUEF:} \quad L \;\rightarrow\; \emptyset \quad / \quad \acute{V}C_0\,O\text{——}\left\{ \begin{array}{l} [-\text{seg}]_1\,C \\ \S \end{array} \right\}$$

FIN-DEL deletes any vowel occuring to the right of the word stress. Because of our formulation of the stress rule (see p. 192) such a vowel can only be a schwa. LIQUEF deletes the final liquid of a morpheme ending with an *OL* cluster when the preceding vowel carries a word stress[58] and when what follows is a pause or a morpheme beginning with a consonant. If the structural description of LIQUEF did not require that the preceding vowel be stressed, the rule would erroneously erase root-final liquids in those future forms of *-er* verbs where FUT-DEL has deleted the thematic vowel. For instance, FUT-DEL optionally rewrites / # sãbl + ər + a # / (*semblera* [sãbləra] 'it will seem') as / # sãbl + r + a # /, which would yield *[sãbra] if LIQUEF were allowed to operate.

An adequate reformulation of EPEN is harder to obtain. If the environment of the rule on p. 212 is generalized to CC——$[-\text{seg}]_1 C$, the rule will correctly operate in / # otr—— + z # ano + z # / (*autres anneaux* ' other rings ') hence [otrəzano], but it will also operate in the future forms of the verbs of the so-called 'third conjugation', and the grammar will derive the ungrammatical form *[pɛrdəra] from the phonological representation / # pɛrd + r + a + t # / (*perdra* 'he will loose'). This can be avoided by restating the environment of the rule as $\acute{V}C_2$——$[-\text{seg}]_1 C$. The new rule is still not factually adequate, however, since it will operate in those infinitive forms of the third conjugation where the ending *-r* is suffixed onto a root ending in a consonant cluster. The rule would for instance derive *[pɛrdər] from / # pɛrd + r # / (*perdre* [pɛrdr] 'to lose '). One observationally adequate formulation is the following:

$$\text{EPEN:} \quad \emptyset \;\rightarrow\; \mathrm{ə} \quad / \quad \acute{V}C_2\text{——}\left\{ \begin{array}{l} \#_1\,C \\ +[-\text{son}] \end{array} \right\} \qquad \begin{array}{l}(a)\\(b)\end{array}$$

---

[58] Vergnaud (1975: 28) was the one to suggest that the preceding vowel is stressed. The rule should be able to operate in words like *arbre* and *ambidextre*, hence the C_0 which occurs between V and O in the environment of the rule.

The second rule of this schema inserts a schwa between a morpheme-final consonant cluster and an obstruent. It takes advantage of the fact that French has three word-final endings which consist of a single consonant, z, t and the infinitive r, and that EPEN operates in front of the obstruents z and t, but not in front of r.

In fact, we think that the real reason why the endings z and t and the word-initial consonants behave in the same way in relation to epenthesis, is because they are both syllable-initial: z is syllable-initial in /enɔrm + z # a-no + z/ (*énormes anneaux* [enɔrm(ə)zano] 'huge rings'), as well as in /enɔrm # zɛbr/ (*énorme zèbre* [enɔrm(ə)zɛbr] 'huge zebra'), and t is syllable-initial in /ekɔrš + t # ɔ̃/ (*écorche-t-on* [ekɔ̃rš(ə)tɔ̃] 'does one flay?') as well as in /ekɔrš # tü/ (*écorches-tu* [ekɔrš(ə)tü] 'do you flay?'). At the point where the epenthesis rule is applicable, the only occurrences of the endings z and t which are still present in the derivations are those which have escaped the truncation rule, i.e. those which establish the *liaison* in the environment ——— # V. But in French, *liaison* consonants belong to the same syllable as the initial vowel of the following word; they are syllable-initial. On the contrary, the r of the infinitive is never syllable-initial: neither when the following word begins with a consonant, since that consonant is then syllable-initial, as the initial l of the article in / # mɔrd + r # # la # mɛ̃/ (*mordre la main* [mɔrd(rə)lamɛ̃] 'to bite the hand'), nor when the following word begins with a vowel. Indeed, if we look at the forms where the infinitive ending r is immediately preceded by a consonantal segment, we see that at the phonetic level this segment is always one of the five following obstruents: p (e.g. in *rompre* [rɔ̃pr] 'to break'), t (e.g. in *battre* [batr] 'to beat'), k (e.g. in *vaincre* [vɛ̃kr] 'to defeat'), d (e.g. in *rendre* [rɑ̃dr] 'to give back', *tordre* [tɔrdr] 'to twist'), v (e.g. in *suivre* [sẅivr] 'to follow'). And it is a well-known fact in French phonology that the clusters pr, tr, kr, dr and vr possess, with a certain number of other OL clusters, the special property that their two consonants are part of the same syllable when they belong to the same word. Thus, in /mɔrd + r # # ɛ̃ # pye/ (*mordre un pied* [mɔrdrɛ̃pye] 'to bite a foot'), the r of the infinitive cannot be syllable-initial, since this implies that the preceding d does not belong to the same syllable. This cannot be the case since we are dealing with a dr group of which the two consonants belong to the same word. To conclude, we propose to reformulate EPEN in the following way:

EPEN: $\emptyset \rightarrow$ ə   / $\acute{V}C_2$ ——— $[- \text{seg}]_1 C$

Condition: the rightmost C is syllable-initial

SCHWA IN CONTIGUOUS SYLLABLES

When several successive syllables contain schwas liable to be deleted by INI and VCE_1, a speaker talking at a normal rate tends to drop as many schwas as is compatible with the principle (P) which will be discussed below. But this is a tendency rather than an absolute necessity. It is common practice to retain two or three schwas in succession without this necessarily implying that one is speaking with particular care: [ãvidətəvwar] *envie de te voir* ‘longing to see you’ [ãvidətərəvwar] *envie de te revoir* ‘longing to see you again’. But as the sequences get longer, so the need to delete schwa increases. All this is to say that it is not possible to distinguish two styles of normal conversation, one which would be characterized by the systematic non-application of INI and VCE_1, and the other by their systematic application.

Consider the sequence *Jacques redevenait (gai)* ‘Jack was becoming (merry) again’, which can be pronounced both [žakrədvənɛ] and [žakrədəvnɛ].[59] The input to VCE[60] is the representation /žak # #rə₁də₂və₃nɛ/ where we have numbered the schwas to facilitate reference to them. VCE_1 cannot operate, for $ə_1$ is preceded by $C\#_1\,C$; on the other hand, $ə_2$ and $ə_3$ are both subject to VCE_2 and as this rule is obligatory, they should both be dropped, whence the final output *[žakrədvnɛ]. In fact, the two schwas are never dropped at the same time. Either $ə_2$ is dropped ([žakrədvənɛ]), or else $ə_3$ ([žakrədəvnɛ]). These two pronunciations are strictly equivalent, both semantically and stylistically. Or again, consider *(tu as) envie de te battre* ‘you feel like fighting’, which can be pronounced [ãvidətbatr], [ãvidətəbatr] or [ãvidtəbatr], but not *[ãvidtbatr], although both schwas are subject to VCE_1. Here are other examples:

tu le retrouves
‘you find him again’

1.	[tülrətruv],	2.	[tülərtruv],
3.	[tülərətruv],	4.	*[tülrtruv].

la queue de ce renard
‘this fox’s tail’

1.	[laködsərnar],	2.	[laködəsrənar],
3.	[laködsərənar],	4.	[laködəsərnar],
5.	[laködəsərənar],	6.	*[laködsrənar],
7.	*[laködəsrnar],	8.	*[laködsrnar].

---

[59] The pronunciation [žakrədəvənɛ] would be more likely when reading aloud than in normal conversation. It is excluded by the fact that VCE_2 is an obligatory rule.

[60] When we wish to refer to both VCE_1 and VCE_2, we will simply use VCE.

envie de te le	1. [ãvidtəldəmãde],	2. [ãvidətlədmãde],
demander[61]	3. [ãvidtələdəmãde],	4. [ãvidətlədəmãde],
'feel like asking	5. [ãvidtələdmãde],	6. [ãvidətəldəmãde],
you'	7. [ãvidətələdmãde],	8. [ãvidətələdəmãde].

These examples show that we can state as follows the principle governing the behaviour of schwas occurring in contiguous syllables and liable to be deleted by the same rule (VCE_1 or VCE_2):

> (P) VCE_1 (or VCE_2) can delete as many schwas as desired, as long as its output does not contain any groups of three consonants $C_1C_2C_3$ where C_2 and C_3 were separated by a schwa in the corresponding input.

Principle (P) is based on an implicit acknowledgement of the fact that the deletion of a schwa by VCE always creates a group of at least two consonants. *(P) does not rule out just any group of three consonants* in the output of VCE, but only certain specific groups of three consonants.[62] VCE creates, for example, a group of three consonants in *prenez le train* [prəneltrɛ̃] 'take the train', and this can take place immediately next to another schwa: *ne le crevez pas* [nəlkrəvepa] 'don't burst it', *plus tard que le scrutin* [plütarkəlskrütɛ̃] 'later than the poll'. As required by the structural description of VCE, such groups only result from the disappearance of schwas preceded by a single consonant and immediately followed by two or more.

The exclusion of certain groups of consonants in the output of VCE cannot be attributed to a general output constraint that would prevent certain sequences from appearing in phonetic representations.[63] For example, in *il veut que ce travail soit bien fait* 'he wants this work to be well done', permissible pronunciations are [...vöksətra...], [...vökəstra...], but not *[...vökstra...], although the sequence [kstr] is present in the phonetic representation of *extraordinaire* [ɛkstrɔrdinɛr] 'extraordinary' and in one of the phonetic representations of *lux(e) trop voyant* [lüks(ə)trovwayã] 'too flashy luxury'. In the first case it is present from the start in the phonological representation and, in the second, it is created by FIN-DEL.

---

[61] For the sake of brevity, we have only given the well-formed pronunciations of this last example.

[62] This does not come out clearly in Grammont's 'law of three consonants' as it is formulated in his *Traité Pratique* (1914: 115): 'the general rule is that it [mute *e*] is only pronounced when it is needed to prevent three consonants from coming together... Its retention or deletion depends essentially on what precedes.'

[63] Cf. p. 215, n. 43.

It can be seen from (P) that the well- or ill-formed character of a group of three consonants in the output of VCE does not depend on the characteristics of the consonants constituting this group, but on the way in which it is created by VCE. The main facts may be summarized as shown below, where word boundaries have been omitted and impossible derivations marked with an asterisk:

$$
\begin{array}{lll}
\text{(A)} & \text{VC\textschwa CC} & \rightarrow & \text{VCCC} \\
\text{*(B)} & \text{VCC\textschwa C} & \rightarrow & \text{VCCC} \\
\text{*(C)} & \text{VC\textschwa C\textschwa C} & \rightarrow & \text{VCCC} \\
\text{(D)} & \text{VC\textschwa C\textschwa C} & \rightarrow & \text{VCC\textschwa C} \\
\text{(E)} & \text{VC\textschwa C\textschwa C} & \rightarrow & \text{VC\textschwa CC} \\
\end{array}
$$

The derivation (B) is impossible because of the very way in which the VCE rules are formulated. It remains to find out how to prevent (C), while allowing (D) and (E).

The problem is the following: we have discovered a certain condition (P) that our grammar must satisfy if it wishes to generate only well-formed sound–meaning pairs. But the grammar we have at hand for the moment does not satisfy (P), since it allows derivations of the type (C). The first idea which comes to mind is that our formulation of VCE is inadequate, and that it could be replaced by another formulation, no less general than the first, but which would exclude derivations of the type (C). The reader will be able to work out that this is impossible. If it is not the formulation of VCE that is in question, it can only be the linguistic theory in whose framework this rule has been formulated. Thus, our inability to account satisfactorily for the behaviour of schwa in French prompts us partially to revise our conception of the organization of grammars in general. We will simply indicate the importance of the problem thus posed, without trying to solve it.

What is being questioned here is the conception we had of the way in which the phonological rules are applied. Taken out of context, phonological rules are no more than a string of symbols set out on paper one after another. It is linguistic theory that enables us to interpret them, providing them, as it were, with directions for use. We will not question what we said on phonological rules in chapter 2, except on one point. Let us see how Chomsky and Halle (1968: 344) conceive the way in which the phonological rules are applied: 'To apply a rule the entire string is first scanned for segments that satisfy the environmental constraints of the rule. After all such segments have been identified in the string, the changes required by the rule are applied simultaneously.'

The point which attracts our attention is the necessity for a rule to operate simultaneously on all relevant points of its input, which we will call the 'principle of simultaneous application'. This principle seems to be open to question, given the behaviour of schwas in $VC\partial C\partial C$ sequences. By virtue of this principle, each schwa should be deleted without considering the fate of schwas situated in contiguous syllables. But in fact we know that one of the schwas can be deleted only if the other has not been deleted. More generally, we cannot admit the principle of simultaneous application without at the same time accepting proposition (Q) as universally true:

> (Q)   When the conditions of the structural description of a rule are satisfied at several points in the same representation, the rule operates at each point without considering what is taking place at other points.

Proposition (Q) has no logical necessity. It is a factual statement that limits the class of possible languages. *A priori*, it is easy to conceive of different modes of application, e.g. (Q') or (Q''):

> (Q')   When the conditions of the structural description of a rule are satisfied in two contiguous syllables of the same representation, the rule only operates on one of these two syllables, chosen randomly. (Q) remains true in all other cases.
>
> (Q'')   Phonological rules only operate in the odd syllables of words (starting from the left).

If (Q') were true, we could expect French words such as *contenter* /kɔntante/ 'to content' to have two alternative pronunciations, [kɔ̃tante] and [kɔntãte], since rule NAS would have to affect either the sequence /ɔnt/ or the sequence /ant/, but not both at the same time. If (Q'') were true, we could expect *contenter* to be pronounced [kɔ̃tante] and *mécontenter* ('to displease') [mekontãte]. Proposition (Q) is, in fact, a good approximation of the truth, and it took time to discover data contradicting it.

To explain the impossibility of the derivation (C) above, suppose that, instead of simultaneously affecting all the segments that satisfy its structural description in a given representation, VCE were applied in as many successive steps as this representation contains schwas subject to it, each new application affecting the output of the preceding one. We will call VCE an iterative rule. The iterative application of VCE is carried out from left to right. Take a sequence like /vu#mə#lə#dit/ *vous me le dites* [vumlədit], [vuməl(ə)dit] 'you tell me so'; VCE_1 begins on the left and first deletes the schwa of *me*, producing /vu # m # lə # dit/. But VCE_1 cannot operate again and delete the schwa of *le*, for, although this schwa was subject to the rule in the original representation, it no longer is once the schwa of *me* has been dropped. In other words, the first application of VCE_1 creates new conditions that prevent it from operating again in the following syllable. In this perspective, the ill-formed character of *[vumldit] has the same origin as that of *[samldi] for *Sam le dit* [samlədi] 'Sam says so': in both cases the schwa of *le* is preceded by two consonants at the moment when it is taken into consideration by the rule. It matters little that the consonant cluster /m # l/ of /vu # m # lə # dit/ comes from a previous application of VCE_1, whereas that of /sam # # lə # di/ is already present when the representation is subject to VCE_1 for the first time. It is essential that the iterative application of VCE be carried out from left to right. If it were from right to left, the first deletion of the schwa of *le* would not prevent the further deletion of the schwa of *me*, since in /vu # mə # l # dit/ this schwa is still subject to VCE_1.[64]

Does this mean that the linguistic theory has to be modified by simply substituting for the principle of simultaneous application another principle by virtue of which all the phonological rules should be iteratively applied from left to right? No, because other languages provide data that cannot be accounted for by iterative rules applying from left to right but seem on the contrary to require iterative application from right to left. All that the facts of French suggest is that the principle of simultaneous application is incorrect, and that it must make way for another principle enabling a rule to reapply, in certain cases, to its own output. But the iteration does not have to take place linearly from left to right or from right to left. Other modes of iterative application are conceivable. In the definitions of these modes, left–right and right–left directions do not play any role but they none the less account for facts like those of French.[65]

Note that, concerning the deletion of schwa, the interaction between two different rules has exactly the same property as the interaction between two successive applications of the same rule. The relative orderings that we have established between the rules FIN-DEL, INI, VCE_1 and VCE_2 are

[64] The deletion or retention of schwas in rows, resulting from the repeated application (from left to right) of the same process, is not a new conception. For example, Bally (1944: 279) declares that the consonant cluster which prevents the deletion of ə can itself be the result of previously deleting an ə. See also De Felice (1950: 18) and Delattre (1966: 24). The same idea has been taken up within the framework of generative phonology by Milner (1967: 281, n. 16), Johnson (1970: 77) and Morin and Friedman (1971: 48–52).
[65] Cf. the references given in n. 67 below.

represented by arrows in the diagram below. Let us once again give the crucial examples that helped us establish these orderings: *je#repars* [žər(ə)par], [žrəpar] 'I'm leaving again' for INI and VCE₁ (p. 211); *devenez* [dəvne], [dvəne] 'become' for INI and VCE₂ (p. 211); *petite#mesure* [pətitməzür] 'small measure' for FIN-DEL and VCE₁ (p. 163); and finally *tu#devenais* [tüdəvnɛ], [tüdvəne] 'you were

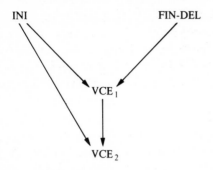

becoming' for VCE₁ and VCE₂ (p. 210). Each example has two schwas occurring in contiguous syllables, and in each case we showed that the behaviour of the schwa on the right depended on the behaviour of the schwa on the left, and the rule liable to affect the schwa on the left was to be applied before the rule liable to affect the schwa on the right. The desired result is always the same: to prevent the deletion of the schwa on the right when the schwa on the left is dropped in *#CəCəC* or *Cə#₁CəC* sequences. By deleting the schwa on the left, the rule ordered first (FIN-DEL, INI or VCE₁) creates new conditions which prevent the rule ordered second (VCE₁ or VCE₂) from deleting the schwa on the right.

These facts argue in favour of some interesting suggestions put forward by Kenstowicz and Kisseberth, according to which the interaction between two successive applications of the same rule would be governed by the same general principles as the interaction between the applications of different rules.[66] We will not go further into the problem posed by the mode of application of the phonological rules, a problem which is in fact far from being satisfactorily solved in spite of all the attention it has been given since

---

[66] Cf. Kenstowicz and Kisseberth (1973). Following Kiparsky (1971) and Kisseberth (1972*b*) they distinguish between 'opaque' and 'transparent' orders of application. The relative ordering which we have established between E-FIN, INI, VCE₁ and VCE₂ is in all cases transparent. Also, with VCE₁ operating iteratively from left to right, the ordering between two applications in adjacent syllables is a transparent one (it would be opaque if VCE₁ were operating from right to left). The same is true for VCE₂.

the publication of *SPE* (1968).[67] Our purpose in raising this problem was first and foremost to show how data taken from a particular language – in this case the behaviour of schwa in French – could be crucial in testing certain universal claims made by a linguistic theory.

To end this section on schwas in contiguous syllables, we will just add a few remarks on the role of polysyllable-final schwas as environments in the operation of rule VCE_1. For some reason, the framework of the VC_2-deletion analysis makes it much easier to grasp intuitively the mechanism at play, and we will thus adopt that analysis here rather than the VC_2-epenthesis analysis,[68] but let it be clear that this choice is only for convenience of exposition. The reader should easily work out for himself that restating everything said here within the VC_2-epenthesis analysis will not change the point at issue. Let us then assume a grammar with the rules FIN-DEL$_a$ and FIN-DEL$_b$ (cf. p. 212), and where all the words which show up phonetically as [XCC] in front of a pause have a final schwa in their underlying representations at the stage of the derivations where FIN-DEL$_a$ becomes applicable (/XCCə/).

The ordering of FIN-DEL$_a$ before VCE_1 entails the prediction that the final schwas which the optional rule FIN-DEL$_a$ has chosen not to erase can serve as a suitable environment for the operation of VCE_1 in a following #CəX# word. And this is indeed what is found in a number of cases. In the sentence *il pourrait presque jeter la balle* 'he could almost throw the ball', the sequence /prɛskə# #žət+e/ has three possible pronunciations: (i) [prɛskəšte][69] – the optional rule FIN-DEL$_a$ has chosen not to operate, hence a sequence /ə# #žə/ meeting the conditions of the rule VCE_1, which then deletes the schwa on the right; (ii) [prɛskəžəte] – FIN-DEL$_a$ has chosen not to operate as in the preceding case, but here the optional rule VCE_1 has chosen not to operate either; (iii) [prɛskžəte] – FIN-DEL$_a$ has deleted the schwa at the end of *presque*, hence a representation where the schwa of *jeter* no longer meets the conditions of VCE_1. We give below the derivations for the first pronunciation and the third one. They illustrate the fact that both rules cannot operate in the same derivation:

	/prɛskə# #žət+e/	/prɛskə# #žət+e/
FIN-DEL$_a$		prɛsk # #žət+e
VCE_1	prɛskə# #ž t+e	
	[prɛskəšte]	[prɛskžəte]

---

[67]   See particularly Anderson (1969, 1974), Johnson (1970), Morin and Friedman (1971), Browne (1972), Kisseberth (1972a), Kenstowicz and Kisseberth (1973), Vergnaud (1972), Jensen and Stong-Jensen (1973).

[68]   On VC_2-deletion and VC_2-epenthesis, see p. 212.

[69]   A late assimilation rule rewrites *ž* as *š* in front of the voiceless *t*.

However, far more frequent are the cases where VCE_1 cannot operate even though the final schwa in the preceding syllable is left intact by FIN-DEL$_a$. Thus /katɔrzə#žətɔ̃/ *quatorze jetons* 'fourteen counters' can be pronounced as [katɔrzəžətɔ̃] and [katɔrzžətɔ̃], but not as *[katɔrzəštɔ̃], in contrast with [prɛskəšte] above, which is grammatical.

Neither reordering our rules nor reformulating them will help us here, for what is at play is something altogether different. In Dell (1978 *b*) we argued that there is a direct correlation between the frequency[70] with which final schwas are deleted by FIN-DEL$_a$ in a given context in speech, and the ability of a schwa spared by FIN-DEL$_a$ in that context to serve as a suitable environment for the operation of VCE_1 in the next syllable. The less frequently final schwas are deleted in a given context, the more easily they can serve as an environment for the operation of VCE_1. For instance, everything being equal, in speech, final schwas are deleted less often after *sk* clusters than after *rz* clusters and correlatively, as seen in the examples above, VCE_1 can delete the rightmost schwa in a sequence /skə#$_1$Cə/ but not in a sequence /rzə#$_1$Cə/.

Given the structure of the language, the speakers have at their disposal two means of deleting as many schwas as possible in order to increase the rate of speech: for the optional rule FIN-DEL$_a$ to operate as often as possible, and for the optional rule VCE_1 to operate as often as possible. Both means can be used simultaneously when in the input to FIN-DEL$_a$ the sequences meeting the conditions of FIN-DEL$_a$ do not overlap with those meeting the conditions of VCE_1, as when /de#pəti+z#ɛ̃sɛktə##marɔ̃/ *des petits insectes marrons* is pronounced [deptizɛ̃sɛktmarɔ̃] 'little brown insects'. When these sequences overlap, i.e. when the conditions of both rules FIN-DEL$_a$ and VCE_1 are met on either side of the same consonant, as in /prɛskə##žət+e/ and /katɔrzə#žətɔ̃/, one must choose to apply one rule or the other, as shown above in the derivations for *presque jeter*.

To put things somewhat metaphorically, it would seem that in the dialect under study schwas meeting the conditions of the optional rule FIN-DEL$_a$ are in general more 'unstable' than those meeting the conditions of the optional rule VCE_1, so that when adjacent syllables contain schwas of both types, priority must be given to the deletion of the most unstable one, i.e. priority must be given to the operation of rule FIN-DEL$_a$, hence the ill-formedness of *[katɔrzəštɔ̃], where this priority has been violated. However there are particular cases where this priority of FIN-DEL$_a$ over

---

[70] On some environmental factors which influence the frequency of the operation of FIN-DEL$_a$ in speech, see p. 198, n. 9.

VCE₁ is cancelled, due to contextual features (such as the nature of the preceding consonant cluster) which make a schwa meeting the conditions of FIN-DEL$_a$ as 'stable' as those meeting the conditions of VCE₁, and the possibility of [prɛskəšte] side by side with [prɛskžəte]would be such a case. For more details we refer the reader to Dell (1978 *b*).

SOME RESIDUAL PROBLEMS, AND A RECAPITULATION OF THE RULES

We have described most of the rules governing the dropping of schwa. There are still a few residual problems to be examined.

Let us first show that ELIS must be applied before INI. We noted (p. 203) that schwa in an initial syllable after a pause is all the more easily dropped the further it is from the main stress of the phrase. We feel that it is easier to pronounce [žlavɛ] for *je lavais* ' I was washing ', than [žlɛ] for *je l'ai* ' I've got it ', and [žlav] for *je lave* ' I wash '; these pronunciations are not impossible, but there is a distinct preference for [žəlɛ] and [žəlav]. If ELIS applies before INI, it first rewrites /§žə#lə#ɛ§/ as /§žə#l#ɛ§/, which consequently places the schwa of *je* in the syllable immediately preceding the one which carries the sentence stress, and thus renders it less easily subject to INI than the schwa of *je* in /§žə#lavɛ§/, which is separated from the sentence stress by one syllable. ELIS also precedes VCE₁ since VCE₁ is applied after INI. Finally, ELIS must precede EPEN. The pronunciation of schwa is almost obligatory at the end of *apporte* in *apporte l'or* [apɔrtəlɔr] ' bring the gold '. As long as the schwa of /lə#ɔr/ has not been elided, the end of the verb does not immediately precede the sentence stress. The preceding considerations also imply that EPEN must be applied to representations where stress has already been assigned by the stress rules, since it is obligatory in some stress contexts and optional in others.[71] Finally, EPEN must be applied after SEM, for, before a pause, we find *énorm(e) brouette* [enɔrm(ə)bruɛt] ' huge wheelbarrow ' but *énorme chouette* [enɔrməšwɛt] ' huge owl ', where *brouette* is phonetically a disyllable, but *chouette* [šwɛt] is a monosyllable. Before SEM operates, both words have disyllabic representations: /bruɛt/ and /šuɛt/.

Let us move on to several problems posed by the behaviour of clitics. This name is given to a certain number of pronouns which group themselves around verbs (*en*, *y*, *se*, *me*, etc.) as well as to the negative particle *ne*. In so-called inverted questions, when a subject pronoun is cliticized after the

[71] Cf. p. 212.

verb, its schwa is obligatorily dropped: *qui est-ce?* [kiɛs] 'who is it?', *qui suis-je?* [kisẅiž] 'who am I?'.[72] Selkirk (1972: 361–3) accounted for the vowel harmony in such forms as *est-il?* 'is he?' ([ɛtil] or [etil]) by positing a readjustment rule which suppresses any word boundary between the verb and subject pronouns which are cliticized after it. This hypothesis perfectly agrees with the fact that these clitics obligatorily lose their schwa. If *suis-je?* is a single word, its final schwa is subject to FIN-DEL as is that of *exige* [egziž] '(he) demands'. Note also that if the postverbal *ce* and *je* were separated from the verb by a word boundary, they would be subject to VCE₁ and one would expect, for example, *où puis-je me laver?* 'where can I wash?' to be pronounced not only [upẅižməlave] but also *[upẅižəmlave].

The clitic *le* poses a different problem. Our present formulation of ELIS is contradicted by the fact that schwa is obligatorily retained in *fais-le attendre* [fɛləatãdr] 'make him wait', *rends-le à Jacques* [rãləažak] 'give it back to Jack'. The impossibility of having *liaison* in *fais-les attendre* [fɛleatãdr] 'make them wait', *rends-les à Jacques* [rãleažak] 'give them back to Jack' shows that, in these sentences, *le* and *les* are followed by two # boundaries. We will therefore reformulate ELIS so that it will only affect schwas that are separated from the following vowel by one boundary at the most:

ELIS: ə → Ø   /——([−seg]) V
(OBL)

We will similarly account for the obligatory retention of schwa in *ce à quoi il faut s'attendre* [səakwa...] 'what one has to expect', *ce en quoi il a tort* [səãkwa...] 'where he is wrong...', by postulating two # boundaries between *ce* and the following preposition, which is confirmed by the impossibility of *liaison* in *celles à qui j'ai parlé* [sɛlaki]/*[sɛlzaki] 'the ones (fem.) I spoke to', *celles en qui j'ai confiance* [sɛlãki...]/*[sɛlzãki...] 'the ones (fem.) I trust'.

Although schwas like those of *fais-le attendre* /fɛ#lə###atãdr/, *ce à quoi (il faut s'attendre)* /§sə##a#kwa.../, obligatorily escape ELIS, they should at least be subject to VCE₁ and INI respectively, and be optionally dropped. And yet this is not the case. Our formulations of VCE₁ and INI are too general. In all the examples that we have adduced in support of these formulations, the #Cə sequence subject to the rules is either the first

---

[72] The inversion of *je* is limited today to a few rote expressions (see Grevisse, 1959: 630).

syllable of a polysyllabic word or a $\#C\partial\#$ monosyllable that is separated from the following word by a single $\#$ boundary. We will reformulate VCE_1 and INI so as to prevent them from affecting any schwa followed by a $\#\#$ sequence:[73]

$$VCE_1: \quad \partial \rightarrow \emptyset \quad / \quad V\#_1C\text{——}([-seg])[+seg]$$
$$(OPT)$$

$$INI: \quad \partial \rightarrow \emptyset \quad / \quad \S\,C\text{——}([-seg])[+seg]$$
$$(OPT)$$

Let us go back to the clitic *le*; two cases must be distinguished. In the first case, *le* immediately precedes a verb or a clitic *en* or *y* belonging to the same verb phrase as that to which it belongs. It is then regularly affected by ELIS and VCE_1:

> *tu l'attends* [tülatã] 'you are waiting for him'
> *tu l(e) vois* [tül(ə)vwa] 'you see him'
> *tu l'en empêches* [tülãnãpɛš] 'you prevent him from doing it'
> *tu l'y forces* [tülifɔrs] 'you make him do it'
> *empêche-l'en* [ãpɛ̌slã] 'prevent him from doing it'
> *force-l'y* [fɔrs(ə)li] 'make him do it'.[74]

In the second case, *le* is not in any of the environments mentioned above. It is then either at the end of a verb phrase, or in front of a clitic (other than *en* or *y*) belonging to the same verb phrase as the one to which it belongs. In that case it is never subject to VCE_1.[75] When *le* is at the end of a verb

---

[73] Vergnaud (1975: 33–4) shows that in order to account for the data of his dialect, which differs on this point from the one we are studying, VCE_1 and INI should be barred from applying to schwas which carry a main phrase stress.

[74] It is essential that the verb or the clitic *en* or *y* which follows *le* belong to the same verb phrase. Contrast *va l'attendre* 'go and wait for him' and *laissez-le attendre* 'let him wait'; *va l'y mettre* 'go and put it there' and *laissez-le y croire* 'let him believe in it'; *va l'en empêcher* 'go and prevent him from doing it' and *laissez-le en parler* 'let him talk about it'. In the first sentence of each pair, *le* is the object of the following infinitive (i.e. it is the object of *attendre*, *mettre* and *empêcher*), and hence it belongs to the same verb phrase as the next word, whose initial vowel triggers elision, as indicated by the apostrophe in conventional spelling. In the second sentence of each pair, *le* is the object complement of the verb *laissez* and is at the end of a verb phrase. It is followed by two boundaries, as can be attested by the fact that the underlying final /z/ of *les* must be deleted in *laissez-les attendre* 'let them wait', *laissez-les y croire* 'let them believe in it' and *laissez-les en parler* 'let them talk about it'.

[75] It is impossible to know how the *le* behaves in relation to ELIS in this environment, since all the clitics it can immediately precede begin with a consonant.

phrase, the fact that it cannot be deleted by VCE_1 is normal, since it is followed by # #; see *rends-le* 'give it back', *rends-moi-le* 'give it back to me', and the examples *laissez-le...* in note 74. On the other hand, when *le* is followed by another clitic belonging to the same verb phrase, the reason that its schwa is retained is unclear: *rends-le-moi, rends-le-leur, rends-le-lui* 'give it back to me/them/him', *tu le leur rends, tu le lui rends* 'you give it back to them/him'. We will suppose that in this environment also *le* is followed by two # boundaries.[76] For the time being, we have no syntactic argument to support this hypothesis, but the syntax of the clitics *le, la, les, lui, leur* in any case poses particular problems that have not yet been solved.

We will also postulate the existence of two # boundaries after *ce* in *ce dont il est question* [sədɔ̃...] 'what it is all about', *ce pour quoi nous luttons* [səpur...] 'what we are fighting for'.

The clitic *ne* (negative particle) poses problems of another kind. Apart from *ne*, there are eight monosyllables in French that have schwa as a vowel:

A: *je, de, ce, que*
B: *me, te, se, le*

Owing to the syntactic structure of French, if *ne* and a member of class A appear one after the other, the order can only be *A # ne*, not **ne # A*. For members of the B class, it is the reverse order: in the same conditions, we have the sequence *ne # B*, not **B # ne*. This generalization holds for all the constituents that do not contain a # # sequence, the only ones which interest us in what follows; the behaviour of schwa in forms such as *# laisse # le # # n(e) # parler qu'à Paul* [lɛslən(ə)parle...] 'let him talk only to Paul' can be attributed to the new formulation of VCE_1 adopted above.

The following empirical generalization can be made concerning the behaviour of schwa in the sequences *A # ne*:

(G)   When in an *A # ne* sequence the schwa of A satisfies the structural description of INI or VCE and the schwa of *ne* satisfies the structural description of VCE, it is the schwa of *ne* which must be dropped, or else both schwas are retained.

It looks as if the deletion of the schwa of *ne* has priority over that of the schwa of the preceding monosyllable. A few examples follow, with others

---

[76] Contrast *prends-le-leur* [prãləlœr] 'take it from them', and *prends l(e) leur* [prãl(ə)lœr] 'take theirs', where schwa can drop as in *prends-l(e) nôtre* 'take ours'. The analogy with *prends l'autre-*[prãlotr] 'take the other', where elision takes place, and with *prends les autres* [prãlezotr] 'take the others', where *liaison* takes place, shows that in *prends l(e) leur* 'take theirs', *le* and *leur* are separated by a single # boundary.

(b′, c′, d′) illustrating the fact that the generalization (G) is only valid for the monosyllable *ne*.

(a)   *ce ne sont pas mes amis*[77] [sənsɔ̃pa...], *[snəsɔ̃pa...] ('they are not my friends')

(b)   *je ne stérilise pas* [žənste...], *[žnəste...] ('I don't sterilize')

(b′) *je le stérilise* [žəlste...], [žləste...] ('I'm sterilizing it')

(c)   *promets de ne le dire qu'à Jean* [prɔmɛdənlədir...], *[prɔmɛdnəldir...] ('promise you'll only tell John')

(c′) *promets de me le dire* [prɔmɛdəmlədir...], [prɔmɛdməldir...] ('promise you'll tell me')

(d)   *plutôt que de ne pas venir* [plütokdənpa...], *[plütokədnəpa...] ('rather than not come')

(d′) *plutôt que de me parler* [plütokdəmparle] [plütokədməparle] ('rather than talk to me')

Pronunciations such as [žnarivpa] *je n'arrive pas* 'I'm not arriving', [sižnarivpa] *si je n'arrive pas* 'If I don't arrive', [dikəžnarivpa] *dis que je n'arrive pas* 'say that I'm not arriving' show that monosyllables are not always exceptions to INI and VCE when they precede *ne*. They are only exceptions if the schwa of *ne* is still present when INI and VCE$_1$ are applicable. The pronunciation [padnəvö]/[padənvö] (*pas de neveu* 'not a nephew') shows on the other hand that (G) is only concerned with the particle *ne*, and not just any word beginning with $\#$ nə-.

A similar tendency can be seen in *ne* $\# B$ sequences and in those where *ne* is followed by a word beginning with $\# C$ə-: the deletion of the schwa of *ne* has priority over that of the schwa of the following syllable:

> *on ne te bat pas* [ɔ̃ntəbapa], *[ɔ̃nətbapa] 'no one is beating you'
> *tu ne demandes pas* [tündəmɑ̃dpa], *[tünədmɑ̃dpa] 'you don't ask'

Of course, the schwa of *ne* only has priority of deletion if it satisfies the structural description of VCE$_1$: *Jacques ne te bat pas* [žaknətbapa] 'Jack doesn't beat you', *Jacques ne demande pas* [žaknədmɑ̃dpa] 'Jack doesn't ask'. When *ne* is preceded by a pause, the schwa in the next syllable is the one which is dropped since *ne* is never subject to INI.[78]

In order to account for these data, the following schema can be posited, which marks as exceptions to INI and VCE$_1$ any schwa that is in a syllable

---

[77] We have not given the pronunciations where all the schwas remain intact: [sənəsɔ̃pa...], etc.
[78] Cf. p. 201, n. 14.

contiguous to an occurrence of *ne*, when the schwa of *ne* itself meets the conditions of VCE_1:

$$\text{NE-EX:} \quad \begin{matrix} \text{ə} \\ \text{(OBL)} \end{matrix} \rightarrow \begin{bmatrix} -\text{INI} \\ -\text{VCE}_1 \end{bmatrix} / \left\{ \begin{matrix} \text{—\#nə\#} \\ V\,\#_1\,\text{nə\#C—} \end{matrix} \right\}$$

NE-EX must be applied after ELIS and of course before INI and VCE_1. This rule accounts for the data, but it gives a poor idea of the mechanisms it purports to describe: the deletion of the schwa of *ne* by VCE_1 has priority over that of schwa in contiguous syllables. It might be wondered whether the deletion of schwa could be attributed to a special rule that would optionally delete schwa in the environment $V\,\#_1\,n$——$\#$. But this solution is untenable. The reader can easily work out for himself that, if this rule were ordered before VCE_1, it would allow the derivation of *[sižndiryɛ̃] for *si je ne dis rien* 'If I don't say anything', and if it were ordered after VCE_1, it would allow the derivation of *[ɔ̃nldipa] for *on ne le dit pas* 'it is not said'.

We will leave this problem without reaching a really satisfactory solution. There is probably a relationship between the curious phonological behaviour of the particle *ne* and the fact that it can always be deleted.[79] Any sentence containing an occurrence of *ne* has a 'colloquial' version obtained by dropping *ne*: *(ne) le laisse pas parler* 'don't let him talk', *il (n')aime que les plats épicés* 'he only likes hot dishes', etc.

To conclude, we will return briefly to two questions that we put aside without having found satisfactory answers to them. The first concerns the behaviour of schwa in front of aspirated *h*. French has a number of exceptional words which begin phonetically with a vowel, but which in many ways behave as if they began with a consonant. These words are traditionally said to begin with an aspirated *h*. Keeping to essentials, let us say that the initial vowel of these words does not allow either elision or *liaison*: *les housses* ('the dust-sheets') is pronounced [leus] and not *[lezus], *le haut* ('the top') is pronounced [ləo] and not *[lo]. One way of accounting for these facts is to suppose, like Schane, that words with aspirated *h* begin in their phonological representations with a certain consonant,[80] let us say $/ʔ/$, and that there exists a phonological rule ordered

---

[79]　The rule responsible for this deletion is a syntactic and not a phonological one.

[80]　Cf. Schane (1967: 45–6; 1968a: 7–8). This solution had already been proposed by Chao (1934), and Bally (1944: 164) talks of a 'zero consonant'. For a systematic review of the arguments in favour of an abstract underlying consonant, cf. Selkirk and Vergnaud (1973). It seems to us that $/ʔ/$ is a more likely candidate than the $/h/$ proposed by Schane because it is used obligatorily by some speakers and optionally by others at the beginning of words with an aspirated *h* when preceded by one ending with a consonant: *il hâche* [ilʔaš] 'he chops'.

after TRUNC and ELIS that deletes all the occurrences of this consonant. One defect of this analysis however is that it does not explain why in many cases an aspirated *h* blocks the operation of FIN-DEL, INI and VCE on a preceding schwa. If an aspirated *h* were simply an initial consonant like any other, a schwa preceding it should be subject to these rules in a regular fashion, as it is in front of any other initial consonant. But this is not so. Schwas preceding a word-internal aspirated *h* can never be deleted, whatever the environment: *rehausse-le* [rəoslə] 'raise it ', *va dehors* [vadɔɔr] 'go outside '; as for those word-final schwas which meet the conditions of FIN-DEL, INI or VCE but precede a word-initial aspirated *h*, whether their retention is optional or obligatory depends on the number of consonants preceding schwa, on the number of # boundaries separating schwa from the word with an aspirated *h*, and on the length of this word:

> *quelle housse* [kɛləus] 'which dust-sheet'
> *quell(e) hauteur* [kɛl(ə)otœr] 'which height'
> *il parle haut* [iparləo] 'he speaks loudly'
> *il parl(e) hardiment* [iparl(ə)ardimã] 'he speaks boldly'
> *il chant(e) haut* [išãt(ə)o] 'he sings loudly'
> *pas de hache* [padəaš] 'no axe'
> *pas d(e) Hollandais* [pad(ə)ɔlãdɛ] 'no Dutchmen', etc.[81]

For what seems to us a step in the right direction we refer the reader to the suggestions in Cornulier (1974) and Morin (1974: 87), which can be interpreted as proposing that morphemes with aspirated *h* are morphemes which begin with a vowel in their underlying representations, but should be marked in the lexicon with a special diacritic feature indicating that the initial vowel of any morpheme so marked cannot belong to the same syllable as a consonant belonging to a preceding morpheme. If the deletion of schwa in a sequence $/Cə[-seg]_1 V/$ results in a reshuffling of syllabic structure which brings the remaining C and V together as constituents of the same syllable, then the proposed diacritic feature would have the effect of blocking all rules whose operation results in such resyllabifications, among which are FIN-DEL, INI and VCE.

---

[81] For an attempt at an overall treatment of the behaviour of schwa in front of words with an aspirated *h* and in front of those like *yaourt* [yaurt] 'yogourt ', *whisky* [wiski] 'whisky ', see Dell (1970: 83–105). Note that a source of new words (masculine and feminine) with an aspirated *h* is the invention of groups of initials whose first letter is *F, H, L, M, N, R* or *S: la RATP, la SNCF, le HLM, le FLN*.

The second question that we will leave aside is the retention of schwa when followed by a liquid and a yod: *chandelier* [šãdəlye] 'candlestick', *chant(e)riez* [šãt(ə)rye] 'you would sing', etc. This problem cannot be treated without entering into the details of fairly complex processes that are responsible for the distribution of semi-vowels in French.[82] Let us just say that, contrary to what is often written on the subject,[83] it is not enough to invoke the 'law of three consonants' (cf. p. 225, n. 62) to account for this phenomenon. We have seen that in general the behaviour of schwa depends on the consonants that precede it, and not on those following it. Also, schwa is not just retained in front of any consonant plus yod group, but only in front of a liquid plus yod group; compare *guichetier* [gišə̸tye] 'turnkey' with *chandelier* [šãdə̲lye]. What is more, this *Ly* group must belong to the same word; see, for example, the difference between *chandelier* and *près de Lyon* [prɛd(ə)lyɔ̃] 'near Lyon'. Lastly, for many speakers, including the author, the behaviour of schwa may vary according to whether the glide following the liquid belongs to the same lexical item or to a verbal ending *-ions*, *-iez*. It is always retained, for example, in *hôtelier* [otə̲lye] 'innkeeper' and *chapelier* [šapə̲lye] 'hatter', whereas it is optionally dropped in *atteliez* [at(ə)lye] 'you harnessed' and *appeliez* [ap(ə)lye] 'you were calling', as long as these words do not carry the main sentence stress. Finally, it still has to be determined what conditions produce pronunciations such as [dəmãdriyɔ̃] for *demanderions* 'we would ask'. It is certainly not enough to say that some speakers find it difficult to distinguish between [OəryV] and [OriyV]. For we can be fairly sure that even those speakers who pronounce [dəmãdriyɔ̃] instead of [dəmãdəryɔ̃] for *demanderions*, never pronounce *[ãbəryɔ̃] for *embryon* [ãbriyɔ̃] 'embryo' or *[friyɔ̃] for *ferions* [fəryɔ̃] 'we would do'.

To conclude, we have set out a recapitulation of the rules arrived at. The page references where the formulation of these rules is discussed can be found in the Index.

ELIS: ə → $\emptyset$ ˎ / ——([−seg])[+syll]
(OBL)

V-E: ə → $\emptyset$ / V ——
(OBL)

---

[82] Cf. p. 218, n. 48.
[83] See e.g. Sten (1966: 32).

E-ADJ: $\left\{\begin{matrix} \text{ə} \\ \text{e} \end{matrix}\right\} \rightarrow \varepsilon \quad / \quad \text{---} \widehat{} C_1 \left\{\begin{matrix} \# \\ C \\ \text{ə}\,[-\text{seg}] \end{matrix}\right\}$
(OBL)

Condition: $C_1 C \neq OL$

SEM: $\begin{bmatrix} +\text{son} \\ +\text{high} \end{bmatrix} \rightarrow [-\text{syll}] \quad / \quad \text{---}V$
(OBL)

TRUNC: $[-\text{son}] \rightarrow \emptyset \quad / \quad \text{---} \left\{\begin{matrix} \left\{\begin{matrix} + \\ \# \end{matrix}\right\} C \\ \#\ \# \end{matrix}\right\}$
(OBL)

NAS: $[+\text{syll}]\ [+\text{nas}] \left\{\begin{matrix} C \\ \# \end{matrix}\right\} \rightarrow [+\text{nas}]\ \emptyset \left\{\begin{matrix} C \\ \# \end{matrix}\right\}$
(OBL)
$\qquad\qquad\quad 1 \qquad\quad 2 \qquad 3 \qquad\qquad 1 \qquad 2 \quad 3$

STR: $V \rightarrow \acute{V} \quad / \quad \text{---}C_0(\text{ə}C_0)\#$
(OBL)

FIN-DEL$_b$: $V \rightarrow \emptyset \quad / \quad \acute{V}C_0\text{---}\#$
(OBL)

EPEN: $\emptyset \rightarrow \text{ə} \quad / \quad \acute{V}C_2\text{---}[-\text{seg}]_1 C$
(OPT)

Condition: the rightmost C is syllable-initial

NE-EX: $\text{ə} \rightarrow \begin{bmatrix} -\text{rule INI} \\ -\text{rule VCE}_1 \end{bmatrix} \left\{\begin{matrix} \text{---}\#\ \text{nə}\ \# \\ V\#_1\,\text{nə}\,\#\,C\text{---} \end{matrix}\right\}$
(OBL)

INI-EX: $\text{ə} \rightarrow [-\text{rule INI}] \quad / \quad \begin{bmatrix} -\text{son} \\ -\text{cont} \end{bmatrix}\text{---}\#_0\begin{bmatrix} -\text{son} \\ -\text{cont} \end{bmatrix}$
(OBL)

INI: $\text{ə} \rightarrow \emptyset \quad / \quad \S\,C\text{---}([-\text{seg}])[+\text{seg}]$
(OPT)

VCE$_1$:
(OPT)
$$\text{ə} \rightarrow \emptyset \;/\; \text{V}\#_1\text{C}\text{—}([-\text{seg}])[+\text{seg}]$$

VCE$_2$:
(OBL)
$$\text{ə} \rightarrow \emptyset \;/\; \text{VC}\text{—}([-\text{seg}])[+\text{seg}]$$

FUT-DEL:
(OPT)
$$\text{ə} \rightarrow \emptyset \;/\; \text{—}+\text{r}+$$

LIQUEF:
(OPT)
$$\begin{bmatrix} +\text{cons} \\ +\text{son} \\ -\text{nas} \end{bmatrix} \rightarrow \emptyset \;/\; \text{V́C}_0[-\text{son}]\text{—}\left\{ \begin{matrix} [-\text{seg}]_1\text{C} \\ \S \end{matrix} \right\}$$

HARM:
(OPT)
$$\begin{bmatrix} +\text{syll} \\ -\text{round} \\ -\text{high} \\ -\text{back} \end{bmatrix} \rightarrow [\alpha\text{low}] \;\Big/\; \text{—}\text{C}_1+\text{C}_0 \begin{bmatrix} +\text{syll} \\ \alpha\,\text{low} \end{bmatrix}$$

e-LOW:
(OPT)
$$\begin{bmatrix} +\text{syll} \\ -\text{high} \\ -\text{round} \end{bmatrix} \rightarrow [+\text{low}] \;\Big/\; \text{—}\text{CC}$$

OBLICONS:
(OUTPUT CONSTRAINT)
$$*[-\text{son}] \begin{bmatrix} +\text{son} \\ +\text{cons} \\ -\text{nas} \end{bmatrix} [+\text{cons}]$$

Conclusion

Having come to the end of this book, some readers may perhaps feel that, compared with other approaches, the one we have developed is relatively abstract and complicated. Is it really necessary to pay such a price if we want to understand what it is that makes speaker–hearers capable of producing and understanding an infinity of sentences that they have never heard before? We will consider these two points, abstraction and complication, in turn.

Let us first consider abstraction. A language is not an object which is accessible by direct observation; it is a system of knowledge whose existence in the brains of speakers we postulate in order to explain what we observe. All that we can observe is the way in which speakers put this knowledge to use when speaking, understanding what is said to them, or answering our questions on the pronunciation of this or that sentence.[1] Our task is not only to describe minutely the data that we gather or to give a principled classification of it, but also to examine it so as to form hypotheses on the exact nature of the system of knowledge which gives rise to these data, a system internalized by speaker–hearers. To describe the phonology of a language is to provide a formal device that fulfils the three following conditions : (i) to establish a correspondence between the set of surface structures of the language in question and the set of corresponding phonetic representations; (ii) to satisfy the general conditions imposed on any grammar by linguistic theory; (iii) to be the simplest[2] device that fulfils

---

[1]   In the present book, only this kind of data have been discussed, but many other kinds of data can be systematically collected and used: for example, by studying language disorders, the way in which children and adults learn languages, spelling systems, whistled or drummed languages, borrowings from one language to another, linguistic changes, secret languages, puns and spoonerisms, versification and singing, etc.

[2]   We insist once again on the fact that here simplicity' is a technical term to be defined precisely *within linguistic theory*, just as are ‘phonological representation’, ‘sonorant’, ‘phonological rule’, etc. Of course we are still far from achieving this goal.

conditions (i) and (ii). This device is composed of a lexicon, i.e. a list of elementary units which can be combined, and a system of rules. The rules are divided into two categories. Some characterize the lexicon as a structured list and indicate certain necessary conditions which the items contained in it must fulfil.[3] Others attribute one or several pronunciations to any combination of these items.

Rules can be conceived of as general propositions that are of the form : ' for any sentence that has the property P to be well-formed, it must have the property Q '. Abstraction inevitably intervenes owing to the fact that the properties in question, P and Q, cannot, in general, be directly defined in terms of the information contained in the phonetic representations alone. One has to take into account the positioning of word or morpheme boundaries, the fact that a morpheme belongs to this or that syntactic or morphological class, the presence of a vowel subject to elision, and so on. All these properties are abstract in the sense that they have no specific correlate at the phonetic level. But there is nonetheless perfectly adequate motivation for positing them when we take an overall view of the language under description (syntax, morphology, lexicon, etc.). Abstraction is not synonymous with arbitrariness or a-priority. The hypothesis according to which the phonological rules apply in a sequence, which is a very abstract hypothesis on the way all human languages function, can and must be empirically motivated. This has been done in chapter 2, where we have shown that this hypothesis must be resorted to in order to describe certain common phonological processes without any loss of generality. Thus using underlying representations that are fairly distant from phonetic ones, or using very abstract hypotheses concerning the organization of grammars, does not reduce our capacity to 'stick' to the data; on the contrary, the only reason why we use abstraction is in order to make sense of the data.

Let us now look at the complexity of the formal device that has to be posited in order to describe the phonology of a language. We are no longer using the word 'complexity' in the technical sense used in linguistic theory, but in the everyday sense of the term : 'difficult to understand because of the number of its parts and the multiplicity of their relations'. The system of knowledge that underlies people's capacity to speak and understand a language is of considerable scope and complexity. It is a pity, but that is how it is. The first imperative which a linguistic theory or the description of a particular language must obey is not to make itself more easily accessible to students. It is to account for the data.

[3]   These are the morpheme structure rules, which define the set of possible allomorphs.

On the level of linguistic theory, a certain degree of complexity is probably inevitable, if we wish to have at our disposal a body of general hypotheses sufficiently rich and specific to limit drastically the set of possible grammars. We can thus reduce the number of grammars compatible with the data of a particular language. At this level the price is worth paying, since it is once and for all. Everything that can be attributed to linguistic theory can be eliminated from the grammar of particular languages.

On the level of the description of particular languages, the result obtained (a grammar or part of a grammar) is not, in the end, very complicated; the complication lies rather in the discussion leading to this result, which consists of eliminating a certain number of competing hypotheses. Once again, the length and difficulty of this discussion is all the greater if the linguistic theory within whose framework we are operating is poor or inexplicit. If the theory is poor, many competing solutions must be considered and eliminated one by one, whereas the role of the theory should be precisely to eliminate from the start most solutions as impossible in principle. If the theory is not very explicit, it fails to define adequately the boundaries of the field of possible hypotheses, resulting in the uncertainties and obscurities which largely contribute to making present linguistic works difficult to approach. It is scarcely necessary to mention that all the linguistic theories previously proposed suffer from these two major defects; the theory which we have presented here at least provides itself with the means of remedying these defects.

A linguistic theory is a system of hypotheses about the nature of language in general, and the description of particular languages is above all a means of testing these hypotheses on an ever increasing range of data, and of looking for data that allow new hypotheses to be devised. Although it undoubtedly represents an advance in comparison with earlier theories, the linguistic theory that we have presented is only an outline of what is still to be constructed. Let us hope that this book will have encouraged some people to contribute to this endeavour.

Bibliography

The initials *QPR* stand for *Quarterly Progress Report*, Research Laboratory of Electronics, Massachusetts Institute of Technology, Cambridge, Mass.

Anderson, S. R. 1969. West Scandinavian vowel systems and the ordering of phonological rules. Unpublished doctoral dissertation, MIT.
   1970. On Grassmann's Law in Sanskrit. *Linguistic Inquiry*, 1.4: 387–96.
   1971. On the description of 'apicalized' consonants, *Linguistic Inquiry*, 2.1: 103–7.
   1974. *The Organization of Phonology*. New York: Academic Press.
Applegate, J. R. 1961. Phonological rules of a subdialect of English, *Word*, 17.2: 186–93.
Aronoff, M. 1976. *Word-Formation in Generative Grammar*. Cambridge, Mass.: MIT Press.
Bach, E. 1968. Two proposals concerning the simplicity metric in phonology, *Glossa*, 2: 128–49.
Bally, C. 1944. *Linguistique générale et linguistique française*. Berne: Francke.
Basbøll, H. 1975. Schwa, jonctures et syllabification dans les représentations phonologiques du Français, *Acta Linguistica Hafniensia*, 16.2.
Bentley, W. H. 1887. *Dictionary and Grammar of the Kongo Language*. London: Trübner.
Bierwisch, M. 1967. Syntactic features in morphology: general problems of so-called pronominal inflection in German, in *To Honor Roman Jakobson, Essays on the Occasion of his Seventieth Birthday*, I, 238–70. The Hague: Mouton.
   1968. Two critical problems in accent rules, *Journal of Linguistics*, 4: 173–8.
Blanche-Benveniste, C. and Chervel, A. 1969. *L'orthographe*. Paris: Maspero.
Bloomfield, L. 1933. *Language*. New York: Holt.
   1939. Menomini morphophonemics, *Travaux du Cercle Linguistique de Prague*, 8: 105–15.
Botha, R. P. 1971. *Methodological Aspects of Generative Phonology*. The Hague: Mouton.
Brame, M. K. 1971. Stress in Arabic and generative phonology, *Foundations of Language*, 7: 556–91.
   ed. 1972. *Contributions to Generative Phonology*. Austin: University of Texas Press.

248   *Bibliography*

1972. On the abstractness of phonology: Maltese ʕ, in Brame, ed., 1972: 22–61.

Bresnan, J. W. 1971. Sentence stress and syntactic transformations, *Language*, 47: 257–81, reprinted in Brame, ed., 1972: 71–107.

1972. Stress and syntax: a reply, *Language*, 48: 326–42.

Bright, W. 1957. *The Karok Language*. University of California Publications in Linguistics no. 13. Berkeley and Los Angeles: University of California Press.

Browne, E. W. 1972. How to apply phonological rules, *QPR*, no. 105: 143–6.

Browne, E. W. and McCawley, J. D. 1965. Srpskohrvatski akcenat, *Zbornik matice srpske za filologiju i lingvistiku* (Novi Sad), 8: 147–51; English trans. under the title 'Serbo-Croatian Accent', in Fudge, ed., 1973: 330–5.

Catford, J. C. 1977. *Fundamental Problems in Phonetics*. Edinburgh: Edinburgh University Press.

Chafe, W. L. 1968. The ordering of phonological rules, *International Journal of American Linguistics*, 34: 115–36.

Chao, Y.-R. 1934. The non-uniqueness of phonemic solutions of phonetic systems, *Bulletin of the Institute of History and Philology, Academia Sinica*, IV, part 4: 363–97, reprinted in Joos, ed., 1957.

Chomsky, N. 1957. *Syntactic Structures*. The Hague: Mouton.

1962. A transformational approach to syntax, in Fodor and Katz, eds., 1964: 211–45.

1964. *Current Issues in Linguistic Theory*. The Hague: Mouton.

1965. *Aspects of the Theory of Syntax*. Cambridge, Mass.: MIT Press.

1966. *Cartesian Linguistics*. New York: Harper and Row.

1967a. The formal nature of language, appendix in E. H. Lenneberg, *Biological Foundations of Language*. New York: Wiley.

1967b. Some general properties of phonological rules, *Language*, 43.1: 102–28.

1972. *Studies on Semantics in Generative Grammar*. The Hague: Mouton.

Chomsky, N. and Halle, M. 1965. Some controversial questions in phonological theory, *Journal of Linguistics*, 1: 97–138.

1968. *The Sound Pattern of English*. New York: Harper and Row.

Chomsky, N. and Miller, G. 1963. Introduction to the formal analysis of natural languages, in R. D. Luce, R. Bush and E. Galanter, eds., *Handbook of Mathematical Psychology*, II, 269–322. New York: Wiley.

Contreras, H. 1969. Simplicity, descriptive adequacy, and binary features, *Language*, 45: 1–8.

Cornulier, B. de. 1974. Expressions disjonctives: *H* et la syllabicité. Paper read at the colloquium Méthodes en Grammaire Française, 6-8 December, Paris. To appear in D. L. Goyvaerts, ed., *Phonology in the 1970's*. Ghent: Story-Scientia.

1977. Le remplacement d'*e* muet par '*è*' et la morphologie des enclitiques, in C. Rohrer, ed., *Actes du Colloque Franco-Allemand de Linguistique Théorique*, 155–80. Tübingen: Niemeyer.

Davis, I. 1966. Review of Newman, 1965. *International Journal of American Linguistics*, 32.1: 82–4.

De Felice, T. 1950. *Éléments de grammaire morphologique*. Paris: Didier.

Delattre, P. 1966. *Studies in French and Comparative Phonetics*. The Hague: Mouton.

Dell, F. 1970. Les règles phonologiques tardives et la morphologie dérivationnelle du français. Unpublished doctoral dissertation, MIT.

1972. Une règle d'effacement de *i* en français, *Recherches Linguistiques*, 1: 63–87. University of Paris VIII-Vincennes.

1973*a*. '*e* muet', fiction graphique ou réalité linguistique?, in S. Anderson and P. Kiparsky, eds., *A Festschrift for Morris Halle*, 26–50. New York: Holt, Rinehart and Winston.

1973*b*. Two cases of exceptional rule ordering, in F. Kiefer and N. Ruwet, eds., *Generative Grammar in Europe*, 141–153. Dordrecht: Reidel.

1976. Schwa précédé d'un groupe obstruante-liquide, *Recherches Linguistiques*, 4, 75–111. University of Paris VIII-Vincennes.

1977. Paramètres syntaxiques et phonologiques qui favorisent l'épenthèse de schwa en français contemporain, in C. Rohrer, ed., *Actes du Colloque Franco-Allemand de Linguistique Théorique*, 141–53. Tübingen: Niemeyer.

1978*a*. Certains corrélats de la distinction entre morphologie dérivationnelle et morphologie flexionnelle dans la phonologie du français, in C. Morin and A. Querido, eds., *Études Linguistiques sur les Langues Romanes. Montreal Working Papers in Linguistics*, 10: 1–10.

1978*b*. Epenthèse et effacement de schwa dans des syllabes contiguës en français, in B. de Cornulier and F. Dell, eds., *Problèmes de phonologie française*, 75–81. Marseille: CNRS.

1979. On *French Phonology and Morphology* and some vowel alternations in French, *Studies in French Linguistics*, I-3: 1–29.

Dell, F. and Selkirk, E. O. 1978. On a morphologically governed vowel alternation in French, in J. Keyser, ed., *Recent Transformational Studies in European Languages. Linguistic Inquiry* Monograph no. 3: 1-51. Cambridge, Mass.: MIT Press.

Denes, P. B. and Pinson, E. N. 1963. *The Speech Chain*. Baltimore: Bell Laboratories; 2nd edn, 1973, New York: Anchor Books.

Derwing, B. L. 1973. *Transformational Grammar as a Theory of Language Acquisition*. Cambridge University Press.

Durand, M. 1936. *Le genre grammatical en français parlé*. Paris: d'Artrey.

Ebeling, C. L. 1960. *Linguistic Units*. The Hague: Mouton.

Fasold, R. W. 1970. Two models of socially significant linguistic variation, *Language*, 46.3: 551–63.

Fidelholtz, J. 1975. Word frequency and vowel reduction in English, in R. E. Grossman, L. J. San and T. J. Vance, eds., *Papers from the Eleventh Regional Meeting, Chicago Linguistic Society*, 200–13. Chicago: Chicago Linguistic Society.

Fodor, J. A. and Katz, J. J. eds., 1964. *The Structure of Language; Readings in the Philosophy of Language*, Englewood Cliffs, NJ: Prentice-Hall.

Fouché, P. 1956. *Traité de prononciation française*. Paris: Klincksieck.

Fudge, E. C., ed. 1973. *Phonology*. Harmondsworth, Middx: Penguin Books.

Goldsmith, J. 1976*a*. Autosegmental phonology. Unpublished doctoral dissertation, MIT.

    1976*b*. An overview of autosegmental phonology, *Linguistic Analysis*, 2: 23–68.

Gougenheim, G. 1935. *Éléments de phonologie française*. Strasbourg: Publications de la Faculté de Lettres de l'Université de Strasbourg.

Grammont, M. 1894. Le Patois de Franche-Montagne et en particulier de Damprichard (Franche-Comté): IV, La loi des trois consonnes, *Mémoires de la Société de Linguistique*, 8: 53–90.

    1914. *Traité pratique de prononciation française*. Paris: Delagrave (quoted from the 1966 edn).

Grevisse, M. 1959. *Le bon usage*. 7th edn. Gembloux: Duculot.

Gross, M. and Lentin, A. 1967. *Notions sur les grammaires formelles*. Paris: Gauthier-Villars. English trans. *Introduction to Formal Grammars*, 1968, New York and Berlin: Springer Verlag.

Haden, E. 1965. Mute *e* in French, *Lingua*, 13: 166–76.

Hale, K. 1965. Some preliminary observations on Papago morphophonemics, *International Journal of American Linguistics*, 31.4: 295–305.

Halle, M. 1959. *The Sound Pattern of Russian*. The Hague: Mouton.

    1962. Phonology in generative grammar, *Word*, 18: 54–72.

    1969. How not to measure length of lexical representations and other matters, *Journal of Linguistics*, 5: 305–8.

    1970. A note on the accentual patterns of the Russian nominal declension, in R. Jakobson and S. Kawamoto, eds., *Studies in General and Oriental Linguistics Presented to Shiro Hattori on the Occasion of His Sixtieth Birthday*, 167–74. Tokyo: TEC Company.

    1971. Remarks on Slavic accentology, *Linguistic Inquiry*, 2.1: 1–19.

    1973*a*. Prolegomena to a theory of word formation, *Linguistic Inquiry*, 4.1: 3–16.

    1973*b*. The accentuation of Russian words, *Language*, 49.2: 312–48.

    1975. On Russian accentuation, *Slavic and East European Journal*, 19.1: 104–11.

Halle, M. and Keyser, S. J. 1967. Les changements phonétiques conçus comme changements de règles, in Schane, ed., 1967: 94–111.

    1971. *English Stress*. New York: Harper and Row.

Halle, M. and Stevens, K. N. 1969. On the feature 'advanced tongue root', *QPR*, no. 94: 209–15.

Harms, R. T. 1968. *Introduction to Phonological Theory*. Englewood Cliffs, NJ: Prentice-Hall.

Harris, J. W. 1969. *Spanish Phonology*. Cambridge, Mass.: MIT Press.

Harris, Z. S. 1951. *Methods in Structural Linguistics*. Chicago: University of Chicago Press (quoted from the 1961 edn: *Structural Linguistics*).

Haudricourt, A. G. and Thomas, J. M.-C. 1967. *La notation des langues; phonétique et phonologie*. Paris: Imprimerie de l'Institut Géographique National.

Hjelmslev, L. 1948. Le système d'expression du français moderne, (résumé basé sur des notes de E. Fischer-Jørgensen), *Bulletin du Cercle Linguistique de Copenhague*, 8–21 (1941–65): 217–24. Copenhagen, 1970, Akademisk Forlag.

Hooper, J. B. 1972. The syllable in phonological theory, *Language*, 48.3: 525–40.

Hyman, L. M. 1970. How concrete is phonology?, *Language*, 46.1: 58–76.

1973. Nupe three years later, *Language*, 49.2: 447–52.

1975. *Phonology. Theory and Analysis.* New York: Holt, Rinehart and Winston.

Hyman, L. M. and Schuh, R. G. 1974. Universals of tone rules: evidence from West Africa, *Linguistic Inquiry*, 5: 81–115.

Iverson, G. K. 1975. The strong alternation condition and Yawelmani phonology, in R. E. Grossman, L. J. San and T. J. Vance, eds., *Papers from the Eleventh Regional Meeting, Chicago Linguistic Society*, 302–12. Chicago: Chicago Linguistic Society.

Jackendoff, R. 1975. Morphological and semantic regularities in the lexicon, *Language*, 51.3: 639–71.

Jakobson, R. 1949. The phonemic and grammatical aspects of language in their interrelations, *Actes du VIᵉ Congrès International des Linguistes, Paris 1949.*

1958. Typological studies and their contribution to historical linguistics, *Proceedings of the VIIIth International Congress of Linguists, Oslo, 1957;* reprinted in Jakobson, 1962: 523–31.

1962. *Selected Writings*, vol. I: *Phonological Studies.* The Hague: Mouton.

1963. *Essais de linguistique générale.* French trans. N. Ruwet, Paris: Editions de Minuit.

Jakobson, R. and Halle, M. 1956. *Fundamentals of Language.* The Hague: Mouton.

Jakobson, R., Fant, G. and Halle, M. 1952. *Preliminaries to Speech Analysis.* Cambridge, Mass.: MIT Press.

Jensen, J. T. and Stong-Jensen, M. 1973. A revised directional theory of rule application in phonology, *QPR*, no. 108: 270–7.

Johnson, D. 1970. *Formal Aspects of Phonological Description.* Project On Linguistic Analysis Reports, Second Series, no. 11. Department of Linguistics, University of California, Berkeley.

Joos, M., ed. 1957. *Readings in Linguistics*, vol. I. Chicago: University of Chicago Press.

Juilland, A. 1965. *Dictionnaire inverse de la langue française.* The Hague: Mouton.

Kahn, D. 1976. Syllable-based generalizations in English phonology. Unpublished doctoral dissertation, MIT.

Kenstowicz, M. 1974. Inflectional accent of the Serbo-Croatian noun, *Studies in the Linguistic Sciences*, 4.1: 80–106.

Kenstowicz, M. and Kisseberth, C. 1970. Rule ordering and the asymmetry hypothesis, *Papers from the Sixth Regional Meeting, Chicago Linguistic Society*, 504–19. Chicago: Chicago Linguistic Society.

1973. The multiple application problem in phonology, in C. W. Kisseberth, ed., *Studies in Generative Phonology*, 13–41. Champaign and Edmonton: Linguistic Research, Inc.

eds., 1973. *Issues in Phonological Theory*. The Hague: Mouton.

Keyser, S. J. 1963. Review of Kurath and McDavid, *The Pronunciation of English in the Atlantic States* (1961), *Language*, 39: 303–16.

Kiefer, F. 1970. *Swedish Morphology*. Stockholm: Skriptor.

1971. Danish verb morphology, *Linguistische Berichte*, 15: 1–11.

1973. *Generative Morphologie des Neufranzösischen*. Tübingen: Niemeyer.

King, R. D. 1969. *Historical Linguistics and Generative Grammar*. Englewood Cliffs, NJ: Prentice-Hall.

Kiparsky, P. 1967. À propos de l'histoire de l'accentuation grecque, in Schane, ed., 1967: 73–93.

1968a. Linguistic universals and linguistic change, in E. Bach and R. T. Harms, eds., *Universals in Linguistic Theory*, 170–202. London and New York: Holt, Rinehart and Winston.

1968b. How abstract is phonology? Bloomington, Ind.: Indiana University Linguistics Club; also in O. Fujimura, ed., *Three Dimensions of Linguistic Theory*. Tokyo: TEC.

1970. Historical linguistics, in J. Lyons, ed., *New Horizons in Linguistics*, 302–15. Harmondsworth, Middx: Penguin Books.

1971. Historical linguistics, in W. O. Dingwall, ed., *A Survey of Linguistic Science*, 577–649. College Park: University of Maryland.

1973a. The inflectional accent in Indo-European, *Language*, 49.4: 794–849.

1973b. Abstractness, opacity, and global rules. Bloomington, Ind.: Indiana University Linguistics Club; also in O. Fujimura, ed., *Three Dimensions of Linguistic Theory*. Tokyo: TEC.

1973c. 'Elsewhere' in phonology, in S. Anderson and P. Kiparsky, eds., *A Festschrift for Morris Halle*, 93–106. New York: Holt, Rinehart and Winston.

1974. A note on the vowel features, *Proceedings of the Fifth Annual Meeting of North Eastern Linguistic Society*, 162–71.

Kisseberth, C. W. 1969a. Theoretical implications of Yawelmani phonology. Unpublished doctoral dissertation, University of Illinois.

1969b. On the abstractness of phonology: the evidence from Yawelmani, *Papers in Linguistics*, 1.2.

1970a. The treatment of exceptions, *Papers in Linguistics*, 2.1.

1970b. On the functional unity of phonological rules, *Linguistic Inquiry*, 1.3: 291–306.

1970c. Review of Kuroda, 1967, *Linguistic Inquiry*, 1.3: 337–45.

1970d. Vowel elision in Tonkawa and derivational constraints, in J. M. Sadock and A. L. Vanek, eds., *Studies Presented to Robert B. Lees by his Students*, 109–137. Edmonton: Linguistic Research, Inc.

1972a. An argument against the principle of simultaneous application of phonological rules, *Linguistic Inquiry*, 3.3: 392–6.

1972*b*. Is rule ordering necessary?, in B. Kachru *et al.* eds, *Issues in Linguistics. Papers in Honor of Henry and Renée Kahane.* Champaign: University of Illinois Press.

Kuroda, S. Y. 1967. *Yawelmani Phonology.* Cambridge, Mass.: MIT Press.

Labov, W. 1969. Contraction, deletion, and inherent variability of the English copula, *Language*, 45.4: 715–62.

1970. The study of language in its social context, *Studium Generale*, 23: 30–87; reprinted in J. Fishman, ed., *Advances in the Sociology of Language* (1971), 152–216. The Hague: Mouton.

1971. Methodology, in W. O. Dingwall, ed., *A Survey of Linguistic Science*, 412–97. College Park: University of Maryland.

1972. *Sociolinguistic Patterns.* Philadelphia: University of Pennsylvania Press.

Ladefoged, P. 1962. *Elements of Acoustic Phonetics.* Chicago: University of Chicago Press.

1964. *A Phonetic Study of West African Languages.* Cambridge: Cambridge University Press.

1971. *Preliminaries to Linguistic Phonetics.* Chicago: University of Chicago Press.

1975. *A Course in Phonetics.* New York: Harcourt, Brace Jovanovich, Inc.

Leben, W. R. 1971. The morphophonemics of tone in Hausa, in C. W. Kim and H. Stahlke, eds., *Papers in African Linguistics.* Edmonton: Linguistic Research, Inc.

1973. Suprasegmental phonology. Unpublished doctoral dissertation, MIT.

1976. Tones in English intonation, *Linguistic Analysis*, 2: 69–107.

Lees, R. B. 1957. Review of Chomsky, 1957, *Language*, 33: 375–408.

Lehiste, I. 1970. *Suprasegmentals.* Cambridge, Mass.: MIT Press.

Léon, P. 1966. Apparition, maintien et chute du 'e' caduc, *La Linguistique*, 2: 111–22.

Leray, F. 1930. La loi des trois consonnes, *Revue de Philologie Française*, 42: 161–84.

Liberman, M. Y. 1975. The intonation system of English. Unpublished doctoral dissertation, MIT.

Liberman, M. Y. and Prince, A. 1977. On stress and linguistic rhythm, *Linguistic Inquiry*, 8.2: 249–336.

Lightner, Th. M. 1973. Against morpheme structure rules and other things, in Kenstowicz and Kisseberth, eds., 1973: 53–60.

Lyons, J. 1970. *Chomsky.* London: Collins.

McCawley, J. D. 1967. Le rôle d'un système de traits phonologiques dans une théorie du langage, in Schane, ed., 1967: 112–23.

1968*a*. *The Phonological Component of a Grammar of Japanese.* The Hague: Mouton.

1968*b*. Review of T. Sebeok, ed., *Current Trends in Linguistics*, vol. III: *Theoretical Foundations* (1966), *Language*, 44.3: 556–93.

1971. On the role of notation in generative phonology. Bloomington, Indiana: Indiana University Linguistics Club.

Malécot, A. 1955. The elision of French mute-e within complex consonantal clusters, *Lingua*, 5: 45–60.

Malmberg, B. 1954. *La phonétique.* Que Sais-je? no. 637. Paris: Presses Universitaires de France.

ed. 1968. *Manual of Phonetics.* Amsterdam: North-Holland.

1969. *Phonétique française.* Malmö: Hermods.

Maran, L. 1971. *Burmese and Jingpho: A Study of Tonal Linguistic Processes.* Occasional Papers of the Wolfenden Society on Tibeto-Burman Linguistics, vol. IV, ed. F. K. Lehman. Urbana: University of Illinois.

Martinet, A. 1945. *La prononciation du français contemporain.* Geneva and Paris: Droz.

1949. Occlusives and affricates with reference to some problems of Romance philology, *Word,* 5: 116–22.

1956. *La description phonologique, avec application au parler franco-provençal d'Hauteville (Savoie).* Geneva: Droz.

1960. *Éléments de linguistique générale.* Paris: Armand Colin.

1962. *A Functional View of Language.* Oxford: Clarendon Press.

1965*a.* *La linguistique synchronique.* Paris: Presses Universitaires de France.

1965*b.* De la morphonologie, *La Linguistique,* 1: 15–30.

1969. *Le français sans fard.* Paris: Presses Universitaires de France.

Martinon, P. 1913. *Comment on prononce le français.* Paris: Larousse.

Matthews, G. H. 1970. Some notes on the proto-siouan continuants, *International Journal of American Linguistics,* 36: 98–109.

Matthews, P. H. 1970. Recent developments in morphology, in J. Lyons, ed., *New Horizons in Linguistics,* 96–114. Harmondsworth, Middx: Penguin Books.

Mende, A. 1880. *Étude sur la prononciation de l'e muet.* London: Trübner.

Michael, D. 1971. A note on some exceptions in Zuni phonology, *International Journal of American Linguistics,* 37.3: 189–92.

Miller, G. A. 1964. Language and psychology, in E. H. Lenneberg, ed., *New Directions in the Study of Language,* 89–107. Cambridge, Mass.: MIT Press.

1970. *The Psychology of Communication, Seven Essays.* Harmondsworth, Middx: Penguin Books.

Milner, J.-C. 1967. French truncation rule, *QPR,* no. 86: 273–83.

Morin, Y. C. 1971. *Computer Experiments in Generative Phonology, Low-Level French Phonology.* Natural Language Studies no. 11. Department of Computer and Communication Sciences, University of Michigan, Ann Arbor.

1972. The phonology of echo-words in French, *Language,* 48: 97–108.

1974. Règles phonologiques à domaine indéterminé: chute de cheva en français, in *Le français dans la région de Montréal, aspects phonétique et phonologique, Cahier de Linguistique no. 4,* 69–88. Montréal: Les Presses de l'Université du Québec.

Morin, Y. C. and Friedman, J. 1971. *Phonological Grammar Tester: Underlying Theory.* Natural Language Studies no. 10. Department of Computer and Communication Sciences, University of Michigan, Ann Arbor.

Newman, P. 1968. The reality of morphophonemics, *Language,* 44.3: 507–15.

Newman, S. 1944. *Yokuts Language of California*. Viking Fund Publications in Anthropology no. 2. New York.

1965. *Zuni Grammar*. University of New Mexico Publications in Anthropology no. 14. Albuquerque.

1967. Zuni grammar: alternative solutions versus weaknesses, *International Journal of American Linguistics*, 33.3: 187–92.

Nyrop, K. 1903. *Grammaire historique de la langue française*, vol. ɪ. Copenhagen: Bojesen.

Perkell, J. S. 1971. Physiology of speech production: a preliminary study of two suggested revisions of the features specifying vowels, *QPR*, no. 102: 123–39.

Perlmutter, D. 1971. *Deep and Surface Structure Constraints in Syntax*. New York: Holt, Rinehart and Winston.

Pike, K. 1948. *Tone Languages*. Ann Arbor: University of Michigan Press.

Pleasants, J. 1956. *Études sur l'e muet*, Paris: Klincksieck.

Postal, P. M. 1968. *Aspects of Phonological Theory*. New York: Harper and Row.

Pulgram, E. 1961. French /ə/: statics and dynamics of linguistic subcodes, *Lingua* 10: 305–25.

Rardin, R. B. 1969. On Finnish vowel harmony, *QPR*, no. 94: 226–31.

Robert, P. 1967. *Le Petit Robert: Dictionnaire alphabétique et analogique de la langue française*. Paris: Société du Nouveau Littré.

Ross, J. R. 1967. *Constraints on Variables in Syntax*. Bloomington: Indiana University Linguistics Club.

1972. A reanalysis of English word stress, in Brame, ed., 1972: 229–323.

Ruwet, N., ed. 1966. *La grammaire générative. Langages* no. 4. Paris: Larousse.

1967. *Introduction à la grammaire générative*. Paris: Plon; English trans. *An Introduction to Generative Grammar*, 1973. Amsterdam: North-Holland.

Sampson, G. 1970. On the need for a phonological base, *Language*, 46.3: 586–626.

Sapir, E. 1925. Sound patterns in language, *Language*, 1: 37–51; reprinted in Sapir, 1949: 33–45.

1933. La réalité psychologique des phonèmes, *Journal de Psychologie Normale et Pathologique*, 30: 247–65; English trans. in Sapir, 1949: 46–60.

1949. *Selected Writings of Edward Sapir*, ed. D. G. Mandelbaum. Berkeley and Los Angeles: University of California Press.

Schane, S. A. 1967. L'élision et la liaison en français, in Schane, ed., 1967: 37–59 (French adaptation of Schane, 1968a: chap. 1).

ed. 1967. *La phonologie générative. Langages* no. 8. Paris: Larousse.

1968a. *French Phonology and Morphology*. Cambridge, Mass.: MIT Press.

1968b. On the abstract character of French 'e muet', *Glossa*, 2.2: 150–63.

1972. The hierarchy for the deletion of French 'e muet', *Linguistics*, 82: 63–9.

Selkirk, E. O. 1972. The phrase phonology of English and French. Unpublished doctoral dissertation, MIT.

Selkirk, E. O. and Vergnaud, J.-R. 1973. How abstract is French phonology?, *Foundations of Language*, 10: 249–54.

Shibatani, M. 1972. The non-cyclic nature of Japanese accentuation, *Language*, 48.3: 584–95.

Smalley, W. A. 1968. *Manual of Articulatory Phonetics*. Tarrytown: Practical Anthropology.

Stanley, R. 1967. Redundancy rules in phonology. *Language*, 43.2: 393–436.

Sten, H. 1966. *Manuel de phonétique française*. Copenhagen: Munksgaard.

Tedlock, D. 1969. The problem of *k* in Zuni phonemics, *International Journal of American Linguistics*, 35.1: 67–71.

Togeby, K. 1951. *Structure immanente de la langue française*. Paris: Larousse.

Troubetzkoy, N. S. 1929. Sur la morphonologie, *Travaux du Cercle Linguistique de Prague*, 1: 85–8.

1931. Gedanken über Morphonologie, *Travaux du Cercle Linguistique de Prague*, 4: 160–3.

1934. Das morphonologische System der russischen Sprache, *Travaux du Cercle Linguistique de Prague*, 5.2.

1939. Grundzüge der Phonologie, *Travaux du Cercle Linguistique de Prague*, 7 (quoted from the French trans. by J. Cantineau: *Principes de phonologie*, 1949. Paris: Klincksieck).

Vachek, J. 1966. *The Linguistic School of Prague*. Bloomington, Ind.: Indiana University Press.

Valdman, A. 1970. Competing models of linguistic analysis: French adjective inflection, *The French Review*, 43.4: 606–23.

Vergnaud, J.-R. 1970. Some properties of the French consonantal system. Unpublished manuscript, MIT.

1972. On the formalization of infinite sets of phonological rules, *QPR*, no. 104: 249–56.

1975. Problèmes formels en phonologie générative, *Rapport de recherches no. 4 du Laboratoire d'Automatique Documentaire et Linguistique*. University of Paris VII and University of Paris VIII-Vincennes.

Walker, W. 1966. Review of Newman, 1965, *Language*, 42: 176–80.

Wang, W. S.-Y. 1967. Phonological features of tone, *International Journal of American Linguistics*, 44: 93–105.

Weinreich, U., Labov, W. and Herzog, M. 1968. Empirical foundations for a theory of language change, in W. Lehmann and Y. Malkiel, eds., *Directions for Historical Linguistics*, 97–195. Austin: University of Texas Press.

Weinrich, H. 1958. *Phonologische Studien zur Romanischen Sprachgeschichte*. Münster: Aschendorff.

Westermann, D. and Ward, I. C. 1933. *Practical Phonetics for Students of African Languages*. London: Oxford University Press.

Williams, E. S. 1976. Underlying tone in Margi and Igbo, *Linguistic Inquiry*, 7.3: 463–84.

Wonderly, W. L. 1951; 1952. Zoque I, II, III, IV and V, *International Journal of American Linguistics*, 17: 1–9, 105–23, 137–62, 235–51 and 18: 35–48.

Woo, N. 1969. *Prosody and Phonology*. Bloomington: Indiana University Linguistics Club.

——— 1970. Tone in Northern Tepehuan, *International Journal of American Linguistics*, 36: 18–30.

Wurzel, W. 1970. Studien zur deutschen Lautstruktur, *Studia Grammatica*, 8.

Zeps, V. J. and Halle, M. 1971. Outline of the accentuation in inflectional paradigms of literary Lithuanian with an appendix on the accentuation of nominal derivatives, *QPR*, no. 103: 139–58.

Zimmer, K. 1969. Markedness and the problem of indeterminacy of lexical representations, *International Journal of American Linguistics*, 35.3: 264–6.

Zwanenburg, W. 1968. Quelques remarques sur le statut phonologique de *e* muet en français moderne, in A. Juilland, ed., *Linguistic Studies Presented to André Martinet, Part Two: Indo-European Linguistics, Word*, 24: 508–18.

Index

When a rule belongs to a language other than French, this is indicated in parentheses. Thus ' ELI (Zuni) ' refers to the elision rule of Zuni, whereas ' ELI ' refers to that of French. An entry such as ' ELIS/EPEN ' indicates the page where it is argued that rule ELIS should be ordered before rule EPEN.